Three Sociological Traditions

SELECTED READINGS

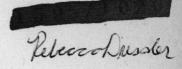

Three Sociological Traditions

SELECTED READINGS

Edited by Randall Collins

New York • Oxford
OXFORD UNIVERSITY PRESS
1985

Copyright © 1985 by Oxford University Press, Inc.
Published by Oxford University Press, Inc.,
200 Madison Avenue
New York, New York 10016

Library of Congress Cataloging in Publication Data
Main entry under title:

Three sociological traditions : selected readings.

   To be used with: Three sociological traditions /
Randall Collins.
   Bibliography: p.
   Includes index.
   1. Sociology—Addresses, essays, lectures.
2. Social conflict—Addresses, essays, lectures.
3. Solidarity—Addresses, essays, lectures.
4. Microsociology—Addresses, essays, lectures.
I. Collins, Randall, 1941–   II. Collins, Randall,
1941–   Three sociological traditions. III. Title:

3 sociological traditions.
HM24.T554 1985   301   84-11277
ISBN 0-19-503521-6

Printing (last digit): 9 8 7 6 5

For my father, Ralph Stokes Collins,
and mother, Maria Zubiller Collins.

PREFACE

Sociology is known for its lack of consensus. Nevertheless, although there is plenty of divisiveness in modern sociology, it is not endless. Amid the countless specialties and viewpoints, there are at least three broad traditions that have developed intellectually and cumulated knowledge within a particular viewpoint over the last century. These three great traditions are the conflict tradition, deriving from Marx, Engels, and Weber; the analysis of the ritual and symbolic bases of social solidarity, which I have called the Durkheimian tradition after its greatest exponent; and the microinteractionist tradition that stretches from Cooley and Mead through the symbolic interactionists and ethnomethodologists to current microsociologies.

The following selections trace the three traditions from their classic statements of principles, through succeeding intellectual generations, up to their continuers and developers of today. The traditions are not static; creative new ideas are still emerging from each of them. I hope this explicit tracing of these lineages, along with my companion volume narrating their history, *Three Sociological Traditions*, will lay to rest the popular notion that sociology has gone nowhere and accomplished nothing across the four or five generations it has been alive.

My aim has been to make the classics of sociology, as well as subsequent mileposts of theory, readily accessible in one place, with their major principles clearly focused by the textual selection and by a brief editorial introduction to each. The titles and most of the subheadings, except in the case of the selections from Goffman, Hagstrom, and Blumer, are the editor's rather than the original authors'.

I would like to thank Ralph Collins, Mark Traugott, and Mary Wagner for assistance with the Hubert and Mauss translation.

San Diego   R.C.
November 1984

CONTENTS

III THE MICRO-INTERACTIONIST TRADITION

Three Sociological Traditions

SELECTED READINGS

I THE CONFLICT TRADITION

Some Main Points of the Conflict Tradition

1800–1840	Classical economics: Ricardo		Hegel	
1840–1870	German historical economics *Realpolitik*		Marx and Engels	
1870–1900		Nietzsche	Engels' dialectical materialism	
1900–1920	Weber Michels		Marxist theories of imperialism	Simmel
1920–1940	Mannheim	Lukacs Gramsci	Frankfurt School Marxist sociologists of science	
1940–1960	Hans Gerth, C. Wright Mills			Functionalist conflict theory: Coser
	Organization theory Stratification theory Political sociology			
1960–	Conflict theory: Dahrendorf Lenski Collins		neo-Marxism: World systems theory Historical sociology of revolutions, social movements, and the state	
	Sex stratification theory			

Materialism and the Theory of Ideology [1846]; The Class Basis of Politics and Revolution [1852]

KARL MARX AND FRIEDRICH ENGELS

• *The roots of modern conflict theory can be traced back to Hegel, Machiavelli, or even further, but for the sociological tradition the founding texts are those of Karl Marx and Friedrich Engels. Not all their works are sociological in the sense that I am concentrating on here (especially the extensive and rather philosophical economics of Marx). Nevertheless, the banner for subsequent conflict theory was first flown in Marx and Engels' phrase from the Com-munist Manifesto (1848): "The history of all hitherto existing society is the history of class struggles."*

The present selections give some of Marx and Engels' key socio-logical principles in relatively pure form: Ideology is shaped by those who control the means of intellectual production; the inner reality of politics is the struggle of different economic class fac-tions over control of the state; political power depends on the material conditions that mobilize a class or else keep it split up in isolated fragments unable to formulate their own class interest. The latter selections, from Marx's The Eighteenth Brumaire of Louis Bonaparte, *describe the process by which the French revolu-tion of 1848, which had overthrown the constitutional monarchy of King Louis Philippe, was itself overthrown in a* coup d'etat *by Louis Bonaparte, the nephew of the great Napoleon. The account not only shows Marx and Engels' sociological thinking at its most realistic, but also Marx's unparalleled gifts as a dramatic writer reporting on, and stirring up, revolution.*

MATERIALISM AND THE THEORY OF IDEOLOGY:
KARL MARX AND FRIEDRICH ENGELS

The premises we begin are not arbitrary ones, not dogmas, but real premises from which abstraction can only be made in the imagination. They are the

Reprinted from Karl Marx and Friedrich Engels, *The German Ideology* (International Publishers, 1947), 6–7, 13–15, 39–41, 58–63, with permission of International Publishers. Originally written in 1846.

real individuals, their activity and the material conditions under which they live, both those which they find already existing and those produced by their activity. These premises can thus be verified in a purely empirical way.

The first premise of all human history is, of course, the existence of living human individuals. Thus the first fact to be established is the physical organization of these individuals and their consequent relation to the rest of nature. Of course, we cannot here go either into the actual physical nature of man, or into the natural conditions in which man finds himself—geological, orohydrographical, climatic and so on. The writing of history must always set out from these natural bases and their modification in the course of history through the action of man.

Men can be distinguished from animals by consciousness, by religion or anything else you like. They themselves begin to distinguish themselves from animals as soon as they begin to *produce* their means of subsistence, a step which is conditioned by their physical organization. By producing their means of subsistence men are indirectly producing their actual material life.

The way in which men produce their means of subsistence depends first of all on the nature of the actual means they find in existence and have to reproduce. This mode of production must not be considered simply as being the reproduction of the physical existence of the individuals. Rather it is a definite form of activity of these individuals, a definite form of expressing their life, a definite *mode of life* on their part. As individuals express their life, so they are. What they are, therefore, coincides with their production, both with *what* they produce and with *how* they produce. The nature of individuals thus depends on the material conditions determining their production.

The fact is that definite individuals who are productively active in a definite way enter into these definite social and political relations. Empirical observation must in each separate instance bring out empirically, and without any mystification and speculation, the connection of the social and political structure with production. The social structure and the State are continually evolving out of the life-process of definite individuals, but of individuals, not as they may appear in their own or other people's imagination, but as they really are; that is, as they are effective, produce materially, and are active under definite material limits, presuppositions and conditions independent of their will.

The production of ideas, of conceptions, of consciousness, is at first directly interwoven with the material activity and the material intercourse of men, the language of real life. Conceiving, thinking, the mental intercourse of men, appear at this stage as the direct efflux of their material behaviour. The same applies to mental production as expressed in the language of the politics, laws,

,morality, religion, metaphysics of a people. Men are the producers of their conceptions, ideas, and so on—real, active men, as they are conditioned by a definite development of their productive forces and of the intercourse corresponding to these, up to its furthest forms. Consciousness can never be anything else than conscious existence, and the existence of men is their actual life-process. If in all ideology men and their circumstances appear upside down as in a *camera obscura*, this phenomenon arises just as much from their historical life-process as the inversion of objects on the retina does from their physical life-process.

In direct contrast to German philosophy which descends from heaven to earth, here we ascend from earth to heaven. That is to say, we do not set out from what men say, imagine, conceive, nor from men as narrated, thought of, imagined, conceived, in order to arrive at men in the flesh. We set out from real, active men, and on the basis of their real life-process we demonstrate the development of the ideological reflexes and echoes of this life-process. The phantoms formed in the human brain are also, necessarily, sublimates of their material life-process, which is empirically verifiable and bound to material premises. Morality, religion, metaphysics, all the rest of ideology and their corresponding forms of consciousness, thus no longer retain the semblance of independence. They have no history, no development; but men, developing their material production and their material intercourse, alter, along with this their real existence, their thinking and the products of their thinking. Life is not determined by consciousness, but consciousness by life. In the first method of approach the starting-point is consciousness taken as the living individual; in the second it is the real living individuals themselves, as they are in actual life, and consciousness is considered solely as *their* consciousness.

The ideas of the ruling class are in every epoch the ruling ideas: that is, the class, which is the "ruling material force" of society, is at the same time its ruling intellectual force. The class which has the means of material production at its disposal, has control at the same time over the means of mental production, so that thereby, generally speaking, the ideas of those who lack the means of mental production are subject to it. The ruling ideas are nothing more than the ideal expression of the dominant material relationships, the dominant material relationships grasped as ideas; hence of the relationships which make the one class the ruling one, therefore the ideas of its dominance. The individuals composing the ruling class possess among other things consciousness, and therefore think. In so far, therefore, as they rule as a class and determine the extent and compass of an epoch, it is self-evident that they do this in their whole range, hence among other things rule also as thinkers, as producers of ideas, and regulate the production and distribution of the ideas of their age: thus their ideas are the ruling ideas of the epoch. For instance, in an age and in a country where royal power, aristocracy and bourgeoisie are contending for mastery and where, therefore, mastery is shared, the doctrine of the separation of powers proves to be the dominant idea and is expressed as an "eternal law." The division of labour, which we saw above as one of the chief forces of history up till now, manifests itself also in the ruling class as the division of mental and material labour, so that inside this class one part appears as the thinkers of the class (its active, conceptive ideologists, who make the perfecting of the illusion of the class about itself their chief source of livelihood), while the others' attitude to these ideas and illusions is more passive and receptive, because they are in reality the active members of this class and have less time to make up illusions and ideas about themselves. Within this class this cleavage can even develop into a certain opposition and hostility between the two parts, which, however, in the case of a practical collision, in which the class itself is endangered, automatically comes to nothing, in which case there also vanishes the semblance that the ruling ideas were not the ideas of the ruling class and had a power distinct from the power of this class. The existence of revolutionary ideas in a particular period presupposes the existence of a revolutionary class; about the premises for the latter sufficient has already been said above.

If now in considering the course of history we detach the ideas of the ruling class from the ruling class itself and attribute to them an independent existence, if we confine ourselves to saying that these or those ideas were dominant, without bothering ourselves about the conditions of production and the producers of these ideas, if we then ignore the individuals and world conditions which are the source of the ideas, we can say, for instance, that during the time that the aristocracy was dominant, the concepts honour, loyalty, and so on, were dominant, during the dominance of the bourgeoisie the concepts freedom, equality, etc. The ruling class itself on the whole imagines this to be so. This conception of history, which is common to all historians, particularly since the eighteenth century, will necessarily come up against the phenomenon that increasingly abstract ideas hold sway, that is ideas which increasingly take on the form of universality. For each new class which puts itself in the place of one ruling before it, is compelled, merely in order to carry through its aim, to represent its interest as the common interest of all the members of society, put in an ideal form; it will give its ideas the form of universality, and represent them as the only rational, universally valid ones. The class making a revolution appears from the very start, merely because it is opposed to a *class*, not as a class but as the representative of the whole of society; it appears as the whole mass of society confronting the one ruling class. It can do this because, to start with, its hegemony:

interest really is more connected with the common interest of all other non-ruling classes, because under the pressure of conditions its interest has not yet been able to develop as the particular interest of a particular class. Its victory, therefore, benefits also many individuals of the other classes which are not winning a dominant position, but only in so far as it now puts these individuals in a position to raise themselves into the ruling class. When the French bourgeoisie overthrew the power of the aristocracy, it thereby made it possible for many proletarians to raise themselves above the proletariat, but only in so far as they became bourgeois. Every new class, therefore, achieves its <u>hegemo</u>ny only on a broader basis than that of the class ruling previously, in return for which the opposition of the non-ruling class against the new ruling class later develops all the more sharply and profoundly. Both these things determine the fact that the struggle to be waged against this new ruling class, in its turn, aims at a more decided and radical negation of the previous conditions of society than could all previous classes which sought to rule.

This whole semblance, that the rule of a certain class is only the rule of certain ideas, comes to a natural end, of course, as soon as society ceases at last to be organized in the form of class-rule, that is to say as soon as it is no longer necessary to represent a particular interest as general or "the general interest" as ruling.

THE RELATION OF STATE AND LAW TO PROPERTY

The first form of <u>property</u>, in the ancient world as in the Middle Ages, is <u>tribal property</u>, determined with the Romans chiefly by war, with the Germans by the rearing of cattle. In the case of the ancient peoples, since several tribes live together in one town, the tribal property appears as State property, and the right of the individual to it as mere *"possession"* which, however, like tribal property as a whole, is confined to landed property only. Real private property began with the ancients, as with modern nations, with personal movable property—(slavery and community) (*dominium ex jure Quiritium*). In the case of the nations which grew out of the Middle Ages, tribal property <u>evolved</u> through various stages—<u>feudal landed property</u>, <u>corporative movable property</u>, manufacture-capital—to <u>modern capital</u>, determined by big industry and universal competition, that is, pure private property, which has cast off all semblance of a communal institution and has shut out the State from any influence on the development of property. To this modern private property corresponds the modern State, which, purchased gradually by the owners of property by means of taxation, has fallen entirely into their hands through the national debt, and its existence has become wholly dependent on the commer-

Cooperation to create structure

cial credit which the owners of property, the bourgeois, extend to it in the rise and fall of State funds on the stock exchange. By the mere fact that it is a *class* and no longer an *estate*, the bourgeoisie is forced to organize itself no longer locally, but nationally, and to give a general form to its mean average interest. Through the emancipation of private property from the community, the State has become a separate entity, beside and outside civil society; but it is nothing more than the form of organization which the bourgeois necessarily adopt both for internal and external purposes, for the mutual guarantee of their property and interests. The independence of the State is only found nowadays in those countries where the estates have not yet completely developed into classes, where the estates, done away with in more advanced countries, still have a part to play, and where there exists a mixture; countries, that is to say in which no one section of the population can achieve dominance over the others. This is the case particularly in Germany. The most perfect example of the modern State is North America. The modern French, English and American writers all express the opinion that the State exists only for the sake of private property, so that this fact has penetrated into the consciousness of the normal man.

Since the State is the form in which the individuals of a ruling class assert their common interests, and in which the whole civil society of an epoch is epitomized, it follows that in the formation of all communal institutions the State acts as intermediary, that these institutions receive a political form. Hence the illusion that law is based on the will, and indeed on the will divorced from its real basis—on free will.

In civil law the existing property relationships are declared to be the result of the general will. The *jus utendi et abutendi* itself asserts on the one hand the fact that private property has become entirely independent of the community, and on the other the illusion that private property itself is based on the private will, the arbitrary disposal of the thing. In practice, the *abuti* has very definite economic limitations for the owner of private property, if he does not wish to see his property and hence his *jus abutendi* pass into other hands, since actually the thing, considered merely with reference to his will, is not a thing at all, but only becomes true property in intercourse, and independently of the right to the thing (a *relationship*, which the philosophers call an idea). This juridical illusion, which reduces law to the mere will, necessarily leads, in the further development of property relationships, to the position that a man may have a title to a thing without really having the thing. If, for instance, the income from a piece of land is lost owing to competition, then the proprietor has certainly his legal title to it along with the *jus utendi et abutendi*. But he can do nothing with it; he owns nothing as a landed proprietor if he has not enough capital besides to cultivate his ground. This illusion of the jurists also explains the fact that for them, as for every codex, it is altogether fortuitous that individuals enter into relationships among themselves (e.g. contracts); it explains why they consider that these relationships can be entered into or not at will, and that their content rests purely on the individual free will of the contracting parties. Whenever, through the development of industry and commerce, new forms of intercourse have been evolved, (e.g. assurance companies etc.) the law has always been compelled to admit them among the modes of acquiring property.

．　　．　　．

Nothing is more common than the notion that in history up till now it has only been a question of *"taking."* The barbarians "take" the Roman Empire, and this fact of "taking" is made to explain the transition from the old world to the feudal system. In this taking by barbarians, however, the question is, whether the nation which is conquered has evolved industrial productive forces, as is the case with modern peoples, or whether their productive forces are based for the most part merely on their association and on the community. Taking is further determined by the object taken. A banker's fortune, consisting of paper, cannot be taken at all, without the taker's submitting to the conditions of production and intercourse of the country taken. Similarly the total industrial capital of a modern industrial country. And finally, everywhere there is very soon an end to taking, and when there is nothing more to take, you have to set about producing. From this necessity of producing, which very soon asserts itself, it follows that the form of community adopted by the settling conquerors must correspond to the stage of development of the productive forces they find in existence; or, if this is not the case from the start, it must change according to the productive forces. By this, too, is explained the fact, which people profess to have noticed everywhere in the period following the migration of the peoples, namely that the servant was master, and that the conquerors very soon took over language, culture and manners from the conquered. The feudal system was by no means brought complete from Germany, but had its origin, as far as the conquerors were concerned, in the martial organization of the army during the actual conquest, and this only evolved after the conquest into the feudal system proper through the action of the productive forces found in the conquered countries. To what an extent this form was determined by the productive forces is shown by the abortive attempts to realize other forms derived from reminiscences of ancient Rome (Charlemagne, etc.).

THE CLASS BASIS OF POLITICS AND REVOLUTION: KARL MARX

ON THE RECURRENCE OF REVOLUTIONS

France is the land where, more than anywhere else, the historical class
struggles were each time fought out to a decision, and where, consequently,
the changing political forms within which they move and in which their
results are summarized have been stamped in the sharpest outlines. The
centre of feudalism in the Middle Ages, the model country of unified monarchy, resting on estates, since the Renaissance, France demolished feudalism
in the Great Revolution and established the unalloyed rule of the bourgeoisie
in a classical purity unequalled by any other European land. And the struggle
of the upward-striving proletariat against the ruling bourgeoisie appeared here
in an acute form unknown elsewhere.

It was precisely Marx who had first discovered the great law of motion of
history, the law according to which all historical struggles, whether they proceed in the political, religious, philosophical or some other ideological domain, are in fact only the more or less clear expression of struggles of social
classes, and that the existence and thereby the collisions, too, between these
classes are in turn conditioned by the degree of development of their economic position, by the mode of their production and of their exchange determined by it. This law, which has the same significance for history as the law
of the transformation of energy has for natural science—this law gave him
here, too, the key to an understanding of the history of the Second French
Republic.

. . .

Hegel remarks somewhere that all facts and personages of great importance
in world history occur, as it were, twice. He forgot to add: the first time as
tragedy, the second as farce. Caussidière for Danton, Louis Blanc for Robes-
pierre, the *Montagne* of 1848 to 1851 for the *Montagne* of 1793 to 1795, the
Nephew for the Uncle. And the same caricature occurs in the circumstances
attending the second edition of the eighteenth Brumaire!

Men make their own history, but they do not make it just as they please;
they do not make it under circumstances chosen by themselves, but under
circumstances directly encountered, given and transmitted from the past. The
tradition of all the dead generations weighs like a nightmare on the brain of

Reprinted from Karl Marx, *The Eighteenth Brumaire of Louis Bonaparte* (International Publishers,
1963), 13–19, 23–24, 46–55, 61–67, 74–76, 83–84, 103–15, 123–31, with permission of International Publishers. Originally published in 1852. The first two paragraphs are from Friedrich Engels'
Preface to the Third German Edition.

the living. And just when they seem engaged in revolutionizing themselves and things, in creating something that has never yet existed, precisely in such periods of revolutionary crisis they anxiously conjure up the spirits of the past to their service and borrow from them names, battle cries and costumes in order to present the new scene of world history in this time-honoured disguise and this borrowed language. Thus Luther donned the mask of the Apostle Paul, the Revolution of 1789 to 1814 draped itself alternately as the Roman republic and the Roman empire, and the Revolution of 1848 knew nothing better to do than to parody, now 1789, now the revolutionary tradition of 1793 to 1795. In like manner a beginner who has learnt a new language always translates it back into his mother tongue, but he has assimilated the spirit of the new language and can freely express himself in it only when he finds his way in it without recalling the old and forgets his native tongue in the use of the new.

The social revolution of the nineteenth century cannot draw its poetry from the past, but only from the future. It cannot begin with itself before it has stripped off all superstition in regard to the past. Earlier revolutions required recollections of past world history in order to drug themselves concerning their own content. In order to arrive at its own content, the revolution of the nineteenth century must let the dead bury their dead. There the phrase went beyond the content; here the content goes beyond the phrase.

The February Revolution was a surprise attack, a *taking* of the old society *unawares*, and the people proclaimed this unexpected *stroke* as a deed of world importance, ushering in a new epoch. On December 2 the February Revolution is conjured away by a cardsharper's trick, and what seems overthrown is no longer the monarchy but the liberal concessions that were wrung from it by centuries of struggle. Instead of *society* having conquered a new content for itself, it seems that the *state* only returned to its oldest form, to the shamelessly simple domination of the sabre and the cowl. This is the answer to the *coup de main*[1] of February 1848, given by the *coup de tête*[2] of December 1851. Easy come, easy go. Meanwhile the interval of time has not passed by unused. During the years 1848 to 1851 French society has made up, and that by an abbreviated because revolutionary method, for the studies and experiences which, in a regular, so to speak, textbook course of development would have had to precede the February Revolution, if it was to be more than a ruffling of the surface. Society now seems to have fallen back behind its point

[1]*Coup de main:* Unexpected stroke.—*Ed.*
[2]*Coup de tête:* Rash act.—*Ed.*

of departure; it has in truth first to create for itself the revolutionary point of departure, the situation, the relations, the conditions under which alone modern revolution becomes serious.

Bourgeois revolutions, like those of the eighteenth century, storm swiftly from success to success; their dramatic effects outdo each other; men and things seem set in sparkling brilliants; ecstasy is the everyday spirit; but they are short-lived; soon they have attained their zenith, and a long crapulent depression lays hold of society before it learns soberly to assimilate the results of its storm-and-stress period. On the other hand, proletarian revolutions, like those of the nineteenth century, criticize themselves constantly, interrupt themselves continually in their own course, come back to the apparently accomplished in order to begin it afresh, deride with unmerciful thoroughness the inadequacies, weaknesses and paltrinesses of their first attempts, seem to throw down their adversary only in order that he may draw new strength from the earth and rise again, more gigantic, before them, recoil ever and anon from the indefinite prodigiousness of their own aims, until a situation has been created which makes all turning back impossible, and the conditions themselves cry out:

Hic Rhodus, hic salta!
[Get it over with!]

THE DEFEAT OF THE PROLETARIAN INSURRECTION

The *bourgeois monarchy* of Louis Philippe can be followed only by a *bourgeois republic*, that is to say, whereas a limited section of the bourgeoisie ruled in the name of the king, the whole of the bourgeoisie will now rule in the name of the people. The demands of the Paris proletariat replied with the *June Insurrection*, the most colossal event in the history of European civil wars. The bourgeois republic triumphed. On its side stood the aristocracy of finance, the industrial bourgeoisie, the middle class, the petty bourgeois, the army, the *lumpenproletariat* organized as the Mobile Guard, the intellectual lights, the clergy and the rural population. On the side of the Paris proletariat stood none but itself. More than three thousand insurgents were butchered after the victory, and fifteen thousand were transported without trial. With this defeat the proletariat passes into the *background* of the revolutionary stage. It attempts to press forward again on every occasion, as soon as the movement appears to make a fresh start, but with ever decreased expenditure of strength and always slighter results. As soon as one of the social strata situated above it gets into revolutionary ferment, the proletariat enters into an alliance with it and so shares all the defeats that the different parties suffer, one after another. But these subsequent blows become the weaker, the greater the surface of society over which they are distributed. The more important leaders of the proletariat in the Assembly and in the press successively fall victims to the courts, and ever more equivocal figures come to head it. In part it throws itself into *doctrinaire experiments, exchange banks and workers' associations, hence into a movement in which it renounces the revolutionizing of the old world by means of the latter's own great, combined resources, and seeks, rather, to achieve its salvation behind society's back, in private fashion, within its limited conditions of existence, and hence necessarily suffers shipwreck.* It seems to be unable either to rediscover revolutionary greatness in itself or to win new energy from the connections newly entered into, until *all classes* with which it contended in June themselves lie prostrate beside it. But at least it succumbs with the honours of the great, world-historic struggle; not only France, but all Europe trembles at the June earthquake, while the ensuing defeats of the upper classes are so cheaply bought that they require bare-faced exaggeration by the victorious party to be able to pass for events at all, and become the more ignominious the further the defeated party is removed from the proletarian party.

The defeat of the June insurgents, to be sure, had now prepared, had levelled the ground on which the bourgeois republic could be founded and built up, but it had shown at the same time that in Europe the questions at issue are other than that of "republic or monarchy." It had revealed that here *bourgeois republic* signifies the unlimited despotism of one class over other classes.

THE TWO FACTIONS OF THE PARTY OF ORDER: LANDED PROPERTY VERSUS URBAN CAPITAL

Before we pursue parliamentary history further, some remarks are necessary to avoid common misconceptions regarding the whole character of the epoch that lies before us. Looked at with the eyes of democrats, the period of the Legislative National Assembly is concerned with what the period of the Constituent Assembly was concerned with: the simple struggle between republicans and royalists. The movement itself, however, they sum up in the one shibboleth: *"reaction"*—night, in which all cats are grey and which permits them to reel off their night watchman's commonplaces. And, to be sure, at first sight the party of Order, reveals a maze of different royalist factions, which not only intrigue against each other—each seeking to elevate its own pretender to the throne and exclude the pretender of the opposing faction—

but also all unite in common hatred of, and common onslaughts on, the "republic." In opposition to this royalist conspiracy the *Montagne*, for its part, appears as the representative of the "republic." The party of Order appears to be perpetually engaged in a "reaction," directed against press, association and the like, neither more nor less than in Prussia, and which, as in Prussia, is carried out in the form of brutal police intervention by the bureaucracy, the *gendarmerie* and the law courts. The "*Montagne*," for its part, is just as continually occupied in warding off these attacks and thus defending the "eternal rights of man" as every so-called people's party has done, more or less, for a century and a half. If one looks at the situation and the parties more closely, however, this superficial appearance, which veils the *class struggle* and the peculiar physiognomy of this period, disappears.

Legitimists and Orleanists, as we have said, formed the two great factions of the party of Order. Was that which held these factions fast to their pretenders and kept them apart from one another nothing but lily and tricolour, House of Bourbon and House of Orleans, different shades of royalism, was it at all the confession of faith of royalism? Under the Bourbons, *big landed property* had governed, with its priests and lackeys; under the Orleans, high finance, large-scale industry, large-scale trade, that is, *capital*, with its retinue of lawyers, professors and smooth-tongued orators. The Legitimate Monarchy was merely the political expression of the hereditary rule of the lords of the soil, as the July Monarchy was only the political expression of the usurped rule of the bourgeois *parvenus*. What kept the two factions apart, therefore, was not any so-called principles, it was their material conditions of existence, two different kinds of property, it was the old contrast between town and country, the rivalry between capital and landed property. That at the same time old memories, personal enmities, fears and hopes, prejudices and illusions, sympathies and antipathies, convictions, articles of faith and principles bound them to one or the other royal house, who denies this? Upon the different forms of property, upon the social conditions of existence, rises an entire superstructure of distinct and peculiarly formed sentiments, illusions, modes of thought and views of life. The entire class creates and forms them out of its material foundations and out of the corresponding social relations. The single individual, who derives them through tradition and upbringing, may imagine that they form the real motives and the starting point of his activity. While Orleanists and Legitimists, while each faction sought to make itself and the other believe that it was loyalty to their two royal houses which separated them, facts later proved that it was rather their divided interests which forbade the uniting of the two royal houses. And as in private life one differentiates between what a man thinks and says of himself and what he really is and does, so in historical struggles one must distinguish still more the phrases and fancies of parties from their real organism and their real interests, their conception of themselves, from their reality. Orleanists and Legitimists found themselves side by side in the republic, with equal claims. If each side wished to effect the *restoration* of its *own* royal house against the other, that merely signified that each of the *two great interests* into which the *bourgeoisie* is split—landed property and capital—sought to restore its own supremacy and the subordination of the other. We speak of two interests of the bourgeoisie, for large landed property, despite its feudal coquetry and pride of race, has been rendered thoroughly bourgeois by the development of modern society. Thus the Tories in England long imagined that they were enthusiastic about monarchy, the church and the beauties of the old English Constitution, until the day of danger wrung from them the confession that they are enthusiastic only about *ground rent*.

THE SOCIAL-DEMOCRATIC PARTY
OF PETTY BOURGEOIS AND WORKERS

As against the coalesced bourgeoisie, a coalition between petty bourgeois and workers had been formed, the so-called *social-democratic* party. The petty bourgeois saw that they were badly rewarded after the June days of 1848, that their material interests were imperilled and that the democratic guarantees which were to ensure the effectuation of these interests were called in question by the counter-revolution. Accordingly, they came closer to the workers. On the other hand, their parliamentary representation, the *Montagne*, thrust aside during the dictatorship of the bourgeois republicans, had in the last half of the life of the Constituent Assembly reconquered its lost popularity through the struggle with Bonaparte and the royalist ministers. It had concluded an alliance with the socialist leaders. In February 1849, banquets celebrated the reconciliation. A joint program was drafted, joint election committees were set up and joint candidates put forward. From the social demands of the proletariat the revolutionary point was broken off and a democratic turn given to them; from the democratic claims of the petty bourgeoisie the purely political form was stripped off and their socialist point thrust forward. Thus arose the *Social-Democracy*. The new *Montagne*, the result of this combination, contained, apart from some supernumeraries from the working class and some socialist sectarians, the same elements as the old *Montagne*, only numerically stronger. However, in the course of development, it had changed with the class that it represented. The peculiar character of the Social-Democracy is epitomized in the fact that democratic-republican institutions are demanded as a means, not of doing away with two extremes, capital and wage labour, but of weakening their antagonism and transforming it into harmony. However different the means proposed for the attainment of this end may be, however much it may be trimmed with more or less revolutionary notions, the content remains the same. This content is the transformation of society in a democratic way, but a transformation within the bounds of the petty bourgeoisie. Only one must not form the narrow-minded notion that the petty bourgeoisie, on principle, wishes to enforce an egoistic class interest. Rather, it believes that the *special* conditions of its emancipation are the *general* conditions within the frame of which alone modern society can be saved and the class struggle avoided. Just as little must one imagine that the democratic representatives are indeed all shopkeepers or enthusiastic champions of shopkeepers. According to their education and their individual position they may be as far apart as heaven from earth. What makes them representatives of the petty bourgeoisie is the fact that in their minds they do not get beyond the limits which the latter do not get beyond in life, that they are consequently driven, theoretically, to the same problems and solutions to which material interest and social position drive the latter practically. This is, in general, the relationship between the *political* and *literary representatives* of a class and the class they represent.

After the analysis given, it is obvious that if the *Montagne* continually contends with the party of Order for the republic and the so-called rights of man, neither the republic nor the rights of man are its final end, any more than an army which one wants to deprive of its weapons and which resists has taken the field in order to remain in possession of its own weapons.

But the democrat, because he represents the petty bourgeoisie, that is, a *transition class*, in which the interests of two classes are simultaneously mutually blunted, imagines himself elevated above class antagonism generally. The democrats concede that a privileged class confronts them, but they, along with all the rest of the nation, form the *people*. What they represent is the *people's rights*; what interests them is the *people's interests*. Accordingly, when a struggle is impending, they do not need to examine the interests and positions of the different classes. They do not need to weigh their own resources too critically. They have merely to give the signal and the *people*, with all its inexhaustible resources, will fall upon the *oppressors*. Now, if in the performance their interests prove to be uninteresting and their potency impotence, then either the fault lies with pernicious sophists, who split the *indivisible people* into different hostile camps, or the army was too brutalized and blinded to comprehend that the pure aims of democracy are the best thing for it itself, or the whole thing has been wrecked by a detail in its execution, or else an unforeseen accident has this time spoilt the game. In any case, the democrat comes out of the most disgraceful defeat just as immaculate as he was innocent when he went into it, with the newly-won conviction that he is bound to win, not that he himself and his party have to give up the old standpoint, but, on the contrary, that conditions have to ripen to suit him.

THE FIGHT OVER THE STATE APPARATUS

It is immediately obvious that in a country like France, where the executive power commands an army of officials numbering more than half a million individuals and therefore constantly maintains an immense mass of interests and livelihoods in the most absolute dependence; where the state enmeshes, controls, regulates, superintends and tutors civil society from its most comprehensive manifestations of life down to its most insignificant stirrings, from its most general modes of being to the private existence of individuals; where through the most extraordinary centralization this parasitic body acquires a ubiquity, an omniscience, a capacity for accelerated mobility and an elasticity which finds a counterpart only in the helpless dependence, in the loose shapelessness of the actual body politic—it is obvious that in such a country the National Assembly forfeits all real influence when it loses command of the ministerial posts, if it does not at the same time simplify the administration of the state, reduce the army of officials as far as possible and, finally, let civil society and public opinion create organs of their own, independent of the governmental power. But it is precisely with the maintenance of that extensive state machine in its numerous ramifications that the *material interests* of the French bourgeoisie are interwoven in the closest fashion. Here it finds posts for its surplus population and makes up in the form of state salaries for what it cannot pocket in the form of profit, interest, rents and honorariums. On the other hand, its *political interests* compelled it to increase daily the repressive measures and therefore the resources and the personnel of the state power, while at the same time it had to wage an uninterrupted war against public opinion and mistrustfully mutilate, cripple, the independent organs of the social movement, where it did not succeed in amputating them entirely. Thus the French bourgeoisie was compelled by its class position to annihilate, on the one hand, the vital conditions of all parliamentary power, and therefore, likewise, of its own, and to render irresistible, on the other hand, the executive power hostile to it.

THE DILEMMAS OF POLITICAL RHETORIC

Whatever amount of passion and declamation might be employed by the party of Order against the minority from the tribune of the National Assembly, its speech remained as monosyllabic as that of the Christians, whose words were to be: Yea, yea; nay, nay! As monosyllabic on the platform as in the press. Flat as a riddle whose answer is known in advance. Whether it was a question of the right of petition or the tax on wine, freedom of the press or free trade, the clubs or the municipal charter, protection of personal liberty or regulation of the state budget, the watchword constantly recurs, the theme remains always the same, the verdict is ever ready and invariably reads: *"Socialism!"* Even bourgeois liberalism is declared *socialistic*, bourgeois enlightenment socialistic, bourgeois financial reform socialistic. It was socialistic to build a railway, where a canal already existed, and it was socialistic to defend oneself with a cane when one was attacked with a rapier.

This was not merely a figure of speech, fashion or party tactics. The bourgeoisie had a true insight into the fact that all the weapons which it had forged against feudalism turned their points against itself, that all the means of education which it had produced rebelled against its own civilization, that all the gods which it had created had fallen away from it. It understood that all the so-called bourgeois liberties and organs of progress attacked and menaced its *class rule* at its social foundation and its political summit simultaneously, and had therefore become *"socialistic."* In this menace and this attack it rightly discerned the secret of Socialism, whose import and tendency it judges more correctly than so-called Socialism knows how to judge itself; the latter can, accordingly, not comprehend why the bourgeoisie callously hardens its heart against it, whether it sentimentally bewails the sufferings of mankind, or in Christian spirit prophesies the millennium and universal brotherly love, or in humanistic style twaddles about mind, education and freedom, or in doctrinaire fashion excogitates a system for the conciliation and welfare of all classes. What the bourgeoisie did not grasp, however, was the logical conclusion that its *own parliamentary regime*, that its *political rule* in general, was now also bound to meet with the general verdict of condemnation as being *socialistic*. As long as the rule of the bourgeois class had not been organized completely, as long as it had not acquired its pure political expression, the antagonism of the other classes, likewise, could not appear in its pure form, and where it did appear could not take the dangerous turn that transforms every struggle against the state power into a struggle against capital. If in every stirring of life in society it saw "tranquillity" imperilled, how could it want to maintain at the head of society a *regime of unrest*, its own regime, the *parlia-*

mentary regime, this regime that, according to the expression of one of its spokesmen, lives in struggle and by struggle? The parliamentary regime lives by discussion; how shall it forbid discussion? Every interest, every social institution, is here transformed into general ideas, debated as ideas; how shall any interest, any institution, sustain itself above thought and impose itself as an article of faith? The struggle of the orators on the platform evokes the struggle of the scribblers of the press; the debating club in parliament is necessarily supplemented by debating clubs in the salons and the pothouses; the representatives, who constantly appeal to public opinion, give public opinion the right to speak its real mind in petitions. The parliamentary regime leaves everything to the decision of majorities; how shall the great majorities outside parliament not want to decide? When you play the fiddle at the top of the state, what else is to be expected but that those down below dance?

Thus, by now stigmatizing as *"socialistic"* what it had previously extolled as *"liberal,"* the bourgeoisie confesses that its own interests dictate that it should be delivered from the danger of its *own rule*; that, in order to restore tranquillity in the country, its bourgeois parliament must, first of all, be given its quietus; that in order to preserve its social power intact, its political power must be broken; that the individual bourgeois can continue to exploit the other classes and to enjoy undisturbed property, family, religion and order only on condition that their class be condemned along with the other classes to like political nullity; that in order to save its purse, it must forfeit the crown, and the sword that is to safeguard it must at the same time be hung over its own head as a sword of Damocles.

BONAPARTE ORGANIZES THE LUMPENPROLETARIAT

As in 1849 so during this year's parliamentary recess, the party of Order had broken up into its separate factions, each occupied with its own Restoration intrigues, which had obtained fresh nutriment through the death of Louis Philippe. The Legitimist king, Henry V, had even nominated a formal ministry which resided in Paris and in which members of the Permanent Commission held seats. Bonaparte, in his turn, was therefore entitled to make tours of the French Departments, and according to the disposition of the town that he favoured with his presence, now more or less covertly, now more or less overtly, to divulge his own restoration plans and canvass votes for himself. On these processions, which the great official *Moniteur* and the little private *Moniteurs* of Bonaparte naturally had to celebrate as triumphal processions, he was constantly accompanied by persons affiliated with the *Society of December 10*. This society dates from the year 1849. On the pretext of founding a benevolent society, the *lumpenproletariat* of Paris had been organized into secret sections, each section being led by Bonapartist agents, with a Bonapartist general at the head of the whole. Alongside decayed *roués* with dubious means of subsistence and of dubious origin, alongside ruined and adventurous offshoots of the bourgeoisie, were vagabonds, discharged soldiers, discharged jailbirds, escaped galley slaves, swindlers, mountebanks, *lazzaroni*, pickpockets, tricksters, gamblers, *maquereaus*, brothel keepers, porters, *literati*, organgrinders, ragpickers, knife grinders, tinkers, beggars—in short, the whole indefinite, disintegrated mass, thrown hither and thither, which the French term *la bohème*; from this kindred element Bonaparte formed the core of the Society of December 10. A "benevolent society"—in so far as, like Bonaparte, all its members felt the need of benefiting themselves at the expense of the labouring nation. This Bonaparte, who constitutes himself *chief of the lumpenproletariat*, who here alone rediscovers in mass form the interests which he personally pursues, who recognizes in this scum, offal, refuse of all classes the only class upon which he can base himself unconditionally, is the real Bonaparte, the Bonaparte *sans phrase*. An old crafty *roué*, he conceives the historical life of the nations and their performances of state as comedy in the most vulgar sense, as a masquerade where the grand costumes, words and postures merely serve to mask the pettiest knavery. Thus on his expedition to Strasbourg, where a trained Swiss vulture had played the part of the Napoleonic eagle. For his irruption into Boulogne he puts some London lackeys into French uniforms. They represent the army. In his Society of December 10, he assembles ten thousand rascally fellows, who are to play the part of the people, as Nick Bottom that of the lion. At a moment when the bourgeoisie itself played the most complete comedy, but in the most serious manner in the world, without infringing any of the pedantic conditions of French dramatic etiquette, and was itself half deceived, half convinced of the solemnity of its own performance of state, the adventurer, who took the comedy as plain comedy, was bound to win. Only when he has eliminated his solemn opponent, when he himself now takes his imperial role seriously and under the Napoleonic mask imagines he is the real Napoleon, does he become the victim of his own conception of the world, the serious buffoon who no longer takes world history for a comedy but his comedy for world history. What the national *ateliers* were for the socialist workers, what the *Gardes mobiles* were for the bourgeois republicans, the Society of December 10 was for Bonaparte, the party fighting force peculiar to him. On his journeys the detachments of this society packing the railways had to improvise a public for him, stage public enthusiasm, roar *vive l'Empereur*, insult and thrash republicans, of course, under the protection of the police. On his return journeys to Paris they had to form the advance guard, forestall counter-demonstrations or disperse them.

PARLIAMENTARY SQUABBLES

We have seen how on great and striking occasions during the months of November and December the National Assembly avoided or quashed the struggle with the executive power. Now we see it compelled to take it up on the pettiest occasions. In the Mauguin affair it confirms the principle of imprisoning People's Representatives for debt, but reserves the right to have it applied only to representatives obnoxious to itself and wrangles over this infamous privilege with the Minister of Justice. Instead of availing itself of the alleged murder plot to decree an enquiry into the Society of December 10 and irredeemably unmasking Bonaparte before France and Europe in his true character of chief of the Paris *lumpenproletariat*, it lets the conflict be degraded to a point where the only issue between it and the Minister of the Interior is which of them has the authority to appoint and dismiss a police commissioner. Thus, during the whole of this period, we see the party of Order compelled by its equivocal position to dissipate and disintegrate its struggle with the executive power in petty jurisdictional squabbles, pettyfoggery, legalistic hairsplitting, and delimitational disputes, and to make the most ridiculous matters of form the substance of its activity. It does not dare to take up the conflict at the moment when this has significance from the standpoint of principle, when the executive power has really exposed itself and the cause of the National Assembly would be the cause of the nation. By so doing it would give the nation its marching orders, and it fears nothing more than that the nation should move. On such occasions it accordingly rejects the motions of the *Montagne* and proceeds to the order of the day. The question at issue in its larger aspects having thus been dropped, the executive power calmly bides the time when it can again take up the same question on petty and insignificant occasions, when this is, so to speak, of only local parliamentary interest. Then the repressed rage of the party of Order breaks out, then it tears away the curtain from the coulisses, then it denounces the President, then it declares the republic in danger, but then, also, its fervour appears absurd and the occasion for the struggle seems a hypocritical pretext or altogether not worth fighting about. The parliamentary storm becomes a storm in a teacup, the fight becomes an intrigue, the conflict a scandal. While the revolutionary classes gloat with malicious joy over the humiliation of the National Assembly, for they are just as enthusiastic about the parliamentary prerogatives of this Assembly as the latter is about the public liberties, the bourgeoisie outside parliament does not understand how the bourgeoisie inside parliament can waste time over such petty squabbles and imperil tranquillity by such pitiful rivalries with the President.

THE ARISTOCRACY OF FINANCE AND
THE INDUSTRIAL BOURGEOISIE

[T]he section of the commercial bourgeoisie which had held the lion's share of power under Louis Philippe, namely, the *aristocracy of finance*, had become Bonapartist. Fould represented not only Bonaparte's interests in the *bourse*, he represented at the same time the interests of the *bourse* before Bonaparte. The position of the aristocracy of finance is most strikingly depicted in a passage from its European organ, the London *Economist*. In its number of February 1, 1851, its Paris correspondent writes:

> Now we have it stated from numerous quarters that above all things France demands tranquillity. The President declares it in his message to the Legislative Assembly; it is echoed from the tribune; is asserted in the journals; it is announced from the pulpit; *it is demonstrated by the sensitiveness of the public funds at the least prospect of disturbance, and their firmness the instant it is made manifest that the executive is victorious*

In its issue of November 29, 1851, *The Economist* declares in its own name:

> The President is the guardian of order, and is now recognized as such on every Stock Exchange of Europe.

The aristocracy of finance, therefore, condemned the parliamentary struggle of the party of Order with the executive power as a *disturbance of order*, and celebrated every victory of the President over its ostensible representatives as a *victory of order*. By the aristocracy of finance must here be understood not merely the great loan promoters and speculators in public funds, in regard to whom it is immediately obvious that their interests coincide with the interests of the state power. All modern finance, the whole of the banking business, is interwoven in the closest fashion with public credit. A part of their business capital is necessarily invested and put out at interest in quickly convertible public funds. Their deposits, the capital placed at their disposal and distributed by them among merchants and industrialists, are partly derived from the dividends of holders of government securities. If in every epoch the stability of the state power signified Moses and the prophets to the entire money market and to the priests of this money market, why not all the more so today, when every deluge threatens to sweep away the old states, and the old state debts with them?

The *industrial bourgeoisie*, too, in its fanaticism for order, was angered by the squabbles of the parliamentary party of Order with the executive power. After their vote of January 18 on the occasion of Changarnier's dismissal, Thiers, Angles, Sainte-Beuve, and so on, received from their constituents, in precisely the industrial districts, public reproofs in which particularly their coalition with the *Montagne* was scourged as high treason to order. If, as we have seen, the boastful taunts, the petty intrigues which marked the struggle of the party of Order with the President merited no better reception, then, on the other hand, this bourgeois party, which required its representatives to allow the military power to pass from its own parliament to an adventurous pretender without offering resistance, was not even worth the intrigues that were squandered in its interests. It proved that the struggle to maintain its *public* interests, its own *class interests*, its *political power*, only troubled and upset it, as it was a disturbance of private business.

THE BUSINESS CRISIS

When trade was good, as it still was at the beginning of 1851, the commercial bourgeoisie raged against any parliamentary struggle, lest trade be put out of humour. When trade was bad, as it continually was from the end of February 1851, the commercial bourgeoisie accused the parliamentary struggles of being the cause of stagnation and cried out for them to stop in order that trade might start again.

.   .   .

In the year 1851, France, to be sure, had passed through a kind of minor trade crisis. . . . [T]he apparent crisis of 1851 was nothing else but the halt which over-production and over-speculation invariably make in describing the industrial cycle, before they summon all their strength in order to rush feverishly through the final phase of this cycle and arrive once more at their starting-point, the *general trade crisis*. During such intervals in the history of trade, commercial bankruptcies break out in England, while in France industry itself is reduced to idleness, being partly forced into retreat by the competition, just then becoming intolerable, of the English in all markets, and being partly singled out for attack as a luxury industry by every business stagnation. Thus, besides the general crisis, France goes through national trade crises of her own, which are nevertheless determined and conditioned far more by the general state of the world market than by French local influences.

Now picture to yourself the French bourgeois, how in the throes of this business panic his trade-crazy brain is tortured, set in a whirl and stunned by rumours of *coups d'état* and the restoration of universal suffrage, by the struggle between parliament and the executive power, by the Fronde war between Orleanists and Legitimists, by the communist conspiracies in the south of France, by alleged *Jacqueries* in the Departments of Nièvre and Cher, by the advertisements of the different candidates for the presidency, by the cheapjack solutions offered by the journals, by the threats of the republicans to uphold the Constitution and universal suffrage by force of arms, by the gospel-preaching émigré heroes *in partibus*, who announced that the world would come to an end on the second Sunday in May 1852—think of all this and you will comprehend why in this unspeakable, deafening chaos of fusion, revision, prorogation, constitution, conspiration, coalition, emigration, usurpation and revolution, the bourgeois madly snorts at his parliamentary republic: "*Rather an end with terror than terror without end!*"

COUP D'ETAT

Bonaparte understood this cry. His power of comprehension was sharpened by the growing turbulence of creditors who, with each sunset which brought settling day, the second Sunday in May 1852, nearer, saw a movement of the stars protesting their earthly bills of exchange. They had become veritable astrologers. The National Assembly had blighted Bonaparte's hopes of a constitutional prolongation of his authority; the candidature of the Prince of Joinville forbade further vacillation.

If ever an event has, well in advance of its coming, cast its shadow before, it was Bonaparte's *coup d'état*. . . . During every parliamentary storm, the Bonapartist journals threatened a *coup d'état*, and the nearer the crisis drew, the louder grew their tone. In the orgies that Bonaparte kept up every night with men and women of the "swell mob," as soon as the hour of midnight approached and copious potations had loosened tongues and fired imaginations, the *coup d'état* was fixed for the following morning. Swords were drawn, glasses clinked, the Representatives were thrown out of the window, the imperial mantle fell upon Bonaparte's shoulders, until the following morning banished the spook once more and astonished Paris learned, from vestals of little reticence and from indiscreet paladins, of the danger it had once again escaped. During the months of September and October rumours of a *coup d'état* followed fast one after the other. Simultaneously, the shadow took on colour, like a variegated daguerreotype. Look up the September and October copies of the organs of the European daily press and you will find, word for word, intimations like the following: "Paris is full of rumours of a *coup d'état*. The capital is to be filled with troops during the night, and the next morning is to bring decrees which will dissolve the National Assembly, declare the Department of the Seine in a state of siege, restore universal suffrage and appeal to the people. Bonaparte is said to be seeking ministers for the execution of these illegal decrees." The letters that bring these tidings always end with the fateful word "*postponed*." The *coup d'état* was ever the fixed idea of Bonaparte. With this idea he had again set foot on French soil. He was so obsessed by it that he continually betrayed it and blurted it out. He was so weak that, just as continually, he gave it up again. The shadow of the *coup d'état* had become so familiar to the Parisians as a spectre that they were not willing to believe in it when it finally appeared in the flesh. What allowed the *coup d'état* to succeed was, therefore, neither the reticent reserve of the chief of the Society of December 10 nor the fact that the National Assembly was caught unawares. If it succeeded, it succeeded despite *his* indiscretion and with *its* foreknowledge, a necessary, inevitable result of antecedent developments.

· · ·

By splitting up into its hostile factions, the party of Order had long ago forfeited its independent parliamentary majority. It showed now that there was no longer any majority at all in parliament. The National Assembly had become *incapable of transacting business*. Its atomic constituents were no longer held together by any force of cohesion; it had drawn its last breath; it was dead.

Cromwell, when he dissolved the Long Parliament, went alone into its midst, drew out his watch in order that it should not continue to exist a minute after the time limit fixed by him, and drove out each one of the members of parliament with hilariously humourous taunts. Napoleon, smaller than his prototype, at least betook himself on the eighteenth Brumaire to the legislative body and read out to it, though in a faltering voice, its sentence of death.

THE VICTORY OF BUREAUCRACY OVER PARLIAMENT

But if the overthrow of the parliamentary republic contains within itself the germ of the triumph of the proletarian revolution, its immediate and palpable result was *the victory of Bonaparte over parliament, of the executive power over the legislative power, of force without phrases over the force of phrases*. In parliament the nation made its general will the law, that is, it made the law of the ruling class its general will. Before the executive power it renounces all will of its own and submits to the superior command of an alien will, to authority. The executive power, in contrast to the legislative power, expresses the heteronomy of a nation, in contrast to its autonomy. France, therefore, seems to have escaped the despotism of a class only to fall back beneath the despotism of an individual, and, what is more, beneath the authority of an individual without authority. The struggle seems to be settled in such a way that all classes, equally impotent and equally mute, fall on their knees before the rifle butt.

But the revolution is thoroughgoing. It is still journeying through purgatory. It does its work methodically. By December 2, 1851, it had completed one half of its preparatory work; it is now completing the other half. First it perfected the parliamentary power, in order to be able to overthrow it. Now that it has attained this, it perfects the *executive power*, reduces it to its purest expression, isolates it, sets it up against itself as the sole target, in order to concentrate all its forces of destruction against it. And when it has done this second half of its preliminary work, Europe will leap from its seat and exultantly exclaim: Well grubbed, old mole!

This executive power with its enormous bureaucratic and military organization, with its ingenious state machinery, embracing wide strata, with a host of officials numbering half a million, besides an army of another half million, this appalling parasitic body, which enmeshes the body of French society like a net and chokes all its pores, sprang up in the days of the absolute monarchy, with the decay of the feudal system, which it helped to hasten. The seignorial privileges of the landowners and towns became transformed into so many attributes of the state power, the feudal dignitaries into paid officials and the motley pattern of conflicting medieval plenary powers into the regulated plan of a state authority whose work is divided and centralized as in a factory. The first French Revolution, with its task of breaking all separate local, territorial, urban and provincial powers in order to create the civil unity of the nation, was bound to develop what the absolute monarchy had begun: centralization, but at the same time the extent, the attributes and the agents of governmental power. Napoleon perfected this state machinery. The Legitimist Monarchy and the July Monarchy added nothing but a greater division of labour, growing in the same measure as the division of labour within bourgeois society created new groups of interests, and, therefore, new material for state administration. Every *common* interest was straightway severed from society, counterposed to it as a higher, *general* interest, snatched from the activity of society's members themselves and made an object of government activity, from a bridge, a schoolhouse and the communal property of a village community to the railways, the national wealth and the national university of France. Finally, in its struggle against the revolution, the parliamentary republic found itself compelled to strengthen, along with the repressive measures, the resources and centralization of governmental power. All revolutions perfected this machine instead of smashing it. The parties that contended in turn for domination regarded the possession of this huge state edifice as the principal spoils of the victor.

But under the absolute monarchy, during the first Revolution, under Napoleon, bureaucracy was only the means of preparing the class rule of the bourgeoisie. Under the Restoration, under Louis Philippe, under the parliamentary republic, it was the instrument of the ruling class, however much it strove for power of its own.

Only under the second Bonaparte does the state seem to have made itself completely independent.

THE DICTATOR AS REPRESENTATIVE OF A
ONCE-REVOLUTIONARY CLASS GONE CONSERVATIVE:
THE PEASANT PROPRIETOR

And yet the state power is not suspended in midair. Bonaparte represents a class, and the most numerous class of French society at that, the *small-holding peasants*.

Just as the Bourbons were the dynasty of big landed property and just as the Orleans were the dynasty of money, so the Bonapartes are the dynasty of the peasants, that is, the mass of the French people. Not the Bonaparte who submitted to the bourgeois parliament, but the Bonaparte who dispersed the bourgeois parliament is the chosen of the peasantry. For three years the towns had succeeded in falsifying the meaning of the election of December 10 and in cheating the peasants out of the restoration of the empire. The election of December 10, 1848, has been consummated only by the *coup d'état* of December 2, 1851.

The small-holding peasants form a vast mass, the members of which live in similar conditions but without entering into manifold relations with one another. Their mode of production isolates them from one another instead of bringing them into mutual intercourse. The isolation is increased by France's bad means of communication and by the poverty of the peasants. Their field of production, the small holding, admits of no division of labour in its cultivation, no application of science and, therefore, no diversity of development, no variety of talent, no wealth of social relationships. Each individual peasant family is almost self-sufficient; it itself directly produces the major part of its consumption and thus acquires its means of life more through exchange with nature than in intercourse with society. A small holding, a peasant and his family; alongside them another small holding, another peasant and another family. A few score of these make up a village, and a few score of villages make up a Department. In this way, the great mass of the French nation is formed by simple addition of homologous magnitudes, much as potatoes in a sack form a sack of potatoes. In so far as millions of families live under economic conditions of existence that separate their mode of life, their interests and their culture from those of the other classes, and put them in hostile opposition to the latter, they form a class. In so far as there is merely a local interconnection among these small-holding peasants, and the identity of their interests begets no community, no national bond and no political organization among them, they do not form a class. They are consequently incapable of enforcing their class interest in their own name, whether through a parliament or through a convention. They cannot represent themselves, they must be represented. Their representative must at the same time appear as their master, as an authority over them, as an unlimited governmental power that protects them against the other classes and sends them rain and sunshine from above. The political influence of the small-holding peasants, therefore, finds its final expression in the executive power subordinating society to itself.

Historical tradition gave rise to the belief of the French peasants in the miracle that a man named Napoleon would bring all the glory back to them. And an individual turned up who gives himself out as the man because he bears the name of Napoleon, in consequence of the *Code Napoléon*, which lays down that *la recherche de la paternité est interdite*. [3] After a vagabondage of twenty years and after a series of grotesque adventures, the legend finds fulfilment and the man becomes Emperor of the French. The fixed idea of the Nephew was realized, because it coincided with the fixed idea of the most numerous class of the French people.

But, it may be objected, what about the peasant risings in half of France, the raids on the peasants by the army, the mass incarceration and transportation of peasants?

Since Louis XIV, France has experienced no similar persecution of the peasants "on account of demagogic practices."

But let there be no misunderstanding. The Bonaparte dynasty represents not the revolutionary, but the conservative peasant; not the peasant that strikes out beyond the condition of his social existence, the small holding, but rather the peasant who wants to consolidate this holding, not the country folk who,

[3] Enquiry into paternity is forbidden.—*Ed.*

linked up with the towns, want to overthrow the old order through their own energies, but on the contrary those who, in stupefied seclusion within this old order, want to see themselves and their small holdings saved and favoured by the ghost of the empire. It represents not the enlightenment, but the superstition of the peasant; not his judgement, but his prejudice; not his future, but his past; not his modern Cevennes, but his modern Vendée.

After the first revolution had transformed the peasants from semi-villeins into freeholders, Napoleon confirmed and regulated the conditions on which they could exploit undisturbed the soil of France which had only just fallen to their lot and slake their youthful passion for property. But what is now causing the ruin of the French peasant is his small holding itself, the division of the land, the form of property which Napoleon consolidated in France. It is precisely the material conditions which made the feudal peasant a small-holding peasant and Napoleon an emperor. Two generations have sufficed to produce the inevitable result: progressive deterioration of agriculture, progressive indebtedness of the agriculturist. The "Napoleonic" form of property, which at the beginning of the nineteenth century was the condition for the liberation and enrichment of the French country folk, has developed in the course of this century into the law of their enslavement and pauperization.

The economic development of small-holding property has radically changed the relation of the peasants to the other classes of society. Under Napoleon, the fragmentation of the land in the countryside supplemented free competition and the beginning of big industry in the towns. The peasant class was the ubiquitous protest against the landed aristocracy which had just been overthrown. The roots that small-holding property struck in French soil deprived feudalism of all nutriment. Its landmarks formed the natural fortifications of the bourgeoisie against any surprise attack on the part of its old overlords. But in the course of the nineteenth century the feudal lords were replaced by urban usurers; the feudal obligation that went with the land was replaced by the mortgage; aristocratic landed property was replaced by bourgeois capital. The small holding of the peasant is now only the pretext that allows the capitalist to draw profits, interest and rent from the soil, while leaving it to the tiller of the soil himself to see how he can extract his wages. The mortgage debt burdening the soil of France imposes on the French peasantry payment of an amount of interest equal to the annual interest on the entire British national debt. Small-holding property, in this enslavement by capital to which its development inevitably pushes forward, has transformed the mass of the French nation into troglodytes.

Besides the mortgage which capital imposes on it, the small holding is burdened by *taxes*. Taxes are the source of life for the bureaucracy, the army,
the priests and the court, in short, for the whole apparatus of the executive
power. Strong government and heavy taxes are identical. By its very nature,
small-holding property forms a suitable basis for an all-powerful and innumerable bureaucracy. It creates a uniform level of relationships and persons
over the whole surface of the land. Hence it also permits of uniform action
from a supreme centre on all points of this uniform mass. It annihilates the
aristocratic intermediate grades between the mass of the people and the state
power. On all sides, therefore, it calls forth the direct interference of this
state power and the interposition of its immediate organs. Finally, it produces an unemployed surplus population for which there is no place either
on the land or in the towns, and which accordingly reaches out for state
offices as a sort of respectable alms, and provokes the creation of state posts.
By the new markets which he opened at the point of the bayonet, by the
plundering of the Continent, Napoleon repaid the compulsory taxes with
interest. These taxes were a spur to the industry of the peasant, whereas now
they rob his industry of its last resources and complete his inability to resist
pauperism. And an enormous bureaucracy, well-gallooned and well-fed, is
the *"idée napoléonienne"* which is most congenial of all to the second Bonaparte. How could it be otherwise, seeing that alongside the actual classes of
society he is forced to create an artificial caste, for which the maintenance of
his regime becomes a bread-and-butter question? Accordingly, one of his first
financial operations was the raising of officials' salaries to their old level and
the creation of new sinecures.

Lastly, the culminating point of the *"idées napoléoniennes"* is the prepon-
derance of the *army*. The army was the *point d'honneur*[4] of the small-holding
peasants, it was they themselves transformed into heroes, defending their new
possessions against the outer world, glorifying their recently won nationhood,
plundering and revolutionizing the world. The uniform was their own state
dress; war was their poetry; the small holding, extended and rounded off in
imagination, was their fatherland, and patriotism the ideal form of the sense of
property. But the enemies against whom the French peasant has now to
defend his property are not the Cossacks; they are the *huissiers*[5] and the tax
collectors. The small holding lies no longer in the so-called fatherland, but in
the register of mortgages. The army itself is no longer the flower of the peasant
youth; it is the swamp-flower of the peasant *lumpenproletariat*. It consists in

[4]Matter of honour, a point of special touch.—*Ed.*
[5]*Huissiers*: Bailiffs.—*Ed.*

large measure of *remplaçants*, of substitutes, just as the second Bonaparte is himself only a *remplaçant*, the substitute for Napoleon.

One sees: *all* "idées napoléoniennes" *are ideas of the undeveloped small holding in the freshness of its youth;* for the small holding that has outlived its day they are an absurdity. They are only the hallucinations of its death struggle, words that are transformed into phrases, spirits transformed into ghosts. But the parody of the empire [*des Imperialismus*] was necessary to free the mass of the French nation from the weight of tradition and to work out in pure form the opposition between the state power and society. With the progressive undermining of small-holding property, the state structure erected upon it collapses. The centralization of the state that modern society requires arises only on the ruins of the military-bureaucratic government machinery which was forged in opposition to feudalism.

The condition of the French peasants provides us with the answer to the riddle of the *general elections of December 20 and 21*, which bore the second Bonaparte up Mount Sinai, not to receive laws, but to give them.

The Origin of Modern Capitalism [1920]

MAX WEBER

• *Max Weber's contributions to conflict theory, as to sociology in general, are voluminous and would require an entire work of their own to excerpt. Weber's main concern throughout his intellectual career, though, was the origins of modern capitalism. There is only one place in his entire works where he summarizes his overall theory: the concluding part of the lectures he gave in the last year of his life,* the General Economic History. *Far less known than* The Protestant Ethic and the Spirit of Capitalism *or indeed than many of his other writings, this work has been a kind of secret handbook of Weber's encompassing vision.*

The portions presented here give Weber's full schema in compressed form. The "rationalized" form that sets off modern capitalism from most other historical types of capitalism is characterized by two points that Marx also stressed: (1) free and propertyless labor *moving in response to the demands of an unrestricted market and* (2) the entrepreneurial organization of capital. *But Weber also insisted that technology and all other factors of production must be* rationalized and calculable *and centralized in the hands of the entrepreneur. These characteristics only came into being on the basis of a* calculable law, *which itself was further dependent on earlier parts of the historical chain of causes, including the* bureaucratic state, *which monopolized the professional means of violence, as well as strong pockets of* legal citizenship rights, *which allowed business interests some leverage against the state. There is also a second great branch of causal connections behind modern capitalism, culminating in a* methodical, nondualistic, and universally applicable economic ethic, *which had its origins in the* Judaic, Greek, and Christian religions. *Weber's more famous* Protestant Ethic, *the subject of his first notable publication, thus comes into the overall scheme as only a late addition to one of the two long chains of historical conditions that were necessary before modern capitalism could emerge.*

Max Weber, *General Economic History* (New York: Greenberg Publishers, 1927), pp. 275–78, 302, 311–16, 322–26, 332–39, 342–44, 352–56, 365–369. Originally published in 1923, from 1920 lectures.

THE MEANING AND PRESUPPOSITIONS OF
MODERN CAPITALISM

Capitalism is present wherever the industrial provision for the needs of a human group is carried out by the method of enterprise, irrespective of what need is involved. More specifically, a rational capitalistic establishment is one with capital accounting, that is, an establishment which determines its income yielding power by calculation according to the methods of modern bookkeeping and the striking of a balance. The device of the balance was first insisted upon by the Dutch theorist Simon Stevin in the year 1698.

It goes without saying that an individual economy may be conducted along capitalistic lines to the most widely varying extent; parts of the economic provision may be organized capitalistically and other parts on the handicraft or the manorial pattern. Thus at a very early time the city of Genoa had a part of its political needs, namely those for the prosecution of war, provided in capitalistic fashion, through stock companies. In the Roman empire, the supply of the population of the capital city with grain was carried out by officials, who however for this purpose, besides control over their subalterns, had the right to command the services of transport organizations; thus the leiturgical or forced contribution type of organization was combined with administration of public resources. Today, in contrast with the greater part of the past, our everyday needs are supplied capitalistically, our political needs however through compulsory contributions, that is, by the performance of political duties of citizenship such as the obligation to military service, jury duty, etc. A whole epoch can be designated as typically capitalistic only as the provision for wants is capitalistically organized to such a predominant degree that if we imagine this form of organization taken away the whole economic system must collapse.

While capitalism of various forms is met with in all periods of history, the provision of the everyday wants by capitalistic methods is characteristic of the occident alone and even here has been the inevitable method only since the middle of the 19th century. Such capitalistic beginnings as are found in earlier centuries were merely anticipatory, and even the somewhat capitalistic establishments of the 16th century may be removed in thought from the economic life of the time without introducing any overwhelming change.

The most general presupposition for the existence of this present-day capitalism is that of rational capital accounting as the norm for all large industrial undertakings which are concerned with provision for everyday wants. Such accounting involves, again, first, the appropriation of all physical means of production—land, apparatus, machinery, tools, and so on, as dis-

posable property of autonomous private industrial enterprises. This is a phenomenon known only to our time, when the army alone forms a universal
exception to it. In the second place, it involves freedom of the market, that
is, the absence of irrational limitations on trading in the market. Such
limitations might be of a class character, if a certain mode of life were
prescribed for a certain class or consumption were standardized along class
lines, or if class monopoly existed, as for example if the townsman were not
allowed to own an estate or the knight or peasant to carry on industry; in
such cases neither a free labor market nor a commodity market exists. Third,
capitalistic accounting presupposes rational technology, that is, one reduced
'o calculation to the largest possible degree, which implies mechanization.
This applies to both production and commerce, the outlays for preparing as
well as moving goods.

The fourth characteristic is that of calculable law. The capitalistic form of
industrial organization, if it is to operate rationally, must be able to depend
upon calculable adjudication and administration. Neither in the age of the
Greek city-state (polis) nor in the patrimonial state of Asia nor in western
countries down to the Stuarts was this condition fulfilled. The royal "cheap
justice" with its remissions by royal grace introduced continual disturbances
into the calculations of economic life . . . The fifth feature is free labor.
Persons must be present who are not only legally in the position, but are also
economically compelled, to sell their labor on the market without restriction.
It is in contradiction to the essence of capitalism, and the development of
capitalism is impossible, if such a propertyless stratum is absent, a class compelled to sell its labor services to live; and it is likewise impossible if only
unfree labor is at hand. Rational capitalistic calculation is possible only on the
basis of free labor; only where in consequence of the existence of workers who
in the formal sense voluntarily, but actually under the compulsion of the whip
of hunger, offer themselves, the costs of products may be unambiguously
determined by agreement in advance. The sixth and final condition is the
commercialization of economic life. By this we mean the general use of
commercial instruments to represent share rights in enterprise, and also in
property ownership.

To sum up, it must be possible to conduct the provision for needs exclusively on the basis of market opportunities and the calculation of net income.
The addition of this commercialization to the other characteristics of capitalism involves intensification of the significance of another factor not yet mentioned, namely speculation. Speculation reaches its full significance only from
the moment when property takes on the form of negotiable paper.

THE DEVELOPMENT OF INDUSTRIAL TECHNIQUE

It is not easy to define accurately the concept of the factory. We think at once of the steam engine and the mechanization of work, but the machine had its forerunner in what we call "apparatus"—labor appliances which had to be utilized in the same way as the machine but which as a rule were driven by water power. The distinction is that the apparatus works as the servant of the man while in modern machines the inverse relation holds. The real distinguishing characteristic of the modern factory is in general, however, not the implements of work applied, but the concentration of ownership of workplace, means of work, source of power and raw material in one and the same hand, that of the entrepreneur. This combination was only exceptionally met with before the 18th century. . . .

The decisive impetus toward capitalism could come only from one source, namely a mass market demand, which again could arise only in a small proportion of the luxury industries through the democratization of the demand, especially along the line of production of substitutes for the luxury goods of the upper classes. This phenomenon is characterized by price competition, while the luxury industries working for the court follow the handicraft principle of competition in quality. The first example of the policy of a state organization entering upon price competition is afforded in England at the close of the 15th century, when the effort was made to undersell Flemish wool, an object which was promoted by numerous export prohibitions.

The great price revolution of the 16th and 17th centuries provided a powerful lever for the specifically capitalistic tendencies of seeking profit through cheapening production and lowering the price. This revolution is rightly ascribed to the continuous inflow of precious metals in consequence of the great overseas discoveries. It lasted from the thirties of the 16th century down to the time of the Thirty Years' War, but affected different branches of economic life in quite different ways. In the case of agricultural products an almost universal rise in price set in, making it possible for them to go over to production for the market. It was quite otherwise with the course of prices for industrial products. By and large these remained stable or rose in price relatively little, thus really falling, in comparison with the agricultural products. This relative decline was made possible only through a shift in technology and economics, and exerted a pressure in the direction of increasing profit by repeated cheapening of production. Thus the development did not follow the order that capitalism set in first and the decline in prices followed, but the reverse; first the prices fell relatively and then came capitalism.

The tendency toward rationalizing technology and economic relations with a view to reducing prices in relation to costs, generated in the 17th century a feverish pursuit of invention. All the inventors of the period are dominated by the object of cheapening production; the notion of perpetual motion as a source of energy is only one of many objectives of this quite universal movement. The inventor as a type goes back much farther. But if one scrutinizes the devices of the greatest inventor of precapitalistic times, Leonardo da Vinci—(for experimentation originated in the field of art and not that of science)—one observes that his urge was not that of cheapening production but the rational mastery of technical problems as such. The inventors of the pre-capitalistic age worked empirically; their inventions had more or less the character of accidents. An exception is mining, and in consequence it is the problems of mining in connection with which deliberate technical progress took place.

A positive innovation in connection with invention is the first rational patent law, the English law of 1623, which contains all the essential provisions of a modern statute. Down to that time the exploitation of inventions had been arranged through a special grant in consideration of a payment; in contrast the law of 1623 limits the protection of the invention to 14 years and makes its subsequent utilization by an entrepreneur conditional upon an adequate royalty for the original inventor. Without the stimulus of this patent law the inventions crucial for the development of capitalism in the field of textile industry in the 18th century would not have been possible.

Drawing together once more the distinguishing characteristics of western capitalism and its causes, we find the following factors. First, this institution alone produced a rational organization of labor, which nowhere previously existed. Everywhere and always there has been trade; it can be traced back into the stone age. Likewise we find in the most varied epochs and cultures war finance, state contributions, tax farming, farming of offices, etc., but not a rational organization of labor. Furthermore we find everywhere else a primitive, strictly integrated internal economy such that there is no question of any freedom of economic action between members of the same tribe or clan, associated with absolute freedom of trade externally. Internal and external ethics are distinguished, and in connection with the latter there is complete ruthlessness in financial procedure; nothing can be more rigidly prescribed than the clan economy of China or the caste economy of India, and on the other hand nothing so unscrupulous as the conduct of the Hindu foreign trader. In contrast with this, the second characteristic of western capitalism is a lifting of the barrier between the internal economy and external economy, between internal and external ethics, and the entry of the commercial principle into the internal economy, with the organization of labor on this basis. Finally, the disintegration of primitive economic fixity is also met with elsewhere, as for example in Babylon, but nowhere else do we find the entrepreneur organization of labor as it is known in the western world.

If this development took place only in the occident the reason is to be found in the special features of its general cultural evolution which are peculiar to it. Only the occident knows the state in the modern sense, with a professional administration, specialized officialdom, and law based on the concept of citizenship. Beginnings of this institution in antiquity and in the orient were never able to develop. Only the occident knows rational law, made by jurists and rationally interpreted and applied, and only in the occident is found the concept of citizen (*civis Romanus, citoyen, bourgeois*) because only in the occident again are there cities in the specific sense. Furthermore, only the occident possesses science in the present-day sense of the word. Theology, philosophy, reflection on the ultimate problems of life, were known to the Chinese and the Hindu perhaps even of a depth unreached by the European; but a rational science and in connection with it a rational technology remained unknown to those civilizations. Finally, western civilization is further distinguished from every other by the presence of men with a rational ethic for the conduct of life. Magic and religion are found everywhere; but a religious basis for the ordering of life which consistently followed out must lead to explicit rationalism is again peculiar to western civilization alone.

CITIZENSHIP

In the concept of citizenship (*Bürgertum*) as it is used in social history are bound up three distinct significations. First, citizenship may include certain social categories or classes which have some specific communal or economic interest. As thus defined the class citizen is not unitary; there are greater citizens and lesser citizens; entrepreneurs and hand workers belong to the class. Second, in the political sense, citizenship signifies membership in the state, with its connotation as the holder of certain political rights. Finally, by citizens in the class sense, we understand those strata which are drawn together, in contrast with the bureaucracy or the proletariat and others outside their circle, as "persons of property and culture," entrepreneurs, recipients of funded incomes, and in general all persons of academic culture, a certain class standard of living, and a certain social prestige.

The first of these concepts is economic in character and is peculiar to western civilization. There are and have been everywhere hand laborers and entrepreneurs, but never and nowhere were they included in a unitary social class. The notion of the citizen of the state has its forerunners in antiquity and in the medieval city. Here there were citizens as holders of political rights, while outside of the occident only traces of this relation are met with, as in the Babylonian patriciate and the Josherim, the inhabitants of a city with full legal rights, in the Old Testament. The farther east we go the fewer are these traces; the notion of citizens of the state is unknown to the world of Islam, and to India and China. Finally, the social class signification of citizen as the man of property and culture, or of one or the other, in contrast with the nobility, on the one hand, and the proletariat, on the other, is likewise a specifically modern and western concept, like that of the bourgeoisie. It is true that in antiquity and in the middle ages, citizen was a class concept; membership in specific class groups made the person a citizen. The difference is that in this use the citizen was privileged in a negative as well as a positive sense. In the positive sense in that he only—in the medieval city for example—might pursue certain occupations; negatively in that certain legal requirements were waived, such as the qualification for holding a fief, the qualification for the tourney, and that for membership in the religious community. The citizen in the quality of membership in a class is always a citizen of a particular city, and the city in this sense, has existed only in the western world, or elsewhere, as in the early period in Mesopotamia, only in an incipient stage. . . .

For the fact that this development took place only in the occident there are two reasons. The first is the peculiar character of the organization for defense. The occidental city is in its beginnings first of all a defense group, an organization of those economically competent to bear arms, to equip and train themselves. Whether the military organization is based on the principle of self-equipment or on that of equipment by a military overlord who furnishes horses, arms and provisions, is a distinction quite as fundamental for social history as is the question whether the means of economic production are the property of the worker or of a capitalistic entrepreneur. Everywhere outside the west the development of the city was prevented by the fact that the army of the prince is older than the city. The earliest Chinese epics do not, like the Homeric, speak of the hero who fares forth to battle in his own chariot, but only of the officer as a leader of the men. Likewise in India an army led by officers marched out against Alexander the Great. In the west the army equipped by the war lord, and the separation of soldier from the paraphernalia of war, in a way analogous to the separation of the worker from the means of production, is a product of the modern era, while in Asia it stands at the apex of the historical development. There was no Egyptian or Babylonian-Assyrian army which would have presented a picture similar to that of the Homeric mass army, the feudal army of the west, the city army of the ancient *polis*, or the medieval guild army.

The distinction is based on the fact that in the cultural evolution of Egypt, western Asia, India, and China the question of irrigation was crucial. The water question conditioned the existence of the bureaucracy, the compulsory service of the dependent classes, and the dependence of the subject classes upon the functioning of the bureaucracy of the king. That the king also expressed his power in the form of a military monopoly is the basis of the distinction between the military organization of Asia and that of the west. In the first case the royal official and army officer is from the beginning the central figure of the process, while in the west both were originally absent. The forms of religious brotherhood and self equipment for war made possible the origin and existence of the city. It is true that the beginnings of an analogous development are found in the east. In India we meet with relations which verge upon the establishment of a city in the western sense, namely, the combination of self equipment and legal citizenship; one who could furnish an elephant for the army is in the free city of Vaiçali a full citizen. In ancient Mesopotamia, too, the knights carried on war with each other and established cities with autonomous administration. But in the one case as in the other these beginnings later disappear as the great kingdom arises on the basis of water regulation. Hence only in the west did the development come to complete maturity.

The second obstacle which prevented the development of the city in the orient was formed by ideas and institutions connected with magic. In India the castes were not in a position to form ritualistic communities and hence a city, because they were ceremonially alien to one another. The same facts explained the peculiar position of the Jews in the middle ages. The cathedral and the eucharist were the symbols of the unity of the city, but the Jews were not permitted to pray in the cathedral or take part in the communion and hence were doomed to form diaspora-communes. On the contrary, the consideration which made it natural for cities to develop in the west was in antiquity the extensive freedom of the priesthood, the absence of any monopoly in the hands of the priests over communion with the gods, such as obtained in Asia. In western antiquity the officials of the city performed the rites, and the resultant proprietorship of the *polis* over the things belonging to the gods and the priestly treasures was carried to the point of filling the priestly offices by auction, since no magical limitations stood in the way as in India. For the later period in the west three great facts were crucial. The first was prophecy among the Jews, which destroyed magic within the confines of Judaism; magical procedure remained real but was devilish instead of divine.

The second fact was the pentecostal miracle, the ceremonial adoption into the spirit of Christ which was a decisive factor in the extraordinary spread of the early Christian enthusiasm. The final factor was the day in Antioch (Gal. 2; 11 ff.) when Paul, in opposition to Peter, espoused fellowship with the uncircumcised. The magical barriers between clans, tribes, and peoples, which were still known in the ancient *polis* to a considerable degree, were thus set aside and the establishment of the occidental city was made possible.

·   ·   ·

The basis of democratization is everywhere purely military in character; it lies in the rise of disciplined infantry, the *hoplites* of antiquity, the guild army in the middle ages. The decisive fact was that military discipline proved its superiority over the battle between heroes. Military discipline meant the triumph of democracy because the community wished and was compelled to secure the co-operation of the non-aristocratic masses and hence put arms, and along with arms political power, into their hands. In addition, the money power plays its role, both in antiquity and in the middle ages.

Parallelism is also manifest in the mode in which democracy establishes itself. Like the state in the beginning, the *popolo* carries on its struggle as a separate group with its own officials. Examples are the Spartan ephors as representatives of the democracy against the kings, and the Roman tribunes of the people, while in the Italian cities of the middle ages the *capitano del popolo*, or *della mercadanzao*, are such officials. It is characteristic of them that they are the first concededly "illegitimate" officials. The consuls of the Italian cities still prefix the *dei gratia* to their titles but the *capitano del popolo* no longer does so. The source of the power of the tribune is illegitimate; he is *sacrocanctus* precisely because he is not a legitimate official and hence is protected only by divine interference, or popular vengeance.

The two courses of development are also equivalent in regard to their purpose. Social and not economic class interests are decisive; it is a question primarily of protection against the aristocratic families. The *popolani* know that they are rich and have fought and won the great wars of the city along with the nobility; they are armed, and hence feel themselves discriminated against and are no longer content with the subordinate class position which they have previously accepted. Similarity exists also, and finally, in the means available to the officials of the separate organization (*Sonderbund*). Everywhere they secure the right of intervention in legal processes in which the plebeians are opposed to the aristocrats. This purpose is served by the right of intercession of the Roman tribune as well as the Florentine *capitano del popolo*, a right which is carried out through appeal or through lynch justice.

The *Sonderbund* sets up the claim that the statutes of the city shall be valid only after they have been ratified by the plebeians, and finally establishes the principle that only that is law which they have determined. The Roman legal principle: *ut quod tributim plebs iussisset populum tenerit* has its counterpart in the Florentine *ordinamenti della giustizia*, and in the exclusion of all non-workers from Lenin's labor dictatorship.

.   .   .

Turning to the question as to the consequences of these relations in connection with the evolution of capitalism, we must emphasize the heterogeneity of industry in antiquity and in the middle ages, and the different species of capitalism itself. In the first place, we are met in the most widely separated periods with a multiplicity of non-rational forms of capitalism. These include first capitalistic enterprises for the purpose of tax farming—in the occident as well as in China and western Asia—and for the purpose of financing war, in China and India, in the period of small separate states; second, capitalism in connection with trade speculation, the trader being entirely absent in almost no epoch of history; third, money-lending capitalism, exploiting the necessities of outsiders. All these forms of capitalism relate to spoils, taxes, the pickings of office or official usury, and finally to tribute and actual need. It is noteworthy that in former times officials were financed as Cæsar was by Crassus and endeavored to recoup the sums advanced through misuse of their official position. All this, however, relates to occasional economic activity of an irrational character, while no rational system of labor organization developed out of these arrangements.

Rational capitalism, on the contrary, is organized with a view to market opportunities, hence to economic objectives in the real sense of the word, and the more rational it is the more closely it relates to mass demand and the provision for mass needs. It was reserved to the modern western development after the close of the middle ages to elevate this capitalism into a system, while in all of antiquity there was but one capitalistic class whose rationalism might be compared with that of modern capitalism, namely, the Roman knighthood. When a Greek city required credit or leased public land or let a contract for supplies, it was forced to incite competition among different interlocal capitalists. Rome, in contrast, was in possession of a rational capitalistic class which from the time of the Gracchi played a determining role in the state. The capitalism of this class was entirely relative to state and governmental opportunities, to the leasing of the *ager publicus* or conquered land, and of domain land, or to tax farming and the financing of political adventures and of wars. It influenced the public policy of Rome in

a decisive way at times, although it had to reckon with the constant antagonism of the official nobility.

The capitalism of the late middle ages began to be directed toward market
opportunities, and the contrast between it and the capitalism of antiquity
appears in the development after the cities have lost their freedom. Here again
we find a fundamental distinction in the lines of development as between
antiquity and medieval and modern times. In antiquity the freedom of the
cities was swept away by a bureaucratically organized world empire within
which there was no longer a place for political capitalism. In the beginning
the emperors were forced to resort to the financial power of the knighthood
but we see them progressively emancipate themselves and exclude the knightly
class from the farming of the taxes and hence from the most lucrative source
of wealth—just as the Egyptian kings were able to make the provisions for
political and military requirements in their realms independent of the capitalist powers and reduce the tax farmers to the position of tax officials. In the
imperial period of Rome the leasing of domain land everywhere decreased in
extent in favor of permanent hereditary appropriation. The provision for the
economic needs of the state was taken care of through compulsory contributions and compulsory labor of servile persons instead of competitive contracts.
The various classes of the population became stratified along occupational
lines and the burden of state requirements was imposed on the newly created
groups on the principle of joint liability.

This development means the throttling of ancient capitalism. A conscript
army takes the place of the mercenaries and ships are provided by compulsory
service. The entire harvest of grain, insofar as regions of surplus production
are concerned, is distributed among the cities in accordance with their needs,
with the exclusion of private trade. The building of roads and every other
service which has to be provided for is laid on the shoulders of specific
personal groups who become attached by inheritance to the soil and to their
occupations. At the end the Roman urban communities, acting through their
mayors in a way not very different from the village community through its
common meeting, demand the return of the rich city councilmen on property
grounds, because the population is jointly responsible for the payments and
services due to the state. These services are subject to the principle of the *origo*
which is erected on the pattern of the ἰδία of Ptolemaic Egypt; the compulsory dues of servile persons can only be rendered in their home commune.
After this system became established the political opportunities for securing
gain were closed to capitalism; in the late Roman state, based on compulsory
contributions (*Leiturgiestaat*) there was as little place for capitalism as in the
Egyptian state organized on the basis of compulsory labor service (*Fronstaat*).

Quite dif   the   the city in the modern era. Here again its
autonomy wa   v. The English city of the 17th and 18th
centuries had   be a   a clique of guilds which could lay
claim only to fina   nd s   ance. The German cities of the
same period, with th   ies, were merely geographical entities (*Landstadt*)   as ordered from above. In the
French cities this developn   n earlier, while the Spanish cities
were deprived of their power   y   , in the insurrection of the *commu-
neros*. The Italian cities found the   ves in the power of the "signory" and
those of Russia never arrived at freedom in the western sense. Everywhere the
military, judicial, and industrial authority was taken away from the cities. In
form the old rights were as a rule unchanged, but in fact the modern city was
deprived of its freedom as effectively as had happened in antiquity with the
establishment of the Roman dominion, though in contrast with antiquity they
came under the power of competing national states in a condition of perpetual
struggle for power in peace or war. This competitive struggle created the
largest opportunities for modern western capitalism. The separate states had to
compete for mobile capital, which dictated to them the conditions under
which it would assist them to power. Out of this alliance of the state with
capital, dictated by necessity, arose the national citizen class, the bourgeoisie
in the modern sense of the word. Hence it is the closed national state which
afforded to capitalism its chance for development—and as long as the national
state does not give place to a world empire capitalism also will endure.

THE RATIONAL STATE

The state in the sense of the rational state has existed only in the western
world. Under the old regime in China a thin stratum of so-called officials, the
mandarins, existed above the unbroken power of the clans and commercial
and industrial guilds. The mandarin is primarily a humanistically educated
literatus in the possession of a benefice but not in the least degree trained for
administration; he knows no jurisprudence but is a fine writer, can make
verses, knows the age-old literature of the Chinese and can interpret it. In the
way of political service no importance is attached to him. Such an official
performs no administrative work himself; administration lies rather in the
hands of the chancery officials. The mandarin is continually transferred from
one place to another to prevent his obtaining a foothold in his administrative
district, and he could never be assigned to his home province. As he does not
understand the dialect of his province he cannot communicate with the public. A state with such officials is something different from the occidental state.

In reality everything is based on the magical theory that the virtue of the empress and the merits of the officials, meaning their perfection in literary culture, keeps things in order in normal times. If a drought sets in or any untoward event takes place an edict is promulgated intensifying the examinations in verse-making, or speeding up legal trials in order to quiet the spirits. The empire is an agrarian state; hence the power of the peasant clans who represent nine-tenths of the economic life—the other one-tenth belonging to commercial and trading guild organizations—is entirely unbroken. In essence things are left to take care of themselves. The officials do not rule but only interfere in the event of disturbances or untoward happenings.

Very different is the rational state in which alone modern capitalism can flourish. Its basis is an expert officialdom and rational law. The Chinese state changed over to administration through trained officials in the place of humanistically cultured persons as early as the 7th and 11th centuries but the change could be only temporarily maintained; then the usual eclipse of the moon arrived and arrangements were transformed in reverse order. It cannot be seriously asserted, however, that the spirit of the Chinese people could not tolerate an administration of specialists. Its development, and that of the rational state, was rather prevented by the persistence of reliance upon magic. In consequence of this fact the power of the clans could not be broken, as happened in the occident through the development of the cities and of Christianity.

The rational law of the modern occidental state, on the basis of which the trained official renders his decisions, arose on its formal side, though not as to its content, out of Roman law. The latter was to begin with a product of the Roman city state, which never witnessed the dominion of democracy and its justice in the same form as the Greek city. A Greek heliast court administered a petty justice; the contestants worked upon the judges through pathos, tears, and abusing their opponents. This procedure was also known in Rome in political trials, as the orations of Cicero show, but not in civil trials where the prætor appointed an *iudex* to whom he gave strict instructions as to the conditions requiring a judgment against the accused or the throwing out of the case. Under Justinian the Byzantine bureaucracy brought order and system into this rational law, in consequence of the natural interest of the official in a law which would be systematic and fixed and hence easier to learn.

With the fall of the Roman empire in the west, law came into the hands of the Italian notaries. These, and secondarily the universities, have on their conscience the revival of Roman law. The notaries adhered to the old contractual forms of the Roman empire and re-interpreted them according to the needs of the time. At the same time a systematic legal doctrine was developed in the universities. The essential feature in the development, however, was the rationalization of procedure. As among all primitive peoples the ancient German legal trial was a rigidly formal affair. The party which pronounced wrongly a single word in the formula lost the case, because the formula possessed magical significance and supernatural evils were feared. This magical formalism of the German trial fitted in with the formalism of Roman law. At the same time the French kingdom played a part through the creation of the institution of the representative or advocate whose task it was especially to pronounce the legal formulas correctly, particularly in connection with the canon law. The magnificent administrative organization of the church required fixed forms for its disciplinary ends in relation to the laity and for its own internal discipline. No more than the bourgeoisie could it take up with the Germanic ordeal or judgment of God. The business man could not permit commercial claims to be decided by a competition in reciting formulas, and everywhere secured exemptions from this legalistic contest and from the ordeal. The church also, after hesitating at first, ended by adopting the view that such procedure was heathenish and not to be tolerated, and established the canonical procedure on lines as rational as possible. This two-fold rationalization of procedure from the profane and spiritual sides spread over the western world. . . .

This formalistic law, is however, calculable. In China it may happen that a man who has sold a house to another may later come to him and ask to be taken in because in the meantime he has been impoverished. If the purchaser refuses to heed the ancient Chinese command to help a brother, the spirits will be disturbed; hence the impoverished seller comes into the house as a renter who pays no rent. Capitalism cannot operate on the basis of a law so constituted. What it requires is law which can be counted upon, like a machine; ritualistic-religious and magical considerations must be excluded.

The creation of such a body of law was achieved through the alliance between the modern state and the jurists for the purpose of making good its claims to power. For a time in the 16th century it attempted to work with the humanists, and the first Greek gymnasia were established with the idea that men educated in them would be suitable for state officials; for political contests were carried out to a large extent through the exchange of state papers and only one schooled in Latin and Greek had the necessary equipment. This illusion was short-lived. It was soon found that the products of the gymnasia were not on that account alone equipped for political life, and the jurists were the final resort. In China, where the humanistically cultured mandarin ruled the field, the monarch had no jurists at his disposal, and the struggle among the different philosophical schools as to which of them formed the best statesmen waged to and fro until finally orthodox Confucianism was victorious.

India also had writers but no trained jurists. In contrast the western world had at its disposal a formally organized legal system, the product of the Roman genius, and officials trained in this law were superior to all others as technical administrators. From the standpoint of economic history this fact is significant in that the alliance between the state and formal jurisprudence was indirectly favorable to capitalism.

The Economic Policy of the Rational State

For the state to have an economic policy worthy of the name, that is one which is continuous and consistent, is an institution of exclusively modern origin. The first system which it brought forth is mercantilism, so-called. Before the development of mercantilism there were two widespread commercial policies, namely, the dominance of fiscal interests and of welfare interests the last in the sense of the customary standard of living.

In the east it was essentially ritualistic considerations, including caste and clan organizations, which prevented the development of a deliberate economic policy. . . .

[C]apitalistic development was not an outgrowth of national mercantilism; rather capitalism developed at first in England alongside the fiscal monopoly policy. The course of events was that a stratum of entrepreneurs which had developed in independence of the political administration secured the systematic support of Parliament in the 18th century, after the collapse of the fiscal monopoly policy of the Stuarts. Here for the last time irrational and rational capitalism faced each other in conflict, that is, capitalism in the field of fiscal and colonial privileges and public monopolies, and capitalism oriented in relation to market opportunities which were developed from within by business interests themselves on the basis of saleable services.

THE EVOLUTION OF THE CAPITALISTIC SPIRIT

In the last resort the factor which produced capitalism is the rational permanent enterprise, rational accounting, rational technology and rational law, but again not these alone. Necessary complementary factors were the rational spirit, the rationalization of the conduct of life in general, and a rationalistic economic ethic.

At the beginning of all ethics and the economic relations which result, is traditionalism, the sanctity of tradition, the exclusive reliance upon such trade and industry as have come down from the fathers. This traditionalism survives far down into the present; only a human lifetime in the past it was futile to double the wages of an agricultural laborer in Silesia who mowed a certain tract of land on a contract, in the hope of inducing him to increase his exertions. He would simply have reduced by half the work expended because with this half he would have been able to earn . . . as much as before. . . . This general incapacity and indisposition to depart from the beaten paths is the motive for the maintenance of tradition.

Primitive traditionalism may, however, undergo essential intensification through two circumstances. In the first place, material interests may be tied up with the maintenance of the tradition. When for example in China, the attempt was made to change certain roads or to introduce more rational means or routes of transportation, the perquisites of certain officials were threatened; and the same was the case in the middle ages in the west, and in modern times when railroads were introduced. Such special interests of officials, land-holders and merchants assisted decisively in restricting a tendency toward rationalization. Stronger still is the effect of the stereotyping of trade on magical grounds, the deep repugnance to undertaking any change in the established conduct of life because supernatural evils are feared. Generally some injury to economic privilege is concealed in this opposition, but its effectiveness depends on a general belief in the potency of the magical processes which are feared.

Traditional obstructions are not overcome by the economic impulse alone. The notion that our rationalistic and capitalistic age is characterized by a stronger economic interest than other periods is childish; the moving spirits of modern capitalism are not possessed of a stronger economic impulse than, for example, an oriental trader. The unchaining of the economic interest merely as such has produced only irrational results; such men as Cortez and Pizarro, who were perhaps its strongest embodiment, were far from having an idea of a rationalistic economic life. If the economic impulse in itself is universal, it is an interesting question as to the relations under which it becomes rationalized and rationally tempered in such fashion as to produce rational institutions of the character of capitalistic enterprise.

Originally, two opposite attitudes toward the pursuit of gain exist in combination. Internally, there is attachment to tradition and to the pietistic relations of fellow members of tribe, clan, and house-community, with the exclusion of the unrestricted quest of gain within the circle of those bound together by religious ties; externally, there is absolutely unrestricted play of the gain spirit in economic relations, every foreigner being originally an enemy in relation to whom no ethical restrictions apply; that is, the ethics of internal and external relations are categorically distinct. The course of development involves on the one hand the bringing in of calculation into the traditional brotherhood,

displacing the old religious relationship. As soon as accountability is established within the family community, and economic relations are no longer
strictly communistic, there is an end of the naive piety and its repression of
the economic impulse. This side of the development is especially characteristic in the west. At the same time there is a tempering of the unrestricted quest
of gain with the adoption of the economic principle into the internal economy. The result is a regulated economic life with the economic impulse
functioning within bounds.

In detail, the course of development has been varied. In India, the restrictions upon gain-seeking apply only to the two uppermost strata, the Brahmins
and the Rajputs. A member of these castes is forbidden to practice certain
callings. A Brahmin may conduct an eating house, as he alone has clean
hands; but he, like the Rajput, would be unclassed if he were to lend money
for interest. The latter, however, is permitted to the mercantile castes, and
within it we find a degree of unscrupulousness in trade which is unmatched
anywhere in the world. Finally, antiquity had only legal limitations on interest, and the proposition *caveat emptor* characterizes Roman economic ethics.
Nevertheless no modern capitalism developed there.

. . .

. . . Judaism was . . . of notable significance for modern rational capitalism, insofar as it transmitted to Christianity the latter's hostility to magic.
Apart from Judaism and Christianity, and two or three oriental sects (one of
which is in Japan), there is no religion with the character of outspoken hostility to magic. Probably this hostility arose through the circumstance that what
the Israelites found in Canaan was the magic of the agricultural god Baal,
while Jahveh was a god of volcanoes, earthquakes, and pestilences. The hostility between the two priesthoods and the victory of the priests of Jahveh discredited the fertility magic of the priests of Baal and stigmatized it with a
character of decadence and godlessness. Since Judaism made Christianity
possible and gave it the character of a religion essentially free from magic, it
rendered an important service from the point of view of economic history. For
the dominance of magic outside the sphere in which Christianity has prevailed
is one of the most serious obstructions to the rationalization of economic life.
Magic involves a stereotyping of technology and economic relations. When
attempts were made in China to inaugurate the building of railroads and
factories a conflict with geomancy ensued. The latter demanded that in the
location of structures on certain mountains, forests, rivers, and cemetery hills,
foresight should be exercised in order not to disturb the rest of the spirits.

Similar is the relation to capitalism of the castes in India. Every new technical process which an Indian employs signifies for him first of all that he leaves his caste and falls into another, necessarily lower. Since he believes in the transmigration of souls, the immediate significance of this is that his chance of purification is put off until another re-birth. He will hardly consent to such a change. An additional fact is that every caste makes every other impure. In consequence, workmen who dare not accept a vessel filled with water from each other's hands, cannot be employed together in the same factory room. Not until the present time, after the possession of the country by the English for almost a century, could this obstacle be overcome. Obviously, capitalism could not develop in an economic group thus bound hand and foot by magical beliefs.

In all times there has been but one means of breaking down the power of magic and establishing a rational conduct of life; this means is great rational prophecy. Not every prophecy by any means destroys the power of magic; but it is possible for a prophet who furnishes credentials in the shape of miracles and otherwise, to break down the traditional sacred rules. Prophecies have released the world from magic and in doing so have created the basis for our modern science and technology, and for capitalism. In China such prophecy has been wanting. What prophecy there was has come from the outside as in the case of Lao-Tse and Taoism. India, however, produced a religion of salvation; in contrast with China it has known great prophetic missions. But they were prophecies by example; that is, the typical Hindu prophet, such as Buddha, lives before the world the life which leads to salvation, but does not regard himself as one sent from God to insist upon the obligation to lead it; he takes the position that whoever wishes salvation, as an end freely chosen, should lead the life. However, one may reject salvation, as it is not the destiny of everyone to enter at death into Nirvana, and only philosophers in the strictest sense are prepared by hatred of this world to adopt the stoical resolution and withdraw from life.

The result was that Hindu prophecy was of immediate significance for the intellectual classes. These became forest dwellers and poor monks. For the masses, however, the significance of the founding of a Buddhistic sect was quite different, namely the opportunity of praying to the saints. There came to be holy men who were believed to work miracles, who must be well fed so that they would repay this good deed by guaranteeing a better reincarnation or through granting wealth, long life, and the like, that is, this world's goods. Hence Buddhism in its pure form was restricted to a thin stratum of monks. The laity found no ethical precepts according to which life should be molded; Buddhism indeed had its decalogue, but in distinction from that of the Jews it gave no binding commands but only recommendations. The most important act of service was and remained the physical maintenance of the monks. Such a religious spirit could never be in a position to displace magic but at best could only put another magic in its place.

In contrast with the ascetic religion of salvation of India and its defective action upon the masses, are Judaism and Christianity, which from the beginning have been plebeian religions and have deliberately remained such. The struggle of the ancient church against the Gnostics was nothing else than a struggle against the aristocracy of the intellectuals, such as is common to ascetic religions, with the object of preventing their seizing the leadership in the church. This struggle was crucial for the success of Christianity among the masses, and hence for the fact that magic was suppressed among the general population to the greatest possible extent. True, it has not been possible even down to today to overcome it entirely, but it was reduced to the character of something unholy, something diabolic. . . .

It is also necessary to distinguish between the virtuoso religion of adepts and the religion of the masses. Virtuoso religion is significant for everyday life only as a pattern; its claims are of the highest, but they fail to determine everyday ethics. The relation between the two is different in different religions. In Catholicism, they are brought into harmonious union insofar as the claims of the religious virtuoso are held up alongside the duties of the laymen as *consilia evangelica*. The really complete Christian is the monk; but his mode of life is not required of everyone, although some of his virtues in a qualified form are held up as ideals. The advantage of this combination was that ethics was not split asunder as in Buddhism. After all the distinction between monk ethics and mass ethics meant that the most worthy individuals in the religious sense withdrew from the world and established a separate community.

Christianity was not alone in this phenomenon, which rather recurs frequently in the history of religions, as is shown by the powerful influence of asceticism, which signifies the carrying out of a definite, methodical conduct of life. Asceticism has always worked in this sense. The enormous achievements possible to such an ascetically determined methodical conduct of life are demonstrated by the example of Tibet. The country seems condemned by nature to be an eternal desert; but a community of celibate ascetics has carried out colossal construction works in Lhassa and saturated the country with the religious doctrines of Buddhism. An analogous phenomenon is present in the middle ages in the west. In that epoch the monk is the first human being who lives rationally, who works methodically and by rational means toward a goal, namely the future life. Only for him did the clock strike, only for him were the hours of the day divided—for prayer. The economic life of the monastic communities was also rational.

But the rational mode of life remained restricted to the monastic circles. The Franciscan movement indeed attempted through the institution of the tertiaries to extend it to the laity, but the institution of the confessional was a barrier to such an extension. The church domesticated medieval Europe by means of its system of confession and penance, but for the men of the middle ages the possibility of unburdening themselves through the channel of the confessional, when they had rendered themselves liable to punishment, meant a release from the consciousness of sin which the teachings of the church had called into being. The unity and strength of the methodical conduct of life were thus in fact broken up. In its knowledge of human nature the church did not reckon with the fact that the individual is a closed unitary ethical personality, but steadfastly held to the view that in spite of the warnings of the confessional and of penances, however strong, he would again fall away morally; that is, it shed its grace on the just and the unjust.

The Reformation made a decisive break with this system. The dropping of the *concilia evangelica* by the Lutheran Reformation meant the disappearance of the dualistic ethics, of the distinction between a universally binding morality and a specifically advantageous code for virtuosi. The other-worldly asceticism came to an end. The stern religious characters who had previously gone into monasteries had now to practice their religion in the life of the world. For such an asceticism within the world the ascetic dogmas of protestantism created an adequate ethics. Celibacy was not required, marriage being viewed simply as an institution for the rational bringing up of children. Poverty was not required, but the pursuit of riches must not lead one astray into reckless enjoyment. Thus Sebastian Franck was correct in summing up the spirit of the Reformation in the words, "you think you have escaped from the monastery, but everyone must now be a monk throughout his life."

The wide significance of this transformation of the ascetic ideal can be followed down to the present in the classical lands of protestant ascetic religiosity. It is especially discernible in the import of the religious denominations in America. Although state and church are separated, still, as late as fifteen or twenty years ago no banker or physician took up a residence or established connections without being asked to what religious community he belonged, and his prospects were good or bad according to the character of his answer. Acceptance into a sect was conditioned upon a strict inquiry into one's ethical conduct. Membership in a sect which did not recognize the Jewish distinction between internal and external moral codes guaranteed one's business honor and reliability and this in turn guaranteed success. Hence the principle "honesty is the best policy" and hence among Quakers, Baptists, and Methodists the ceaseless repetition of the proposition based on experience that God would take care of his own. "The Godless cannot trust each other across the road; they turn to us when they want to do business; piety is the surest road to wealth." This is by no means "cant," but a combination of religiosity with consequences which were originally unknown to it and which were never intended.

It is true that the acquisition of wealth, attributed to piety, led to a dilemma, in all respects similar to that into which the medieval monasteries constantly fell; the religious guild led to wealth, wealth to fall from grace, and this again to the necessity of re-constitution. Calvinism sought to avoid this difficulty through the idea that man was only an administrator of what God had given him; it condemned enjoyment, yet permitted no flight from the world but rather regarded working together, with its rational discipline, as the religious task of the individual. Out of this system of thought came our word "calling," which is known only to the languages influenced by the Protestant translations of the Bible. It expresses the value placed upon rational activity carried on according to the rational capitalistic principle, as the fulfillment of a God-given task. Here lay also in the last analysis the basis of the contrast between the Puritans and the Stuarts. The ideas of both were capitalistically directed; but in a characteristic way the Jew was for the Puritan the embodiment of everything repugnant because he devoted himself to irrational and illegal occupations such as war loans, tax farming, and leasing of offices, in the fashion of the court favorite.

This development of the concept of the calling quickly gave to the modern entrepreneur a fabulously clear conscience,—and also industrious workers; he gave to his employees as the wages of their ascetic devotion to the calling and of co-operation in his ruthless exploitation of them through capitalism the prospect of eternal salvation, which in an age when ecclesiastical discipline took control of the whole of life to an extent inconceivable to us now, represented a reality quite different from any it has today. The Catholic and Lutheran churches also recognized and practiced ecclesiastical discipline. But in the Protestant ascetic communities admission to the Lord's Supper was conditioned on ethical fitness, which again was identified with business honor, while into the content of one's faith no one inquired. Such a powerful, unconsciously refined organization for the production of capitalistic individuals has never existed in any other church or religion, and in comparison with it what the Renaissance did for capitalism shrinks into insignificance.

The religious root of modern economic humanity is dead; today the concept of the calling is a *caput mortuum* in the world. Ascetic religiosity has been displaced by a pessimistic though by no means ascetic view of the world, such as that portrayed in Mandeville's Fable of the Bees, which teaches that private vices may under certain conditions be for the good of the public. With the complete disappearance of all the remains of the original enormous religious pathos of the sects, the optimism of the Enlightenment which believed in the harmony of interests, appeared as the heir of Protestant asceticism in the field of economic ideas; it guided the hands of the princes, statesmen, and writers of the later 18th and early 19th century. Economic ethics arose against the background of the ascetic ideal; now it has been stripped of its religious import. It was possible for the working class to accept its lot as long as the promise of eternal happiness could be held out to it. When this consolation fell away it was inevitable that those strains and stresses should appear in economic society which since then have grown so rapidly. This point had been reached at the end of the early period of capitalism, at the beginning of the age of iron, in the 19th century.

Power Divisions as the Basis of Class Conflict [1959]

RALF DAHRENDORF

• *Ralf Dahrendorf's* Class and Class Conflict in Industrial Society *(1959) set off the modern debate over conflict theory. Dahrendorf is known for his polemical attack on functionalist theories of
society, but his work is also a profound—one might say
heretical—revision of the Marxian theory of classes. Dahrendorf
sets out to write Marx's unfinished chapter on classes, of which
only a fragment survives in the posthumous Part 3 of* Capital.
*Marx mistook a historically specific form of class and class con-
flict for the basis of class conflict in general, according to Dahrendorf; Marx had founded class on the ownership or nonownership
of capital, but in fact this was only the specific form that power
took within the society of his time. The more generic division is
between those who have power and those who lack power. Thus,
any formal organization and any society have class divisions and
potential conflicts—between those who give orders and those who
have to take orders. Socialist societies (one might think of modern
Poland) have classes as well as capitalist societies, although they
are not based on ownership of capital. Dahrendorf then proceeds
to lay out a series of hypotheses on the conditions that mobilize or
inhibit the outbreak of overt conflicts among classes.*

MARX'S MODEL

What are the structural conditions of the formation of social classes? For simplicity's sake I shall treat this aspect of Marx's theory of class with reference to
his analysis of capitalist society, since the question remains undecided for the
time being whether this theory can be applied to other types of society at all.

Marx states quite clearly that class conflicts do not originate in differences of
income, or of the sources of income. His classes are not tax classes in the
sense of the Roman censors. Rather, the determinant of classes is "property."
Property, however, must not be understood in terms of purely passive wealth,
but as an effective force of production, as "ownership of means of production"

Reprinted from *Class and Class Conflict in Industrial Society*, pp. 20–23, 64, 71, 125–26, 136–41,
165–88, 200–201, 237–40, by Ralf Dahrendorf, with permission of the publishers, Stanford
University Press. Copyright 1959 by the Board of Trustees of the Leland Stanford Junior University.

and its denial to others. In this sense, the "relations of production," i.e., the authority relations resulting from the distribution of effective property in the realm of (industrial) production, constitute the ultimate determinant of the formation of classes and the development of class conflicts. The capitalists possess factories and machines, and buy the only property of the proletarians, their labor power, in order to produce a surplus value with these means of production and augment their capital.

But our question cannot be answered all that easily. The role of property in Marx's theory of class poses a problem of interpretation, and on this interpretation the validity of Marx's theory of class stands or falls. Does Marx understand, by the relations of property or production, the relations of factual control and subordination in the enterprises of industrial production—or merely the authority relations in so far as they are based on the legal title of property? Does he conceive of property in a loose (sociological) sense—that is, in terms of the exclusiveness of legitimate control (in which the manager also exercises property functions)—or merely as a statutory property right in connection with such control? Is property for Marx a special case of authority—or, vice versa, authority a special case of property? These questions are of considerable significance. If one works with the narrow concept of property, class conflict is the specific characteristic of a form of production which rests on the union of ownership and control. In this case a society in which control is exercised, for example, by state functionaries, has by definition neither classes nor class conflicts. If, on the other hand, one works with the wider concept of property, class structure is determined by the authority structure of the enterprise, and the category of class becomes at least potentially applicable to all "relations of production."

Marx does not always make his answer to our questions entirely clear. But it can be shown that his analyses are essentially based on the narrow, legal concept of property. This procedure, and this procedure only, enables Marx to link his sociology with his philosophy of history—a brilliant attempt, but at the same time a fault that robs his sociological analyses of stringency and conviction, a fault made no more acceptable by the fact that orthodox Marxists have remained faithful to their master in this point to the present day.

The most striking evidence for this interpretation can be found in the preliminary attempts at an analysis of the new form of ownership characteristic of joint-stock companies which Marx presents in Volume III of *Capital*. Marx is here explicitly concerned with the phenomenon that is commonly described today as the separation of ownership and control. He discusses what he calls the "transformation of the really functioning capitalist into a mere director, an administrator of alien capital, and of the owners of capital into mere owners, mere money capitalists." "In joint-stock companies, function is separated from capital ownership; thereby labor is entirely separated from ownership of the means of production, and of surplus labor." Now, hard though it is for ordinary minds to see why this change in the size and legal structure of industrial enterprises should end the conflict between entrepreneurs who can command and workers who have to obey (the conflict that Marx postulates for the "pure" capitalist enterprise), Marx ascribes to the joint-stock company a peculiar place in history. Time and again he describes the joint-stock company as "private production without the control of private property," as "the elimination of capital as private property within the capitalist mode of production itself," and even as the "abolition of the capitalist mode of production within the capitalist mode of production itself." For him, the joint-stock company is "a necessary point on the way to reconverting capital into the property of the producers, this no longer being the private property of individual producers but their associated property, that is, immediate social property." It is a "point on the way to the transformation of all functions in the process of reproduction hitherto connected with capital ownership into mere functions of the associated producers, into social functions." The joint-stock company, in other words, is halfway to the communist—and that means classless—society.

One of the critical pivots of Marx's theory of class is the undisputed identification of economic and political power and authority. Although classes are founded on the "relations of production," that is, the distribution of effective property in the narrow sphere of commodity production, they become socially significant only in the political sphere. But both these spheres are inseparable. "The political power" of a class arises for Marx "from the relations of production." The relations of production are "the final secret, the hidden basis of the whole construction of society"; industrial classes are *eo ipso* also social classes, and industrial class conflict is political class conflict. Nowhere has Marx explicitly discussed the basis of this empirical proposition—nor has he seen sufficiently clearly that it is an empirical proposition rather than a postulate or premise. The thesis that political conditions are determined by industrial conditions seems to stem, for him, from the generalized assertion of an absolute and universal primacy of production over all other structures of economy and society. It is evident that a postulate of this kind requires empirical test; how it fares in this test will have to be shown.

[T]he equalization of status resulting from social developments of the past century has contributed greatly to changing the issues and diminishing the intensity of class conflict. By way of extrapolation—fairly wild extrapolation, I may say—some authors have visualized a state in which there are no classes and no class conflicts, because there is simply nothing to quarrel about. I do not think that such a state is ever likely to occur. But in order to substantiate this opinion, it is necessary to explore the structural limits of equality, that is, to find the points at which even the most fanatic egalitarian comes up against insurmountable realities of social structure. One of these is surely the variety of human desires, ideas, and interests, the elimination of which is neither desirable nor likely. But while this is important, it is not as such an element of social structure. I shall suggest in this study that the fundamental inequality of social structure, and the lasting determinant of social conflict, is the inequality of power and authority which inevitably accompanies social organization.

[I]n post-capitalist as in capitalist industrial enterprises there are some whose task it is to control the actions of others and issue commands, and others who have to allow themselves to be controlled and who have to obey. Today as a hundred years ago there are governments, parliaments, and courts the members of which are entitled to make decisions that affect the lives of many citizens, and there are citizens who can protest and shift their vote but who have to abide by the law. Insofar as either of these relations can be described as one of authority, I would claim that relations of domination and subordination have persisted throughout the changes of the past century. Again, I believe that we can go even further. The authority exercised in both capitalist and post-capitalist society is of the same type; it is, in Weber's terms, "rational authority" based "on the belief in the legality of institutionalized norms and the right of command on the part of those invested with authority by these norms." From this condition many others, including the necessity of bureaucratic administration, follow. But these are based above all on the fundamental social inequality of authority which may be mitigated by its "rational" character, but that nevertheless pervades the structure of all industrial societies and provides both the determinant and the substance of most conflicts and clashes.

SOCIOLOGICAL CRITIQUE OF MARX

Marx succeeded in tracing conflicts that effect change back to patterns of social structure. For him, social conflicts were not random occurrences which forbid explanation and therefore prediction. Rather, he believed these conflicts to be necessary outgrowths of the structure of any given society and, in particular, of capitalist society. It is doubtful whether Marx, by assuming property relations to be the structural origin of conflict, was right in the substance of his analysis. But this does not diminish the analytical achievement of tracing in the structure of a given society the seeds of its supersedure. The idea of a society which produces in its structure the antagonisms that lead to its modification appears an appropriate model for the analysis of change in general.

Secondly, Marx properly assumed the dominance of one particular conflict in any given situation. Whatever criticism may be required of the Marxian theory, any theory of conflict has to operate with something like a two-class model. There are but two contending parties—this is implied in the very concept of conflict. There may be coalitions, of course, as there may be conflicts internal to either of the contenders, and there may be groups that are not drawn into a given dispute; but from the point of view of a given clash of interests, there are never more than two positions that struggle for domination. We can follow Marx in this argument (which, for him, is often more implicit than explicit) even further. If social conflicts effect change, and if they are generated by social structure, then it is reasonable to assume that of the two interests involved in any one conflict, one will be pressing for change, the other one for the *status quo*. This assumption, again, is based on logic as much as on empirical observation. In every conflict, one party attacks and another defends. The defending party wants to retain and secure its position, while the attacking party has to fight it in order to improve its own condition. Once again, it is clear that these statements remain on a high level of formality. They imply no reference to the substance or the origin of conflicting interests. But, again, it will prove useful to have articulated the formal prerequisites of Marx's and, indeed, of any theory of conflict.

With these formal points, however, our agreement with Marx ends. Although the heuristic purpose and general approach of his theory of class can and must be sustained, this is not the case with respect to most other features of this theory. Only by rejecting these can we hope to clear the way for a more useful theory of class conflict in industrial societies.

Property and Social Class: Marx Rejected

For Marx, the determinant of social classes was effective private property in the means of production. In all essential elements, his theory of class is based on this definition of the concept of class. We have seen, meanwhile, that precisely this tie between the concept of class and the possession of, or exclusion from, effective private property limits the applicability of class theory to a relatively short period of European social history. A theory of class based on the division of society into owners and nonowners of means of production loses its analytical value as soon as legal ownership and factual control are separated. For this reason, any effective supersedure of Marx's theory of class has to start at this point. Now, it is one of the central theses of this study that such a supersedure is possible if we replace the possession, or nonpossession, of effective private property by the exercise of, or exclusion from, authority as the criterion of class formation. Renner, Schumpeter, Burnham, Djilas, and others have prepared the ground for this decision; by contrast to most of these we shall not confine the notion of authority to the control of the means of production, but consider it as a type of social relations analytically independent of economic conditions. The authority structure of entire societies as well as particular institutional orders within societies (such as industry) is, in terms of the theory here advanced, the structural determinant of class formation and class conflict. The specific type of change of social structures caused by social classes and their conflicts is ultimately the result of the differential distribution of positions of authority in societies and their institutional orders. Control over the means of production is but a special case of authority, and the connection of control with legal property an incidental phenomenon of the industrializing societies of Europe and the United States. Classes are tied neither to private property nor to industry or economic structures in general, but as an element of social structure and a factor effecting change they are as universal as their determinant, namely, authority and its distribution itself. On the basis of a concept of class defined by relations of authority, a theory can be formulated which accounts for the facts described by Marx as well as for the changed reality of post-capitalist society.

At several points of our investigation it has become apparent how many doubts and objections can be raised against Marx's treatment of the relationship between property and social class. In presenting Marx's theory, in describing the phenomenon of the separation of ownership and control, and in discussing Burnham's inferences from this phenomenon and Djilas's analysis of Communist totalitarianism, we have seen how, by connecting the concept of class with private property (and thereby capitalism), Marx renders this concept fit for inclusion in his philosophical conception of history but unfit for the sociological analysis even of the conflicts with which he was concerned. Marx, too, is concerned with relations of authority; indeed, he explicitly refers to these when he describes class conflicts generated by the structure of the industrial enterprise. But Marx believed that authority and power are factors which can be traced back to a man's share in effective private property. In reality, the opposite is the case. Power and authority are irreducible factors from which the social relations associated with legal private property as well as those associated with communal property can be derived. Burnham, and above all Geiger, have rightly stressed that property is in its sociological aspect in the first place a permission to exclude others from control over an object. It is therefore (Weber) a "chance to find obedience with defined persons for an order" (in this case a prohibition), that is, a form of authority. But property is by no means the only form of authority; it is but one of its numerous types. Whoever tries, therefore, to define authority by property defines the general by the particular—an obvious logical fallacy. Wherever there is property there is authority, but not every form of authority implies property. Authority is the more general social relation.

This formal argument is not, however, the only reason for substituting for Marx's definition of classes by private property one by a man's share in authority; this generalization is necessary, also, for the sake of the empirical applicability of the theory of class. For this purpose, it is moreover necessary to separate radically the concept of authority from its narrow application to the control over economic means of production. Just as property is formally, thus control over the means of production is empirically but a special case of those general relations of authority which, according to our conception, lie at the base of class formation and class conflict. Why this extension is empirically necessary will be shown in detail in the following section of this chapter, where we deal with the relation between industrial and social authority structures. However, this much can be stated even without a more detailed discussion: that a theory of group conflict the central category of which is defined by a man's share in the control of the means of production can apply only to the sphere of industrial production. In any case, its significance for structure change would be even more restricted than is the significance of the theory of class.

To say that classes are based on a man's share in legitimate power is not to formulate an empirical hypothesis. If this were so, it would presuppose an independent definition of the concept of class. It is rather a definition which, in a preliminary way, we can state as follows: classes are social conflict groups the determinant (or *differentia specifica*) of which can be found in the participation in or exclusion from the exercise of authority within any imperatively coordinated association. In this sense, classes differ from other conflict groups which rest on religious, ethnic, or legal differences. In principle, a definition is of course an arbitrary decision. If it is logically unassailable, it cannot be refuted by empirical facts. Yet the definition proposed here is more than a terminological decision without empirical consequences. We shall see that this decision alone opens up many new possibilities for the analysis of social conflicts.

If we define classes by relations of authority, it is *ipso facto* evident that "economic classes," that is, classes within economic organizations, are but a special case of the phenomenon of class. Furthermore, even within the sphere of industrial production it is not really economic factors that give rise to class formation, but a certain type of social relations which we have tried to comprehend in the notion of authority. Classes are neither primarily nor at all economic groupings.

It is less easy to determine the relation between classes as authority groups and the system of social stratification. In the first place, it is important to realize that there is no one-to-one correlation between class structure and social stratification in the sense that classes result from people's place in the hierarchy of stratification. The analyses of class and of social stratification are essentially independent subjects of sociological inquiry. On the other hand, there is between them a significant indirect connection which results from the fact that authority, the determinant of class, is at the same time one of the determinants of social status. It can be demonstrated that there is an empirical tendency for the possession of authority to be accompanied, within certain limits and with significant exceptions, by high income and high prestige, and, conversely, for the exclusion from authority to be accompanied by relatively low income and prestige. Indeed, it is one of the distinguishing features of authority that it can become an instrument for the satisfaction of other desires and needs and for the attainment of directly gratifying social rewards. Thus, there is in most societies a tendential, if not unequivocal, correlation between the distribution of authority and the system of social rewards that underlies stratification. In this sense, but only in this sense, the partial parallelism between the lines of class division and those of social stratification may be an empirical fact. One might go further and regard this parallelism as probable, as it could be argued that a certain correspondence between people's share in authority and in social rewards in general is a functional imperative of relatively stable societies. But no parallelism between structures of class and stratification can be postulated. Classes can be identical with strata, they can unite several strata within them, and their structure can cut right through the hierarchy of stratification.

For purposes of clarity it seemed advisable to state, in the strongest possible terms, the way in which class is independent of property, economic conditions, and social stratification. In the abstract, no qualification need be made to this statement. Fortunately, however, empirical conditions do not usually reproduce the simplicity of our assumptions and theories. Although the idea of property, of the relationships that have to do with production, and of the hierarchy of social stratification is, in each instance, clearly distinct from the idea of class, these factors have a great deal to do with the realities of social class and class conflict. Without doubt, the fact that at the time Marx wrote there were capitalists who simultaneously owned and controlled their enterprises contributed greatly to the formation of classes and the antagonism between them. Similarly, the fact that it is possible to identify the powerful with the wealthy cannot be overlooked in class analysis. While the connection between property and social class is not one of definition or mutual dependence, it is one that affects the empirical course of class conflict. If distinctions of property are superimposed on distinctions of class, class conflict is likely to be more violent than if these two lines of social differentiation diverge. An analogous argument could be made for class and social stratification. In fact, this is one of many points at which Marx has transformed a correct empirical observation into a false and useless assumption by arbitrarily generalizing what was characteristic only of the comparatively short historical period which he lived to see.

Power and Authority

From the point of view of the integration theory of social structure, units of social analysis ("social systems") are essentially voluntary associations of people who share certain values and set up institutions in order to ensure the smooth functioning of cooperation. From the point of view of coercion theory, however, the units of social analysis present an altogether different picture. Here, it is not voluntary cooperation or general consensus but enforced constraint that makes social organizations cohere. In institutional terms, this means that in every social organization some positions are entrusted with a right to exercise control over other positions in order to ensure effective coercion; it means, in other words, that there is a differential distribution of power and authority. One of the central theses of this study consists in the assumption that this differential distribution of authority invariably becomes the determining factor of systematic social conflicts of a type that is germane to class conflicts in the traditional (Marxian) sense of this term. The structural origin of such group conflicts must be sought in the arrangement of social roles endowed with expectations of domination or subjection. Wherever there are such roles, group conflicts of the type in question are to be expected. Differentiation of groups engaged in such conflicts follows the lines of differentiation of roles that are relevant from the point of view of the exercise of authority. Identification of variously equipped authority roles is the first task of conflict analysis; conceptually and empirically all further steps of analysis follow from the investigation of distributions of power and authority.

In conflict analysis we are concerned *inter alia* with the generation of conflict groups by the authority relations obtaining in imperatively coordinated associations. Since imperative coordination, or authority, is a type of social relation present in every conceivable social organization, it will be sufficient to describe such organizations simply as associations. Despite prolonged terminological discussions, no general agreement has been attained by sociologists on the precise meaning of the categories "organization," "association," and "institution." If I am not mistaken in my interpretation of the trend of terminological disputes, it appears justifiable to use the term "association" in such a way as to imply the coordination of organized aggregates of roles by domination and subjection. The state, a church, an enterprise, but also a political party, a trade union, and a chess club are associations in this sense. In all of them, authority relations exist; for all of them, conflict analysis is therefore applicable. If at a later stage we shall suggest restriction to the two great associations of the state and the industrial enterprise, this suggestion is dictated merely by considerations of empirical significance, not logical (or definitional) difference. In looking at social organizations not in terms of their integration and coherence but from the point of view of their structure of coercion and constraint, we regard them as (imperatively coordinated) associations rather than as social systems. Because social organizations are also associations, they generate conflicts of interest and become the birthplace of conflict groups.

I have assumed in the preceding remarks that authority is a characteristic of social organizations as general as society itself. Despite the assertion of Renner—and other modern sociologists—that in some contemporary societies the exercise of authority has been eliminated and replaced by the more anonymous "rule of the law" or other nonauthoritative relations, I should indeed maintain that authority is a universal element of social structure. It is in this sense more general than, for example, property, or even status. With respect to postcapitalist industrial society, I hope to establish this position more unambiguously in the final chapters of this study. Generally speaking, however, the universality of authority relations would seem evident as soon as we describe these relations in a "passive" rather than in an "active" sense. Authority relations exist wherever there are people whose actions are subject to legitimate and sanctioned prescriptions that originate outside them but within social structure. This formulation, by leaving open who exercises what kind of authority, leaves little doubt as to the omnipresence of some kind of authority somehow exercised. For it is evident that there are many forms and types of authority in historical societies. There are differences of a considerable order of magnitude between the relations of the citizen of classical Athens and his slaves, the feudal landlord and his villeins and serfs, the nineteenth-century capitalist and his workers, the secretary of a totalitarian state party and its members, the appointed manager of a modern enterprise and its employees, or the elected prime minister of a democratic country and the electorate. No attempt will be made in this study to develop a typology of authority. But it is assumed throughout that the existence of domination and subjection is a common feature of all possible types of authority and, indeed, of all possible types of association and organization.

In referring to the ugly face of authority as a "zero-sum" concept, Parsons brings out one further aspect of this category which is essential for our considerations. By zero-sum, Parsons evidently means that from the point of view of the disruptive "functions" of authority there are two groups or aggregates of persons, of which one possesses authority to the extent to which the other one is deprived of it. This implies—for us, if not for Parsons—that in terms of the coercion theory of society we can always observe a dichotomy of positions in imperatively coordinated associations with respect to the distribution of authority. Parsons, in his critique of Mills, compares the distribution of authority to the distribution of wealth. It seems to me that this comparison is misleading. However unequally wealth may be distributed, there always is a continuum of possession ranging from the lowest to the highest rank. Wealth is not and cannot be conceived as a zero-sum concept. With respect to authority, however, a clear line can at least in theory be drawn between those who participate in its exercise in given associations and those who are subject to the authoritative commands of others. Our analysis of modern societies in later chapters will show that empirically it is not always easy to identify the border line between domination and subjection. Authority has not remained unaffected by the modern process of division of labor. But even here, groups or aggregates can be identified which do not participate in the exercise of authority other than by complying with given commands or prohibitions. Contrary to all criteria of social stratification, authority does not permit the construction of a scale. So-called hierarchies of authority (as displayed, for example, in organization charts) are in fact hierarchies of the "plus-side" of authority, that is, of the differentiation of domination; but there is, in every association, also a "minus-side" consisting of those who are subjected to authority rather than participate in its exercise.

In two respects this analysis has to be specified, if not supplemented. First, for the individual incumbent of roles, domination in one association does not necessarily involve domination in all others to which he belongs, and subjection, conversely, in one association does not mean subjection in all. The dichotomy of positions of authority holds for specific associations only.

In a democratic state, there are both mere voters and incumbents of positions of authority such as cabinet ministers, representatives, and higher civil servants. But this does not mean that the "mere voter" cannot be incumbent of a position of authority in a different context, say, in an industrial enterprise; conversely, a cabinet minister may be, in his church, a mere member, that is, subject to the authority of others. Although empirically a certain correlation of the authority positions of individuals in different associations seems likely, it is by no means general and is in any case a matter of specific empirical conditions. It is at least possible, if not probable, that if individuals in a given society are ranked according to the sum total of their authority positions in all associations, the resulting pattern will not be a dichotomy but rather like scales of stratification according to income or prestige. For this reason it is necessary to emphasize that in the sociological analysis of group conflict the unit of analysis is always a specific association and the dichotomy of positions within it.

As with respect to the set of roles associated with an individual, total societies, also, do not usually present an unambiguously dichotomic authority structure. There are a large number of imperatively coordinated associations in any given society. Within every one of them we can distinguish the aggregates of those who dominate and those who are subjected. But since domination in industry does not necessarily involve domination in the state, or a church, or other associations, total societies can present the picture of a plurality of competing dominant (and, conversely, subjected) aggregates. This, again, is a problem for the analysis of specific historical societies and must not be confounded with the clearer lines of differentiation within any one association. Within the latter, the distribution of authority always sums up to zero, that is, there always is a division involving domination and subjection.

I have introduced, as a structural determinant of conflict groups, the category of authority as exercised in imperatively coordinated associations. While agreeing with Marx that source and level of income—even socioeconomic status—cannot usefully be conceived as determinants of conflict groups, I have added to this list of erroneous approaches Marx's own in terms of property in the means of production. Authority is both a more general and a more significant social relation. The former has been shown in our critique of Marx; the latter will have to be demonstrated by subsequent considerations and analyses. The concept of authority is used, in this context, in a specific sense. It is differentiated from power by what may roughly be referred to as the element of legitimacy; and it has to be understood throughout in the restricted sense of authority as distributed and exercised in imperatively coordinated associations. While its "disruptive" or conflict-generating consequences are not the only aspect of authority, they are the one relevant in terms of the coercion model of society. Within the frame of reference of this model, (1) the distribution of authority in associations is the ultimate "cause" of the formation of conflict groups, and (2), being dichotomous, it is, in any given association, the cause of the formation of two, and only two, conflict groups.

The first of these statements is logically an assumption, since it underlies scientific theories. It cannot as such be tested by observation; its validity is proven, rather, by its usefulness for purposes of explanation. We shall derive from this assumption certain more specific hypotheses which, if refuted, would take the assumption with them into the waste-paper basket of scientific theories. We assume in this sense that if we manage to identify the incumbents of positions of domination and subjection in any given association, we have identified the contenders of one significant type of conflicts—conflicts which occur in this association at all times.

As to the second statement, the one concerned with the dichotomy of authority positions in imperatively coordinated associations, it is not, I suggest, either an assumption or an empirical hypothesis, but an analytical statement. It follows from and is implicit in the very concept of authority that within specified contexts some have authority and others not. If either nobody or everybody had authority, the concept would lose its meaning. Authority implies both domination and subjection, and it therefore implies the existence of two distinct sets of positions or persons. This is not to say, of course, that there is no difference between those who have a great deal and those who have merely a little authority. Among the positions of domination there may be, and often is, considerable differentiation. But such differentiation, while important for empirical analysis, leaves unaffected the existence of a border line somewhere between those who have whatever little authority and the "outs."

. . .

That "the realization of a socialist society" constitutes "the true interest of labor" is indeed an assertion for the (empirical) premises of which "the proof is missing." An assumption of this kind cannot be introduced by way of a postulate. The substance of socially structured "objective" interests can be described only in highly formal terms: they are interests in the maintenance or modification of a *status quo*. Our model of conflict group formation involves the proposition that of the two aggregates of authority positions to be distinguished in every association, one—that of domination—is characterized by an interest in the maintenance of a social structure that for them conveys authority, whereas the other—that of subjection—involves an interest in changing a social condition that deprives its incumbents of authority. The two interests are in conflict.

Max Weber has convincingly demonstrated that the problem of maintaining or changing given structures of authority can be expressed, both conceptually and empirically, in terms of the basis of legitimacy of relations of authority. From our assumption of an at least latent conflict of interests in every imperatively coordinated association, it follows that the legitimacy of authority must always be precarious. There always is one aggregate of positions and their incumbents which represents the institutionalized doubt in the legitimacy of the *status quo* of the distribution of authority. In this sense, the proposition that there are "objective" interests in changing any given structure of authority might also be expressed in terms of the potential illegitimacy of all relations of authority. Empirically, group conflict is probably most easily accessible to analysis if it be understood as a conflict about the legitimacy of relations of authority. In every association, the interests of the ruling group are the values that constitute the ideology of the legitimacy of its rule, whereas the interests of the subjected group constitute a threat to this ideology and the social relations it covers.

Quasi-Groups and Interest Groups: Theoretical Conditions of Conflict Group Formation

We have postulated two conflicting orientations of latent interests as characteristic of the role structure of imperatively coordinated associations. By implication, this means, of course, that the authority positions equipped with expected interests as well as their incumbents have at least one attribute in common. In a significant sense, the occupants of identical authority positions, that is, either of positions of domination or of positions of subjection, find themselves in a common situation. Being united by a common, potentially permanent, characteristic, they are more than mere masses or incoherent quantities. At the same time, the incumbents of like authority positions in an association do not in any sociologically tenable sense constitute a group. Just as all doctors, or all inhabitants of Berlin, do not as such constitute social groups, the occupants of positions with identical latent interests are not a group. For groups, a feeling of belongingness is as constitutive as a minimum of organization; but both are explicitly not demanded by the concept of latent interests. The aggregates of incumbents of positions with identical role interests are at best a potential group. Following M. Ginsberg we shall use for this particular type of social grouping the term *quasi-group*. "Not all collectivities or aggregates form groups. Groups are masses of people in regular contact or communication, and possessing a recognizable structure. There are other aggregates or portions of the community which have no recognizable structure, but whose members have certain interests or modes of behavior in common, which may at any time lead them to form themselves into definite groups. To this category of quasi-groups belong such entities as social classes, which, without being groups, are a recruiting field for groups, and whose members have certain characteristic modes of behavior in common."

.   .   .

In what sense are interest groups, such as political parties, to be regarded as representative of the quasi-groups that can be inferred behind them? Can the same quasi-group become a recruiting field for several interest groups? In principle, the possibility intimated by the latter question has to be answered in the affirmative. From the point of view of conflict theory, competing trade unions of, say, Christian and Socialist description originate from the same quasi-group. Empirically, interest groups are always smaller than their recruiting fields, the quasi-groups. They are subsets of the sets constituted by quasi-groups; and the identity of set and subset remains a limiting case. One might compare the relation of the two with that of the members and the voters of one political party. Furthermore, a number of specific intervening variables may disturb the immediacy of the relation between given quasi-groups and interest groups. While quasi-groups, being in the nature of a theoretical construction, are unequivocally defined, organized interest groups may supplement the interests accruing from authority structures by a multitude of other and independent goals and orientations. This is merely another expression for the fact that interest groups are "real phenomena," and that, like all such phenomena, they cannot be completely described by one attribute. Thus, the theory of group conflict involves no statement about the empirical variety of interest groups. It concentrates on one of their aspects: on their function in social conflicts as units of manifest interests which can be explained in terms of latent role interests and their aggregation in quasi-groups.[1]

Quasi-Groups and Interest Groups:
Empirical Conditions of Conflict Group Formation

"It is a matter of no small interest," Ginsberg adds to his definition of quasi-groups, "to determine at what point these looser configurations crystallize into associations." The categories of quasi-group and interest group mark the two

---

[1] To illustrate this rather abstract formulation: for the theory of conflict, socialist parties are of interest not as instruments of workers' education or as clublike associations, but merely as forces in social conflicts. The same party may function in many ways other than as an interest group, but only the latter aspect is in question in the present analysis.

foci of the analysis of conflict group formation, but they do not describe the connecting lines between them. It will now be our task to examine the conditions under which a "class in itself" becomes a "class for itself." Perhaps the negative side of this problem is of even greater importance. We shall want to ascertain the conditions under which the organization of interest groups does not take place despite the presence of quasi-groups of latent interests in an imperatively coordinated association. This is evidently a matter of ascertaining possible intervening variables which we shall comprehend under the collective term of "structural conditions of organization."

In dealing with the empirical process of development of classes Marx has touched upon this problem at many points. Among these there is one which is particularly illuminating for our present context. At the end of his essay on the 18th of Brumaire of Louis Bonaparte, Marx is dealing with "the most numerous class of French society, the small independent peasants." Marx states, to begin with, that these peasants, by virtue of their situation, their conditions of existence, their way of life, and their (latent) interests, constitute a "class," namely, a quasi-group. One would therefore expect a political organization or interest group to grow out of their midst. However, precisely this did not happen. In so far as the identity of the (latent) interests of the peasants "does not produce a community, national association and political organization, they do not constitute a class." In explaining this surprising fact, Marx refers to conditions of the kind of the intervening variables in question here: "The small independent peasants constitute an enormous mass, the members of which live in the same situation but do not enter into manifold relations with each other. Their mode of production isolates them from each other instead of bringing them into mutual intercourse. This isolation is strengthened by the bad state of French means of communication and by the poverty of the peasants . . . Every single peasant family is almost self-sufficient . . . and thus gains its material of life more in exchange with nature than in intercourse with society." The brilliant conclusion Marx draws from this analysis—namely, that Louis Bonaparte is trying to justify his claim for power by reference to this quasi-group of peasants whose interests are condemned to latency—will concern us less here than the problem impressively demonstrated by it. Under certain conditions, quasi-groups may persist as such without interest groups emerging from them. What are these conditions, and under which conditions do interest groups come to be formed?

It is a commonplace that groups cannot exist without members and, in that sense, without a personnel. Moreover, since we have postulated the presence of a personnel in the quasi-groups from which interest groups emerge, this condition does not at first sight appear to be a genuine intervening variable. It is, indeed, not the total membership of an interest group which is in question here, but that sector of the membership which can be described as the leading group or cadre. For an organized interest group to emerge from a quasi-group, there have to be certain persons who make this organization their business, who carry it out practically and take the lead. Every party needs its founders. The availability of founders in this sense, however, is by no means given in our model nor can it be. It is an additional empirical condition of conflict group formation. As such it is a necessary, although not sufficient, condition of organization. To stipulate a leading group as a prerequisite of the organization of interest groups must not be misunderstood to mean that conflict groups are based on the goals and actions of a handful of leaders. The availability of possible organizers, founders, and leaders is essentially a technical prerequisite which must be satisfied for unorganized quasi-groups to be transformed into organized interest groups. The organizers are one of the ferments, not the starting point or cause of organization. That without them organization is impossible has been demonstrated convincingly—in so far as it is not self-evident—by Marx at the place in the "18th Brumaire" quoted above, and above all in the "Communist Manifesto."

Marx has realized, also, that the creation of a charter is not an automatic process. Malinowski defines the charter of an organization as the "system of values for the pursuit of which human beings organize." In the particular case of conflict groups these values consist of what we have called "manifest interests." While latent interests are nonpsychological orientations implicit in the social structure of roles and positions, manifest interests are articulate, formulated (or at least formulable) programs. They entail specific claims related to given structures of authority. The articulation and codification of such interests is again a process that presupposes certain conditions. Either there must be a person or circle of persons who take on themselves the task of articulation and codification, or, alternatively, an "ideology," a system of ideas, must be available which in a given case is capable of serving as a program or charter of groups. As evidence for the first, it seems sufficient to refer to the role of the political ideologist Marx for the organization of the socialist movement; as evidence of the latter alternative, to the role of a certain interpretation of Calvinism for early English capitalists. Ideologies understood as articulated and codified manifest interests are again but a technical condition of organization. Ideologies do not create conflict groups or cause conflict groups to emerge. Yet they are indispensable as obstetricians of conflict groups, and in this sense as an intervening variable.

Even if we are given not only quasi-groups with common latent interests, but leaders and ideologies as well—if, in other words, the technical conditions of organization are present—it is still not justified to make the empirical inference that interest groups will be formed. A second category of prerequisites which have to be satisfied for organization to be possible will be described here as the *political conditions of organization*. The totalitarian state is probably the most unambiguous illustration of a social situation in which these conditions are not fulfilled, and in which therefore at least oppositional interest groups cannot emerge despite the presence of quasi-groups and latent interests.[2] Where a plurality of conflicting parties is not permitted and their emergence suppressed by the absence of freedom of coalition and by police force, conflict groups cannot organize themselves even if all other conditions of their organization are present. The study of the possibilities and actual types of group conflict under such conditions is a problem of sociological analysis of the highest importance. There is a starting point, here, of the analysis not only of "underground movements" and the development of revolutions, but more generally of structure and dynamics of totalitarian states. But this type of problem can be merely intimated here, since we are for the time being concerned with formulating the general structural conditions of organization. We can maintain that the political permissibility of organization is one of the additional intervening prerequisites of conflict group formation.

Apart from technical and political conditions, some, in the narrow sense, *social conditions of organization* are of importance for the formation of interest groups. Among these we find the condition of communication between the "members" of quasi-groups emphasized by Marx in the case of French peasants. If an aggregate within an association can be described as a community of latent interests, is also provided with the technical and political possibilities of organization, but is so scattered topologically or ecologically that a regular connection among the members of the aggregate does not exist and can be established only with great difficulty, then the formation of an organized interest group is empirically most unlikely. However, important as this premise of organization is, the generalization seems tenable that its significance is steadily diminishing in industrial societies with a highly developed system of means of communication. In advanced industrial societies this condition may be assumed to be generally given; it enters, therefore, into the analysis of conflict group formation as a constant.

This is not the case, however, with another social condition of organization

---

[2]Technically similar conditions obtain in many preindustrial societies. In terms of the political conditions of organization the restriction of this study to industrial societies can be well illustrated. In all preindustrial societies group conflict is seriously impeded by the absence of certain political conditions (the political "citizenship rights"). It would be a matter for separate analysis to investigate forms of group conflict in these societies.

the implications of which will occupy us a good deal more. Empirically, the formation of organized interest groups is possible only if recruitment to quasi-groups follows a structural pattern rather than chance. By this condition, the group described by Marx as *lumpenproletariat* is excluded from conflict group formation. Persons who attain positions relevant for conflict analysis not by the normal process of the allocation of social positions in a social structure, but by peculiar, structurally random personal circumstances, appear generally unsuited for the organization of conflict groups. Thus the lowest stratum of industrial societies is frequently recruited in manifold but structurally irrelevant ways: by delinquency, extreme lack of talent, personal mishaps, physical or psychological instability, and so on. In this case, the condition of structural recruitment is not satisfied, and conflict group formation cannot be expected.

From the empirical conditions of the organization of conflict groups thus briefly sketched, we can, by way of generalization, derive a number of social constellations which are unfavorable if not prohibitive for conflict group formation and group conflict. Here, again, I shall confine myself to giving an indication. One constellation resisting conflict group formation, namely, that of the totalitarian state, is directly given in the formulated conditions. A second important constellation can be defined by combining several of the factors mentioned. If imperatively coordinated associations are either themselves just emerging or subject to radical change, the probability is small that the quasi-groups derived from their authority structure will lead to coherent forms of organization. Examples for this may be seen in the early stages of industrial development, or in societies immediately after social revolutions (such as the Soviet Union in the 1920's). In both cases authority structures, latent interests, and quasi-groups are present. But in both cases it seems reasonable to assume that the absence of leaders and ideologies as well as the still unpatterned and unnormalized recruitment to the relevant positions stand in the way of conflict group formation. In this sense, it seems feasible to attempt to reformulate Marx's problem of the gradual formation of classes in the course of industrialization.

The empirical conditions of organization have been described here as prerequisites of conflict group formation. However, their effect goes beyond the process of emergence of conflict groups. These factors are relevant, also, as variables affecting organized interest groups. They must then be understood, of course, as continua which permit gradations. A relative lack of technical, political, and social conditions of organization can hamper organized interest groups in their operation, and it can, indeed—which is apparent in the case of the political conditions—result in their disintegration.

Subjected conflict groups must therefore not be visualized as essentially unorganized masses without effective force. In analogy to the characteristics of ruling groups we can state (a) that they do not necessarily comprise the majority of the members of an association, (b) that their members are not necessarily connected by "properties" or a "culture" beyond the interests that bind them into groups, and (c) that their existence is always related to particular associations, so that one society may display several subjected conflict groups. Beyond these, one distinguishing feature of subjected groups must be emphasized. The Marxian expression "suppressed classes" might appear to mean that any such group is characterized by the attributes which Marx ascribed to, or found present in, the proletariat of his time. However, this implication is by no means intended here. "Pauperism," "slavery," absolute exclusion from the wealth and liberty of society is a possible but unnecessary attribute of the incumbents of roles of subjection. Here, again, the connection is indeterminate, that is, variable, and its particular pattern can be established only by empirical observation and for particular associations. It is not only conceivable that members of the subjected group of one association belong to the dominating group of another association, it is above all possible that "suppressed classes" enjoy, despite their exclusion from legitimate power, an (absolutely) high measure of social rewards without this fact impeding their organization as interest groups or their participation in group conflicts. Even a "bourgeoisified proletariat" can function as a subjected conflict group, for conflict groups and group conflicts are solely based on the one criterion of participation in or exclusion from the exercise of authority in imperatively coordinated associations. Difficult as it may be for minds schooled in Marx to separate the category of "suppressed class" from the ideas of poverty and exploitation, a well-formulated theory of group conflict requires the radical separation of these spheres.

The Theory of Social Classes and Class Conflict

1. The approach of this study has to be understood in terms of two premises— one formal, one substantive—which, although they are of a meta-theoretical or methodological nature, provide the necessary frame of reference of its elements.

1.1. The heuristic purpose of the approach proposed in the present study is the explanation of structure changes in terms of group conflict. This purpose is therefore neither purely descriptive nor related to problems of integration and coherence in or of society.

1.2. In order to do justice to this heuristic purpose it is necessary to visualize society in terms of the coercion theory of social structure, that is, change and conflict have to be assumed as ubiquitous, all elements of social structure have to be related to instability and change, and unity and coherence have to be understood as resulting from coercion and constraint.

2. Within this frame of reference, the theory of social classes and class conflict involves a number of concepts to be defined.

2.1. "*Authority* is the probability that a command with a given specific content will be obeyed by a given group of persons" (Weber).

2.1.1. By *domination* shall be understood the possession of authority, that is, the right to issue authoritative commands.

2.1.2. By *subjection* shall be understood the exclusion from authority, that is, the duty to obey authoritative commands.

2.2. "An association shall be called *imperatively coordinated association* insofar as its members are, by virtue of a prevailing order, subject to authority relations" (Weber).

2.3 Orientations of behavior which are inherent in social positions without necessarily being conscious to their incumbents (role expectations), and which oppose two aggregates of positions in any imperatively coordinated association, shall be called *latent interests*.

2.4. *Quasi-group* shall mean any collectivity of individuals sharing positions with identical latent interests without having organized themselves as such.

2.5. *Manifest interests* shall mean orientations of behavior which are articulate and conscious to individuals, and which oppose collectivities of individuals in any imperatively coordinated association.

2.6. *Interest group* shall mean any organized collectivity of individuals sharing manifest interests.

2.7. By *social class* shall be understood such organized or unorganized collectivities of individuals as share manifest or latent interests arising from and related to the authority structure of imperatively coordinated associations. It follows from the definitions of latent and manifest interests that social classes are always conflict groups.

2.8. Any antagonistic relationship between organized collectivities of individuals that can be explained in terms of patterns of social structure (and is not, therefore, sociologically random) shall be called *group conflict*.

2.9. *Class conflict* shall mean any group conflict that arises from and is related to the authority structure of imperatively coordinated associations.

2.10. Any deviation of the values (normative structure) or institutions (factual structure) of a unit of social analysis at a given point of time $(T + n)$ from those of a preceding point of time (T) shall be called *structure change*, insofar as it involves the incumbents of positions of domination.

2.10.1. By *radicalness of structure change* shall be understood the significance of consequences and ramifications of structure change.

2.10.2 By *suddenness of structure change* shall be understood the extent to which incumbents of positions of domination are replaced.

3. The formation of conflict groups of the class type follows a pattern that can be described in terms of a model involving the following partly analytical, partly hypothetical steps:

3.1. In any imperatively coordinated association, two, and only two, aggregates of positions may be distinguished, that is, positions of domination and positions of subjection.

3.2. Each of these aggregates is characterized by common latent interests; the collectivities of individuals corresponding to them constitute quasi-groups.

3.3. Latent interests are articulated into manifest interests; and the quasi-groups become the recruiting fields of organized interest groups of the class type.

3.3.1. Articulation of manifest interests and organization of interest groups can be prevented by the intervention of empirically variable conditions of organization.

3.3.2. Among the conditions of organization, technical conditions (personnel, charter), political conditions (freedom of coalition), and social conditions (communication, patterned recruitment) can be distinguished. To these, certain nonstructural psychological conditions (internalization of role interests) may be added.

4. The course of group conflict of the class type also follows a pattern that can be described in terms of a model involving both analytical and hypothetical elements.

4.1. Once the formation of conflict groups of the class type is complete, they stand, within given associations, in a relation of group conflict (class conflict).

4.1.1. The intensity of class conflict varies on a scale (from 0 to 1) according to the operation of certain factors.

4.1.1.1. The intensity of class conflict decreases to the extent that the conditions of class organization are present.

4.1.1.2. The intensity of class conflict decreases to the extent that class conflicts in different associations are dissociated (and not superimposed).

4.1.1.3. The intensity of class conflict decreases to the extent that different group conflicts in the same society are dissociated (and not superimposed).

4.1.1.4. The intensity of class conflict decreases to the extent that the distribution of authority and the distribution of rewards and facilities in an association are dissociated (and not superimposed).

4.1.1.5. The intensity of class conflict decreases to the extent that classes are open (and not closed).

4.1.2. The violence of class conflict varies on a scale (from 0 to 1) according to the operation of certain factors.

4.1.2.1. The violence of class conflict decreases to the extent that the conditions of class organization are present.

4.1.2.2. The violence of class conflict decreases if absolute deprivation of rewards and facilities on the part of a subjected class gives way to relative deprivation.

4.1.2.3. The violence of class conflict decreases to the extent that class conflict is effectively regulated.

4.2. Group conflict of the class type effects structure changes in the associations in which it occurs.

4.2.1. The radicalness of structure change co-varies with the intensity of class conflict.

4.2.2. The suddenness of structure change co-varies with the violence of class conflict.

Three Arenas of Economic Conflict [1967]

NORBERT WILEY

• *Norbert Wiley's 1967 article is one of the most important modern developments of Weberian sociology. Wiley parallels Dahrendorf in that both of them revived themes of Marxian and conflict
theory after decades of relative neglect. But Wiley and Dahrendorf represent each of the two wings of a debate about how
conflict theory should proceed: along the routes of economic conflict or power conflict. Dahrendorf rejected Marx's economic
model for a broader process based on divisions of power, thus
moving Marxism in a more Weberian direction. Wiley proceeds
in the opposite way. He uses a little-noticed section of Weber's
theory of classes to argue that economic conflicts do not have to
be jettisoned just because the political history of the United
States has not centered on conflicts between workers and capitalist employers. There are also two other forms of economic class
conflict: (1) between debtors and creditors and (2) between consumers and sellers. It is the latter two that have dominated U.S.
history, from the agrarian movements of the nineteenth centu y
(debtor-creditor conflict) to the black ghetto uprisings of the 196 s
(consumer-seller conflict).*

In Weber's view, as it appears in his essay on "Class, Status and Party,"
economic class is multidimensional, and there are as many bases for class
differentiation as there are forms of competitive relationship in the economy.
It is true that he gave a great analytic emphasis to the dimension of the labor
market and the struggle over the price of labor, for that issue has been most
salient during the industrialization of Western Europe. Accordingly, he distinguished those who live by exploiting capital property from those who live by
selling services and made further distinctions within each of those two major
classes. He was also concerned, however, with the relations between debtors
and creditors, buyers and sellers, and landlords and tenants, and he recognized the possibility that economic classes might be formed along the dimen-

From Norbert Wiley, "America's Unique Class Politics: The Interplay of the Labor, Credit, and
Commodity Markets," *American Sociological Review* 32 (August 1967), pp. 531–41. Reprinted by
permission of the American Sociological Association.

sions of the credit and commodity markets as well as the labor market. In speaking of the history of European class conflict he points out that, "the struggle in which class situations are effective has progressively shifted from consumption credit toward, first, competitive struggles in the commodity market and, then, toward price wars on the labor market".[1] It seems clear, then, that Weber visualized the economic class system as a constellation of related dimensions, any one of which might become the major focus of class conflict under the right historical conditions.

Weber did not pay much attention to the relations among these three areas of class conflict or to the possibility of a historical reversal, which might again make debtor and consumer protest central. But from the viewpoint of the 1960s, and especially in the United States, it is obvious that economic struggles are not confined to the issue of the price of labor and that the future will bring even more complexity in the class order.

We will follow Weber in distinguishing three major dimensions of the class system: (1) the labor market, which is the source of the conflict among occupational and property-owning groups, (2) the credit or money market, which is the basis for the conflict between debtors and creditors, and (3) the commodity market, which is the basis for the conflict between buyers and sellers, and landlords and tenants. Accordingly, anyone who participates in all three markets is a member of three distinct economic classes and may participate in class conflict along three distinct axes. These three lines of conflict are not equally important at any one time in the industrialization process or in the business cycle, nor do distinct interest groups always form around each issue. Nevertheless, all three conflicts are deeply imbedded in capitalism, and the historic problems of economic ethics—those of usury, the just price and the living wage—are manifested squarely in the three markets.

Weber's perspective permits the invention of a number of new class concepts, and, if our intention were the formal development of this theory, we would systematically draw out these concepts. Instead, our purpose is to analyze American politics, and we will concentrate on concepts that serve this purpose. One such concept is that of inconsistencies in the class order itself, apart from any inconsistencies that might exist in the status order. Class inconsistency can exist either for the individual or for the system. Beginning with individual inconsistency, this pattern will be defined in relation to its opposite, the consistent pattern.

There are two consistent sets of class attributes, the propertied and the

[1] Hans H. Gerth and C. Wright Mills (eds.), *From Max Weber* (New York: Oxford University Press, 1958), p. 185.

non-propertied. The propertied set is that of employer-creditor-seller; the non-propertied that of employee-debtor-buyer. All other sets entail a mixture of the propertied and the non-propertied, or non-membership in one or more markets, or membership on both the propertied and non-propertied sides in one or more markets, or some combination of these. It will be assumed that all sets, other than the two consistent ones, are likely to involve a conflict of economic interest for the person, and it is in this sense that we refer to them as inconsistent. The extent of inconsistency reflects the degree to which the three axes of class conflict divide a population at different points, and to that extent a society will have a built-in source of cross-pressures.

It might be asked if conflict of economic interest cannot exist also within the "consistent" sets of propertied and non-propertied. Certainly this always exists to some extent, but we are assuming that at the level of the individual it will usually be easier to find harmony among a "consistent" than among an "inconsistent" set of class interests. However, if, in the society as a whole, there are substantial conflicts of interest among debtors, workers and buyers, or among creditors, employers and sellers, we will refer to this situation as class inconsistency within the system. The two types of class inconsistency, individual and systematic, are independent of each other to some extent, but if there is a great deal of individual inconsistency it will tend to create inconsistency at the systematic level also. If, for example, the debtors are a different group from the workers, the two sets of interests will be more likely to diverge and conflict. Also, if there is a rentier-creditor group different from the employer group, a systematic conflict of interest is likely to appear on the propertied side.

A society with a systematic inconsistency in its class structure may have political qualities which derive from this inconsistency, just as an individual with inconsistent class interests may find his political interests affected by this situation. This expanded conception of class allows one to see various combinations of class interests and conflict and to frame new hypotheses concerning class and politics.

Class Conflict in American History. Central to the history of class conflict in America is the paradox previously mentioned. The most vigorous class action, particularly in political life, has come from small agrarian capitalists, especially the wheat farmers of the Great Plains, while the urban workers, with their clearer class interest and stronger organizational potential, have been less militant. To describe these phenomena in Weber's terms, a distinction must be made among varieties of class interests. The farmers were pursuing their class interests in the credit and commodity markets and not in the labor market, for the most important class memberships of American farmers were as debtors and sellers. Being farm owners they were neither employees, nor, to any important extent, employers. Thus American class conflict has gone on largely outside the labor market, and the relative tranquility of the urban workers has given our history an unusual distribution of class action.

The problem of the American worker's lack of attraction to socialism can be examined more sharply if we distinguish among types of socialism. Within our frame of reference there are three pure forms of socialism: debtor, consumer and proletariat socialism. The common feature is that in each case the government controls the relevant market in the interest of the poorer class. With debtor socialism, government owns or controls credit institutions; with consumer socialism, the distribution of commodities; and with proletariat socialism, capital property. The agrarian radicals, even when most militant, as at certain times and places during the Populist Movement, were by no means complete socialists. They wanted elements of debtor and commodity socialism but not proletariat socialism, even though some Populist literature made vague demands in that direction. Certainly the Populists showed no interest in having themselves placed on collective farms.

On the other hand, the American government has taken its strongest socialist actions, limited as they are, along the line of commodity socialism by providing a variety of cheap or free services in the health, education and welfare areas. Not the least of the commodity controls has been the provision of price supports for the farmers. Debtor socialism has been less developed, and proletarian socialism, with the outright nationalization of capital property, least of all. Of course the impact of any socialistic measure, on any of the three dimensions, is not only in government control but in the question of which class benefits, and from this point of view the meaning of existing government controls in the United States is quite controversial.

The problem of the urban worker can now be restated as follows: why has the urban working class not supported proletarian socialism? Social thinkers have answered this question in a variety of ways, and several special American conditions which had a subduing effect on the working class have been cited. Our perspective suggests a new factor, or perhaps a new way of looking at something long recognized. *The United States has had a highly inconsistent class structure with a largely different subordinate class along each dimension of class conflict.* This has disunified American radicalism, for the militant debtor class has been in conflict of interest with the proletarian class. The main class issue of the farmers was that of credit and commodity prices; the main issue of the workers was wages and working conditions. The two streams of radicalism were at odds over membership, class interest, and therefore organizational and political programs.

In the technical terms of this paper, the farmers and workers both had inconsistent sets of class attributes, for the farmers lacked a clear interest in the labor market and the workers lacked interest in the credit market. This individual inconsistency was so widespread, and structured in such a way, that there was a clash between debtor and worker needs. For instance, inflation, while it would have relieved farmer debt and increased farmer selling power, would have meant little more than increased commodity prices for the urban workers.

This conflict was not entirely clear at the time, for both groups identified themselves under the heading of "producing classes" and both identified their opponent as big business, the plutocracy or the "money power". Yet the two sections of the producing class were quite distinct in their relation to property, and the concessions they wanted from their common enemy were also distinct, if not incompatible. From the point of view of big business, a divide and conquer strategy was built into the American class system, and this is nowhere seen more clearly than in the critical 1896 Presidential election in which the farmers backed Bryan and inflation while the workers supported McKinley and the tariff.

We are saying, then, that the absence of urban support for socialism was due partly to the centrality of the agrarian reform movement in American politics. During industrialization, the American farmer displayed a militancy not seen in the farmers of any other industrializing nation of the time. In England, for example, the decline of small agriculture and the enclosure movement preceded industrialization. In the United States, however, small agriculture grew with early industrialization, and a large agrarian class was available to spearhead the protest movement. The industrial revolution increased the consistency of the class structure in England, while it decreased it in the United States. The normal response of a consistent lower class, centered around proletarian interests, is socialism; the normal response of an inconsistent lower class, centered around several inconsistent interests, is something more diffuse and less radical than socialism. This diffuseness is well illustrated by the American case, for the strength of the agrarian protest blurred the class consciousness and the political interest of the American lower classes generally, weakened both lines of radicalism, and gave business interests a working control of the federal government until 1932.

RIGHT-WING MOVEMENTS

The question of the radical right is one of the most investigated and least illuminated matters in political sociology. The question of why these groupings appeared, or reappeared, after World War II, and what social forces support them is still unclear. There are difficulties at the more elementary level of political classification as well. Do these groups have enough in common to be placed in the same category, do their programs share anything more than anti-Communism, does the support of each tend to come from the same segments of the population, or at least the same general social forces? The changes in the radical right, from the early 1950s to the middle 1960s, have not made analysis any easier, for the right's orientation has shifted from the anti-Communism of Senator McCarthy, to the crusade against welfare state legislation of the John Birch Society, and finally to the anti-desegregation position of the Southern groups that backed Goldwater. These ideological shifts seem to have brought substantial shifts in the sources of popular support. Considering the complexities of this question, it does not seem likely that any single theory would be able to explain it.

The hypothesis we will submit is an attempt to clarify only one factor, one that arises from the class system, which may push people toward right-wing groups. No doubt it interacts with other factors, and its influence may not be the statistically most important at any one time, but we think it is a continuously predisposing factor. This hypothesis is built on a paper by Martin Trow entitled "Small Businessmen, Political Tolerance, and Support for McCarthy."[2] Trow shows, from a sample survey of Bennington, Vermont, that small businessmen supported McCarthy more strongly than did either manual workers or the salaried middle class. More importantly, he shows that certain economic attitudes, which appeared most frequently among the small business group, were good predictors of pro-McCarthy attitudes. These were attitudes of hostility toward both big business and labor unions. Trow calls this set of attitudes "19th century liberalism," and he reasons that people holding this backward-looking view probably feel unrepresented by any of the major pressure groups and political parties of contemporary life. It follows that they might have been especially attracted to the negativism and opposition to powerful institutions which McCarthy expressed.

Trow's research finds a source of support for McCarthy in the secular decline of small business, pressed between labor unions and big business, and the generalized economic hostility which this decline brought about. This interpretation is extended and translated into our frame of reference in the following hypothesis: *People with inconsistent class attributes are especially prone to support right-wing groups.* It will be recalled that there are two consistent sets of attributes, the propertied set of employer-creditor-seller and the non-propertied set of employee-debtor-buyer. All others are inconsistent.

[2]In *American Journal of Sociology* 64 (November 1958), pp. 270–81.

Small businessmen along with farmers are the classic mixed types, for while both make their living by selling, they also do capital buying from powerful sellers, and their incomes are often affected as much by buying as by selling. In addition, they are often heavily in debt and may be employers of labor, at least sporadically. Both groups, consequently, are afflicted with economic cross-pressures and cannot identify their interests with either big business or labor unions.

If the political disaffection of small businessmen is due to the mechanism we have described, it should be possible to find other forms of this mechanism in other segments of the population which exhibit a similar tendency toward the right wing. For example, a factor of this kind may be operating among some manual workers. The strong response of manual workers to McCarthy and some of the other right-wing groups has been difficult to explain, since these groups often oppose labor unions and welfare state legislation. Their response cannot be attributed to the greater intolerance or authoritarianism of manual workers, since there is some doubt that they are more intolerant on political matters. But beyond that, it has been shown that political intolerance and support for right-wing groups have only a weak relationship to each other.

Our hypothesis predicts that workers who have a stake in capital property in some respect would be drawn to the right wing. This could take the form of a second job, or a wife's job, in small business, a sales "route," or part-time farming, or it could be some sort of direct capital investment in neighborhood real estate or corporate securities. Such people might be moving socially, up or down, or they might just be carrying two jobs or lines of economic activity, with no thought of mobility. In any case, they are in a mixed class position, on the nonpropertied side in the labor market and on the propertied side in the commodity or credit market. The investment might be an extremely modest one, or even only in the planning stage, and still affect the class attachments and political actions of these people.

It follows that such people might experience much the same cross pressures as the small businessman or farmer in relation to big business and labor and to the two major political parties. This group of workers might also be quite Republican, despite their political uneasiness, opposed to welfare state legislation, attached to the Protestant Ethic and religiously fundamentalistic. In a recent paper, Lipset reviewed four major polls on McCarthyism and concluded that among manual workers, especially the Republican ones, support for McCarthy increased with income. He suggests that "Perhaps the higher-income people within lower occupational or educational strata were precisely those who were most drawn to an ideology that attacked as pro-Communist both liberal lower-class-based politics and moderate, conservative old upper-class-elitist groups."[3] We would add that perhaps these higher income manual workers were often responding to the mixed class pressures of my hypothesis.

Turning to the category of retired people, especially those living on small incomes, it is not difficult to see how they might experience economic cross pressures and react irrationally. They are no longer attached to organized labor or any other occupational group, and upon retirement their class interests shift entirely to the credit and commodity markets.

Finally let us consider the salaried middle class. This group was among the weakest supporters of McCarthy but it seems to be giving stronger support, relatively speaking, to the John Birch Society. On the face of it, this group is consistently on the nonpropertied side, just as manual workers are. Yet there are many small, and some large, investors in this group. More importantly, it is the salaried middle class that often becomes psychologically identified with the interests of big business. The result is that people who are typically employee-debtor-buyers may perceive themselves as employer-debtor-buyers. Thus they place themselves in the class position not of big business, but of small business, and evidently experience many of the political pressures of the old middle classes.

People in all of these positions—farmers, manual workers, retirees, and even the salaried middle class—thus may sometimes find themselves under the same kind of class pressures that Trow singled out for the case of small business. There is good reason to expect unusual political consequences from these situations, for they do not present clear cues for conventional political action. When class attachments are inconsistent, there is no single source of pressure, no clear source of trouble and no reasonable target. Pursuit of class interest becomes ambiguous, not only because class interests are scattered, but because *there is no class enemy*. All the powerful groups are, in some respect, enemies, and no single form of opposition will give emotional, let alone rational, satisfaction. It is not surprising if the political response carries a hostility toward all major institutions and suggests comparison with the clinical condition of paranoia at times.

It is the mixed position in particular that produces what C. Wright Mills called the inability to see the relation between private troubles and public issues. More generally, it follows that the people caught between bureaucracies and class interests are a greater source of irrationality than the people solidly located within bureaucracies. Mannheim argued that the growth of

[3]Seymour Martin Lipset, "Three Decades of the Radical Right: Coughlinites, McCarthyites, and Birchers," in Daniel Bell (ed.), *The Radical Right* (New York: Doubleday, 1964), pp. 373–446.

rational bureaucracy decreases the political rationality of the ordinary person employed within a bureaucracy. As he put it, the growth of functional rationality decreases substantive rationality. This may be true for the response to crisis situations, such as characterized Europe between the two World Wars, but in non-crisis situations, such as post-war United States, it is apparently the mixed-class types, without a solid bureaucratic attachment, who are most pressured into the irrational political response.

This hypothesis is not incompatible with many of the social and psychological theories of the right wing. Many of the mixed-class types are, for example, in a mixed status position as well, and much of the status instability in the United States is the social expression of an underlying class inconsistency, as with the worker-landlord or worker-farmer. And, of course, status inconsistency, with its resentments and frustrations, would intensify the frustrations of an underlying economic inconsistency.

Similarly, there is a kind of alienation in not being clearly attached to any of the powerful bureaucracies, but this form of alienation comes, not from the growth of bureaucracy and mass society, but from the unevenness of this growth.

These social and psychological factors, then, may move in the same direction as the underlying economic cross pressures. But they are mediating and not originating forces, and they are usually brought into play by the class base.

Throughout this section we have drawn on the notion of individual class inconsistency. This was in contrast to the previous section where the major concept was systematic class inconsistency at the level of social structure. This shift in emphasis reflects a shift in the political importance of these two factors in the last seventy years or so. During this period, the United States class system has become progressively more consistent on the structural level as the labor unions and big business have grown, as the old middle classes have declined as an interposing force between business and labor, and as the major political parties have taken clearer class positions. During this time the incidence of individual inconsistency also declined, mainly because of the decline of the old middle class. The result, though, is that the remaining class inconsistents are in a much more ambiguous and free-floating class position than they were during the earlier period, when they had the stability of numbers and less powerful opposition. Their economic interest is not as clear as before, so they are less likely to pursue interest politics and more likely to vent general resentments on the entire institutional system. This does not mean, however, that as the old middle classes decline still further this general source of right-wing support will disappear, for the other mixed-class types that we discussed are not declining.

THE NEGRO PROTEST MOVEMENT

Like the previous problems we considered, the Negro protest movement is difficult to define in traditional political categories. It is not simply a case of class conflict, for even though Negroes are typically in a consistent lower class situation, some Negroes of all classes are on the one side, just as some whites of all classes are on the other. Nor is it purely a case of racial or status conflict, for the issues are not empty status symbols; they are solidly economic and cut into all spheres of economic life. In fact, it is this very economic diffuseness, this spilling over beyond the familiar category of jobs and working conditions, in combination with the status issue, which makes the Negro revolution unique in our political history.

It is illuminating to regard the economic side of this movement as a special form of class conflict in the commodity market, in other words as a conflict between buyers and sellers, landlords and tenants, government agencies and commodity recipients. The concrete grievances of Negroes often center around the need for commodities, which they either cannot afford or are not permitted to buy or rent, and much of the non-violent action, such as sit-ins, has been an attempt to obtain forbidden commodities and to secure complete freedom within this market. When these actions have been most militant, as in the rioting and store looting of recent summers or the rent strikes in some urban slums, the economic side of the conflict has been squarely in the commodity market.

This is not to say that the major economic disabilities of Negroes are in the commodity market, even when this market is conceived quite broadly. Certainly unemployment, low wages and other labor market troubles are the Negroes' most serious economic problem. But sometimes the response is incommensurate with the stimulus, because something mediates. The commodity market in the United States is the economic area most saturated with status and symbolic values, and the pure status conflict or "tribal" confrontation between Negroes and whites finds issues in the commodity market more easily than in other areas. Commodity protests define the interaction of status and class conflict in this case. This response, moreover, is in line with what might be expected from a people with only a marginal allegiance to the working class and a predominantly "lumpenproletariat" mentality.

This leads to a theoretical question about the lumpenproletariat generally. I think it is a mistake to regard this bottom-of-the-heap group as declassed or lacking in class interest. This may be true in labor market terms, but if we consider that the extreme poor are always buyers and almost always debtors, we can see a distinct class interest in these other areas. What the lumpenproletariat lack is not class interest or economic grievances. They lack organization, and the self-respect and political commitment that can come only from organization. If they could organize around their existing class interests, no one would make the mistake of saying they are without class or objective political interest.

The organization of propertyless elements for purposes of collective action has usually centered around type of job and place of work. But the Negro protest movement is showing that this organization can occur outside of the labor market, on other bases. There are indications that the Negro poor can now be organized and made a political force more easily than the white poor, for the Negroes have found an organizational weapon lacking to the whites. This weapon is skin color itself, and it is backed up by the residential ghetto with its many small organizations, its grapevines and other communication networks. Color and segregation give a unity and an organizational potential which the white poor do not have. We are not saying these mechanisms are a sufficient condition for the Negro protest movement. Rather, they are organizational resources which are intensifying a movement which began for quite different reasons. Negro organization is building on these unifying bases, much as the industrial labor unions were built on the unifying elements of the factory itself and its working conditions. But the Negro response, by virtue of the resources it has to work with, has been drawn to the commodity market. This is the area of most visible grievance, most degrading deprivation, and, above all, most unifying resentment.

The special class orientation and organizational needs of Negroes help explain why they have been drawn to ethnic solidarity and black nationalism in a way that other American ethnic groups were not. Broadly speaking, the labor movement has been the vehicle of protest for most other American ethnic groups. But because of the Negroes' rural backgrounds, marginal employment situation and the discrimination in the unions themselves, this vehicle of protest has not been available to Negroes. Accordingly, as a larger proportion of Negroes enter the stable working class, one might expect their protest to lose its emphasis on the commodity market, on racial unity, and to merge with the labor movement generally.

The Negro revolution, then, can be visualized as a combination of status conflict and mixed class conflict, with the primary class dimension being in the commodity market up until now. From another point of view, this revolution resembles the tradition of agrarian radicalism, for while both movements are forms of economic class conflict, they operate largely outside the labor market and are not explicable from a narrowly Marxist viewpoint.

CONCLUSION

In this paper we have tried to develop the Weberian theory of class and class
conflict, relating it to selected problems of American politics. The central
argument can be stated as follows: because of the special way in which industrialization occurred in the United States, there has been an unusual degree of
inconsistency in the economic class structure, and, with important transformations, this pattern has persisted and has led to several political patterns of
uniquely American quality. To explain these patterns, political sociology
needs a more comprehensive economic theory than presently exists. The
prevailing economic theories of Marxism and utilitarian liberalism were in-
vented during a period of relatively uncomplicated economic life and were
shaped especially by British experience. Clearly, the economic influences on
politics are now extremely complex, and it would be unfortunate if the importance of economic factors were not fully recognized merely because the available theories were obsolete. It is our opinion that a more adequate theory can
be developed, along the lines suggested in this paper, from the ideas of Max
Weber. Once this has been done, a better framework will be available for the
interpretation of such non-economic factors as status conflict, religion, psychological tensions and the like.

A Theory of Inequality [1966]

GERHARD E. LENSKI

• *Gerhard Lenski's* Power and Privilege *(1966) was the first systematic triumph for conflict sociology. For decades American sociologists of various persuasions had been posturing about making sociology into a science, but there remained a dearth of genuine theories that actually explained anything. Lenski presented not only a generalized explanatory theory, but also a conflict theory, of a central social phenomenon: the degree of inequality or equality in the distribution of wealth within a society. True to the best scientific method, Lenski made comparisons among the relevant empirical cases: in this instance, the entire range of human societies. Lenski's categorization of types of societies has become classic: hunting-and-gathering, primitive horticulture, advanced horticulture, agrarian, and industrial. It is based on basic productive technologies, and captures far more of the relevant dimensions of historical difference among societies than Marx's alleged stages: "primitive communism" (a confused, early view of the anthropological evidence that mixed hunting-and-gathering and horticultural—that is, tribal, generally stateless—societies), "slavery," "feudalism" (both of which were mainly agrarian in Lenski's sense), and finally "capitalism" (a subtype within industrial societies). On this basis, Lenski lays down several basic laws of distribution: The amount of inequality grows with the size of the* economic surplus *in society, but also with (and under certain conditions is overridden by) the* concentration of political power. *The last factor parallels Dahrendorf's emphasis on power as a determining factor in class conflicts.*

The starting point in every sociological discussion of the nature of man is the deceptively simple assertion that *man is a social being obliged by nature to live with others as a member of society.* On this proposition at least, radicals and conservatives agree, and this serves as the *first postulate* in our general theory.

To say that man is a social being is not to deny that a few individuals withdraw from society and live as hermits. The human race could not survive on this basis, however, since its chief weapon in the struggle for existence has always been culture, and culture is uniquely a social product. Social life is essential not only for the survival of the species but also for the maximum satisfaction of human needs and desires. Through cooperative activity men can satisfy many needs and desires which could never be met otherwise and can satisfy most other needs much more efficiently, that is, with greater return for less effort or other investment.

If our first postulate is relatively noncontroversial, the same cannot be said of the second. It takes us directly into the realm of one of the bitterest disputes between radicals and conservatives—the dispute concerning the origin of evil. As noted in the last chapter, the radical view of man and society steadily gained in popularity and intellectual respectability after the English revolution of the seventeenth century. In an era of European growth and expansion, this optimistic view, which postulated society as the source of evil, found increasing acceptance, especially among intellectuals. Since the rise of Nazism and the outbreak of World War II, however, the trend has been halted and, for the first time in roughly three centuries, the pendulum seems to be moving in the opposite direction. On every hand the evidence mounts that the evil in men's actions is rooted more deeply than radical theorists had supposed. Neither the French Revolution nor the Russian produced the utopias that were promised despite revolutionary institutional change. Though the patterns of men's lives have been changed greatly by the social and technological revolutions of modern times, egoism, selfishness, and cruelty continue to loom large.

Paralleling the argument from modern history is that from contemporary psychology, where current theory and research undermine our faith in the natural goodness of man no less than do political events. Recent research reveals the human infant as an extremely self-centered creature, motivated solely by his own needs and desires. If we rid ourselves of the romantic aura which surrounds babies in our society, we discover that they are totally involved in reducing the various tensions created by their biological nature and the environment. Their early actions are simply trial-and-error probings to discover methods of reducing or relieving these tensions.

In time, of course, the normal child learns to take the wishes of others into account. But this does not mean that he is any less motivated to maximize his own satisfactions. Rather, it means that he has learned that the attainment of his own goals is inextricably linked with the interests of others. For example, a boy who acquires a taste for baseball soon finds that he can satisfy this taste

only by cooperating with others who share his enthusiasm. Because he cooper-
ates with them and obeys the rules of the game we should not assume that he
is no longer seeking to maximize his own satisfactions. On the contrary, we
can be sure he is!

Children's games afford far more insights into the nature of social organization than is usually recognized. In particular, they demonstrate the process by
which institutions with their elements of cooperation and morality and their
concepts of right and justice can emerge from the actions of an originally
unorganized aggregation of individuals each selfishly seeking to maximize his
own personal satisfactions. To achieve this maximization individuals are
forced to work (and play) together, but they find that this can be rewarding
only if the activity takes place within the framework of a system of rules
which, above all else, protects the cooperative activity itself. This can only be
done if certain basic rights are guaranteed to all of the essential participants;
for example, each boy is guaranteed his turn at bat. This may seem to entail
some sacrifice on the part of the stronger or abler participants, but really it
does not, since the only alternative is the cessation of the cooperative activity
and all its benefits. Thus, for them, as for the other participants, adherence to
the rules can be accounted for merely as a form of *enlightened self-interest*.

Many years ago William Graham Sumner coined the phrase "antagonistic
cooperation" to call attention to this paradoxical feature of human life. As he
pointed out, men are "brought into association and held there by compulsion"—the compulsion of self-interest. He declared that "it is quite as wrong
to assume mutual good-will as the basis of human cooperation as it would be
to suppose its existence between the bee and the clover or the rhinoceros and
the tick bird." In his opinion, "most cooperation has in it . . . suppressed
antagonisms that are overborne by practical advantage." While he may have
overstated the case somewhat, it is especially applicable in the case of those
forms of social organization which are so large and complex that they embrace
total strangers.

If one is fond of paradox and irony, one might go further and argue that
cooperation itself is one of the basic sources of conflict in human life. If man
were a solitary species, with each individual living apart from all the rest
except for mating, as is the case with certain animals, there would be far less
conflict among men. If each produced only for himself and there were no
division of labor and exchange of goods, one of the major sources of human
strife would be eliminated. By contrast, when men join forces in a cooperative
enterprise, whether it be a family or total society, both the opportunity and the
motivation for conflict are greatly increased. This is an aspect of the social
scene which most conservative theorists have neglected.

We cannot argue, however, that simple self-interest, enlightened or otherwise, is the only motivating force in human affairs. When we take an objective view, we recognize that the problem is more complicated than this. Self-sacrifice *is* an observable reality no less than self-seeking: parents *do* sacrifice for their children and soldiers for their buddies.

From the moral standpoint, these forms of action are highly commendable. Nevertheless, as some of the more insightful observers of the human scene have pointed out, such actions involve a strong element of self-seeking. Jesus pointed this out to his followers at one point where he said, "If you love only those who love you, what credit is that to you? Even tax collectors do that." Many actions appear as sacrifices only when the larger context is ignored. Seen in context, such actions appear as parts of a mutually beneficial system of exchanged favors.

Whatever else is true of this kind of sacrificial action, it is not disinterested. Such actions are seldom taken on behalf of strangers, nor do we expect it. Rather, they presuppose the existence of highly valued and rewarding interpersonal ties between the parties involved. For lack of a better term, we might call this pattern of action "partisan self-sacrifice" and the interests served by it "partisan group interests" to differentiate it from the disinterested pattern of self-sacrifice involved in truly altruistic action.

There is one other aspect of this matter deserving note. Groups which generate sacrificial action by their members in their relations with one another typically foster a very different pattern of action in relations with outsiders. In fact, it sometimes seems that the stronger the sacrificial tendencies in *intragroup* relations, the weaker such tendencies in *intergroup* relations. This means that our *judgments about the frequency and importance of sacrificial action in human life are a function of the social level on which we focus.* If we make the family or some other primary group the object of our analysis, we are far more likely to be impressed by the evidences of self-sacrifice than if we examine a large and complex nation. When we view human action in this broader perspective, as we shall in this volume, we soon discover that these groups which generate so much sacrificial action in their internal relations are often capable of the most ruthless pursuit of their partisan group interests when dealing with outsiders, even though the latter are members of the same society.

Another questionable form of self-sacrifice is the practice of *noblesse oblige*. The well-to-do in some societies accept certain obligations, such as charity, almsgiving and public service, which yield no obvious returns for themselves. Again, however, the element of self-interest intrudes. For the very wealthy, philanthropy costs relatively little but usually yields substantial dividends. It is one of the few trustworthy routes to honor and prestige, and for those who have everything else, this can be important. . . . Also, as the Lynds demonstrated in their famous study of Middletown, philanthropy can be made to pay handsome political and economic dividends. This is not to say that all charitable actions are prompted by self-interest but only that the element of self-interest is not incompatible with philanthropy. A more serious question which must be directed at charitable action concerns its relative importance in the total economy. Charitable donations usually represent only a small fraction of all expenditures; like icing on a cake, their visibility is no measure of their substance.

Lest it seem that all human action is motivated solely by self-interest, it must be affirmed that some is clearly motivated by a genuine concern for others, with no overtones of self-interest. Clearly there are forces in human experience which are capable of evoking the response of *unselfish or altruistic love*. However, since in most persons this pattern of response has only a limited development, altruistic action is most likely to occur in the minor events of daily life where little is at stake. Apparently many men develop a genuine desire to be generous and kind in their dealings with others but find it "impossible" to act in this way when much is at stake. Thus altruistic action is concentrated on the level of lesser events and decisions, and is infrequent on the level of major social decisions. In fact, it appears that one can state as a generalization that *the frequency of altruistic action varies inversely with the magnitude of the values involved*.

This is not to say that men are immoral when major values are at stake. Rather, it points to the need to differentiate between two kinds of morality, *pragmatic morality* and *ideal morality*. Pragmatic morality is the basis of all popular moral codes, and is based on the recognition that men need one another, and therefore condemns many kinds of harmful actions, especially those which threaten to undermine the social order. Ideal morality, by contrast, has never been accepted as the basis of any popular moral code, since it not only condemns harmful actions but requires that men love others as they love themselves and without regard to possible rewards.

This does not mean that altruism, or unselfish love, is of little or no importance. It is extremely important from both the psychological and moral standpoints, and human existence would be much poorer and harsher if it were absent. It is not, however, a major determinant of the distribution of power and privilege.

Thus, when one surveys the human scene, one is forced to conclude that *when men are confronted with important decisions where they are obliged to choose between their own, or their group's, interests and the interests of others, they nearly always choose the former*—though often seeking to hide this fact from themselves and others. This is the *second postulate* in our theory. As is evident, it leans far in the direction of the conservative position with its skeptical view of the innate goodness of man.

Before leaving this controversial postulate, it may be well to point out that the exchange system and the division of labor in all the more complex societies serve as veils which largely hide this ugly truth. In complex societies men seldom see the consequences of their own economic and political actions. Rather, they observe the workings of the impersonal market system, which favors some and penalizes others. Success or failure thus appears to result from impersonal forces, or forces so complex that the influence of any single individual becomes negligible. This helps to foster the myth that man is by nature good and kind.

The *third postulate* in our theory pertains to the objects of men's strivings. Some, such as the air we breathe, are readily available to all, but most are not. *Most are in short supply*—that is, the demand for them exceeds the available supply.

This is a normal feature of the world of nature. Though we often speak of nature's bounty, the fact remains that all living things have a reproductive capacity which, in view of the limited supply of food and other resources, makes it inevitable that large numbers will die well before the end of their normal life span and most of the others live close to the margin of subsistence.

To some extent man has been able to free himself from these difficulties. Thousands of years ago he learned to increase his food supply and, more recently, he has learned to control reproduction. Yet while man enjoys certain advantages when compared with other living things, he also suffers from certain disadvantages. Unlike the various plants and animals, *man has an insatiable appetite for goods and services*. No matter how much he produces and consumes, he always desires more. This is true chiefly because the goods and services he consumes have a *status value* as well as a utilitarian value. If automobiles were simply a means of transportation, a society able to control its reproduction could eventually satisfy this demand. However, automobiles are also status symbols; hence there is no limit to the demand for their improvement and for the goods and services utilized in their production. The very nature of status striving makes it inevitable that the demand will exceed the supply: those of lower status constantly strive to equal those of higher status and those of higher status always seek to preserve the difference. Given these conditions, satiation is impossible no matter how much man increases production or restricts population increase.

If our first three postulates are correct, that is, if man is a social being, and if most of his important actions are motivated by self-interest or partisan group interest, and if many or most of the objects of his striving are in short supply, then it follows logically that *a struggle for rewards will be present in every human society*. This struggle need not always assume violent forms. On the contrary, it can be carried on within the framework of some system of rules. However, the absence of violence does not mean that the struggle is any less real or serious for the parties involved.

TWO LAWS OF DISTRIBUTION

When one seeks to build a theory of distribution on the postulates about the nature of man and society set forth in the last chapter, one soon discovers that these lead to a curious, but important, *dualism*. If those postulates are sound, one would predict that almost all the products of men's labors will be distributed on the basis of two seemingly contradictory principles, *need* and *power*.

In our discussion of the nature of man, it was postulated that where important decisions are involved, most human action is motivated either by self-interest or by partisan group interests. This suggests that power alone governs the distribution of rewards. This cannot be the case, however, since we also postulated that most of these essentially selfish interests can be satisfied only by the establishment of cooperative relations with others. Cooperation is absolutely essential both for survival and for the efficient attainment of most other goals. In other words, men's selfish interests compel them to remain members of society and to share in the division of labor.

If these two postulates are correct, then it follows that *men will share the product of their labors to the extent required to insure the survival and continued productivity of those others whose actions are necessary or beneficial to themselves*. This might well be called the first law of distribution, since the survival of mankind as a species depends on compliance with it.

This first law, however, does not cover the entire problem. It says nothing about how any *surplus*, that is, goods and services over and above the minimum required to keep producers alive and productive, which men may be able to produce will be distributed. This leads to what may be called the second law of distribution. If we assume that in important decisions human action is motivated almost entirely by self-interest or partisan group interests, and if we assume that many of the things men most desire are in short supply, then, as noted before, this surplus will inevitably give rise to conflicts and struggles aimed at its control. If, following Weber, we define power as the probability of persons or groups carrying out their will even when opposed by others, then it follows that *power will determine the distribution of nearly all of the surplus possessed by a society.* The qualification "nearly all" takes account of the very limited influence of altruistic action which our earlier analysis of the nature of man leads us to expect.

This second law points the way to another very important relationship, that between our two chief variables, power and privilege. If privilege is defined as possession or control of a portion of the surplus produced by a society, then it follows that *privilege is largely a function of power, and to a very limited degree, a function of altruism.* This means that to explain most of the distribution of privilege in a society, we have but to determine the distribution of power.

To state the matter this way suggests that the task of explaining the distribution of privilege is simple. Unfortunately, this is not the case since there are many forms of power and they spring from many sources. Nevertheless, the establishment of this key relationship reduces the problem to more manageable proportions, since it concentrates attention on one key variable, power. Thus if we can establish the pattern of its distribution in a given society, we have largely established the pattern for the distribution of privilege, and if we can discover the causes of a given distribution of power we have also discovered the causes of the distribution of privilege linked with it.

To put the matter this way is to invite the question of how the third basic element in every distributive system, *prestige,* is related to power and privilege. It would be nice if one could say that prestige is a simple function of privilege, but unfortunately this does not seem to be the case. Without going into a complex analysis of the matter at this point, the best that can be said is that empirical evidence strongly suggests that *prestige is largely, though not solely, a function of power and privilege, at least in those societies where there is a substantial surplus.* If this is true, it follows that even though the subject of prestige is not often mentioned in this volume, its pattern of distribution and its causes can largely be deduced from discussion of the distribution of power and privilege and their causes in those societies where there is an appreciable surplus.

Graphically, the relationship between these three variables, as set forth in the propositions above, can be depicted in this way:

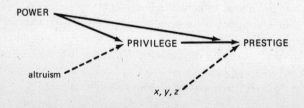

The solid lines indicate major sources of influence, the dashed lines secondary sources.

To make this diagram complete, one other dashed line should probably be added, indicating some feedback from prestige to power. Thus a more accurate representation of the relationships would look like this:

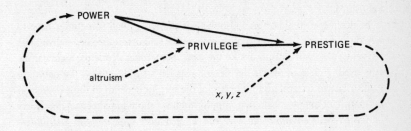

Power is the key variable in the triad from the causal and explanatory standpoint. Hence, it is with this variable that we shall be primarily concerned in the analysis which follows.

THE VARIABLE ASPECTS OF DISTRIBUTIVE SYSTEMS

As the statement of the two laws indicates, the second law does not have any effect on the distributive process until the conditions specified in the first have been satisfied. Until the necessities of life have been made available to enough productive, mutually interdependent members of the group, there is no surplus to be fought over and distributed on the basis of power. Thus, as a first hypothesis we would be led to predict that *in the simplest societies, or those which are technologically most primitive, the goods and services available will be distributed wholly, or largely, on the basis of need.*

As the productivity of societies increases, the possibility of producing a surplus steadily increases, though it should be noted that the existence of a surplus is not a function of technological advance alone. Even though we cannot say that the surplus available to a society increases proportionately with advances in the level of technology, such advances increase the probability that there will be a surplus and also that there will be a sizable surplus. Hence, as a second hypothesis we are led to predict that *with technological advance, an increasing proportion of the goods and services available to a society will be distributed on the basis of power.*

It should also be noted that classifying societies on the basis of the nature of their technology does not imply that all those in a single category have *identi-*

cal distributive systems any more than that all oligopolistic markets function the same way. Obviously there are variations within each societal type just as within each type of market, and an effort will be made to identify and account for the more important of them. However, these may be thought of as *second-order variations*, which are best dealt with after the first-order variations have been established and the internal uniformities associated with them clearly delineated.

In dealing with these second-order variations we shall sometimes have to rely on inductive logic to establish both causal and descriptive generalizations. However, this will not always be the case. Sometimes deductive logic can be employed. For example, if the size of a society's surplus affects the nature of its distributive system, and if the size of the surplus depends to some degree on the nature of the physical environment, then we should predict that *differences in the physical environment will lead to secondary differences in distributive systems.* More specifically, the richer the environment, the larger the surplus and the greater the importance of power in the distributive process.

There are also reasons for predicting that the influence of environmental differences will be greater in primitive societies than in those which are technologically more advanced. To begin with, technological advance makes possible the geographical expansion of societies, and the larger the territory occupied by a society, the less the probability that the total environment will be extremely favorable or unfavorable and the greater the probability that it will include a mixture of favorable and unfavorable land. Hence, environmental variation should be less among the larger, technologically advanced societies than among the smaller, more primitive. In addition, technological advance frequently means the development of alternative solutions to the various problems of production. Technologically advanced societies, therefore, should be less hampered by environmental limitations than primitive societies are, and thus *environmental variation should have less effect on the level of productivity in advanced societies than in primitive.*

Another important source of secondary variation has been identified by Stanislaw Andrzejewski in his important but neglected book, *Military Organization and Society.* As he has shown, both deductive logic and empirical data indicate that *the degree of inequality in societies of a given level of technological development tends to vary inversely with what he calls "the military participation ratio,"* that is *the proportion of the adult male population utilized in military operations.* Where most adult males are utilized for such purposes, the degree of inequality tends to be less than in those in which military needs are supplied by a small force of military specialists. Thus, this factor can also be used to explain some of the secondary variations which are found among societies of the same technological type.

FORCE AND ITS TRANSFORMATION

As a starting point, it may be well to return briefly to one of the postulates introduced in the last chapter. There it was assumed that survival is the chief goal of the great majority of men. If this is so, then it follows that *the ability to take life is the most effective form of power.* In other words, more men will respond more readily to the threat of the use of *force* than to any other. In effect, it constitutes the final court of appeals in human affairs; there is no appeal from force in a given situation except the exercise of superior force. Hence force stands in the same relationship to other forms of power as trumps to the other suits in the game of bridge, and those who can exercise the greatest force are like those who control trumps.

This fact has been recognized by countless observers of the human scene in every age. As Pascal put it, "Not being able to make that which is just strong, man has made that which is strong just." Cicero made the same point when he said, "Laws are dumb in the midst of arms," and Hobbes asserted that "Covenants without the sword are but words, and of no strength to secure a man at all."

This principle is also recognized by the leaders of nations, the practical men of affairs. Every sovereign state restricts, and where possible prohibits, the independent exercise of force by its subjects. States may be tolerant of many things, but never of the growth of independent military organizations within their territories. The reason is obvious: any government which cannot suppress each and every forceful challenge to its authority is overthrown. Force is the foundation of sovereignty.

If force is the foundation of political sovereignty, it is also the foundation of the distributive system in every society where there is a surplus to be divided. Where coercive power is weak, challenges inevitably occur, and the system is eventually destroyed and replaced by another based more firmly on force. Men struggling over control of the surplus of a society will not accept defeat so long as there is a higher court of appeals to which they may take their case with some likelihood of success and profit to themselves.

The principle involved here is essentially the same as the principle of escalation with which modern military men are so concerned. Small wars based on small weapons inevitably grow into more deadly wars utilizing more deadly weapons if, by advancing the level of conflict, one of the parties anticipates turning defeat into victory. Similarly, in the case of conflicts within societies, the parties involved are always motivated to take the issue to the final court of appeals so long as there is the likelihood of benefiting by it. While men will not resort to armed revolution for trivial gains, when control over the entire surplus of a society is involved, the prospect is more enticing. The attractiveness varies directly with the weakness of the current regime.

Nevertheless, as Edmund Burke, the famed English conservative, recognized, "The use of force alone is but temporary. It may subdue for a moment; but it does not remove the necessity of subduing again: and a nation is not governed, which is perpetually to be conquered." Though force is the most effective instrument for seizing power in a society, and though it always remains the foundation of any system of inequality, it is not the most effective instrument for retaining and exploiting a position of power and deriving the maximum benefits from it. Therefore, regardless of the objectives of a new regime, once organized opposition has been destroyed it is to its advantage to make increasing use of other techniques and instruments of control, and to allow force to recede into the background to be used only when other techniques fail.

If the new elite has materialistic goals and is concerned solely with self-aggrandizement, it soon discovers that the rule of might is both inefficient and costly. So long as it relies on force, much of the profit is consumed by the costs of coercion. If the population obeys only out of fear of physical violence, a large portion of the time, energy, and wealth of the elite are invariably consumed in the effort to keep it under control and separate the producers from the product of their labors. Even worse, honor, which normally ranks high in the scale of human values, is denied to those who rule by force alone.

If materialistic elites have strong motives for shifting from the rule of might to the rule of right, ideologically motivated elites have even stronger. If the visions and ideals which led them to undertake the terrible risks and hardships of revolution are ever to be fulfilled, the voluntary cooperation of the population is essential, and this cannot be obtained by force. Force is, at best, the means to an end. That end, the establishment of a new social order, can never be fully attained until most members of society freely accept it as their own. The purpose of the revolution is to destroy the old elite and their institutions, which prevent the fulfillment of this dream. Once they are destroyed, an ideological elite strives to rule by persuasion. Thus *those who seize power by force find it advantageous to legitimize their rule once effective organized opposition is eliminated.* Force can no longer continue to play the role it did. It can no longer function as the private resource of a special segment of the population. Rather it must be transformed into a public resource used in the defense of law and order.

This may seem to be the equivalent of saying that those who have at great risk to themselves displaced the old elite must now give up all they have won. Actually, however, this is not at all necessary since, with a limited exercise of intelligence, force can be transformed into authority, and might into right.

There are various means by which this transformation can be effected. To begin with, by virtue of its coercive power, a new elite is in a good position to rewrite the law of the land as it sees fit. This affords them a unique opportunity, since by its very nature law is identified with justice and the rule of right. Since legal statutes are stated in general and impersonal terms, they appear to support abstract principles of justice rather than the special interests of particular men or classes of men. The fact that laws exist prior to the events to which they are applied suggests an objective impartiality which also contributes to their acceptance. Yet laws can always be written in such a way that they favor some particular segment of society. Anatole France saw this clearly when he wrote, "The law in its majestic equality forbids the rich as well as the poor to sleep under bridges, to beg in the street, and to steal bread."

As should be evident, those in the employ of the elite are rewarded in proportion to the value of their services to the elite, and the scarcity of the supply of replacements. Contrary to such functionalist theorists as Kingsley Davis and Wilbert Moore, these roles are not rewarded in proportion to their contribution to the common good. It is the needs of the elite, not the needs of the total society, which determine the demand curve for such services. *The distribution of rewards in a society is a function of the distribution of power, not of system needs.* This is inevitable in such imperfect systems as human societies.

Every system of power and privilege also sets in motion a deadly *struggle for survival among the offspring of the common people*, except in those societies which are able to control reproduction or in which there is a temporary shortage of population such as may be created by major plagues, famines, or other disasters. Unhappily, mankind has always been able to produce more offspring than society can maintain, especially when the economic surplus is skimmed off by a privileged elite. Usually there has not been land enough for every farmer's son to farm, nor farmers enough for every farmer's daughter to marry. Hence some of the common people of almost every generation have been reduced to the status of beggars, criminals, and prostitutes. Such persons have usually had short lives, since at this level the competition for survival is intense. From the standpoint of the elite, the struggles which developed among the common people have been a matter of little concern, since human fecundity always insured an ample supply of qualified producers. In fact, these struggles probably served the interests of the elite by diverting attention from their own exploitative role, thus affording them a considerable measure of security against popular protest and revolution.

CLASSES

[P]ower takes many forms and these cannot always be reduced to a meaningful common denominator. An individual may have large property holdings without occupying a correspondingly important and powerful office and vice versa. Similarly, an individual may occupy an important and powerful role in one institutional system but not in others.

In view of this, it is clear that the term "class" should not be defined too narrowly. More can be gained by defining the term broadly and then distinguishing carefully between different kinds of classes. Therefore, we might best define a class as *an aggregation of persons in a society who stand in a similar position with respect to some form of power, privilege, or prestige.*

This is *not* to say that all types of classes are equally important for theoretical and analytical purposes. On the contrary, if our goal is to answer the question of "who gets what and why?" and if our analysis of the last two chapters has any validity at all, *power* classes must be our chief concern. The distribution of privilege and prestige seem largely determined by the distribution of power, at least in those societies in which a significant surplus is produced.

In the last chapter we also saw that power manifests itself in two basic forms, force and institutionalized power. The latter, in turn, can be subdivided into the power of position and the power of property. Building on this, a power class may be defined as *an aggregation of persons in a society who stand in a similar position with respect to force or some specific form of institutionalized power.* . . . Though the definition does not say so explicitly, *the members of every power class share certain common interests with one another, and these shared interests constitute a potential basis for hostility toward other classes.* This follows as a logical corollary of the fact that what unites the members of a class is their common possession, control, or utilization of something which affects their chances of fulfilling their wishes and desires. Given our earlier assumptions about the nature of man, it follows that all members of a given class have a vested interest in protecting or increasing the value of their common resource and in reducing the value of competitive resources which constitute the bases of other classes.

This is not to say that the members of a class always have a conscious awareness of their common interest, much less that they act collectively on the basis of it. Nor are they always consciously or overtly hostile to members of other classes. These are possibilities which may be realized, but there is nothing inevitable about them.

CITIZENSHIP: A POTENTIALLY UNIQUE RESOURCE

In an earlier period the rights of citizenship were reserved for the few and citizenship, like other resources, did divide men into classes. Sometimes citizenship divided the members of societies into citizens and noncitizens, other times into first- and second-class citizens. This traditional pattern can be seen in the early history of this country, when the population was divided into enfranchised citizens, unenfranchised freemen, and slaves. Each stood in a different relation to the state, with enfranchised citizens in the most favored position and slaves in the least.

Today slavery has disappeared in advanced industrial societies and the right of franchise has been extended to include nearly all adults. As a result, citizenship tends to be a resource which all share alike.

Since citizenship is shared by all, one might suppose that it no longer has any special relevance for the student of stratification. This is not the case, however. Citizenship continues to figure prominently in the distributive process. Those who lack other kinds of resources, together with those who, for ideological reasons, believe in social equality, have combined to fight for the enhancement of the value of citizenship at the expense of those resources which generate inequality. This struggle is evident in recent controversies involving the issue of property rights versus human rights. Those who advocate the primacy of human rights over property rights typically advocate the enlargement of the rights of citizenship at the expense of the traditional rights of property. Their opponents take the opposite position. Thus the struggle becomes not merely a struggle between classes, but also a struggle between class systems and thus between differing principles of stratification.

Historically oriented students of stratification will recognize that the modern era is not completely unique in this, since in preindustrial societies the less powerful classes often fought the more powerful classes in the same way, and not without some success. At the very least, they often succeeded in establishing certain uniform legal rights, including the right to a public trial based on an established body of law. Sometimes they were even able to establish the right of all men to protection from extortionary and irregular taxation and other abuses. To be sure, men of property and position usually fought to prevent such rights from being established and to undermine them if they were. Usually they were successful in these efforts. Only in the more advanced industrial societies of the modern era, however, is citizenship simultaneously a resource of *major* importance and one shared by all.

In many ways this centuries-old effort to enhance the value of common citizenship can be viewed as an attempt to reestablish the ascendancy of *need* over *power* as the dominant principle of distribution. As noted in the last chapter, in those societies which are technologically most primitive, need, rather than power, is the chief determinant of "who gets what." With technological advance and the growing capacity to produce a surplus, power became the chief determinant. Today, an organized effort is being made to restore the importance of need. Ironically, however, it appears that this reversal can occur only if the advocates of need can mobilize more power than the advocates of power. This is because advanced industrial societies, unlike primitive hunting and gathering societies, have a surplus and thus their distributive pattern is not dictated by economic necessity. Thus one is led to the conclusion that if need should ever be restored to the position of dominance, it would not rest on the same foundation as that on which it rested in technologically primitive societies.

The Dynamics of Distributive Systems

On the basis of the postulates set forth . . . one would predict that *the degree of inequality in distributive systems will vary directly with the size of a society's surplus*. Some modification of this general pattern could develop, however, when conditions permit persons who individually lack power to combine and organize, and thus to develop a collective counterbalance to those with greater individual power. Such developments seem most probable in democratic nations with an egalitarian or socialist ideology.

EQUALITY IN SOCIETIES WITH NO SURPLUS

Of all the various characteristics shared by hunting and gathering societies, the one of key importance for students of stratification is the absence of any appreciable economic surplus. According to the first and second laws of distribution . . . men are free to monopolize or expropriate only that portion of the product of the group which is not required to sustain the producers. If this is true, and if hunting and gathering societies are incapable of producing any appreciable economic surplus, then our theory leads us to predict that there will be relative equality in these societies, at least with respect to the distribution of goods and services.

The facts support this prediction. If any single feature of the life of hunting and gathering societies has impressed itself upon observers, it is the relative equality of the members. In fact, many untrained observers have reported perfect equality in certain of these societies. While the more careful observations of trained observers force us to reject these extreme claims, the fact remains that the distributive process in hunting and gathering societies is radically different from that in industrial societies such as our own, or the agrarian societies from which industrial societies have so recently emerged.

The Andaman Islanders provide a good illustration of a relatively pure and uncontaminated hunting and gathering society, and one which has not developed even the more rudimentary forms of horticulture. In writing of their economic life, Radcliffe-Brown reports that "it approaches to a sort of communism." Land, the basic resource of the group, is communally owned, thus insuring equal access to the necessities of life. While the produce of the land and all portable property are privately owned, the Andamanese have customs which offset the usual effects of private ownership. For example, though all food is private property, "everyone who has food is expected . . . to give to those who have none." The result is that "practically all of the food obtained is evenly distributed through the whole camp, the only inequality being that the younger men do not fare so well as their elders." In the case of other forms of privately owned property, an egalitarian distribution is assured by the Andamanese custom of exchanging presents. This practice, when combined with the tradition of according honor to persons who are generous with their possessions, insures near equality in the distribution of goods. In such a society a man stands to gain more by sharing than by hoarding.

While no one hunting and gathering society is completely representative of all, a person familiar with the distribution of goods in Andamanese society is not likely to be greatly surprised by what he finds in most of the others. In those societies, too, one finds a close approximation to equality in the distribution of goods. This is usually achieved, as among the Andamanese, by the communal ownership of land and by some type of institutionalized redistributive process. Often there is some limited inequality, with certain segments of the population faring a bit better than others. In the case of the Andamanese the old men enjoy some advantage over the younger. Among the Siriono, the senior wife in a polygynous family and her children are reported to fare somewhat better than the junior wife and hers. In some societies men fare better than women. These differences, however, represent little more than secondary variations on the basic theme of substantial equality.

The distribution of prestige is a very different matter from the distribution of goods. Here there is no problem of short supply, and inequality does not threaten the group's chances of survival. As a consequence, the unequal distribution of honor tends to be the rule rather than the exception in hunting and gathering societies, just as our theory would lead us to expect. However, for reasons which will become evident shortly, the degree of prestige inequality falls far short of that with which members of more advanced societies are familiar.

Once again we may turn to Andamanese society as one which is reasonably typical, at least in the more basic aspects of the matter. Radcliffe-Brown, the leading authority on these people, reports that honor and respect are accorded to three kinds of people: (1) older people, (2) people endowed with supernatural powers, and (3) people with certain valued personal qualities, notably, "skill in hunting and warfare, generosity and kindness, and freedom from bad temper." Though it is not completely clear from Radcliffe-Brown's account, there is some indication that men are more likely than women to be highly honored.

Such inequality might properly be called "functional inequality." In other words, the benefits and honors enjoyed by the few represent *a return for services rendered to the many under conditions free from any form of social coercion or man-made shortage.* This can be seen most clearly in the case of an individual who is honored for his skill in hunting and for his generosity. The less able members of the group reward such a person with prestige and influence in exchange for a share in the game he kills. By this spontaneous and uncoerced exchange, those who are generously endowed by nature with talent and energy are stimulated to produce more, and those who are not have greater assurance of obtaining the necessities of life. The alternative would be deprivation, suffering, and possible death for the less able, and, for the more able, surfeit of food and loss of prestige and the respect of others. Thus, *potentially disastrous inequalities in subsistence are transformed into inequalities in prestige and influence, a much safer and more satisfying arrangement.*

One may question whether *all* the inequality in honor and influence in Andamanese and similar societies results in genuine gains for the less favored. For example, are the services of most primitive medicine men of real value to others? This leads into an area of possible disagreement. One observer may feel that the peace of mind a skillful shaman creates for his patients justifies the prestige he receives, while another may not. In this situation it may be wiser to rely on the natives' judgment of the matter and differentiate between functional and nonfunctional inequality on the basis of the relative freedom of the individuals involved. If the exchange is free of man-made coercive elements, then it is reasonable to view such inequality as is generated as functional. If one takes this approach, it is clear that most of the inequality evident in primitive hunting and gathering groups is of just this type.

In hunting and gathering societies, prestige usually goes hand in hand with political influence. The reasons for this are not hard to find. Government by coercion is an impossibility in these societies. The leader of the group is not supported by a force of specialists in violence who are dependent on his favor and therefore motivated to follow his orders. All men are trained and equipped for fighting and the same weapons and training are available to all. The only differences among them are those inherent in the physical constitutions and personalities of the individuals and, while a single man who is unusually well endowed by nature may be the equal, or even the master, of two less favorably endowed men, he is not likely to be able to coerce or defend himself against three who join forces against him. Furthermore, dissatisfied followers may always desert their leader and attach themselves to another band. It follows, therefore, that government must be by persuasion. This means that in any situation in which there is no one obviously correct course of action, effective leadership is possible only if a majority of the population is predisposed to follow the direction of certain individuals and to reject that of others. In short, the limited political development of these societies creates a situation in which honor and respect are necessary prerequisites to political influence.

The same conditions which make honor and respect necessary qualifications for political influence also serve to limit the extent of political inequality possible. The extremes of political domination and subordination are impossible in a society where men must govern by persuasion.

REVERSAL OF A BASIC TREND

[T]he appearance of mature industrial societies marks the first significant reversal in the age-old evolutionary trend toward ever increasing inequality.

The evidence supporting these assertions takes several basic forms. To begin with, a comparison of the political systems of agrarian and industrial societies makes it clear that political power is much more concentrated in the former. In agrarian societies, the powers of government were nearly always vested in the hands of the few; the great majority were *wholly excluded* from the political process. In industrial societies this is a minority pattern, limited only to those societies in the earlier stages of industrialization and to those ruled by totalitarian parties. In the majority of industrial societies, all adult citizens not only enjoy voting privileges but, far more important, the right to organize politically to promote their own special interests or beliefs, even when these are in opposition to the interests or beliefs of those in power. While this does not mean that all inequalities in political power are eliminated or the democratic millennium ushered in, it does mean a significant reduction in political inequality and a substantial diffusion of political power, both of which are readily evident when these societies are compared with agrarian. This can be seen most clearly in the case of the Scandinavian democracies, where Socialist Parties have been the dominant political force in recent decades, but the pattern is also evident in countries such as the United States and France, where the political influence of the lower classes has not been nearly so great. It should also be noted that even in some of those industrial societies where democracy was not permitted, as in post-Stalinist Russia or Peron's Argentina, the political elite used much of its power to promote programs designed to benefit the lower classes, a practice virtually unknown in agrarian societies.

A second indication of declining inequalities can be found in data on the distribution of income. Earlier we saw evidence which indicated that in agrarian societies the top 1 or 2 per cent of the population, usually received *not less than half* of the total income of the nation. In the case of industrial societies the comparable figure is substantially less. According to official governmental reports, the top 2 per cent of the population of democratic nations receives about 10 per cent of the total personal cash income after taxes. For example, British figures for 1954 indicate that the top 2 per cent received 8.5 per cent of the total income after taxes; Swedish figures for 1950 show the top 1.8 per cent received 9.9 per cent before taxes; Danish figures for 1949 show the top 1.1 per cent received 10.3 per cent *before taxes*; United States figures for 1958 show the top 1.3 per cent received 8.1 per cent, and the top 2.3 per cent received 11.6 per cent, *before taxes*.

These figures cannot, of course, be taken at face value. As a number of recent writers have pointed out, they do not include many billions of dollars of income, sometimes because of fraud and evasion by taxpayers, but more often because the tax statutes do not define certain forms of income as income. . . . Taking the higher estimate for underreporting by the upper-income group, that is, $15 billion, we arrive at the conclusion that, before taxes, 15.5 per cent of the personal income of the American people went to the top 2.3 per cent.

Even this figure, however, is far short of the 50 per cent estimated to be the elite's share of the gross national product in agrarian societies. This difference arises, in part, because the revenues of government are included in agrarian societies but not in industrial. On first inspection this may seem both arbitrary and unjust. Actually it is neither. In agrarian societies government functions almost entirely, as we have seen, as an instrument of, by, and for the few. In modern industrial societies, this is no longer the case. While it is true that the upper classes still benefit disproportionately from the actions of government in every industrial society, it is also true that the masses of ordinary citizens benefit to an extent undreamed of in the agrarian societies of the past, or even in those which still survive.

It is impossible to determine with any precision what percentage of the benefits of government go to the top 2 per cent of the population and what percentage to the remainder in industrial societies. However, even if one were to assume that they went *entirely* to the elite, the total would still fall short of the agrarian figure of 50 per cent. . . . [W]hile it may not be possible to determine precisely what percentage of the gross national product is enjoyed by the top 2 per cent in mature industrial societies, it is safe to conclude that the percentage is considerably less than in agrarian. In fact, it is probably no more than half so large, and quite possibly less than that.

Since the foregoing estimates are all based on data from democratic nations, one may properly ask whether the situation in totalitarian states is not different. This question is not easily answered owing to the paucity of trustworthy quantitative data. However, such as we have indicates that in the Soviet Union, at least, income inequality is substantially less than in the United States. . . . Thus, it appears that the Soviet Union provides no exception to the conclusion about the historic decline in income inequality formulated on the basis of data from democratic nations.

CAUSES OF THE REVERSAL

From the theoretical standpoint, the decline in political and economic inequality associated with the emergence of industrial societies is extremely important. This constitutes a reversal in a major historical trend, and the reasons for this reversal are by no means obvious. On the contrary, given the increased productivity of industrial societies and the growth in the powers of the state, one would normally predict even greater inequality than in agrarian societies. The fact that the opposite occurred indicates either that one or more of the basic postulates with which we began is in error, or that other factors are at work which were not taken into account (or, at least, not sufficiently) in our original, highly general formulation. The evidence, as I shall show, favors the latter interpretation, indicating again the serious difficulties which attend any effort to develop a general theory by purely deductive means.

Among the factors not considered in our earlier assumptions about the nature of man and society, was the relationship between technological and cultural complexity on the one hand, and administrative efficiency on the other. In modern industrial societies, technology in particular, and culture in general, are far more complex than in even the most advanced agrarian societies. In fact, they are so complex that it is no longer possible for those in positions of high command to begin to understand the work of all those beneath them. In effect, there is a growing "ignorance" on the part of those in positions of command. This is not to say that those in authority in industrial societies are less intelligent or knowledgeable than their counterparts in agrarian societies, but rather that they are masters of *a smaller proportion* of what they need to know to maintain effective control over those beneath them. Thus, because of the many gaps in their knowledge, they are often compelled either to issue commands based on insufficient information, or to leave matters to the discretion of their subordinates, thus opening the door to encroachments on their prerogatives. In the former case, authority is preserved, but at the expense of efficiency and productivity, while in the latter case a measure of authority is sacrificed to increase efficiency and productivity. In short, *the relationship between productivity and authority appears to be curvilinear in industrial societies, at least up to the present time.* Thus, unless political authorities are willing and able to sacrifice productivity, it is unlikely that they will be able to rely on the technique of command to the extent their agrarian counterparts did. However, to the degree that they delegate authority or rely on market mechanisms, they facilitate the diffusion of power and privilege.

A second factor which seems to have contributed to the reversal in the historic trend toward greater inequality is *the rapidity and magnitude of the increases in productivity.* In societies in which the gross national product and per capita income are rapidly rising, and promise to continue rising, elites find themselves in the paradoxical situation in which they can maximize their *net* input of rewards by responding to pressures from below and making certain concessions. By granting the lower classes some share in the economic surplus, they can reduce worker hostility and the accompanying losses from strikes, slowdowns, and industrial sabotage. In an expanding economy, an elite can make economic concessions in *relative* terms without necessarily suffering any loss in *absolute* terms. In fact, if the concessions are not too large, and the rate of the economy's growth is great enough, relative losses can even be accompanied by *substantial* absolute gains. For example, an elite would enjoy a substantially greater income if it took 40 per cent of the gross national product in a $100 billion economy, than if it stubbornly fought to maintain a 50 per cent share and thereby held the economy at the $50 billion level. *If we assume that the majority of men would willingly make modest relative concessions for the sake of substantial absolute gains, and if we also assume that leading members of the elites in industrial societies have an awareness of the benefits they can obtain from concessions, then we can only predict they will make them.*

A willingness to make concessions may also be encouraged by the principle of marginal utility. This principle serves as a reminder that the first million dollars normally has greater value to a man than any subsequent million he may acquire. In societies with very productive economies, many members of the elite may be prepared to make some *economic* concessions in order to maximize other kinds of rewards, such as safety, respect, and leisure. In other words, after a certain level of wealth has been attained, elites may prefer to sacrifice a portion of the economic surplus in order to reduce hostility and the dangers of revolution, and to win for themselves a greater measure of respect and affection. Or, they may find it impossible to maintain tight control over political and economic organizations and at the same time enjoy the benefits of leisure, and so permit a portion of the economic surplus to pass into other hands. In short, *because elites have multiple goals, and are not concerned with maximizing material rewards alone, they may be willing to make certain economic concessions in a highly productive and expanding economy.*

Yet another factor which has played a role in reducing inequality is the development of new and highly effective methods of birth control. In the past, the natural tendency of the human race to multiply usually had the effect of offsetting whatever economic gains might otherwise have resulted from technological advance. Numbers tended to increase up to the carrying power of the economy *except as limited by the development of tyrannical political systems which diverted the "economic surplus" to the elite at the expense of further population increase.* One consequence, of course, was the large and wretched class of expendables, whose very presence served to prevent any substantial long-run improvement in the lot of the peasants and artisans with whom they constantly competed for employment.

Today the situation is rapidly changing, and promises to change even more in the future. For the first time in history, mankind has found safe, simple, and effective means of controlling population growth. In societies where these have been most widely used, the rate of population growth has been slowed to the point where real and substantial gains in per capita income have been achieved in a fairly short time, thus reducing the intensity of the competitive pressures. Now, for almost the first time in centuries, the lower classes are able to bargain for wages in markets no longer perennially glutted with labor. This development has almost certainly contributed to the decline in inequality.

Another factor that has probably contributed to the decline in inequality is the great expansion in human knowledge. In the past, the dominant class chiefly needed unskilled labor, and thanks to human fecundity, this was always plentiful. This put the vast majority of men in a poor bargaining position, and hence the price of labor was minimal. Today, in the more advanced industrial societies, the situation is radically changed. Because of the great functional utility of so much of the new knowledge, a host of occupational specialists have appeared who are not interchangeable to any great degree. This introduces into the labor market certain rigidities which favor the sellers of labor, especially in an era in which the demand for technical skills is rapidly rising. Furthermore, even if the dominant classes could obtain the necessary labor for a subsistence wage, it is doubtful that this would prove expedient. The efficiency of work requiring mental effort or alertness can be seriously reduced when those performing it are not physically fit. Two men working at 50 per cent efficiency in this situation are not the equal of one man working at top efficiency, as in work requiring brute strength alone. Moreover expensive machines and tight production schedules are vulnerable to the mistakes of inattentive workers to a degree that is not characteristic of agrarian societies. These factors all prevent the dominant classes from driving the wages of this increasingly numerous segment of the population down to the subsistence level, and prevent the system from reaching the level of economic inequality that is found in agrarian societies, both past and present.

The egalitarian trend in modern industrial societies is evident in the *political* area no less than in the economic. In many respects the trend toward greater political equality is more surprising than the corresponding economic trend, because the struggle for political power is essentially a zero-sum "game," i.e., gains by one party necessarily entail corresponding losses by opponents. The struggle for privilege, on the other hand, is a positive-sum "game," thanks to the constantly rising level of productivity. Thus in the political realm the privileged classes cannot accept losses in relative terms and still realize absolute gains.

All the reasons for the spread of democratic government are still not completely understood. Obviously, it has not been dictated by economic necessity, as shown by the vigor of a number of nondemocratic, totalitarian nations. On the other hand, the relative frequency of democratic government in industrial states and its virtual absence in agrarian, strongly indicate some connection. Specifically, this suggests that industrialization creates conditions favorable to the growth of democracy, but does not make it inevitable.

One favorable condition is the spread of literacy and the extension of education. An illiterate peasantry lacking access to mass media of information is in a poor position to participate in the political process; a literate middle and working class with many media of information available is much more favorably situated. Advances in the level of living have a similar effect. Peasants and artisans living at, or near, the subsistence level cannot afford the luxury of sustained political activity; workers in an industrial society have more leisure, energy, and money to devote to this. Still another factor favoring the growth of democracy is the modern pattern of warfare which involves the entire population to an extent unknown in agrarian societies. As many observers have noted, the traditional distinction between the military and civilian segments of the population has been almost obliterated, and military men have come to regard urban centers of production as prime military targets. If Andrzejewski and other writers are correct, this trend should have an egalitarian influence, since inequality tends to be most pronounced where military activities are limited to the few.

More important than any of these, however, has been the rise and spread of *the new democratic ideology* which asserts that the state belongs to the people. This ideology is not simply a reflection of changing economic conditions, though, as we have seen, it has been affected by them. Rather, the historical record indicates it had its origin in religious and philosophical developments of the seventeenth century and spread rather widely in the eighteenth century in countries which were still thoroughly agrarian in character, for example, the United States and France. In fact, there appears to be as much justification for the thesis that this new ideology contributed to the emergence of industrial societies as for the converse.

In any case, this new ideology became an important force in the political life of industrial societies. It captured the imagination of all kinds of men, even some of the political elite, thus making the traditional monopoly of political power increasingly untenable. As the democratic ideology spread, those who governed had to make substantial concessions in order to avoid massive challenges to their power—challenges which would have been costly to resist, and might even have led to their overthrow. The idea that the state should be the servant of all the people continues to be a major force in the modern era, mobilizing the egoistic impulses of the disadvantaged classes in an idealistic cause, thereby uniting morality and egoism in a manner reminiscent of their union under the banner of "the divine right of kings," but with the opposite effect.

Wherever democratic theory has become institutionalized, a dramatic new possibility has arisen: *now the many can combine against the few, and even though individually the many are weaker, in combination they may be as strong or stronger.* With this development, the door is opened to a host of revolutionary developments in the distributive realm.

THE GENERAL THEORY REEXAMINED

In the light of the evidence presented . . .one can give an essentially affirmative answer to the basic question of the validity of the general theory presented
in the introductory chapters. The most basic characteristics of distributive
systems do appear to be shaped by the interaction of those *constant elements* in
the human situation which we identified earlier and the *variable element of
technology*. As hypothesized, the influence of these factors appears to be mediated by a series of social organizational factors whose variation is greatly
influenced by prior variations in technology. It was this systematic covariation,
of course, which made possible the development of the societal typology,
which proved so valuable.

The high degree of support for the theory was not completely unexpected
because of the manner in which the theory was constructed. Despite some
appearances to the contrary, the theory presented in the early chapters was not
a simple exercise in deductive logic. Rather, it represented the end product of
an already extensive process of both induction and deduction. In a sense, the
theory was designed to fit the facts, or at least those facts with which I was
familiar when I began writing this volume. However, the theory with which I
began writing was not the same that I had taught ten years previously. On the
contrary, over the course of that decade I constantly shifted and modified my
theoretical position to try to get a better fit between theory and data. In the
process I found myself shifting from what was basically a functionalist position
to what I have called a synthetic or synthesizing position. In other words, I
found an increasing need to incorporate hypotheses and postulates which had
little or no part in the functionalist tradition, yet without wholly abandoning
the latter.

In the light of the evidence set forth . . . it appears that the general theory
corresponds reasonably well with the evidence, but the correspondence is not
perfect and certain modifications and changes are necessary. To begin with,
our survey of advanced horticultural and agrarian societies indicates that the
relationship between technology and political organization is not so simple as
anticipated. In these societies one finds significant variations in level of political development associated with apparently limited variations in technology.
This suggests that we must think of the level of technological advance either as
a *necessary*, but not *sufficient*, cause of political advance, or as the generator
of a "threshold effect," whereby a limited advance in technology causes (or
makes possible) a major advance in political organization. Perhaps both apply.
In any case, it is clear that at certain levels of technological development, a
considerable degree of variation in political development becomes possible.

This has significant consequences for the distributive process because the level of political development is clearly a major determinant of the character of distributive systems.

A second modification which is indicated is a distinction at the analytical level between the concepts "technology" and "economy." In retrospect, it appears that these two terms were often used interchangeably in the preceding chapters. In the majority of instances this caused no great difficulty because differences in economy, i.e., the economic organization of a society, usually parallel differences in technology, that is, the cultural means by which a society relates to its environment. Thus, a hunting and gathering technology is accompanied by a hunting and gathering economy. Difficulties arise, however, in the case of societal types standing on comparable levels of technological development, as in the case of agrarian and maritime societies. Here, the same elements of technology appear to be available to both, but certain elements are emphasized in one and neglected in the other. The reasons for this reflect, in part at least, the influence of environmental factors, though other factors are probably also at work. Economic variations which occur independently of technological variations appear to have effects on distributive systems comparable to those produced by political variations. Hence, we might more accurately portray the links in the causal chain as follows:[1]

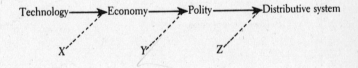

In addition, of course, there are elements of feedback operating, which further complicates relations.

In addition to demonstrating the importance of technology and social organization in the shaping of distributive systems, our findings also demonstrate the influence of other factors. . . . Two of these stand out because of their widespread importance: (1) *variations in ideology*, and (2) *variations in the personal attributes of political leaders*.

Ideology seems to have its greatest impact in the more advanced societies. Ideological variations of great magnitude and importance for distributive systems presuppose the existence of specialists in ideology, supported by appropriate religious and political institutions. These developments seem to have their

[1] The symbols X, Y, and Z are included as a reminder that our theory assumes that other factors exercise an influence at each point in the causal chain.

beginnings in advanced horticultural societies, while coming to full flower
only in industrial societies.

The importance of ideology was seen most clearly in the somewhat unexpected halting, and possible reversal, of the trend toward increasing social
inequality, so pronounced in the evolution from hunting and gathering to
agrarian societies. . . . [I]t was predicted that the degree of inequality in distributive systems would vary directly with the size of a society's surplus. This
was qualified in tentative fashion to make allowance for the possibility that
persons who lacked power individually might, through organization, develop a
measure of countervailing power; and it was "predicted" (not without some
awareness of the facts) that this would be most likely in democratic nations
with an egalitarian or socialistic ideology. Though it was not possible to
develop any quantitative measure of overall inequality, the evidence which we
reviewed strongly suggests that the average level of inequality in the most
advanced industrial societies is no greater than that in the average advanced
agrarian society, and probably less. Graphically, the evolutionary pattern appears to resemble the pattern in Figure 1.

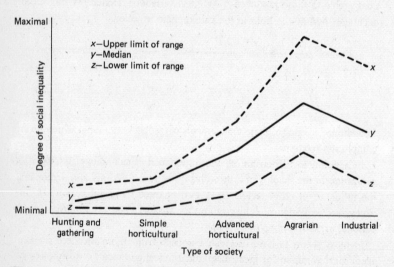

Figure 1   Degree of social inequality by type of society.

The Political Economy of Culture [1979]

RANDALL COLLINS

• By the 1960s and 1970s, sociological research had hit on stratification as a central topic. Within this, by far the most popular
area to study was social mobility or, in the more ideological
terminology of some researchers, "status attainment." By focusing
on recent industrial societies, this research laid tremendous stress
on education as a much more important determinant of an individual's occupational success than his or her social class background. The following selection is the theoretical section from my
own presentation of evidence for a deeper understanding of education in the stratification process. It attempts to demonstrate
that education does not primarily provide technical skills, but
rather a currency of social membership in the status groups that
control higher occupational levels. Occupational positions, sociologically speaking, are really a form of appropriation of various
kinds of income as "positional property." The class structure,
thus, is divided into markets for "productive labor" and "political
labor." The economy of these occupational markets is shaped by
the degree of inflation in the cultural currency turned out by the
educational sector.

[G]eneral issues of stratification include: how people get occupational positions,
and from them, the financial and material rewards that make up the distribution
of wealth. The question then arises, Who gets what out of this process? The
technical—functional theory by which the prominence of education has been
explained offers a general perspective on this process of occupational stratification: people obtain positions by competing on a market for skills, and they are
paid in proportion to the marginal return upon the products of their labor.
Those whose labor skills are relatively most productive of highly desired goods
and services receive the greatest returns. Yet the evidence amassed in the previous chapters against the meritocratic interpretation of education in careers also
casts strong doubts upon the more general formulation.

From Randall Collins, *The Credential Society* (New York: Academic Press, 1979), pp. 49–72.
Reprinted with permission of Academic Press.

This same evidence suggests an alternative explanation. People are actively concerned with the process of gaining and controlling occupational power and income, not merely (or even primarily) with using skills to maximize production. This is not to say that no one is involved in productive work, but as we have seen, it is difficult to assess merit in most organizations, especially at white-collar levels, and the social organization of workers operates fairly deliberately to prevent accurate assessment. The workers with the greatest technical skills are not the best paid, but they are found mainly in the lower–middle levels of organizations (and side branches of the middle levels); the most important routes to power and income are through the realms of organizational politics and administration.

PRODUCTIVE LABOR AND POLITICAL LABOR

That is to say, there is not only *productive labor*, but there is also *political labor*. By the latter, I mean primarily efforts within the maneuverings of organizational politics. Productive labor is responsible for the material production of wealth, but political labor sets the conditions under which the wealth is appropriated. To the extent that one is paid for one's productive contribution, this does not happen automatically but because political labor has shaped the organizational structure and the labor market to make this possible. More generally, just how occupational incomes are distributed depends upon the political labor surrounding the work process.

Political labor is above all a matter of forming social alliances within and sometimes across organizations, and of influencing others' views of the realities of work. Both processes go on together, and via the same means: Social networks are formed by the process of communications, and the constructing of social realities is also a matter of communications. Both are crucially determined by cultural resources. The outcomes of organizational politics are the shaping of incomes, jobs, and the structures of organizations themselves.

This is done in three ways. First, as we have seen, there is the control of gatekeeping—the entry requirements into an occupation. Second, there is the structure of the career channel within the organization—whether it is a dead end, promotes in a self-contained branch, allows for transfers and rotations, allows potential promotion to the top level of authority, and so on. Third and most generally, there is the shaping of the "position" itself—what kinds of work are grouped together or separated off as distinct duties of an individual worker, how many people are deemed necessary at such positions; what degrees of tenure and what method of pay is adopted (piece rate, hourly, monthly, commission, etc.).

In all of these, the political process may involve several groups within the organization. Most obviously, there is the interest of the managers themselves in formulating entry requirements, career sequences, and positions. They do this not only with an eye for costs and productive efficiency, but also for the utility of various arrangements in controlling their subordinates. Managers are concerned with shaping their own positions and careers as well. Since they are involved in a political process within the organization, managers must do this shaping in alliance with others, and often in opposition to rival individuals and groups. Hence much of position shaping may be complex and reactive, with results unlike what any particular party to the struggle intended.

This is all the more true when we consider that not only managers with line authority, but also other participants in organizations engage in shaping positions. Professional and technical specialists, even without explicit decision-making authority, have considerable influence by their ability to "expertly" define what technical problems exist or will be encountered, and hence what numbers of specialists with what qualifications are needed. Officially powerless manual workers demonstrate an even more potent weapon for position shaping. Their informal organization of the work group controls how hard they will work and hence their rate of output, thus indirectly determining how many workers of a given sort are "needed." Formally, unions and professional associations can demand certain entrance requirements and job descriptions, and sometimes even career channels; informally, workers can control selection by ostracizing or subverting members of particular groups, either influencing entry requirements or creating further subspecialties within the organization for undesirable workers. And all these processes interact, so that the shape of an organization and the distribution of income it generates is the result of a complex of struggles.

This process is hidden if we view organizations and occupations through the lenses of the ideological categories used in struggles within them. Organizations are commonly defined as places where work is done; their structure is regarded as a way of dividing the labor, and occupations are considered to be work roles. But the work that is done and the way it is divided up are not the neutral bases of positions and structures; rather they are to be appropriated or shunted off to others as power resources permit.

Consider the blue collar–white collar distinction. This actually means the distinction between wage and salary modes of payment (as technicians and even "professionals" on the "white-collar" side may do most of their work with their hands), which is to say, a difference in degrees of job tenure. Wage positions are explicitly more short-term, salary positions more long-term, and they thus differ in lesser or greater protection from the vicissitudes of the employment market. The distinction also reflects different career channels; usually each is a separate employment sector with entry jobs at the bottom and no provision for promotion from one sector to the other. Given the existence of this organizational divide, subsequent maneuverings for advantage tend to reinforce the structure, as when long-term blue-collar employees press for seniority rules governing promotion into protected jobs just below this line. The fact that certain organizations (such as U.S. police departments) promote from the bottom up shows that an alternative structure is possible and that the particular kinds of power arrangements produce the prevailing dichotomous pattern. Similarly, the separate hierarchies for clerical workers in most modern organizations are based on little more than sexual segregation, usually with a separate pay scale; under different power conditions these could be organized into quite a different set of career channels and work responsibilities. In fact, before the introduction of female secretaries in the late nineteenth century, secretarial positions were not differentiated from other administrative jobs and had the promotional possibilities of the aide-de-camp or the apprentice.

The distinction between *productive* and *political labor*, then, is crucial for understanding how organizations are shaped and, as a result, how people are stratified. The distinction separates the two major social classes: the working class engaged in productive labor, and the dominant class engaged in political labor. Both classes expend energy, but it is the subordinated class that produces the wealth, whereas the dominant class determines its distribution.

Yet the division between productive labor and political labor is an abstract one; in empirical reality, the same person may do both. Consider the range of modern occupations. Some are almost completely devoted to material work, producing food, housing, clothes, and other essentials. Others are devoted entirely to activities of domination, exercising or threatening the use of force (the military, the police). Some concentrate on acting to gain and defend political offices and sinecures (which may exist widely in nongovernment organizations as well as in government ones) and others on producing cultural resources (as in the educational and communications industries). Other occupations are in an intermediate zone, for material production involves not only the physical labor of production, but also the labor of transportation and distribution, and the lighter talking-and-paperwork labor of planning both production and distribution. The people who carry out these activities, though—the white-collar sector in organizations—are not engaged in these activities alone. We must not be misled by our everyday definitions of what a job is, for the sole legitimate definitions are in terms of productive labor. In fact, many white-collar activities involve the political labor of attempting to control others and defending one's own autonomy from their control. Probably the greater part of clerical activities are devoted to communications of this sort—conferences, paperwork, reports, records—that bear little relation to material production but are part of the incessant political maneuvering, under the guise of planning and distributing (but also often called "personnel administration"), to take the initiative in the realm of domination, or simply to fill time with the appearance of working.

Thus we have an analytical distinction between the two kinds of activities, productive and political. Any job may be apportioned between the two in varying degrees. The "working-class" aspect (productive labor) and the "dominant-class" aspect (political labor) may both appear in the same job. It is the relative mixture of class conditions within each individual's daily life that produces various forms of class cultures and attitudes toward authority; as the evidence indicates,[1] individuals vary across the range of attitudinal mixtures according to their particular cases. Hence the actual population does not necessarily fall into clear-cut class-wide allegiances but rather into much smaller local interest groups. It should be borne in mind that even positions toward the core of the materially productive sector have their political elements. Important sectors of blue-collar workers (especially the upper working class) have cultural and organizational resources that they use to influence their situations, both formally through unions and even more importantly, informally in the social relations of the work place. As a result, they can introduce some nonwork into their job time by collectively controlling the work pace; they can monopolize to some degree the easier or more remunerative jobs; or they can increase their security of tenure.

The overall structure of the modern occupational world may be conceived as a range of variations in the possession of "political" resources for controlling the conditions of work and appropriating the fruits of production; hence it can be seen as a range of mixtures of productive work with political work. At one end are relatively unprotected laborers, subject directly to the market for productive labor; at the other are pure political laborers engaged in the activities of the ideological, financial, and governmental superstructure. The upper ranges of the working class and the middle ranges of the administrative class contain mixed activities, the former using the resources of organizational politics to reduce the strains and reap the benefits of productive work, the latter building an elaborate screen of administrative politics around a productive core of planning and distributive activities.

[1]Randall Collins, *Conflict Sociology: Toward an Explanatory Science* (New York: Academic Press, 1975), pp. 61–87.

SINECURES AND POSITIONAL PROPERTY

Social classes may be distinguished by the amount of property they possess, but the most important form of such "property" is not limited to the traditional notion of material and financial possessions. Rather it is how "positions" are shaped that constitutes the most immediate form of property in the labor market, and it is by the shaping of such positions that income is distributed. The term *position* is only a metaphor (although it is widely accepted and taken for granted) for the seemingly object-like immutability of a collection of behavioral patterns that are reserved for particular individuals under particular conditions of tenure. Indeed, material and financial *property* is a similar metaphor, for the property relation is a behavioral one, a particular degree of tenure of action toward certain objects and persons, not a physical relationship of owner to thing. It is *property in positions* that is crucial in determining most of class organization and class struggle in everyday life. For material and financial property (if we except home ownership) is concentrated within a quite small group, but property in positions shapes class relations throughout the population and has a wide range of variations. The actual details of economic conflict are carried out on this level.

Technological change, within this context, has a peculiar result. It does not raise the skill requirements of most jobs very much; the great majority of all jobs can be learned through practice by almost any literate person. The number of esoteric specialties "requiring" unusually extensive training or skill is relatively small. The "system" does not "need" or "demand" a certain kind of performance; it "needs" what it gets, because "it" is nothing more than a slipshod way of talking about the way things happen to be at the time. How hard people work, and with what dexterity and cleverness, depends on how much other people can require them to do and on how much they can dominate other people. What the advance of technology *does* do, rather, is increase the total wealth produced and lead to intense struggles over the shaping of property in occupational positions, not because of the necessities of *production* but because of the struggles over the *distribution* of the increased wealth.

We live in an era in which our machinery and our organizational techniques are very powerful, capable of supporting everyone at a comfortable standard of living with relatively little physical effort. This prospect has been contemplated for quite some time, sometimes with hope, sometimes with anger against the forces impeding it, sometimes with fear of ensuing boredom and purposelessness. But in fact, the shift toward a predominantly leisure society does not seem to be happening, or at least it is happening so slowly that it seems like little has changed. Most people still work a fairly long work week; at the highest job levels, very long work weeks (over 55 hours in a substantial portion of this group); a large proportion of married women work; many people hold several jobs.[2]

Why? The paradox is resolved if we recall that the most prominent form of leisure in our society is the most undesirable: unemployment. People work because that is the main way that wealth is distributed. The welfare system for the support of nonworkers, despite the outcries of its opponents, redistributes very little.[3] The reason some people are wealthy is that they or their families have jobs that control the biggest organizations with the most money. Others have at least a middling foothold in the system of organizational property that supports us. People without jobs (or with a succession of marginal positions) are without power over the main property resources of our society (and usually without political influence as well), and that is the reason they are poor.

In relation to our hypothetical high-leisure technocracy, then, the crucial question becomes: *Who would control it?* The answer is clear: Those few who did work in a mass-leisure society would get most of the wealth. Michels' discovery that the persons who control the administrative machinery of a political party get most of the benefits from it is paralleled here on a larger scale. It is for this reason that we have not moved toward a high-leisure society, despite our technological capacity for doing so. We have elaborated a largely superfluous structure of more or less easy jobs, full of administrative make-work and featherbedding because modern technology allows it and because of political pressures from the populace wanting work. Thus we have the enormous structure of government employment (including education), the union sector protected by elaborate work regulations, and the huge work forces of our corporate oligopolies keeping themselves busy seeking new products to justify their jobs. In effect, leisure has been incorporated into the job itself. Advanced technology, far from demanding hard work and long training from everyone, has made occupational demands more and more superficial and arbitrary.

Bensman and Vidich[4] have given one set of reasons why it has been possible to move toward this "sinecure society": the very productivity of our technology has created the now widely recognized "Keynesian" problem of keeping up consumer demand and thus fending off economic depression. The massive

---

[2]Harold L. Wilensky, "The Uneven Distribution of Leisure," *Social Problems* 9 (1961): 32–56.
[3]Donald M. Pilcher, *The Sociology of Income Distribution*. Unpublished dissertation, Univ. of California, San Diego, 1976.
[4]Joseph Bensman and Arthur J. Vidich, *The New American Society* (New York: Quadrayle Books, 1971).

expansion of government employment is one way in which this has come about. The support given by government to the tertiary sector by dispensing an increasing number of licenses for franchises and professional monopolies is another. Private sinecures also exist within the biggest manufacturing corporations, with their extensive educational requirements and staff divisions, their leisure perquisites in the forms of sales conventions and motivational and retraining programs. Much of the control apparatus of big organizations, even if it is established in the name of productive efficiency, increases the nonproductive sinecure component. Elaborate planning and cost-accounting divisions add their own expense to the organization and transfer wealth to their own members; so do agencies for compliance with insurance regulations and law enforcement. In all these areas, the struggle for control, both from above and from below, elaborates the political sector of organizations at every step. The more claims made upon insurance companies, the more union grievances or minority discrimination complaints, the larger becomes the institutionalized sector of positions that deal with such matters, adding yet more members of the organization who struggle to enhance their own positional property. The sinecure sector feeds upon struggles over control of itself.

One might ask why the rationality of the economic market does not drive out such wastefulness, forcing the organizations that engage in it out of business. In major sectors of the economy, this process does not hold. Government organizations are not subject to competition and are seldom subject to effective political pressures for economizing. And the large corporations are the very organizations that can best afford such internal redistribution, for they hold oligopolistic controls over their markets, often supported by favorable governmental policies; external competition does nothing to make them reduce their internal costs, while the scope of bureaucratic complexity and the separation of stock ownership from direct control make them accountable to no one but themselves. Ironically, it is these highly protected organizations that technocratic apologists like Galbraith[5] think are prosperous because of their technological advance, whereas the smaller organizations that are not protected from the market are consigned to insecurity and relative poverty because of their technological backwardness. This is only repeating the gloating of the sinecure sector in the terms of its own ideology.

To speak of the prevalence of sinecures and of essentially "luxury" or "waste" production in a time of economic downturn may seem incongruous, but only from the point of view of a technocratic ideology. Economic crises due to inflation and deficiencies in aggregate demand may, in fact, be the very

[5]John Kenneth Galbraith, *The New Industrial State* (Boston: Houghton Mifflin, 1967).

results of the inequality of a sinecure system. The coexistence of material wealth and leisure for some, with economic hardships for others, and perhaps anxiety for all, is hardly unprecedented in economic history. The high productivity of the technology does not disappear in an economic crisis, for crises are ultimately in the sphere of distribution, not of production.

The "political" realm, then, is found within all organizations and occupational networks, not merely in the formal government structure, and the major part of the redistribution of wealth, under the pressure of intermittent overproduction crises, has taken the form of reshaping property in occupational positions. This has come about both by expanding the numbers of people allowed into the political superstructure, especially the governmental and culture-producing sides of it, and by increasing the amount of nonwork within the occupational structure generally.

Weber would no doubt agree with this line of analysis. Although he had no opportunity to observe the power relations of advanced industrial society, his historical work makes abundant use of the concept of *prebends*—positions distinguished for the purpose of monopolizing their incomes. With the greater honesty of societies lacking an industrial-style technocratic ideology, these were simply referred to as "livings," and often were openly bought and sold, combined or subdivided, purely for fiscal considerations and under the shifting conditions of power. In the twentieth century, the market for such positions had disguised its nature, without undergoing a fundamental change; instead of direct purchase of office, one invests in educational credentials, which in turn (subject to the "monetary" vicissitudes of this cultural currency system) are used to purchase a job protected from various aspects of labor market competition.

The term *sinecure* itself had a respectable tone in medieval society, for it indicated the ideal "living" one could purchase from pope or king.[6] Today the term becomes disreputable, for it offends the notions of meritocracy by which the modern system of monopolization is legitimated. But the importance of this structural arrangement is, if anything, even more important in a wealthy industrial society where leisure has migrated into the interior of virtually all jobs to a greater or lesser degree. It is most obvious in the slow pace of government bureaucracies, less so in the competitive grind of some schools and in the political infighting over monopolistic privileges themselves. But this kind of effort—the work put into creating or defending conditions to avoid work—is analytically distinct from the work that leads to material results. The distinction of preindustrial societies is still in evidence, between the aristocracy, fighting or politicking to maintain or enhance their position, and the

---

[6]To be "*sine curia*" was to hold the income of a parish without responsibility for the "cure of souls."

commoners, whose materially productive work the aristocrats are struggling to dominate. In industrial America, aristocrats and commoners still exist, sometimes within the compass of a single job.[7]

The principal questions for us then, are: What determines how people in organizations can shape positional property? What are the resources of organizational politics, and above all, on what basis can we predict how such resources will be distributed both in space and in time? The major weapon of any form of politics is the capacity to form alliances and to impress others with a given definition of reality. These are the effects of culture, and these effects form their clearest pattern when culture is distributed by its own structure of exchange. We have, then, two important market realms instead of one: the market for economic goods and services, and the market for culture. Economic and cultural markets are not separated as base and superstructure; they are distinguished only as ends and means, and it is the means—the resources of group organization and struggle—that create the lineups in struggles for advancement. Cultural weapons penetrate the economic sphere at an intimate level, shaping the behavior patterns and barriers that constitute "positions." The appropriation of incomes is determined by where these barriers are formed. Stratification, on its most material level, is shaped by the cultural market, and it is to this that we now turn.

THE CULTURAL MARKET

Culture is both a good in itself and a social resource. In everyday life, it takes the form of the style of physical appearances and the expressions of thoughts and emotions through communications and especially in conversation. Culture thus serves to dramatize one's self-image, to set moods, to mentally re-create past realities and to create new ones. Whatever subject holds the floor in a conversation, however fleetingly, has a corresponding degree of shared mental reality. As such, it provides the temporarily dominant definition of the social situation and hence of operative social structure.

Conversation may be conceived as cultural exchange, the negotiation of partners to talk with and topics to be given sway. The empirical details of

[7]The prevailing informal tone of the two realms of productive and political labor is revealing. Among manual workers with any control over their own work pace, the standing jokes are usually an ironic "Hey, get to work!" or "Done any work today?" Among professionals and managers, on the other hand, the prevailing style is to appear extremely busy, loaded down with outstanding commitments. Those who are required to do genuine productive work are cynical and detached about the nature of organizational politics, while the organizational politicians must play it straight, claiming to exert endless efforts in their struggles for control, and of course disguising these efforts under the ideology of productivity.

social relationships of different sorts come down to the different sorts of conversation that people carry out with one another: purely external relationships
confined to minimal exchanges upon practical matters, or more significant ties
based upon talk containing larger proportions of discussion, ideological debate, entertainment, gossip, or personal topics. The consequences of everyday
cultural exchange, then, are the formation and reproduction of social groups
and formal organizations. In different terminology, cultural resources are the
basis of associational communities, which Weber called status groups. They
might also be called consciousness communities, since their distinguishing
feature is the expression of utterances in shared symbols with reality-defining
effects for the persons involved.

One advantage of calling them consciousness communities rather than
status groups is to remind us that such communities take a variety of forms.
They range in duration from brief, temporary relations to continually repeated
ones, and they range in intensity from weak to very strong interpersonal
commitments. The size of the community can vary from small local groups
up through larger communities in which most individuals have direct contacts
with only a relatively few others, but who have the bond of being potential
friends because of a common culture. The usual conception of a status group,
or more loosely, of a social class, actually fits this latter case: This is not to say
that everyone in the group knows everyone else, but their commonalities make
their association easy when they do encounter one another. Ethnic groups are
generally status groups of this kind. And finally, consciousness communities
may vary in degree of self-consciousness, from associations carried on without
explicit self-definition, through the self-consciousness that comes with the
giving of group names, to the highly formalized group identity when a group
institutionalizes itself with periodic meetings, regulations, and legal charters.

Cultural exchanges are the empirical means by which all organized forms
of stratification are enacted and by which the class struggle over work and
material goods is carried out. Culture produces both horizontal and vertical
relations. Persons with common cultural resources tend to form egalitarian ties
as friends or co-members of a group. Such groups, as we have seen, are major
actors within the struggles to control organizations, whether over work pace,
gatekeeping criteria, the definition of positional duties and perquisites, assessment of merit, or personal advancement. Such struggles need have little of a
clandestine or conspiratorial tone to them; informal groups are manifested
simply in casual conversation, usually without great self-consciousness or deliberation, but nevertheless can add up to very strong consensus about common courses of action. Formal and self-conscious versions of associational
communities are also important in maneuverings for material advantage, as in

the case of occupations that have organized themselves into professional or commercial associations or trade unions.

The ability of occupational categories to form consciousness communities of one degree or another is determined by how similar their cultural resources are, whereas the scope and power of the community thus formed depend in part upon the nature of their resources for defining reality, as well as upon the other resources that these mediate. Cultural resources enter into the process of stratification in another way as well. Hierarchical relations among nonequals are also immediately enacted in face-to-face conversational exchanges. Although background resources ultimately tend to determine domination and subordination in such encounters, they do so mainly by being brought to bear through the symbolic interchange of the moment. Cultural expressions are a way of defining reality and may define both a horizontal bond among equals and a vertical relation among unequals. Usually this is done by the dominant person controlling the conversational interaction, picking the topic and influencing what is said about it, affecting the underlying emotional tone, and thus controlling the cognitive and moral definitions of reality. Among the resources for doing this successfully are access to channels of information and other social networks and the vocabulary and rhetorical style to impress others with allegedly superior (and possibly esoteric) knowledge and power. Thus cultural resources not only form the groups that struggle over control of social organization, but also tend to determine the hierarchic relations among these groups.

Indigenous and Formal Production of Culture

Culture is produced in two different ways: in the experiences of everyday interaction themselves or by specialized culture-producing organizations. Indigenous cultural production goes on all the time in the worlds of work, home, and leisure alike. Every experience is potential conversational material, and every conversation generates further capacities to speak in certain styles and to peddle one's acquired information, entertainment value, and emotions in further exchanges. Much of these conversational resources, though, tend to be specific to particular individuals and situations. Information about one's own experiences or about the practical matters at hand, gossip about one's acquaintances, standing jokes and styles of joking—these are resources for local barter markets for culture. Such resources are not readily transferable to other situations; if cultural resources mediate group ties, indigenously produced resources produce local ties among limited numbers of specific individuals. If cultural resources construct shared social realities, the realities these create are inextensive and fragmentary.

Moreover, such resources may cumulate, but they tend to do so in a circular flow. Personal experiences and conversational contacts generate conversational resources, which can be used to keep up existing social relations and negotiate new ones of the same type. It is possible that individuals may move on the borderlines of their usual contacts and thus encounter new situations, thereby generating new conversational resources, which could be used to build different social ties. Such cultural and associational movement, though, is likely to be slow and sporadic when based only on purely indigenous cultural resources derived from the immediate situation. Thus indigenously produced culture tends conservatively to reproduce itself and a given pattern of social relations. Such cultures as a whole tend to change only when some exogenous processes, such as political or economic catastrophes, radically change the conditions of life. But even here, the circular flow of culture and group structure tends to stabilize any new developments. This kind of culture is not a force for change, or strictly speaking, an independent causal factor in its own right.

Culture may also be produced by specialized organizations. Churches and other religious associations were historically among the first such organizations in which full-time specialists devoted themselves to symbolic expressions. Professional entertainers constitute another type of specialized culture producer, as do, especially importantly for our purposes, schools. Such specialized agencies of cultural production have several effects. By comparison with indigenous cultural production, they can much more readily generate new forms of culture—partly because the internal exigencies and struggles over control within culture-producing organizations tend to shape their products in new directions, and partly because their members' full-time and self-conscious absorption with culture gives them much more refined skills. And cultural innovation, especially vis-à-vis any particular indigenous culture, is likely to be especially strong the more that specialized culture-producing organizations constitute a larger network or market among themselves. Such formal culture-producing agencies, then, become exogenous sources of change within the cultural sphere, and by extension, in the realm of group structures.

Thus developments of religious culture have been crucial in forming new political and economic organizations at various times in world history. In Weber's fully developed historical theory, the culture of the universalistic world religions transcended the family and tribal–ethnic base of organization, made possible the rise of the bureaucratic state, and eventually led to the "rationalized" capitalist economy. Similarly, it can be argued that the mass news media of the industrial era generated a new form of politics based on the ideologically oriented group and that the popular music media were a crucial organizational basis for the youth revolt of the 1960s and 1970s. Schools have been especially important for forming new group structures, ranging from the creation of the gentry class of traditional China to the formation of specialized occupational enclaves in contemporary America.

Formally produced culture is not only more innovative than indigenous culture, but it also allows the creation of much larger and more self-conscious communities. This type of culture is propagated more widely across different local situations, tends to be made up of more abstract concepts and symbols, and it creates more generalized references. Formally produced culture deals less with specific individuals and situations and more with the commonalities across many situations. Its images, even if concrete, tend to symbolize every individual or to symbolize the aggregate of individuals as an organized unit. Formal culture is more widely useful than indigenous culture; it can relatively quickly negotiate ties among individuals who otherwise have little in common to exchange. Thus formal culture has been the basis for impersonal bureaucratic organizations, for generating political loyalties to an overarching state, for mobilizing mass occupational groups and large-scale social movements.

If indigenously produced culture supports local barter markets, formally produced culture operates more nearly as a monetary currency. It is more widely negotiable (that is, it is a medium of exchange) and can be used on a much wider basis for assessing reputations (that is, it acts as a store of value). A true currency-like system of cultural "money" only comes into existence with a further transformation, however: when formal culture-producing organizations not only broadcast their cultural products, but also give formal summary announcements of the quantity of cultural goods an individual has acquired from them (that is, to develop the monetary analogy further, they act as measurable units of account). Thus religious attainments have sometimes been summarized by titles of sainthood and other distinctions, and the culture acquired in schools has been summarized by grades and certificates. Once these formal summaries are available, they may be substituted for the full display of the culture itself. In a further transformation, they may become subject to their own high-level economy, just as the value of organizational incomes can be transformed into stocks, which themselves are bought and sold on a specialized stock market subject to its own market forces. Once this occurs, the purely quantitative relations among these second- or third-order currencies become major determinants of their value and can affect their use in more primitive markets irrespective of their actual underlying content.

In other words, the more formalized the culture-producing organization, the more its culture tends to resemble a currency, and the more the cultural economy becomes subject to specifically monetary effects. The "price" of the social memberships that culture can "buy" may undergo inflation, due to an exogenous increase in monetary "supply"; conversely, price deflation is also conceivable. The conditions and effects of these, and their interdynamics with the material economy, will be considered next.

Determinants of Cultural Currency Production

How much cultural currency is produced is determined by several causes. First, it depends on how much material wealth is siphoned into specialized culture-producing organizations: that is, how much of the material economy is invested in the cultural economy. Thus richer societies in world history have generally been able to afford more churches and monasteries, more professional entertainment, and more schooling. Rich societies have not *necessarily* done this; the mobilizing and innovating effects of cultural organizations have sometimes been resisted by traditional rulers (as in various periods in the history of China and Russia, for example), and in some situations the populace has preferred to spend its wealth more heavily on direct material consumption. Wealth is a facilitating factor, not a determinative one.

Second, culture-producing organizations have been affected by inventions of special technologies for cultural production and transmission. The invention of writing itself, improved implements and paper, book printing, and the modern media of electronic communications and information storage have all affected the specialized production of culture. These effects, though, have not all been uniformly in the direction of increasing the amount of formal cultural production. Some of them (such as modern television broadcasting), because of their concentrated pattern of ownership, may have tended to keep cultural production within quite narrow limits and even to reduce the overall variety and amount of culture in society as a whole. Such technological changes have been relatively infrequent in world history and hence have operated primarily as background for more dynamic factors within any given historical time.

The major determinant of the amount of formal cultural production, and especially the determinant of relatively short-run variations in it, has been the degree of competition among cultural producers and also among cultural consumers. Both the history of religions and the history of education show the pattern: Religious movements and schools have proliferated where governments were relatively weak and decentralized; they have been kept under stricter limitations where centralized governments were strong. This is so even though centralized governments have often adopted a state religion, or, in modern times, a compulsory public school system, as a basis for bureaucratic administration and control of the population. But such governments have usually favored a single religion and repressed its rivals; their educational policies as well have tended to keep the educational system small. In contrast, it has been weak governments, unable to intervene to control the cultural market, that have allowed competitive cultural production to expand on its own.

Effects of Cultural Currency Production

A large-scale production of formal culture transforms the whole society. In effect, the populace invests large quantities of the goods derived from the material economy into the cultural economy with the hope of bettering their social position in all spheres. The struggle to control the occupational realm, whether by the direct shaping of positions, as in the modern world, or by building control over the economy through the development of a strong state (as is generally the case in the preindustrial world), can be carried on most effectively by groups that control superior organizational resources. A large and widely dispersed supply of cultural currency makes resources available to many groups in the population for organizing themselves in this struggle, which may then result in the proliferation of monopolized occupational enclaves. We see this tendency especially in late medieval Europe, as the expansion of formal religious currencies was followed by considerable organization building, both by local princes and by monopolizing guilds within an ever-increasing number of occupational specialties. Similarly, the continued expansion of religious sects in India fostered a long-term tendency for castes to split into subcastes, as larger occupational groups split into religiously sanctioned subgroups. The increasing access to formal educational credentials has shaped numerous occupational enclaves in the modern American economy.

But the outcome of such a process of widening educational opportunities may bring little or no change in the order of stratification among groups. If previously dominant groups maintain a head start in the race for cultural resources, they may well end up with just as commanding a position in a culture-based stratification system as in a more primitive economically or politically based one. Moreover, the expansion of the entire system of cultural production, without a commensurate expansion in the number of desirable occupational positions, brings about an inflation in the cultural price of the older positions. For example, expanded numbers of students presented themselves for the civil service examinations in China from the sixteenth through the nineteenth centuries, but the number of government positions was kept virtually constant. Hence the cultural price rose—an examination system was elaborated, eventually becoming a series of examinations that might take a scholar 30 years to pass. Another period of credential inflation occurred around 1800 in Germany when a mass of applicants for government positions crowded the universities; the pressure resulted in a reform that extended educational requirements to more positions. And Weber noted the inflationary tendency in bureaucratic employment requirements in Europe in his day. In other words, the fact that cultural goods are resources for struggle over positions in the material realm means that there may be limits upon what various groups can buy, and hence overproduction crises are possible within purely cultural markets as well.

To study these sorts of possibilities, we must turn to the interaction between cultural markets and the economy of material production.

1. Increasing investment in cultural goods can bring about an expansion in material production. This can happen where cultural goods are used to build larger social networks of coordination and domination in such a way as to make possible greater economic exchange; thus the investment of cultural goods in building the superstructures of horticultural, agrarian, and the beginnings of industrial societies often tended to help expand the material economy and increase its productiveness. Or, within a modern industrial economy (and within agrarian economies too), a period of expansion of cultural markets may stimulate material production by creating an atmosphere of confidence and growth; it might especially help to overcome a chronic crisis of material overproduction/underconsumption by opening up a new area of material investment (in the material basis of culture production) and by generally loosening stagnant organizational arrangements. This can happen even if the interaction between cultural supply and demand is the "inflationary" equilibrium noted above, in which the payoffs in domination that cultural investors seek do not come about because the relative standing of the investors does not change.

Such stimulating effects on the material economy depend upon there being unused material capacity for expansion. The potential resources and markets must be there; the situation should lack only the organizational interconnections or the wave of psychological confidence necessary to bring them together. Lacking this, an expansion of the cultural economy will have entirely different effects.

2. Increasing investment in cultural goods may bring about an increase in the degree of domination in a society. In one sense, this tended to be true in the long run for all the shifts from hunting and gathering, to primitive horticultural, to advanced horticultural, to agrarian types of societies; all of these, although they probably experienced an initial growth in material production

through the organization of religious, or otherwise culturally cemented super-structures, ended up with a typical structure of material distribution that was markedly more unequal than the previous type. Probably each went through an initial period of expanding overall production; then the investment of portions of this in a cultural and military superstructure resulted in greater inequality than before, and eventually the society settled into a pattern of economic stagnation. This was certainly the difficulty experienced by most agrarian societies in breaking through into industrialization; the structure of domination was such that markets were generally limited to luxury goods for the elite, and the mass consumer markets required to make mass production worthwhile had little chance of being established.

The shift to industrial society required that some pressures for redistribution take place in a prior agrarian society, and it is possible that cultural markets had a place in this. (Weber's thesis about Christianity might be interpreted in this sense.) In the long run, though, it is likely that industrial societies also undergo at least the structural possibility of repeating the earlier patterns: Cultural resources can become structured in such a way that they enforce economic domination and inequality rather than economic expansion, and hence they can contribute to economic stagnation. Industrial societies have not really existed long enough for us to have much evidence on these possibilities. One thing that seems clear is that the level of inequality enforced in industrial societies is lower than that in agrarian societies; but it is also clear that the new level does not recede constantly but reaches a plateau at which it remains fairly stable.[8] For the United States, that plateau was reached by the time of World War II; the massive expansion of the cultural market since then has had little effect on the overall pattern of inequality. (This also seems to be the case in the histories of other twentieth-century industrial societies.)

Within the context of the material economy of material production, the growth of a cultural economy that settles into a constant level of domination will tend to exacerbate the underlying problem of overproduction/underconsumption. (In an agrarian economy, the similar use of culture for domination will block the growth of any mass market and hence any shift to industrialism; there are important elements of this in the stagnant quasi-agrarian–quasi-industrial economies of Latin America and elsewhere in the Third World today.) Thus we find that expanded cultural economies can result in economic growth or economic stagnation or even crisis. If the cause of the first alternative is the existence of unused material capacities and readily accessible markets, the cause of the second alternative may be the nonexistence of such

[8]Pilcher, *op. cit.*

conditions; or it may be a particular way in which the cultural economy is structured. About this second possibility, we know little as yet.

3. The cultural market might result in some redistribution of material goods. This seems to have been true in the early phase of industrialization and perhaps in some periods in earlier societies as well. This comes about first by the redistribution of goods to the segment of the middle class that is involved in cultural production; a growth in the number of teachers (or priests, monks, etc.) is itself a widening of the number of people employed in the superstructure. The general expansion of the culture-producing industries throughout most of the twentieth century in the United States is thus· one element in redistribution of material resources that otherwise would have gone to the previously smaller group of dominants in the political sector. Furthermore, educational credentials have been invested in expanding autonomous professional enclaves, as well as the productively superfluous component of the administrative sector, and have helped shape occupations in such a way as to help leisure migrate into the interior of jobs. The growth of the nonproductive, white-collar sector has been achieved above all through the mechanism of investing cultural resources (educational credentials) in occupational property. Thus an expansion of the cultural market, even though it has not changed the overall proportions of the distribution of wealth, has led to an expansion in the number of people who are dependent upon the "political" sector (the "sinecure sector"), who receive their material goods by way of the structure of domination rather than the structure of production.

Once that revolution was carried out, it has seemingly had no further effects. Yet the number of people employed in the sinecure sector has constantly risen, even during the period when the degree of inequality in distribution has changed little. There are probably two offsetting processes going on simultaneously here: (a) the shift into the sinecure sector has brought about a continuous redistribution; and (b) at the same time, the tendency of the sector of domination as a whole versus the sector of production has been to create greater inequality. The continuous process of technological overproduction and financial centralization has kept the economy in a chronic state of operation below capacity, since it has kept down overall consumer demand. The growth of the sinecure sector has been just enough to offset this, to maintain a rough equilibrium around a constant degree of inequality. Short-run shifts in employment in either sector, wars, and other such phenomena have moved the economy briefly and marginally on either side of this equilibrium, but the long-range pattern is remarkably constant.

4. Finally, we may imagine the possibility of an extreme redistribution of material goods brought about by an expansion of cultural markets. This might happen, for example, if cultural movements became so widespread that they mobilized virtually the entire active population. The organizations that would be built upon these cultural resources could no longer be so hierarchic; cultural resources would be so common that no one would be unduly impressed by those held by others. This tendency might be considered to be a revolutionary one. But any revolution that maintained a centralized organization would itself be antithetical to the centripetal tendencies of universal cultural equality and would either act to set up a new cultural elite (for example, by establishing new standards of culture, such as revolutionary party membership, whose eliteness is upheld by the resources of domination) or would fail to maintain its own centralization. For the interests of individual investors in cultural resources are always in the direction of inflating their own subjective prestige; this is done, if possible, by trying to dominate others in the objective world, but lacking that, it is done by creating one's own autonomous enclave in which one's personal cultural standards alone have to be noticed. In a situation of mass mobilization (one that is more than an ephemeral episode), individuals might come to see that their increase in relative status vis-à-vis the previous dominants is no longer of any value except to make the former elites equal to the majority; the tendency would then be to withdraw into private spheres in which their own personal idiosyncracies make the best subjective impression. Under these conditions, we may expect that the social organization would tend to fragment. There would no longer be any dominant cultural currency; ethnically or religiously heterogeneous empires would fall apart into monoethnic states;[9] modern status groups would go their private ways and

---

[9] For example, the unity of multiethnic medieval Europe under the papacy disintegrated into national states. The devaluation of the spiritual credit of the centralized church played a central part in this disintegration—a disintegration that we have come to take for granted so much that we forget that Europe in the thirteenth century could very well have laid the basis for modernization as a single unified state. But the universities, the key to the emerging papal bureaucracy, underwent enormous inflation in the price of their credentials, as the number of years to achieve the higher degrees giving employment in the higher ranks of the church increased from 6 to 16 years. From the fourteenth century onward (and lasting until the nineteenth century in many places), student enrollments dropped sharply, a number of the higher faculties disappeared in many places, and intellectual and cultural life migrated to other institutions. With the destruction of its former monopoly over culture production, the centralizing papacy was severely weakened and eventually lost its monopoly even over religion to a series of schisms in the fourteenth and fifteenth centuries and to the Protestant churches of the sixteenth century. The final split, interestingly enough, was set off by a reaction to the devaluation of an even more explicit form of spiritual currency, the sale of indulgences—certificates of spiritual pardon for sins, redeemable in purgatory. These were sold in larger and larger quantities as time went on in order to meet deficits in the papal budget. Martin Luther led the attack on one particularly blatant selling campaign in Germany as their monetary prices and moral acceptability declined with increasing volume; the result was the end of the unified cultural currency entirely and the end of the papal efforts at a pan-European state.

ignore the prestige claims of others. A true cultural revolution is inherently anarchistic; the attainment of any very high degree of equality of cultural resources tends to result in social decentralization.

The various material results of cultural markets, then, are often likely to be disappointing for the investors. Sometimes, if excess material productive capacity is there to be brought into action, an expanding cultural market will help the overall productiveness of the economy. But cultural goods are above all resources of domination; especially in an inflationary cycle of relative status competition, the result is likely to be the crystallization of a pattern of domination at a level of relative material inequality that cannot be broken. It is possible that at some periods the cultural market does bring redistribution, at least for those who can use it to enter fully into the "political" sinecure sector, but this redistribution is likely to be episodic, limited to shifts in goods from the higher to the middle sectors of the elite, and offset in modern economies by a countervailing tendency for economic processes to increase inequality. Finally, in the areas and cases where a truly equal distribution of cultural goods is approached, the result is likely to be the destruction of the standardized currency and a dissolution of the system into many smaller parts.

Sensing these various outcomes, various groups may attack, withdraw from, or try to limit or destroy the cultural market. Dominant elites, fearing redistributive consequences, may attempt to hold down cultural production; ironically, however, it is often their own policies of external military expansion that force them to rely on cultural mobilization of their own population as a motivational and economic fund-raising device (as in nineteenth-century Russia), and thus bring about their own downfall. It sometimes happens that a new internal middle class, heavily investing in the means of cultural mobilization, has displaced an older upper class by instituting a regime of their own domination. Sometimes there has been a popular revulsion against an inflationary credential market, leading to a refusal to buy any more cultural goods and even leading to a violent destruction of the culture-producing agency. In its most extreme form, this is exemplified by the Protestant reformation; in milder forms, it is exemplified by a somewhat earlier reaction in medieval Europe against the selling of credentials by the universities, and a similar development in America in the early 1970s.

The underlying cause for this revulsion against an inflationary credential market is probably to be found in the interaction between the cultural market and the material market. Perhaps the short-term cycles in the material economy and the more long-term cycles of the cultural economy coincide at particular points that makes it no longer materially promising, or even bearable, for people to invest very heavily in cultural goods. A downturn in the material economy coinciding with a point of particularly obvious overinflation of the costs of cultural prestige may be the formula for an anticultural revolution. And since cultural resources are the crucial building blocks of what is distinctive about societies, these crises may be very important indeed. Given a reaction of sufficient proportions, these may turn out to be the major turning points in history.

CONCLUSION

The cultural market, then, is a key to the class struggles over control of material production. To the extent that competitive cultural and economic markets exist at all, the success of any particular contenders in these struggles is determined not so much by their own resources as by the relationships between production and consumption of all groups in both the cultural and economic spheres. The differences between an expanding cultural market that leads to material expansion and one that leads to crisis or fragmentation are largely quantitative variations depending on the interplay among a number of conditions. In general, one might suppose that simultaneous crises of cultural and economic markets would be the equivalent of the epoch-making revolutionary crisis in Marxian theory. This may be true, although a theory of revolutions of this scope has hardly begun to be worked out.

But in more limited ways, the expansion of the cultural economy seems to move counter to the Marxian model of increasing class mobilization. The Marxian model proposes the development of a homogeneous culture among workers, brought to self-consciousness of a common interest through participation in a common economic struggle against a single enemy. The culture that is thus elevated into a general proletarian consciousness is not an abstract and externally imposed one, but is based upon the commonalities of the everyday experience of the worker. In this sense, as Lukacs stated, the proletarian class consciousness is the destruction of abstract and reified consciousness. But the expansion of formal cultural currency has precisely the opposite effects. A formal currency is doubly abstract—both as a specialized set of symbols transcending ordinary local experience and in the cryptic marks of cultural attainment summarized in educational degrees. Consciousness in a cultural currency system of this degree of formalization is directed away from the material realities of work experience and into the purely relative values of the cultural currency at that point in its market's history.

The effects of widespread cultural currency upon the occupational realm are not to unify it, but to divide it. Specialized occupational groups come increasingly into possession of resources for monopolizing positions for their own local advantage. At most, cultural currency leads to the development of self-conscious and organized groups of workers within particular specialties. This, too, is a form of class conflict, for the workers can be seen as struggling in the throes of a capitalist economy for economic survival, as well as for economic advantage. The difference is that a cultural currency makes the conflict irreparably multisided, each occupational group against the other, and tends toward increasing fragmentation rather than toward consolidation into two opposing blocs. A common cultural currency, while it may reduce ethnic differences, thus reproduces the equivalent of an ethnically segregated division of labor. Education, as I have argued elsewhere, might very well be called pseudoethnicity.

A theory of cultural markets, then, may prove relevant to salvaging Marx's insights on class conflict and revolution, although in a far more cynical form. Class conflict may be even more pervasive, and less historically revolutionary, than had been supposed.

Class and Status Group in a World System Perspective
[1983]

GIOVANNI ARRIGHI, TERENCE HOPKINS,
AND IMMANUEL WALLERSTEIN

• *One of the most important intellectual changes of the last 15
years has been a shift toward a world-system perspective. Previously, conservative and middle-of-the-road sociologists saw each
society going through its own stages of "development" or "modernization" whereas Marxists concentrated on economic contradictions and class conflicts within separate states. The world-system
perspective has totally changed these conceptions. A society's
"development" or lack of "development," in this view, does not
depend on what stage it has reached, but on the dominant or
subordinant "core" and "semiperipheral" or "peripheral" position
it occupies in the world network of economics and power. Similarly, revolutions are not so much produced from within as they
are results of structural pressures from outside. Immanuel Wallerstein is one of the architects of world-system theory; in this
selection, he and his collaborators, Giovanni Arrighi and
Terence Hopkins, argue that the central sociological concepts of
the conflict tradition, Marx and Engels' classes and Max
Weber's status groups, must themselves be seen as products of
structural positions in the world system.*

In his well-known but often neglected conclusion to Book I of *The Wealth of
Nations*, Adam Smith defined the interests of "the three great, original and
constituent orders of every civilized society," that is, those who live by rent,
those who live by wages, and those who live by profit (1961: I, 276). His
argument was that the interests of the first two orders coincide with the general
interest of society because, according to his analysis, the real value of both
rents and wages rises with the prosperity and falls with the economic decline of
society. The interests of profit earners, on the other hand, are different from,

From Giovanni Arrighi, Terence K. Hopkins, and Immanuel Wallerstein, "Rethinking the Concepts of Class and Status-Group in a World-System Perspective," *Review* VI, 3, Winter 1983, 283–
304. Copyright 1983 Research Foundation of SUNY. Reprinted by permission of Sage Publications,
Inc.

and even opposite to, such general social interest because to widen the market and to narrow the competition are always in the interest of merchants and manufacturers. And, while to "widen the market may frequently be agreeable enough to the interest of the public; . . . to narrow the competition must always be against it, and can serve only the dealers, by raising their profits above what they naturally would be, to levy, for their own benefit, an absurd tax upon the rest of their fellow-citizens" (1961: I, 278).

Profit-earners not only have an interest contrary to the general one. They also have a better knowledge of their interest and a greater power and determination in pursuing it than those who live by either rent or wages. The indolence of landowners, "which is the natural effect of the ease and security of their situation, renders them too often, not only ignorant, but incapable of that application of mind which is necessary in order to foresee and understand the consequences of any public regulation" (1961: I, 276–77). As for the wage-earner, "he is incapable either of comprehending the general social interest, or of understanding its connection with his own" (1961: I, 277). Moreover, in the public deliberations, "his voice is little heard and less regarded, except upon some particular occasions, when his clamour is animated, set on, and supported by his employers, not for his, but their own particular purposes" (1961: I, 277). Profit-earners, on the other hand, particularly those who employ the largest amount of capital, draw to themselves by their wealth the greatest share of the public consideration. Moreover, since during their whole lives they are engaged in plans and projects, they have a more acute understanding of their particular interest than the other orders of society.

The Wealth of Nations being a work of legislation, the purpose of this "class analysis" was to warn the Sovereign against the dangers involved in following the advice and yielding to the pressures of merchants and master manufacturers. As the head of the national household, he should instead strengthen the rule of the market over civil society, thereby achieving the double objective of a more efficient public administration and a greater well-being of the nation.

It is not our purpose here to assess the soundness of the advice given by Smith to the national householder or of the substantive analysis on which it was based. Rather, we want to point out those aspects of his analysis that can be considered as paradigmatic of political economy and that we can find duplicated in contemporary class analyses.

First, the tripartite social order of which he spoke was a predicate of a particular kind of society, that defined by the territorial reach of a definite Sovereign or State. These were the states of Europe as they had been and were being formed within mutually exclusive domains operating within an interstate system.

Secondly, his social orders (or classes) were defined on the basis of property relations. The ownership of land, of capital, and of labor-power define his three great orders of society. Among the proprietors of capital, what some today would call a "fraction" of capital (merchants and master manufacturers) is singled out for special treatment in view of its political-economic power, of its greater self-awareness of its own interests, and of the opposition of its interests to the general social well-being.

Thirdly, the interests of each of the social orders classes were identified with its market situation; that is, both their competitive opportunities in relation to each other as classes (and of individuals within each class to each other), and the costs and benefits to each of them of monopoly power within markets, understood as restriction to entry. In *Wealth of Nations*, Smith limited the subjective ground of collective action by a class to these market interests. Monopoly power in the product as well as in factor markets was traced back to the creation or tolerance of restrictions to entry on the part of the Sovereign/ State.

Fourthly, market relations were defined within or between national economic spaces. Class conflicts and alignments were thus limited to struggles within each state for influence/control over its policies. The unit of analysis, in other words, was the nation-state, which determined both the context and the object of class contradictions.

Fifthly, a "relative autonomy" of state actions in relation to class interests and powers was presupposed. The enactment of laws and regulations by the state was continuously traced to the powers and influence of particular classes or "fractions" thereof. But the Sovereign was assumed to be in a position to distance himself from any particular interest to promote some form of general interest, reflecting and/or generating a consensus for this general interest.

If we contrast this analytical framework with that associated with Karl Marx's *critique* of political economy (that is, of Smith and other classical economists), we notice two consequential shifts of focus: a shift away from state-defined economic spaces to world economic space on the one hand, and a shift away from the marketplace to the workplace on the other.

The first shift implied that the market was no longer seen as enclosed within (or "embedded" in) each nation-state as an independent economic space, and that the world-economy was no longer conceived of as an interstate economy linking discrete national economic spaces. Rather, nation-states were seen as jurisdictional claims in a unitary world market. By effecting the socialization of labor on a world scale, the world market determined the most general context of the class contradictions and therefore of the class struggles of capitalist society, which Marx defined by its constitutive orders, the bourgeoisie and the proletariat. "The modern history of capital dates from the creation in the sixteenth century of a world-embracing commerce and world-embracing market" (1959: 146). "This market has given an immense development to commerce, to navigation, to communication by land. This development has, in its turn, reacted on the extension of industry; and in proportion as industry, commerce, navigation, railways extended, in the same proportion the bourgeoisie developed, increased its capital, and pushed into the background every class handed down from the Middle Ages" (1967: 81).

This was not a mere matter of trade relations between Sovereign states. Rather the developing bourgeoisie "compels all nations, on pain of extinction, to adopt the bourgeois modes of production; it compels them to introduce what it calls civilization into their midst, that is, to become bourgeoisie themselves. In one word, it creates a world after its own image" (1967: 84). The world so created was characterized by a highly stratified structure of domination and had more than market interests as subjective grounds for collective action. "Just as it has made the country dependent on the towns, so it has made barbarian and semi-barbarian countries dependent on the civilized ones, nations of peasants on nations of bourgeois, the East on the West" (1967: 84).

The second shift implied that the antagonism between the two great classes into which, according to Marx, bourgeois society as a whole tends to split, the bourgeoisie and the proletariat, was no longer traced to relations in the product or factor markets but to relations in production. In order to define the interests of the nation and of its component classes, Smith took leave of the pin factory whose scenario opens *The Wealth of Nations* to follow the interplay of supply and demand in the marketplace and of class interests in the national political arena. Marx in his critique of political economy took us in the opposite direction. We take leave not of the shop floor but of the noisy sphere of the marketplace (and, we may add, of the political arena), "where everything takes place on the surface and in view of all men," and follow the owner of the means of production and the possessor of labor power "into the hidden abode of production, on whose threshold there stares us in the face 'No admittance except on business'" (1959: 176). In this hidden abode of production, Marx discovered two quite contradictory tendencies that implied two quite different scenarios of class struggle and social transformation.

The first was the one generally emphasized in Marxist literature after Marx: even if we assume that in the marketplace the relationship between the owners of the means of production and the owners of labor-power appears as a relationship between equals, in the sense that the commodities they bring to the market tend to exchange at their full cost of production/reproduction (which, of course, is not always or even normally the case), the relationship would still be a fundamentally unequal one. This is so because of the longer-run effects of capitalist production on the relative value and the relative bargaining power of capital and labor. Capitalist production, that is, is seen as a process that tends to reduce the value of labor-power (its real costs of reproduction) and simultaneously to undermine the bargaining power of its possessors, so that the advantages of the reduction of labor's costs of reproduction tend to accrue entirely to capital.

This tendency obviously poses problems of realization of the growing mass of surplus labor that capital appropriates in production. These problems periodically manifest themselves in crises of overproduction that are overcome on the one hand "by enforced destruction of a mass of productive forces; on the other, by conquest of new markets, and by the more thorough exploitation of the old ones. That is to say, by paving the way for more destructive crises, and by diminishing the means whereby crises are prevented" (1967: 86).

It would seem from the above that the unequal relation between labor and capital, continuously reproduced and enhanced in the workplace, leads capital either to self-destruction in the marketplace or to a greater development of the world-economy, both extensively (incorporations) and intensively. Given a finite globe, the more thorough this development, the greater the self-destructiveness of capital.

In this scenario labor plays no role in precipitating capitalist crises except in a negative sense: it is its growing subordination in the workplace, and consequent weakening of bargaining power in the marketplace, that are ultimately responsible for the outbreak of the "epidemic of overproduction," as Marx called it. Labor, or its social personification, the proletariat, plays an active role only in transforming the self-destructiveness of capital into political revolution. The increasing precariousness of working and living conditions induces proletarians to form combinations against the bourgeoisie.

> Now and then the workers are victorious, but only for a time. The real fruit of their battles lies, not in the immediate result, but in the ever-expanding union of the workers. . . .
>
> This organization of the proletarians into a class, and consequently into a political party, is continuously being upset again by the competition between the workers themselves. But it ever rises up again, stronger, firmer, mightier. . . .
>
> Altogether collisions between the classes of the old society further, in many ways, the course of development of the proletariat. The bourgeoisie finds itself involved in a constant battle. At first with the aristocracy;

later on, with those portions of the bourgeoisie itself, whose interests have become antagonistic to the progress of industry; at all times, with the bourgeoisie of foreign countries. In all these battles it sees itself compelled to appeal to the proletariat, to ask for its help, and thus, to drag it into the political arena (1967: 90).

Alongside this scenario, however, as we indicated, Marx suggested another one, quite distinct in its unfolding. Both in the *Manifesto* and in *Capital* we are told that, along with the growing mass of misery, oppression, and degradation, the strength of the working class grows too, not so much as a result of political organization aimed at counteracting its structural weakness, but rather as a result of the very process of capitalist production.

> Along with the constantly diminishing number of the magnates of capital . . . grows the mass of misery, oppression, slavery, degradation, exploitation, but with this too grows the revolt of the working-class, a class always increasing in numbers, and disciplined, united, organized by the very mechanism of the process of capitalist production itself (1959: 763).

> The essential condition for the existence, and for the sway of the bourgeois class, is the formation and augmentation of capital; the condition for capital is wage labor. Wage labor rests exclusively on competition between the laborers. The advance of industry, whose involuntary promoter is the bourgeoisie, replaces the isolation of the laborers, due to competition, by their revolutionary combination, due to association. The development of Modern Industry, therefore, cuts from under its feet the very foundation on which the bourgeoisie produces and appropriates products (1967: 93–94).

Here, therefore, the strengthening of labor in the work place is the cause of the crisis of capital.

As we know, Marx never managed to reconcile these two contradictory tendencies that he discovered in the abode of production, let alone to work out fully and systematically all their implications for the analysis of class contradictions in capitalist society. Instead, Marx, in some of his historical writings, and many followers in their theoretical writings, gave up the critique of political economy and reverted to the Smithian paradigm of class analysis, reviving, rather than carrying out the critique of, political economy.

In the case of Marx, this retreat is most evident in his writings on the class struggle in France, in which class interests are defined in terms of a national political-economic space, and what goes on in the abode of production simply does not come into the picture at all. Obviously, Marx himself thought that the shift of focus he was advancing to analyze the overall, long-term tendencies of capitalist society had a limited relevance for the concrete analysis of a concrete instance of class struggle at a relatively low stage of development of such tendencies.

Moreover, even at the theoretical level, the shift of focus away from the noisy sphere of political economy did not imply any belittlement of the nation-state as the main locus of political power, that is, of the monopoly of the legitimate use of violence over a given territory. This power embodied in nation-states, whatever its origins, could obviously be used, and has indeed generally been used, simultaneously in two directions: as an aggressive/defensive instrument of intra-capitalist competition in the world-economy, and as an aggressive/defensive instrument of class struggle in national locales. True, the growing density and connectedness of world economic networks on the one hand, and the displacement of class contradictions from the marketplace to the workplace on the other, would ultimately make nation-states "obsolete" from both points of view. In outlining this tendency, however, Marx was only defining the situation that the capitalist world economy would asymptotically approach in the very long run. The farther the class struggle was from the projected asymptote, the more it would take on a political/national character. Even the proletariat, the class which in his view had neither country nor nationality, had first of all to wage a national struggle:

> Since the proletariat must first of all acquire political supremacy, must rise to be the leading class of the nation, must constitute itself *the* nation, it is, so far, itself national, though not in the bourgeois sense of the word (1967: 102).

Marx's empirical retreat into political economy did not, however, entail a corresponding retreat at the theoretical level. It simply implied a recognition of the distance separating the historical circumstances of nineteenth-century Europe from the asymptotic circumstances projected in the *Manifesto* and in *Capital*.

Far more than this was implicit in the retreat into/revival of political economy by Marxists after Marx, however. The most striking characteristic of the *theories* of finance and monopoly capital, of imperialism and of state capitalism, that begin to develop at the turn of the century and are later synthesized in canonical form by Lenin, is that they take us back to the noisy sphere of political economic relations. Their main concerns are the forms of capitalist competition, and the class contradictions identified are those defined in terms of market interests and state power. However much such formulations may or may not be justified in terms of the political strategies of the time, we are concerned here with their elevation by epigones into theoretical advances rather than pragmatic retreats from Marx's critique of Smithian political economy.

This theoretical retreat into political economy had some justification in the tendencies that came to characterize the capitalist world-economy around the turn of the century. The growing unity of the world market presupposed by Marx's paradigmatic shift began to be undermined by the re-emergence of state protectionist/mercantilist policies. These policies increasingly transferred world capitalist competition from the realm of relations among enterprises to the realm of relations among states. As a consequence, war and national/imperial autarky came to the fore and in pragmatic terms shaped the scenario of the world-economy. Connected with this tendency, the high concentration and centralization of capital characteristic of most of the new leading/core sectors of economic activity led to a resurgence of practices, often backed by state power, that restricted competition within the national/imperial segments into which the world-economy was splitting. States thus returned to the forefront of world-economic life, and monopoly in and through the Sovereign became once again the central issue around which conflicts and alignments among classes and fractions thereof revolved. This situation, that has broadly characterized the first half of the twentieth century, undoubtedly warranted a revival of political economy as the most relevant theoretical framework for the short/medium-term analysis of class contradictions and conflicts.

We should not be surprised, therefore, to find that the conception of class conflicts and alliances advanced by Lenin fits better theoretically into the Smithian than the Marxian paradigm: the monopoly power of a "fraction" of capital (finance capital and large scale industry, as opposed to Smith's merchants and master manufacturers employing large capitals) is singled out as the main determinant of waste and exploitation as well as of interimperialist rivalries and war (the enmity among nations, in Smithian parlance). It follows that all "popular classes," including the non-monopolistic fractions of capital, can be mobilized by the party of the proletariat (the "new prince," as Gramsci would have said) to wrest political power from the monopolistic fractions of capital—a prescription analoguous to Smith's suggestion that the enlightened Sovereign could count on the support of all other orders of society in pursuing the general interest against the particular interest of large merchants and manufacturers.

This, however, is not all that was involved in the theoretical retreat of
Marxists back into political economy. Monopoly capitalism and imperialism
were not treated for what they ultimately turned out to be—a cyclical resurgence of mercantilist policies, connected with the crisis of British world hegemony and with intensifying tendencies toward overproduction. If they had been
treated in this way, the retreat into political economy would have merely implied a recognition of the fact that the path leading the capitalist world-economy
to the ideal-typical asymptote envisaged in Marx's critique of political economy
was characterized by cycles and discontinuities that could increase, even for
relatively long periods, the distance separating historical circumstances from
such an asymptote. Instead, monopoly capitalism and imperialism were theor-
ized as the highest and final stage of the capitalist world-system, that is, as
themselves representing the asymptote. In this way, Marxism as canonized by
Lenin has come to be perversely identified as (and therefore with) political
economy.

Weber's writings on processes of group-formation in the modern world are
undoubtedly among the most extensive available. For present purposes we
limit our attention to his highly influential contrast of classes and status-groups
(Stände). The contrasted categories were at once an advance over the class
analysis projected by Marx and a retreat from it. They were an advance
because of the juxtaposition of status-group formation to class formation. They
were a retreat because of the restriction of the processes, and the resulting
elemental forms of social structure, to existent "political communities" (which
"under modern conditions . . . are 'states' ") (1968: 904). We require in our
work on modern social change the kind of juxtaposition Weber constructed.
But, in order to have it, we need to free it from the assumptions he made.
And, in order to do that, we need to examine those assumptions.

Modern sociology would have us believe that Weber wrote an essay on
class, status, and party. He did nothing of the sort. It would furthermore
have us believe that he juxtaposed class and status-group as two separate
dimensions of something called stratification in modern societies, both in
turn separate from the state (construed as the realm of "parties"), which he
also did not do. We first then must set to one side these imposed readings in
order to see what Weber did do and so allow ourselves to examine the
assumptions he did make.

This preliminary exercise can fortunately be quite brief. In the Roth-
Wittich edition of *Economy and Society* (Weber, 1968), Chapter IX in Part
Two is entitled "Political Communities." This chapter is provided with six
sections, each titled, the sixth of which is entitled, "The distribution of power
within the political community," and subtitled, "class, status, party." It is this

section of this chapter that appears in Hans Gerth and Wright Mills, *Essays from Max Weber* (1946) as itself a "chapter" (there, Chapter VII) with its subtitle, "class, status, party," as its full title. As someone once said, much may be lost in translation.[1]

For Weber in Chapter IX of *Economy and Society*, there were two and only two possible basic ways for the distribution of power in political communities (that is, in the modern world, states) to be structured: it can be either class-structured or status-group-structured. For "power" (undifferentiated here) to be class-structured, the factual distribution of goods and services within the political community or state in question must be market-organized. If so, or in so far as it is so, the distribution of life-chances among the members of the political community (and others in its territory) is determined by their relative position ("class situation") in the organizing complex of market relations, the basic categories of which are "property" and "lack of property". Alternatively for "power" to be status-group-structured the factual distribution of goods and services within the political community or state in question must be prestige-organized. If so, or in so far it is so, the distribution of life-chances among the members of the political community (and others) is determined by their membership ("status situation") in the organizing complex of honorifically ranked communal groups, the basic categories of which are "positively esteemed" and "negatively esteemed."

While depicted as if positively different, a class-structured distribution of power within a political community differs from a status-group-structured distribution only in one governing respect, namely, whether the distribution of goods and services is effected through market relations (= "class-structured") or instead through non-market relations (= "status-group-structured"), that is, residually.[2] The two stated elemental ways in which a given political community may be socially structured, then, were for Weber central categories to use in tracing historically the rise of the market, that is, the historical displacement by market relations of any and all other kinds of social relations through which the "factors" of production are recurrently brought together, the result-

---

[1]Weber scholars will know that most headings in the Roth-Wittich edition were provided not by Weber but by the editors of the writings combined to form *Economy and Society*. The key sentences from the section under discussion are for present purposes two:

> The structure of every legal order directly influences the distribution of power, economic or otherwise, within its respective [political] community (1968: 926).

> Now: "classes", "status groups", and "parties" are phenomena of the distribution of power within a [political] community (1968: 927).

[2]It is not until Polanyi (in *The Great Transformation* [1957] and subsequent writings) gave positive content to "non-market forms of integration" that this residual category began to receive systematic conceptual elaboration.

ing products are "circulated", the embodied surpluses are "realized" and appropriated, and the material means of subsistence are "distributed." To the extent that relations among status-groups organize and mediate these flows, the market (the complex of market relations) does not, and classes in his terms are unformed. To the extent that the market organizes the flows, status-group relations do not, and status-groups are unformed (or better, "eroded," since the historical transformation from feudalism to capitalism in Europe underpins the contrast).

Still, even given the one-dimensionality of the distinction, it retained in its elaboration a matter of central importance, that of an sich/für sich derived from Marx. Weber made use of it in a particular manner. Classes in relation to one another, in a given political community, are an sich by definition but not thereby für sich. Here he followed quite unambiguously the pre-Marx conventional political economy, seeing immediate class interests as given by market position and hence as theoretically indeterminate, so far as collective action is concerned, whether it be directly in relation to other classes or indirectly through their relation to the apparatus of the political community (state). Theoretically, something in addition to class interests must be introduced if one is to account for (continuous) collective class action and so therefore, too, for its absence. Status-groups in relation to one another, in contrast, are by definition groups, definitionally endowed with the capacity to act collectively in relation to one another and to act on their respective behalfs in relation to the state.

The definitional difference was not arbitrary for Weber. A political community entails by construction "value systems" (1968: 902), in accordance with which its constituent elements have more or less legitimacy, prestige, and so on, in comparison with one another, and with reference to which they have more or less pride, solidarity, or capacity to act collectively in relation with one another. A status-group structuring of the distribution of power, because the constituent groups are arrayed honorifically by rank, confers on each more or less prestige and pride, and through that the solidarity and capacity to act collectively in relation to one another. A class structuring of this distribution of power, in contrast, because of the market principle—which, in its operations for Weber, either eliminates all considerations of honor from its relations or is constrained in its working by them—provides its constituent classes with no necessary solidarity in their relation with one another and hence no necessary capacity for collective action in or on these relations. In short, and to go a bit beyond Weber in this summary, status-groups are constituents of and thereby carriers of a moral order, in Durkheim's sense. Classes are not; if they become so, it is in virtue of processes fundamental by, different from, and not entailed in, those that constitute them as classes in relation to one another.[3]

All of this is subject to the very strict proviso that we are examining the possible social structurings of the distribution of power *within* a constituted political community, a state under modern conditions. Weber himself, however, earlier opened up the possibility of freeing the contrasted categories of class and status-group from this highly constraining premise of their construction. In Section Three, headed "Power prestige and the 'Great Powers,' " he asserted that states in relation to one another "may pretend to a special 'prestige,' and their pretensions may influence" the conduct of their relations with one another. "Experience teaches," he continues,

> that claims to prestige have always played into the origins of wars. Their part is difficult to gauge: it cannot be determined in general, but it is very obvious. The realm of "honor," which is comparable to the "status order" *within* a social structure, pertains also to the *interrelations of political structures* (1968: 911; italics added).

But extending the scope of stratifying processes[4] so that their operation within the interstate system of the world-economy is "comparable" to their suggested operation within one of its units (a political community, whether sovereign state or colony) runs into deeply serious difficulties. An illustration of this claim is all that time and space here permit.

Weber, in a "fragment" on "The Market" (Chapter VII of Part Two in the Roth-Wittich edition [1968: 635–40]), distinguished appropriately and sharply between two fundamentally different kinds of "monopolies" encountered within a given political community. On the one side are "the monopolies of status-groups [which] excluded from their field of action the mechanism of the market." On the other side are the "capitalistic monopolies which are acquired in the market through the power of property." The difference is ellipti-

---

[3]Weber's one theoretical claim in this section. Section Six of the Chapter "Political Communities," reads thus:

> As to the general economic conditions making for the predominance of stratification by status, only the following can be said. When the bases of the acquisition and distribution of goods are relatively stable, stratification by status is favored. Every technological repercussion and economic transformation threatens stratification by status and pushes the class situation into the foreground. Epochs and countries in which the naked class situation is of predominant significance are regularly the periods of technical and economic transformations. And every slowing down of the change in economic stratification leads, in due course, to the growth of status structures and makes for resuscitation of the important role of social honor (1968: 938).

[4] We have departed from Weber's use of "stratification." For a provisional and programmatic formulation of the concept, "stratifying processes," see Hopkins & Wallerstein (1981).

cally specified: "The beneficiary of a monopoly by a status-group restricts, and maintains his power against, the market, while the rational-economic monopolist rules through the market" (1968: 639). The general difficulty we alluded to may be exemplified as follows. Supposing that, among our interrelated and honor-oriented states, the government of one creates a "monopoly" within its borders for its few local (national) producers of, say, automobiles, by so raising the import duties on automobiles produced elsewhere in the world that they are no longer price-competitive. They are, as is said, "priced out of the market," which amounts to saying that the government in question has restricted, and maintained its power against, the world-market for automobiles. Do we construe that situation as comparable on the world scene to a status-group monopoly within a political community, or to a class-formed capitalistic monopoly? Or is it a bit of both—class-like because of the rational appropriation of profit opportunities by the automobile firms who persuaded the government to introduce the restrictions; and status-group-like because of the sentiments of national pride and prestige marshalled in support of and generated by the policy?

We suspect the latter. But, if we are right, Weber's sharply etched structural distinction, between class-structured and status-group-structured distributions of power within political communities, becomes a fused concept when put to use in the examination of processes of group-formation in the modern world-system. And we shall have to ground anew processes of class-formation and processes of status-group formation, in order to see them on occasion as fused and reinforcing sets of processes rather than being restricted by their original and careful formulation as necessarily diametrically opposed in their operation.

The intellectual pressure to reify groups, to presume their permanency and longevity, is difficult to resist. For one thing, most self-conscious groups argue as part of their legitimizing ideology not merely their preeminence (in one way or another) but their temporal priority over competing groups. Groups that are self-conscious, that seem to act collectively in significant ways, often seem very solid and very resilient. We too often lose from sight the degree to which this solidarity, this reality, is itself the product of the group's activities in relations with others, activities that in turn are made possible by and have a direct impact upon the rest of social reality. The very activities of groups in relation to one another serve to change each substantially and substantively, and in particular to change their respective boundaries and their distinguishing and defining characteristics.

Permit us to suggest an analogy. If one has a wheel of mottled colors, one that includes the whole range of the color spectrum, and if one spins the wheel, it will appear more and more like a solid white mass as the speed increases. There comes a point of speed where it is impossible to see the wheel as other than pure white. If, however, the wheel slows down, the white will dissolve into its component separate colors. So it is with groups, even (and perhaps especially) those most central of institutional structures of the modern world-system—the states, the classes, the nations, and/or ethnic groups.[5] Seen in long historical time and broad world space, they fade into one another, becoming only "groups". Seen in short historical time and narrow world space, they become clearly defined and so form distinctive "structures".

The distinction between classes *an sich* and classes *für sich* is helpful insofar as it recognizes that the self-consciousness of classes (and other groups) is not a constant but a variable. We must, however, draw on Marx and Weber one step further and recognize with them that the very existence of particular historical groups in relation to one another is not given but is also a variable. It may be objected that no one ever assumed that a class or an ethnic group *always* existed, and that everyone knows that for every group there is of course a moment of its coming into existence (however difficult this may be to specify). But this is not the point we are making.

At some moment of historical time the bourgeoisie (the world bourgeoisie or a local version in a given area or of a given people), the Brahmin caste, the Hungarian nation, and the religious community of Buddhists all came (or evolved) into existence. Are we to assume that each just continued to exist from that point on? We are contending that there is a sense in which all these groups are in fact constantly being recreated such that over time we have genuinely new wine in old bottles, and that the emphasis on the continuity and primordiality of the group's existence, though it may be of considerable ideological value to its members as such, is of very little analytic value to us as observers. The transition from feudalism to capitalism cannot be explained by the struggle of classes that came into real current existence only as the result of that transition. Civil war in Lebanon cannot be explained by the struggle of religious groups who have come into real *current existence* largely as a result of that civil war.

What intelligent analysis therefore requires is that we uncover the processes by which groups (and institutions) are constantly recreated, remolded, and eliminated in the ongoing operations of the capitalist world-economy, which is an actual social system that came into historical existence in the "long" sixteenth century primarily in Europe, and which subsequently has been expanded in space so that it now includes all other geographical areas of the globe. The relational concept and, therefore, the actual structures of classes

---

[5]This theme is developed in Wallerstein (1980).

and ethnic-groups have been dependent on the creation of the modern states. The states are the key political units of the world-economy, units that have been defined by and circumscribed by their location in the interstate system. And this system has served as the evolving political superstructure of the world-economy.

In the original loci of the capitalist world-economy, the birth of diplomacy, of so-called international law, and of state-building ideologies (such as absolutism) all coincide with the early functioning of the world-economy. Of course, these states rapidly found themselves in a hierarchical network of unequal strength. As new areas became incorporated into this capitalist world-economy, the existing political structures of such areas were commonly reshaped in quite fundamental ways (including even the definition of their territorial and "ethnic" or national boundaries) so that they could play their expected roles in the relational network of the interstate system. These states had to be too weak to interfere with the flow of the factors of production across their boundaries, and therefore with the peripheralization of their production processes. Hence, in some cases, pre-existing political structures had to be "weakened." But the states also had to be *strong* enough to ensure the very same flow, the same peripheralization. Hence, in other cases, pre-existing political structures had to be "strengthened." But weakened or strengthened, these recreated or entirely newly-created incorporated states ended up as state-structures that were weak relative to the states specializing in core production processes within the world-economy.

The classes and the ethnic/national groups or groupings that began to crystallize were crystallized, so to speak, from three directions. They defined themselves primarily in relation to these state-structures that commanded the largest amount of armed force and access to economic possibilities, either through the direct distribution of ever-increasing tax income or through the creation of structured possibilities of preferential access to the market (including training). They were defined by those in the centers of these structures (and in the centers of the world-system as a whole). And they were perceived by competitive groups in their relational setting.

Three kinds of groups emerged in relation to these state-structures—class, national, and ethnic groups. While classes *an sich* developed in terms of the relation of households to the real social economy, which in this case was a capitalist *world*-economy, a class *für sich* is a group that makes conscious claims of class membership, which is a claim to a place in a particular political order. Such a class could therefore only grow up in relation to a given political entity. When E. P. Thompson (1964) writes about the making of the English working class, he is writing about the conditions under which urban proletarians within a jurisdiction called "England" came to think of themselves as English workers and to act politically in this capacity. The class "made" itself, as he emphasizes, not only by the evolution of objective economic and social conditions, but by the ways in which some (many) people reacted to these conditions.

Of course, the extent to which there emerged an English rather than a British working class already indicated that a key political choice had been made. The Irish workers, for example, were thereby defined as a different group. Thus, the construction of a "class" was *ipso facto* part of the construction of at least two "nationalities," the English and the Irish. Nor did this particular story stop there. For we are still seeing today the later consequences of these early developments. Protestant urban proletarians in Northern Ireland do not today think of themselves as "Irish." Instead they call themselves "Protestants," or "Ulstermen," or (least likely) "Britons," or even all three. It is clear that, in reality, to be a "Protestant" and to be an "Ulsterman" is in this situation virtually synonomous; to be a "Catholic" and to be "Irish" is the same. To be sure, there are Protestants, and even Jews, resident in Dublin who think of themselves as Irish. This doesn't mitigate the meaning of the religious terms in Northern Ireland.

If now some political organization comes along and insists on banning the use of religious terminology in favor, let us say, of the exclusive use of class terminology, such a group is arguing in favor of a particular political resolution of the conflict. Were such a group to succeed, the reality of the religious groups as social entities might rapidly recede in Northern Ireland, as they have in many other areas of the world. An example would be Switzerland, where people primarily identify as members of linguistic groups and only in a minor way as members of religious groups.

Is there an Indian bourgeoisie? This is not a question of essences, but of existential reality. It is a political question that divides Indian entrepreneurs among themselves. To the extent that we can say that there exists an Indian bourgeoisie, as opposed to merely members of the world bourgeoisie who happen to hold Indian passports, it is because there is a belief on the part of these bourgeois that the Indian state-apparatus has or could have an important role in assuring their "class" interests vis-à-vis both both workers in India and bourgeois in other areas of the world.

The whole line between classes as they are constructed and status-groups of every variety is far more fluid and blurred than the classic presumption of an antinomy between class and status-group has indicated. It is in fact very hard to know when we are dealing primarily with the one rather than with the other. This is especially true when political conflict becomes acute, and this is one of the reasons why the lines between social movements and national movements have become increasingly difficult to disentangle and are perhaps unimportant to discern.

Furthermore, even among traditionally defined status-groups, it is not sure that it is very useful to distinguish "nations" from other kinds of "ethnic groups." A "nation" seems to be nothing but a political claim that the boundaries of a state should coincide with those of a given "ethnic group." This is used to justify either secessionist movements or unification movements. In point of fact, if we were to use a strict definition of the concept "nation," we would be hard-pressed to find even one "nation-state" in the entire world-system. This indicates that "nation" is more the description of an aspiration, or of a tendency, than of an existing phenomenon. Whenever the political claim (and/or definition by others) is less than that of state sovereignty, we tend to call this group an "ethnic group," whatever the basis of this claim, be it common language, common religion, common skin color, or fictive common ancestry.

The actual history of the construction (reconstruction, remolding, destruction) of classes, nations, and ethnic groups—including the pressure both of "external" groups to create these groups and of the "internal" desire of putative groups to create themselves—is a history of the constant rise and fall of the intensity of these political claims in cultural clothing. There is no evidence that, over the several hundred years of the existence of the capitalist world-economy, one particular genre of claim has grown at the expense of others; each genre seems to have held its own. It would seem, therefore, that assertions about primordiality are in fact ideological. This is not to say that there has not been systemic development. For example, nothing herein argued is inconsistent with the proposition that there has been growing class polarization in the capitalist world-economy. But such a proposition would be referring to classes *an sich*, that is, at the level of the real social economy, the capitalist world-economy. Rather, this analysis should be seen as an argument that group formations (solidarities) are processes of the capitalist world-economy, and are among the central underlying forms of the more narrowly manifest efforts at political organization.

In recent years, social scientists of various intellectual schools have begun to return to Marx's critique of political economy, but in ways that go beyond the mechanical usages of class analysis that formed the ideology of the Second and Third Internationals and beyond the equally mechanical concept of primordial status-groups that dominated the developmentalist ideology of U.S.-dominated world social science in the 1950's and 1960's.

On the one hand, in the era of U.S. hegemony (roughly 1945–70), the unity of the world market analytically presupposed by Marx (when he observed an era of British hegemony), and which was thought to have disappeared in the late nineteenth century, was in fact progressively reconstituted. The so-called transnationals sought to operate with minimal constraint by state-political apparatuses. Though the concentration of capital increased even further, its transnational expansion out of the American core became a major factor in the intensification of world market competition and in the consolidation of the unity of the world market. In this context the role played by states changed radically, though not everywhere to the same extent. Particularly outside of the Communist world, the emphasis in their action changed from territorial expansion and restriction of inter-enterprise competition within and across national/imperial boundaries to strengthening the competitive edge of their territories as locales of production and to sustaining the transnational expansion of their respective national capitals. They thereby contributed to the enhancement of the density and connectedness of world-economic networks that, in turn, undermined their ability to influence/control economic activity even within their own borders.

On the other hand, the anti-systemic movements have more and more taken on the clothing of "national liberation movements," claiming the double legitimacy of nationalist anti-imperialism and proletarian anti-capitalism. This has given them great strength as mobilizing movements. But, insofar as they have come to power in specific state structures operating within the interstate system, they have been caught in the constraints of this system that has led to conflicts within and among such "post-revolutionary" states among other things.

A cogent analysis of existing trends within the world-system requires both a return to basics in terms of an analysis of the operational mechanisms of capitalism as a mode of production, and a reconceptualization of the operational mechanisms of the social groups (that are formed, are reformed, and of course also disappear) that compete and conflict within this capitalist world-economy, as it continues to evolve and to transform itself.

REFERENCES

Hopkins, Terence K. & Wallerstein, Immanuel (1981). "Structural Transformations of the World-Economy," in R. Rubinson, ed., *Dynamics of World Development*. Beverly Hills: Sage Publications, 249–59.

Marx, Karl (1959). *Capital*, Vol. I. Moscow: Foreign Languages Publishing House.

Marx, Karl & Engels, Friedrich (1967). *The Communist Manifesto*. London: Penguin.

Polanyi, Karl (1957). *The Great Transformation*. Boston: Beacon Press.

Smith, Adam (1961). *The Wealth of Nations*, Vol. 1. London: Methuen.

Thompson, E. P. (1964). *The Making of the English Working Class*. New York: Pantheon.

Wallerstein, Immanuel (1980). "The States in the Institutional Vortex of the Capitalist World-Economy," *International Social Science Journal*, XXXII, 4, 743–81.

Weber, Max (1946). *Essays from Max Weber*, ed. H. Gerth & C. W. Mills. New York: Oxford Univ. Press.

Weber, Max (1968). *Economy and Society*, ed. G. Roth & C. Wittich. New York: Bedminster Press.

II THE DURKHEIMIAN TRADITION

Some Main Points of the Durkheimian Tradition

	Macro wing			Micro wing
1740–1770	Montesquieu			
1770–1800	Revolutionary *philosophes*			
1800–1830	Saint-Simon			Reactionary defenders of religion: De Bonald, De Maistre
1830–1860	Comte's positivism			
	Utilitarian influence: John Stuart Mill			
1860–1890	Herbert Spencer			Crowd psychologists
				Classicists and anthropologists: Frazer Fustel de Coulanges
1890–1920	Durkheim			Anthropology of rituals: Mauss
1920–1960				Cambridge scholars of classical religion
	Functionalists Merton Parsons	Levi-Strauss's structuralism		British social anthropology: Radcliffe-Brown Lloyd Warner
1960–		Bourdieu's cultural capital theory		Goffman's interaction rituals
				Ritual and stratification: Bernstein Mary Douglas Collins
				Durkheimian sociology of science: Hagstrom Bloor

Precontractual Solidarity [1893]; Social Rituals and Sacred Objects [1912]

EMILE DURKHEIM

• *Emile Durkheim may well be sociology's greatest theorist to date. That is not to say all his theories have always proved right or fruitful; some lineages of his intellectual followers, in my opinion (such as the functionalist and evolutionist traditions), pick up more of the fallacies and ideological elements in Durkheim than his strengths. But Durkheim also provides the classic breakthrough insights of sociology, the great "aha!" experiences: of realization that social order and rational thought itself rest on a nonrational foundation; that this substructure is a flow of emotions determined by the density of social interactions and especially by the tightly focused mutual actions of rituals; that symbols like gods are charged with moral energies by the group whose membership they reflect. Following are some key arguments of Durkheim's relentlessly logical and systematic theoretical analysis.*

THE PRE-CONTRACTUAL BASIS OF SOCIAL SOLIDARITY

[If society were based solely on social contracts] . . . the typical social relation would be the economic, stripped of all regulation and resulting from the entirely free initiative of the parties. In short, society would be solely the stage where individuals exchanged the products of their labor, without any action properly social coming to regulate this exchange.

Is this the character of societies whose unity is produced by the division of labor? If this were so, we could with justice doubt their stability. For if interest relates men, it is never for more than some few moments. It can create only an external link between them. In the fact of exchange, the various agents remain outside of each other, and when the business has been completed, each one retires and is left entirely on his own. Consciences are only superficially in contact; they neither penetrate each other, nor do they adhere. If we look further into the matter, we shall see that this total harmony of interests

Reprinted with permission of the Free Press, a Division of Macmillan, Inc., from Emile Durkheim, *The Division of Labor in Society* (New York: Free Press, 1964), pp. 203–204, 212–214, 275–280, 287–291, 345–350; originally published 1893.

conceals a latent or deferred conflict. For where interest is the only ruling force each individual finds himself in a state of war with every other since nothing comes to mollify the egos, and any truce in this eternal antagonism would not be of long duration. There is nothing less constant than interest. Today, it unites me to you; tomorrow, it will make me your enemy. Such a cause can only give rise to transient relations and passing associations. We now understand how necessary it is to see if this is really the nature of organic solidarity.

To be sure, when men unite in a contract, it is because, through the division of labor, either simple or complex, they need each other. But in order for them to co-operate harmoniously, it is not enough that they enter into a relationship, nor even that they feel the state of mutual dependence in which they find themselves. It is still necessary that the conditions of this co-opera-tion be fixed for the duration of their relations. The rights and duties of each must be defined, not only in view of the situation such as it presents itself at the moment when the contract is made, but with foresight for the circum-stances which may arise to modify it. Otherwise, at every instant, there would be conflicts and endless difficulties. We must not forget that, if the division of labor makes interests solidary, it does not confound them; it keeps them distinct and opposite. Even as in the internal workings of the individual organism each organ is in conflict with others while co-operating with them, each of the contractants, while needing the other, seeks to obtain what he needs at the least expense; that is to say, to acquire as many rights as possible in exchange for the smallest possible obligations.

It is necessary therefore to pre-determine the share of each, but this cannot be done according to a preconceived plan. There is nothing in the nature of things from which one can deduce what the obligations of one or the other ought to be until a certain limit is reached. Every determination of this kind can only result in compromise. It is a compromise between the rivalry of interests present and their solidarity. It is a position of equilibrium which can be found only after more or less laborious experiments. But it is quite evident that we can neither begin these experiments over again nor restore this equi-librium at fresh expense every time that we engage in some contractual rela-tion. We lack all ability to do that. It is not at the moment when difficulties surge upon us that we must resolve them, and, moreover, we can neither foresee the variety of possible circumstances in which our contract will involve itself, nor fix in advance with the aid of simple mental calculus what will be in each case the rights and duties of each, save in matters in which we have a very definite experience. Moreover, the material conditions of life oppose themselves to the repetition of such operations. For, at each instant, and often at the most inopportune, we find ourselves contracting, either for something we have bought, or sold, somewhere we are traveling, our hiring of one's services, some acceptance of hostelry, and so on. The greater part of our relations with others is of a contractual nature. If, then, it were necessary each time to begin the struggles anew, to again go through the conferences necessary to establish firmly all the conditions of agreement for the present and the future, we would be put to rout. For all these reasons, if we were linked only by the terms of our contracts, as they are agreed upon, only a precarious solidarity would result.

But contract-law is that which determines the juridical consequences of our acts that we have not determined. It expresses the normal conditions of equilibrium, as they arise from themselves or from the average. A résumé of numerous, varied experiences, what we cannot foresee individually is there provided for, what we cannot regulate is there regulated, and this regulation imposes itself upon us, although it may not be our handiwork, but that of society and tradition. It forces us to assume obligations that we have not contracted for, in the exact sense of the word, since we have not deliberated upon them, nor even, occasionally, had any knowledge about them in advance. Of course, the initial act is always contractual, but there are consequences, sometimes immediate, which run over the limits of the contract. We co-operate because we wish to, but our voluntary co-operation creates duties for us that we did not desire.

.   .   .

A corollary of all that has preceded is that the division of labor can be effectuated only among members of an already constituted society.

In effect, when competition places isolated and estranged individuals in opposition, it can only separate them more. If there is a lot of space at their disposal, they will flee; if they cannot go beyond certain boundaries, they will differentiate themselves, so as to become still more independent. No case can be cited where relations of pure hostility are transformed, without the intervention of any other factor, into social relations. Thus, as among individuals of the same animal or vegetable species, there is generally no bond, the war they wage has no other result than to diversify them, to give birth to dissimilar varieties which grow farther apart. It is this progressive disjunction that Darwin called the law of the divergence of characters. But the division of labor unites at the same time that it opposes; it makes the activities it differentiates converge; it brings together those it separates. Since competition cannot have determined this conciliation, it must have existed before. The individuals among whom the struggle is waged must already be solidary and feel so. That is to say, they must belong to the same society. That is why, where this feeling of solidarity is too feeble to resist the dispersive influence of competition, the latter engenders altogether different effects from the division of labor. In countries where existence is too difficult because of the extreme density of the population, the inhabitants, instead of specializing, retire from society, either permanently or temporarily and leave for other countries.

To represent what the division of labor is suffices to make one understand that it cannot be otherwise. It consists in the sharing of functions up to that time common. But this sharing cannot be executed according to a preconceived plan. We cannot tell in advance where the line of demarcation between tasks will be found once they are separated, for it is not marked so evidently in the nature of things, but depends, on the contrary, upon a multitude of circumstances. The division of labor, then, must come about of itself and progressively. Consequently, under these conditions, for a function to be divided into two exactly complementary parts, as the nature of the division of labor demands, it is indispensable that the two specializing parts be in constant communication during all the time that this dissociation lasts. There is no other means for one to receive all the movement the other abandons, and which they adapt to each other. But in the same way that an animal colony whose members embody a continuity of tissue form one individual, every aggregate of individuals who are in continuous contact form a society. The division of labor can then be produced only in the midst of a pre-existing society. By that, we do not mean to say simply that individuals must adhere materially, but it is still necessary that there be moral links between them. First, material continuity by itself produces links of this kind, provided it is durable. But, moreover, they are directly necessary. If the relations becoming established in the period of groping were not subject to any rule, if no power moderated the conflict of individual interests, there would be chaos from which no new order could emerge. It is thought, it is true, that everything takes place through private conventions freely disputed. Thus, it seems that all social action is absent. But this is to forget that contracts are possible only where a juridical regulation, and, consequently, a society, already exists.

Hence, the claim sometimes advanced that in the division of labor lies the fundamental fact of all social life is wrong. Work is not divided among independent and already differentiated individuals who by uniting and associating bring together their different aptitudes. For it would be a miracle if differences thus born through chance circumstance could unite so perfectly as to form a coherent whole. Far from preceding collective life, they derive from it. They can be produced only in the midst of a society, and under the pressure of social sentiments and social needs. That is what makes them essentially harmonious. There is, then, a social life outside the whole division of labor, but which the latter presupposes. That is, indeed, what we have directly established in showing that there are societies whose cohesion is essentially due to a community of beliefs and sentiments, and it is from these societies that those whose unity is assured by the division of labor have emerged. The conclusions of the preceding book and those which we have just reached can then be used to control and mutually confirm each other. The division of physiological labor is itself submitted to this law; it never appears except in the midst of polycellular masses which are already endowed with a certain cohesion.

For a number of theorists, it is a self-evident truth that all society essentially consists of co-operation. Spencer has said that a society in the scientific sense of the word exists only when to the juxtaposition of individuals co-operation is added. We have just seen that this so-called axiom is contrary to the truth. Rather it is evident, as Auguste Comte points out, "that co-operation, far from having produced society, necessarily supposes, as preamble, its spontaneous existence." What bring men together are mechanical causes and impulsive forces, such as affinity of blood, attachment to the same soil, ancestral worship, community of habits, and so on. It is only when the group has been formed on these bases that co-operation is organized there.

Further, the only co-operation possible in the beginning is so intermittent and feeble that social life, if it had no other source, would be without force and without continuity. With stronger reason, the complex co-operation resulting from the division of labor is an ulterior and derived phenomenon. It results from internal movements which are developed in the midst of the mass, when the latter is constituted. It is true that once it appears it tightens the social bonds and makes a more perfect individuality of society. But this integration supposes another which it replaces. For social units to be able to be differentiated, they must first be attracted or grouped by virtue of the resemblances they present. This process of formation is observed, not only originally, but in each phase of evolution. We know, indeed, that higher societies result from the union of lower societies of the same type. It is necessary first that these latter be mingled in the midst of the same identical collective conscience for the process of differentiation to begin or recommence. It is thus that more complex organisms are formed by the repetition of more simple, similar organisms which are differentiated only if once associated. In short, association and co-operation are two distinct facts, and if the second, when developed, reacts on the first and transforms it, if human societies steadily become groups of co-operators, the duality of the two phenomena does not vanish for all that.

If this important truth has been disregarded by the utilitarians, it is an error rooted in the manner in which they conceive the genesis of society. They suppose originally isolated and independent individuals, who, consequently, enter into relationships only to co-operate, for they have no other reason to clear the space separating them and to associate. But this theory, so widely held, postulates a veritable *creatio ex nihilo.*

It consists, indeed, in deducing society from the individual. But nothing we know authorizes us to believe in the possibility of such spontaneous generation. According to Spencer, for societies to be formed within this hypothesis, it is necessary that primitive units pass from the state of perfect independence to that of mutual dependence. But what can have determined such a complete transformation in them? Is it the prospect of the advantages presented by social life? But they are counterbalanced, perhaps more than counterbalanced, by the loss of independence, for, among individuals born for a free and solitary life, such a sacrifice is most intolerable. Add to this, that in the first social types social life is as absolute as possible, for nowhere is the individual more completely absorbed in the group. How would man, if he were born an individualist, as is supposed, be able to resign himself to an existence clashing violently with his fundamental inclination? How pale the problematical utility of co-operation must appear to him beside such a fall! With autonomous individualities, as are imagined, nothing can emerge save what is individual, and, consequently, co-operation itself, which is a social fact, submissive to social rules, cannot arise. Thus, the psychologist who starts by restricting himself to the ego cannot emerge to find the non-ego.

Collective life is not born from individual life, but it is, on the contrary, the second which is born from the first. It is on this condition alone that one can explain how the personal individuality of social units has been able to be formed and enlarged without disintegrating society. Indeed, as, in this case, it becomes elaborate in the midst of a pre-existing social environment, it necessarily bears its mark. It is made in a manner so as not to ruin this collective order with which it is solidary. It remains adapted to it while detaching itself. It has nothing anti-social about it because it is a product of society. It is not the absolute personality of the monad, which is sufficient unto itself, and could do without the rest of the world, but that of an organ or part of an organ having its determined function, but which cannot, without risking dissolution, separate itself from the rest of the organism. Under these conditions, co-operation becomes not only possible but necessary. Utilitarians thus reverse the natural order of facts, and nothing is more deceiving than this inversion. It is a particular illustration of the general truth that what is first in knowledge is last in reality. Precisely because co-operation is the most recent fact, it strikes sight first. If, then, one clings to appearance, as does common sense, it is inevitable that one see in it the primary fact of moral and social life.

But if it is not all of ethics, it is not necessary to put it outside ethics, as do certain moralists. As the utilitarians, the idealists have it consist exclusively in a system of economic relations, of private arrangements in which egotism is the only active power. In truth, the moral life traverses all the relations which constitute co-operation, since it would not be possible if social sentiments, and, consequently, moral sentiments, did not preside in its elaboration.

TWO FORMS OF COLLECTIVE CONSCIENCE: CONCRETE AND ABSTRACT

In a small society, since everyone is clearly placed in the same conditions of existence, the collective environment is essentially concrete. It is made up of beings of all sorts who fill the social horizon. The states of conscience representing it then have the same character. First, they are related to precise objects, as this animal, this tree, this plant, this natural force, etc. Then, as everybody is related to these things in the same way, they affect all consciences in the same way. The whole tribe, if it is not too widely extended, enjoys or suffers the same advantages or inconveniences from the sun, rain, heat, or cold, from this river, or that source, etc. The collective impressions resulting from the fusion of all these individual impressions are then determined in form as well as in object, and, consequently, the common conscience has a defined character. But it changes its nature as societies become more voluminous. Because these societies are spread over a vaster surface, the common conscience is itself obliged to rise above all local diversities, to dominate more space, and consequently to become more abstract. For not many general things can be common to all these diverse environments. It is no longer such an animal, but such a species; not this source, but such sources; not this forest, but forest *in abstracto*.

Moreover, because conditions of life are no longer the same everywhere, these common objects, whatever they may be, can no longer determine perfectly identical sentiments everywhere. The collective resultants then no longer have the same sharpness, and the more so in this respect as their component elements are more unlike. The more differences among individual portraits serving to make a composite portrait, the more indecisive the latter is. True it is that local collective consciences can keep their individuality in the midst of the general collective conscience and that, as they comprise less space, they more easily remain concrete. But we know they slowly tend to vanish from the first, in so far as the social segments to which they correspond are effaced.

The fact which perhaps best manifests this increasing tendency of the common conscience is the parallel transcendence of the most essential of its elements, I mean the idea of divinity. In the beginning, the gods are not distinct from the universe, or rather there are no gods, but only sacred beings, without their sacred character being related to any external entity as their source. The animals or plants of the species which serves as a clan-totem are the objects of worship, but that is not because a principle *sui generis* comes to communicate their divine nature to them from without. This nature is intrinsic with them; they are divine in and of themselves. But little by little religious forces are detached from the things of which they were first only the attributes, and become hypostatized. Thus is formed the notion of spirits or gods who, while residing here or there as preferred, nevertheless exist outside of the particular objects to which they are more specifically attached. By that very fact they are less concrete. Whether they multiply or have been led back to some certain unity, they are still immanent in the world. If they are in part separated from things, they are always in space. They remain, then, very near us, constantly fused into our life. The Graeco-Latin polytheism, which is a more elevated and better organized form of animism, marks new progress in the direction of transcendence. The residence of the gods becomes more sharply distinct from that of men. Set upon the mysterious heights of Olympus or dwelling in the recesses of the earth, they personally intervene in human affairs only in somewhat intermittent fashion. But it is only with Christianity that God takes leave of space; his kingdom is no longer of this world. The dissociation of nature and the divine is so complete that it degenerates into antagonism. At the same time, the concept of divinity becomes more general and more abstract, for it is formed, not of sensations, as originally, but of ideas. The God of humanity necessarily is less concrete than the gods of the city or the clan.

Besides, at the same time as religion, the rules of law become universal, as well as those of morality. Linked at first to local circumstances, to particularities, ethnic, climatic, and so on, they free themselves little by little, and with the same stroke become more general. What makes this increase of generality obvious is the uninterrupted decline of formalism. In lower societies, the very external form of conduct is predetermined even to the details. The way in which man must eat, dress in every situation, the gestures he must make, the formulae he must pronounce, are precisely fixed. On the contrary, the further one strays from the point of departure, the more moral and juridical prescriptions lose their sharpness and precision. They rule only the most general forms of conduct, and rule them in a very general manner, saying what must be done, not how it must be done. Now, all that is defined is expressed in a definite form. If collective sentiments had the same determination as formerly, they would not be expressed in a less determined manner. If the concrete details of action and thought were as uniform, they would be as obligatory.

It has often been remarked that civilization has a tendency to become more rational and more logical. The cause is now evident. That alone is rational which is universal. What baffles understanding is the particular and the concrete. Only the general is thought well of. Consequently, the nearer the common conscience is to particular things, the more it bears their imprint, the more unintelligible it also is. That is why primitive civilizations affect us as they do. Being unable to subsume them under logical principles, we succeed in seeing only bizarre and fortuitous combinations of heterogeneous elements. In reality, there is nothing artificial about them. It is necessary only to seek their determining causes in sensations and movements of sensibility, not in concepts. And if this is so, it is because the social environment for which they are made is not sufficiently extended. On the contrary, when civilization is developed over a vaster field of action, when it is applied to more people and things, general ideas necessarily appear and become predominant there. The idea of man, for example, replaces in law, in morality, in religion, that of Roman, which, being more concrete, is more refractory to science. Thus, it is the increase of volume in societies and their greater condensation which explain this great transformation.

But the more general the common conscience becomes, the greater the place it leaves to individual variations. When God is far from things and men, his action is no longer omnipresent, nor ubiquitous. There is nothing fixed save abstract rules which can be freely applied in very different ways. Then they no longer have the same ascendancy nor the same force of resistance. Indeed, if practices and formulae, when they are precise, determine thought and movements with a necessity analogous to that of reflexes, these general principles, on the contrary, can pass into facts only with the aid of intelligence. But, once reflection is awakened, it is not easy to restrain it. When it has taken hold, it develops spontaneously beyond the limits assigned to it. One begins by putting articles of faith beyond discussion; then discussion extends to them. One wishes an explanation of them; one asks their reasons for existing, and, as they submit to this search, they lose a part of their force. For reflective ideas never have the same constraining force as instincts. It is thus that deliberated movements have not the spontaneity of involuntary movements. Because it becomes more rational, the collective conscience becomes less imperative, and for this very reason, it wields less restraint over the free development of individual varieties.

THE SOCIAL NATURE OF THE HUMAN INDIVIDUAL

With societies, individuals are transformed in accordance with the changes produced in the number of social units and their relations.

First, they are made more and more free of the yoke of the organism. An animal is almost completely under the influence of his physical environment; its biological constitution predetermines its existence. Man, on the contrary, is dependent upon social causes. Of course, animals also form societies, but, as they are very restricted, collective life is very simple. They are also stationary because the equilibrium of such small societies is necessarily stable. For these two reasons, it easily fixes itself in the organism. It not only has its roots in the organism, but it is entirely enveloped in it to such a point that it loses its own characteristics. It functions through a system of instincts, of reflexes which are not essentially distinct from those which assure the functioning of organic life. They present, it is true, the particular characteristic of adapting the individual to the social environment, not to the physical environment, and are caused by occurrences of the common life. They are not of different nature, however, from those which, in certain cases, determine without any previous education the necessary movements in locomotion. It is quite otherwise with man, because the societies he forms are much vaster. Even the smallest we know of are more extensive than the majority of animal societies. Being more complex, they also change more, and these two causes together see to it that social life with man is not congealed in a biological form. Even where it is most simple, it clings to its specificity. There are always beliefs and practices common to men which are not inscribed in their tissues. But this character is more manifest as the social mass and density grow. The more people there are in association, and the more they react upon one another, the more also does the product of these reactions pass beyond the bounds of the organism. Man thus finds himself placed under the sway of causes *sui generis* whose relative part in the constitution of human nature becomes ever more considerable.

Moreover, the influence of this factor increases not only in relative value, but also in absolute value. The same cause which increases the importance of the collective environment weakens the organic environment in such a manner as to make it accessible to the action of social causes and to subordinate it to them. Because there are more individuals living together, common life is richer and more varied, but for this variety to be possible, the organic type must be less definite to be able to diversify itself. We have seen, in effect, that the tendencies and aptitudes transmitted by heredity became ever more general and more indeterminate, more refractory consequently, to assuming the form of instincts. Thus, a phenomenon is produced which is exactly the inverse of that which we observe at the beginning of evolution. With animals, the organism assimilates social facts to it, and, stripping them of their special nature, transforms them into biological facts. Social life is materialized. In man, on the contrary, and particularly in higher societies, social causes substitute themselves for organic causes. The organism is spiritualized.

The individual is transformed in accordance with this change in dependence. Since this activity which calls forth the special action of social causes cannot be fixed in the organism, a new life, also *sui generis*, is superimposed upon that of the body. Freer, more complex, more independent of the organs which support it, its distinguishing characteristics become ever more apparent as it progresses and becomes solid. From this description we can recognize the essential traits of psychic life. To be sure, it would be exaggerating to say that psychic life begins only with societies, but certainly it becomes extensive only as societies develop. That is why, as has often been remarked, the progress of conscience is in inverse ratio to that of instinct. Whatever may be said of them, it is not the first which breaks up the second. Instinct, the product of the accumulated experience of generations, has a much greater resistive force to dissolution simply because it becomes conscious. Truly, conscience only invades the ground which instinct has ceased to occupy, or where instinct cannot be established. Conscience does not make instinct recede; it only fills the space instinct leaves free. Moreover, if instinct regresses rather than extends as general life extends, the greater importance of the social factor is the cause of this. Hence, the great difference which separates man from animals, that is, the greater development of his psychic life, comes from his greater sociability. To understand why psychic functions have been carried, from the very beginnings of the human species, to a degree of perfection unknown among animal species, one would first have to know why it is that men, instead of living in solitude or in small bands, were led to form more extensive societies. To put it in terms of the classical definition, if man is a reasonable animal, that is because he is a sociable animal, or at least infinitely more sociable than other animals.

This is not all. In so far as societies do not reach certain dimensions nor a certain degree of concentration, the only psychic life which may be truly developed is that which is common to all the members of the group, which is found identical in each. But, as societies become more vast and, particularly, more condensed, a psychic life of a new sort appears. Individual diversities, at first lost and confused amidst the mass of social likenesses, become disengaged, become conspicuous, and multiply. A multitude of things which use to remain outside consciences because they did not affect the collective being become objects of representations. Whereas individuals used to act only by involving one another, except in cases where their conduct was determined by physical needs, each of them becomes a source of spontaneous activity. Particular personalities become constituted, take conscience of themselves. Moreover, this growth of psychic life in the individual does not obliterate the psychic life of society, but only transforms it. It becomes freer, more extensive, and as it has, after all, no other bases than individual consciences, these extend, become complex, and thus become flexible.

Hence, the cause which called forth the differences separating man from animals is also that which has forced him to elevate himself above himself. The ever growing distance between the savage and the civilized man has no other source. If the faculty of ideation is slowly disengaged from the confused feeling of its origin, if man has learned to formulate concepts and laws, if his spirit has embraced more and more extensive portions of space and time, if, not content with clinging to the past, he has trespassed upon the future, if his emotions and his tendencies, at first simple and not very numerous, have multiplied and diversified, that is because the social milieu has changed without interruption. In effect, unless these transformations were born from nothing, they can have had for causes only the corresponding transformations of surrounding milieux. But, man depends only upon three sorts of milieux: the organism, the external world, society. If one leaves aside the accidental variations due to combinations of heredity,—and their role in human progress is certainly not very considerable,—the organism is not automatically modified; it is necessary that it be impelled by some external cause. As for the physical world, since the beginning of history it has remained sensibly the same, at least if one does not take account of novelties which are of social origin. Consequently, there is only society which has changed enough to be able to explain the parallel changes in individual nature.

It is not, then, audacious to affirm that, from now on, whatever progress is made in psycho-physiology will never represent more than a fraction of psychology, since the major part of psychic phenomena does not come from organic causes. This is what spiritualist philosophers have learned, and the great service that they have rendered science has been to combat the doctrines which reduce psychic life merely to an efflorescence of physical life. They have very justly felt that the first, in its highest manifestations, is much too free and complex to be merely a prolongation of the second. Because it is partly independent of the organism, however, it does not follow that it depends upon no natural cause, and that it must be put outside nature. But all these facts whose explanation we cannot find in the constitution of tissues derive from properties of the social milieu. This hypothesis assumes, at least, very great probability from what has preceded. But the social realm is not less natural than the organic realm. Consequently, because there is a vast region of conscience whose genesis is unintelligible through psycho-physiology alone, we must not conclude that it has been formed of itself and that it is, accordingly, refractory to scientific investigation, but only that it derives from some other positive science which can be called socio-psychology. The phenomena which would constitute its matter are, in effect, of a mixed nature. They have the same essential characters as other psychic facts, but they arise from social causes.

It is not necessary, then, with Spencer, to present social life as a simple resultant of individual natures, since, on the contrary, it is rather the latter which come from the former. Social facts are not the simple development of psychic facts, but the second are in large part only the prolongation of the first in the interior of consciences. This proposition is very important, for the contrary point of view exposes the sociologist, at every moment, to mistaking the cause for the effect, and conversely. For example, if, as often happens, we see in the organization of the family the logically necessary expression of human sentiments inherent in every conscience, we are reversing the true order of facts. On the contrary, it is the social organization of the relations of kinship which has determined the respective sentiments of parents and children. They would have been completely different if the social structure had been different, and the proof of this is, in effect, that paternal love is unknown in a great many societies.[1] One could cite many other examples of the same error.[2] Of course, it is a self-evident truth that there is nothing in social life which is not in individual consciences. Everything that is found in the latter, however, comes from society. The major part of our states of conscience would not have been produced among isolated beings and would have been produced quite otherwise among beings grouped in some other manner. They come, then, not from the psychological nature of man in general, but from the manner in which men once associated mutually affect one another, according as they are more or less numerous, more or less close. Products of group life, it is the nature of the group which alone can explain them. Of course, they would not be possible if individual constitutions did not lend themselves to such action, but individual constitutions are only remote conditions, not determinate causes. Spencer in one place compares the work of the

---

[1] This is the case in societies where the matriarchal family rules.

[2] To cite only one example of this,—religion has been explained by the movements of individual feeling, whereas these movements are only the prolongation in the individual of social states which give birth to religion. We have developed this point further in an article in the *Révue Philosophique, Etudes de science sociale*, June, 1886. Cf. *Année Sociologique*, Vol. II, pp. 1–28.

sociologist to the calculation of a mathematician who, from the form of a
certain number of balls, deduces the manner in which they must be combined
in order to keep them in equilibrium. The comparison is inexact and does not
apply to social facts. Here, instead, it is rather the form of all which determines that of the parts. Society does not find the bases on which it rests fully
laid out in consciences; it puts them there itself.[3]

SOCIAL RITUALS AND SACRED OBJECTS

In a general way, it is unquestionable that a society has all that is necessary to
arouse the sensation of the divine in minds, merely by the power that it has
over them; for to its members it is what a god is to his worshippers. In fact, a
god is, first of all, a being whom men think of as superior to themselves, and
upon whom they feel that they depend. Whether it be a conscious personality,
such as Zeus or Jahveh, or merely abstract forces such as those in play in
totemism, the worshipper, in the one case as in the other, believes himself
held to certain manners of acting which are imposed upon him by the nature
of the sacred principle with which he feels that he is in communion. Now
society also gives us the sensation of a perpetual dependence. Since it has a
nature which is peculiar to itself and different from our individual nature, it
pursues ends which are likewise special to it; but, as it cannot attain them
except through our intermediacy, it imperiously demands our aid. It requires
that, forgetful of our own interest, we make ourselves its servitors, and it
submits us to every sort of inconvenience, privation and sacrifice, without
which social life would be impossible. It is because of this that at every instant
we are obliged to submit ourselves to rules of conduct and of thought which
we have neither made nor desired, and which are sometimes even contrary to
our most fundamental inclinations and instincts.

Even if society were unable to obtain these concessions and sacrifices from
us except by a material constraint, it might awaken in us only the idea of a
physical force to which we must give way of necessity, instead of that of a

Reprinted with permission of the Free Press, a Division of Macmillan, Inc., from Emile Durkheim,
The Elementary Forms of the Religious Life (New York: Free Press, 1965), pp. 236–252, 262–264.
Originally published 1912.

[3]This is a sufficient reply, we believe, to those who think they prove that everything in social life is
individual because society is made up only of individuals. Of course, society has no other substratum, but because individuals form society, new phenomena which are formed by association are
produced, and react upon individual consciences and in large part form them. That is why, although
society may be nothing without individuals, each of them is much more a product of society than he
is its maker.

moral power such as religions adore. But as a matter of fact, the empire which it holds over consciences is due much less to the physical supremacy of which it has the privilege than to the moral authority with which it is invested. If we yield to its orders, it is not merely because it is strong enough to triumph over our resistance; it is primarily because it is the object of a venerable respect.

We say that an object, whether individual or collective, inspires respect when the representation expressing it in the mind is gifted with such a force that it automatically causes or inhibits actions, *without regard for any consideration relative to their useful or injurious effects.* When we obey somebody because of the moral authority which we recognize in him, we follow out his opinions, not because they seem wise, but because a certain sort of physical energy is imminent in the idea that we form of this person, which conquers our will and inclines it in the indicated direction. Respect is the emotion which we experience when we feel this interior and wholly spiritual pressure operating upon us. Then we are not determined by the advantages or inconveniences of the attitude which is prescribed or recommended to us; it is by the way in which we represent to ourselves the person recommending or prescribing it. This is why commands generally take a short, peremptory form leaving no place for hesitation; it is because, in so far as it is a command and goes by its own force, it excludes all idea of deliberation or calculation; it gets its efficacy from the intensity of the mental state in which it is placed. It is this intensity which creates what is called a moral ascendancy.

Now the ways of action to which society is strongly enough attached to impose them upon its members, are, by that very fact, marked with a distinctive sign provocative of respect. Since they are elaborated in common, the vigour with which they have been thought of by each particular mind is retained in all the other minds, and reciprocally. The representations which express them within each of us have an intensity which no purely private states of consciousness could ever attain; for they have the strength of the innumerable individual representations which have served to form each of them. It is society who speaks through the mouths of those who affirm them in our presence; it is society whom we hear in hearing them; and the voice of all has an accent which that of one alone could never have. The very violence with which society reacts, by way of blame or material suppression, against every attempted dissidence, contributes to strengthening its empire by manifesting the common conviction through this burst of ardour. In a word, when something is the object of such a state of opinion, the representation which each individual has of it gains a power of action from its origins and the conditions in which it was born, which even those feel who do not submit themselves to it. It tends to repel the representations which contradict it, and it keeps them at a distance; on the other hand, it commands those acts which will realize it, and it does so, not by a material coercion or by the perspective of something of this sort, but by the simple radiation of the mental energy which it contains. It has an efficacy coming solely from its psychical properties, and it is by just this sign that moral authority is recognized. So opinion, primarily a social thing, is a source of authority, and it might even be asked whether all authority is not the daughter of opinion. It may be objected that science is often the antagonist of opinion, whose errors it combats and rectifies. But it cannot succeed in this task if it does not have sufficient authority, and it can obtain this authority only from opinion itself. If a people did not have faith in science, all the scientific demonstrations in the world would be without any influence whatsoever over their minds. Even to-day, if science happened to resist a very strong current of public opinion, it would risk losing its credit there.

Since it is in spiritual ways that social pressure exercises itself, it could not fail to give men the idea that outside themselves there exist one or several powers, both moral and, at the same time, efficacious, upon which they depend. They must think of these powers, at least in part, as outside themselves, for these address them in a tone of command and sometimes even order them to do violence to their most natural inclinations. It is undoubtedly true that if they were able to see that these influences which they feel emanate from society, then the mythological system of interpretations would never be born. But social action follows ways that are too circuitous and obscure, and employs psychical mechanisms that are too complex to allow the ordinary observer to see when it comes. As long as scientific analysis does not come to teach it to them, men know well that they are acted upon, but they do not know by whom. So they must invent by themselves the idea of these powers with which they feel themselves in connection, and from that, we are able to catch a glimpse of the way by which they were led to represent them under forms that are really foreign to their nature and to transfigure them by thought.

But a god is not merely an authority upon whom we depend; it is a force upon which our strength relies. The man who has obeyed his god and who for this reason, believes the god is with him, approaches the world with confidence and with the feeling of an increased energy. Likewise, social action does not confine itself to demanding sacrifices, privations and efforts from us. For the collective force is not entirely outside of us; it does not act upon us wholly from without; but rather, since society cannot exist except in and through individual consciousness, this force must also penetrate us and organize itself within us; it thus becomes an integral part of our being and by that very fact this is elevated and magnified.

There are occasions when this strengthening and vivifying action of society is especially apparent. In the midst of an assembly animated by a common passion, we become susceptible of acts and sentiments of which we are incapable when reduced to our own forces; and when the assembly is dissolved and when, finding ourselves alone again, we fall back to our ordinary level, we are then able to measure the height to which we have been raised above ourselves. History abounds in examples of this sort. It is enough to think of the night of the Fourth of August, 1789, when an assembly was suddenly led to an act of sacrifice and abnegation which each of its members had refused the day before, and at which they were all surprised the day after. This is why all parties political, economic or confessional, are careful to have periodical reunions where their members may revivify their common faith by manifesting it in common. To strengthen those sentiments which, if left to themselves, would soon weaken, it is sufficient to bring those who hold them together and to put them into closer and more active relations with one another. This is the explanation of the particular attitude of a man speaking to a crowd, at least if he has succeeded in entering into communion with it. His language has a grandiloquence that would be ridiculous in ordinary circumstances; his gestures show a certain domination; his very thought is impatient of all rules, and easily falls into all sorts of excesses. It is because he feels within him an abnormal over-supply of force which overflows and tries to burst out from him; sometimes he even has the feeling that he is dominated by a moral force which is greater than he and of which he is only the interpreter. It is by this trait that we are able to recognize what has often been called the demon of oratorical inspiration. Now this exceptional increase of force is something very real; it comes to him from the very group which he addresses. The sentiments provoked by his words come back to him, but enlarged and amplified, and to this degree they strengthen his own sentiment. The passionate energies he arouses re-echo within him and quicken his vital tone. It is no longer a simple individual who speaks, it is a group incarnate and personified.

Besides these passing and intermittent states, there are other more durable ones, where this strengthening influence of society makes itself felt with greater consequences and frequently even with greater brilliancy. There are periods in history when, under the influence of some great collective shock, social interactions have become much more frequent and active. Men look for each other and assemble together more than ever. That general effervescence results which is characteristic of revolutionary or creative epochs. Now this greater activity results in a general stimulation of individual forces. Men see more and differently now than in normal times. Changes are not merely of shades and degrees; men become different. The passions moving them are of such an intensity that they cannot be satisfied except by violent and unrestrained actions, actions of superhuman heroism or of bloody barbarism. This is what explains the Crusades, for example, or many of the scenes, either sublime or savage, of the French Revolution. Under the influence of the general exaltation, we see the most mediocre and inoffensive bourgeois become either a hero or a butcher. And so clearly are all these mental processes the ones that are also at the root of religion that the individuals themselves have often pictured the pressure before which they thus gave way in a distinctly religious form. The Crusaders believed that they felt God present in the midst of them, enjoining them to go to the conquest of the Holy Land; Joan of Arc believed that she obeyed celestial voices.

But it is not only in exceptional circumstances that this stimulating action of society makes itself felt; there is not, so to speak, a moment in our lives when some current of energy does not come to us from without. The man who has done his duty finds, in the manifestations of every sort expressing the sympathy, esteem or affection which his fellows have for him, a feeling of comfort, of which he does not ordinarily take account, but which sustains him, none the less. The sentiments which society has for him raise the sentiments which he has for himself. Because he is in moral harmony with his comrades, he has more confidence, courage and boldness in action, just like the believer who thinks that he feels the regard of his god turned graciously towards him. It thus produces, as it were, a perpetual sustenance of our moral nature. Since this varies with a multitude of external circumstances, as our relations with the groups about us are more or less active and as these groups themselves vary, we cannot fail to feel that this moral support depends upon an external cause; but we do not perceive where this cause is nor what it is. So we ordinarily think of it under the form of a moral power which, though immanent in us, represents within us something not ourselves: this is the moral conscience, of which, by the way, men have never made even a slightly distinct representation except by the aid of religious symbols.

In addition to these free forces which are constantly coming to renew our own, there are others which are fixed in the methods and traditions which we employ. We speak a language that we did not make; we use instruments that we did not invent; we invoke rights that we did not found; a treasury of knowledge is transmitted to each generation that it did not gather itself, etc. It is to society that we owe these varied benefits of civilization, and if we do not ordinarily see the source from which we get them, we at least know that they are not our own work. Now it is these things that give man his own place among things; a man is a man only because he is civilized. So he could not escape the feeling that outside of him there are active causes from which he gets the characteristic attributes of his nature and which, as benevolent powers, assist him, protect him and assure him of a privileged fate. And of course he must attribute to these powers a dignity corresponding to the great value of the good things he attributes to them.

Thus the environment in which we live seems to us to be peopled with forces that are at once imperious and helpful, august and gracious, and with which we have relations. Since they exercise over us a pressure of which we are conscious, we are forced to localize them outside ourselves, just as we do for the objective causes of our sensations. But the sentiments which they inspire in us differ in nature from those which we have for simple visible objects. As long as these latter are reduced to their empirical characteristics as shown in ordinary experience, and as long as the religious imagination has not metamorphosed them, we entertain for them no feeling which resembles respect, and they contain within them nothing that is able to raise us outside ourselves. Therefore, the representations which express them appear to us to be very different from those aroused in us by collective influences. The two form two distinct and separate mental states in our consciousness, just as do the two forms of life to which they correspond. Consequently, we get the impression that we are in relations with two distinct sorts of reality and that a sharply drawn line of demarcation separates them from each other: on the one hand is the world of profane things, on the other, that of sacred things.

Also, in the present day just as much as in the past, we see society constantly creating sacred things out of ordinary ones. If it happens to fall in love with a man and if it thinks it has found in him the principal aspirations that move it, as well as the means of satisfying them, this man will be raised above the others and, as it were, deified. Opinion will invest him with a majesty exactly analogous to that protecting the gods. This is what has happened to so many sovereigns in whom their age had faith: if they were not made gods, they were at least regarded as direct representatives of the deity. And the fact that it is society alone which is the author of these varieties of apotheosis, is evident since it frequently chances to consecrate men thus who have no right to it from their own merit. The simple deference inspired by men invested with high social functions is not different in nature from religious respect. It is expressed by the same movements: a man keeps at a distance from a high personage; he approaches him only with precautions; in conversing with him, he uses other gestures and language than those used with ordinary mortals. The sentiment felt on these occasions is so closely related to the religious sentiment that many peoples have confounded the two. In order to explain the consideration accorded to princes, nobles and political chiefs, a sacred character has been attributed to them. In Melanesia and Polynesia, for example, it is said that an influential man has *mana*, and that his influence is due to this *mana*. However, it is evident that his situation is due solely to the importance attributed to him by public opinion. Thus the moral power conferred by opinion and that with which sacred beings are invested are at bottom of a single origin and made up of the same elements. That is why a single word is able to designate the two.

In addition to men, society also consecrates things, especially ideas. If a belief is unanimously shared by a people, then, for the reason which we pointed out above, it is forbidden to touch it, that is to say, to deny it or to contest it. Now the prohibition of criticism is an interdiction like the others and proves the presence of something sacred. Even to-day, howsoever great may be the liberty which we accord to others, a man who should totally deny progress or ridicule the human ideal to which modern societies are attached, would produce the effect of a sacrilege. There is at least one principle which those the most devoted to the free examination of everything tend to place above discussion and to regard as untouchable, that is to say, as sacred: this is the very principle of free examination.

This aptitude of society for setting itself up as a god or for creating gods was never more apparent than during the first years of the French Revolution. At this time, in fact, under the influence of the general enthusiasm, things purely laïcal by nature were transformed by public opinion into sacred things: these were the Fatherland, Liberty, Reason. A religion tended to become established which had its dogmas, symbols, altars and feasts. It was to these spontaneous aspirations that the cult of Reason and the Supreme Being attempted to give a sort of official satisfaction. It is true that this religious renovation had only an ephemeral duration. But that was because the patriotic enthusiasm which at first transported the masses soon relaxed. The cause being gone, the effect could not remain. But this experiment, though short-lived, keeps all its sociological interest. It remains true that in one determined case we have seen society and its essential ideas become, directly and with no transfiguration of any sort, the object of a veritable cult.

All these facts allow us to catch glimpses of how the clan was able to awaken within its members the idea that outside of them there exist forces which dominate them and at the same time sustain them, that is to say in fine, religious forces: it is because there is no society with which the primitive is more directly and closely connected. The bonds uniting him to the tribe are much more lax and more feebly felt. Although this is not at all strange or foreign to him, it is with the people of his own clan that he has the greatest number of things in common; it is the action of this group that he feels the most directly; so it is this also which, in preference to all others, should express itself in religious symbols.

But this first explanation has been too general, for it is applicable to every sort of society indifferently, and consequently to every sort of religion. Let us attempt to determine exactly what form this collective action takes in the clan and how it arouses the sensation of sacredness there. For there is no place where it is more easily observable or more apparent in its results.

The life of the Australian societies passes alternately through two distinct phases. Sometimes the population is broken up into little groups who wander about independently of one another, in their various occupations; each family lives by itself, hunting and fishing, and in a word, trying to procure its indispensable food by all the means in its power. Sometimes, on the contrary, the population concentrates and gathers at determined points for a length of time varying from several days to several months. This concentration takes place when a clan or a part of the tribe is summoned to the gathering, and on this occasion they celebrate a religious ceremony, or else hold what is called a corrobbori in the usual ethnological language.

These two phases are contrasted with each other in the sharpest way. In the first, economic activity is the preponderating one, and it is generally of a very mediocre intensity. Gathering the grains or herbs that are necessary for food, or hunting and fishing are not occupations to awaken very lively passions. The dispersed condition in which the society finds itself results in making its life uniform, languishing and dull. But when a corrobbori takes place, everything changes. Since the emotional and passional faculties of the primitive are only imperfectly placed under the control of his reason and will, he easily loses control of himself. Any event of some importance puts him quite outside himself. Does he receive good news? There are at once transports of enthusiasm. In the contrary conditions, he is to be seen running here and there like a madman, giving himself up to all sorts of immoderate movements, crying, shrieking, rolling in the dust, throwing it in every direction, biting himself, brandishing his arms in a furious manner, and so on. The very fact of the concentration acts as an exceptionally powerful stimulant. When they are once come together, a sort of electricity is formed by their collecting which quickly transports them to an extraordinary degree of exaltation. Every sentiment expressed finds a place without resistance in all the minds, which are very open to outside impressions; each re-echoes the others, and is re-echoed by the others. The initial impulse thus proceeds, growing as it goes, as an avalanche grows in its advance. And as such active passions so free from all control could not fail to burst out, on every side one sees nothing but violent gestures, cries, veritable howls, and deafening noises of every sort, which aid in intensifying still more the state of mind which they manifest. And since a collective sentiment cannot express itself collectively except on the condition of observing a certain order permitting co-operation and movements in unison, these gestures and cries naturally tend to become rhythmic and regular; hence come songs and dances. But in taking a more regular form, they lose nothing of their natural violence; a regulated tumult remains tumult. The human voice is not sufficient for the task; it is reinforced by means of artificial processes: boomerangs are beaten against each other; bull-roarers are whirled. It is probable that these instruments, the use of which is so general in the Australian religious ceremonies, are used primarily to express in a more adequate fashion the agitation felt. But while they express it, they also strengthen it. This effervescence often reaches such a point that it causes unheard-of actions. The passions released are of such an impetuosity that they can be restrained by nothing. They are so far removed from their ordinary conditions of life, and they are so thoroughly conscious of it, that they feel that they must set themselves outside of and above their ordinary morals. The sexes unite contrarily to the rules governing sexual relations. Men exchange wives with each other. Sometimes even incestuous unions, which in normal times are thought abominable and are severely punished, are now contracted openly and with impunity. If we add to all this that the ceremonies generally take place at night in a darkness pierced here and there by the light of fires, we can easily imagine what effect such scenes ought to produce on the minds of those who participate. They produce such a violent super-excitation of the whole physical and mental life that it cannot be supported very long: the actor taking the principal part finally falls exhausted on the ground.

.   .   .

One can readily conceive how, when arrived at this state of exaltation, a man does not recognize himself any longer. Feeling himself dominated and carried away by some sort of an external power which makes him think and act differently than in normal times, he naturally has the impression of being himself no longer. It seems to him that he has become a new being: the decorations he puts on and the masks that cover his face and figure materially in this interior transformation, and to a still greater extent, they aid in determining its nature. And as at the same time all his companions feel themselves transformed in the same way and express this sentiment by their cries, their gestures and their general attitude, everything is just as though he really were transported into a special world, entirely different from the one where he ordinarily lives, and into an environment filled with exceptionally intense forces that take hold of him and metamorphose him. How could such experiences as these, especially when they are repeated every day for weeks, fail to leave in him the conviction that there really exist two heterogeneous and mutually incomparable worlds? One is that where his daily life drags wearily along; but he cannot penetrate into the other without at once entering into relations with extraordinary powers that excite him to the point of frenzy. The first is the profane world, the second, that of sacred things.

So it is in the midst of these effervescent social environments and out of this effervescence itself that the religious idea seems to be born. The theory that this is really its origin is confirmed by the fact that in Australia the really religious activity is almost entirely confined to the moments when these assemblies are held. To be sure, there is no people among whom the great solemnities of the cult are not more or less periodic; but in the more advanced societies, there is not, so to speak, a day when some prayer or offering is not addressed to the gods and some ritual act is not performed. But in Australia, on the contrary, apart from the celebrations of the clan and tribe, the time is nearly all filled with lay and profane occupations. Of course there are prohibitions that should be and are preserved even during these periods of temporal activity; it is never permissible to kill or eat freely of the totemic animal, at least in those parts where the interdiction has retained its original vigour; but almost no positive rites are then celebrated, and there are no ceremonies of any importance. These take place only in the midst of assembled groups. The religious life of the Australian passes through successive phases of complete lull and of superexcitation, and social life oscillates in the same rhythm. This puts clearly into evidence the bond uniting them to one another, but among the peoples called civilized, the relative continuity of the two blurs their relations. It might even be asked whether the violence of this contrast was not necessary to disengage the feeling of sacredness in its first form. By concentrating itself almost entirely in certain determined moments, the collective life has been able to attain its greatest intensity and efficacy, and consequently to give men a more active sentiment of the double existence they lead and of the double nature in which they participate.

But the explanation is still incomplete. We have shown how the clan, by the manner in which it acts upon its members, awakens within them the idea of external forces which dominate them and exalt them; but we must still demand how it happens that these forces are thought of under the form of totems, that is to say, in the shape of an animal or plant.

It is because this animal or plant has given its name to the clan and serves it as emblem. In fact, it is a well-known law that the sentiments aroused in us by something spontaneously attach themselves to the symbol which represents them. For us, black is a sign of mourning; it also suggests sad impressions and ideas. This transference of sentiments comes simply from the fact that the idea of a thing and the idea of its symbol are closely united in our minds; the result is that the emotions provoked by the one extend contagiously to the other. But this contagion, which takes place in every case to a certain degree, is much more complete and more marked when the symbol is something simple, definite and easily representable, while the thing itself, owing to its dimensions, the number of its parts and the complexity of their arrangement, is difficult to hold in the mind. For we are unable to consider an abstract entity, which we can represent only laboriously and confusedly, the source of the strong sentiments which we feel. We cannot explain them to ourselves except by connecting them to some concrete object of whose reality we are vividly aware. Then if the thing itself does not fulfil this condition, it cannot serve as the accepted basis of the sentiments felt, even though it may be what really aroused them. Then some sign takes it place; it is to this that we connect the emotions it excites. It is this which is loved, feared, respected; it is to this that we are grateful; it is for this that we sacrifice ourselves. The soldier who dies for his flag, dies for his country; but as a matter of fact, in his own consciousness, it is the flag that has the first place. It sometimes happens that this even directly determines action. Whether one isolated standard remains in the hands of the enemy or not does not determine the fate of the country, yet the soldier allows himself to be killed to regain it. He loses sight of the fact that the flag is only a sign, and that it has no value in itself, but only brings to mind the reality that it represents; it is treated as if it were this reality itself.

Now the totem is the flag of the clan. It is therefore natural that the impressions aroused by the clan in individual minds—impressions of dependence and of increased vitality—should fix themselves to the idea of the totem rather than that of the clan: for the clan is too complex a reality to be represented clearly in all its complex unity by such rudimentary intelligences. More than that, the primitive does not even see that these impressions come to him from the group. He does not know that the coming together of a number of men associated in the same life results in disengaging new energies, which transform each of them. All that he knows is that he is raised above himself and that he sees a different life from the one he ordinarily leads. However, he must connect these sensations to some external object as their cause. Now what does he see about him? On every side those things which appeal to his senses and strike his imagination are the numerous images of the totem. They are the waninga and the nurtunja, which are symbols of the sacred being. They are churinga and bull-roarers, upon which are generally carved combinations of lines having the same significance. They are the decorations covering the different parts of his body, which are totemic marks. How could this image, repeated everywhere and in all sorts of forms, fail to stand out with exceptional relief in his mind? Placed thus in the centre of the scene, it becomes representative. The sentiments experienced fix themselves upon it, for it is the only concrete object upon which they can fix themselves. It continues to bring them to mind and to evoke them even after the assembly has dissolved, for it survives the assembly, being carved upon the instruments of the cult, upon the sides of rocks, upon bucklers, etc. By it, the emotions experienced are perpetually sustained and revived. Everything happens just as if they inspired them directly. It is still more natural to attribute them to it for, since they are common to the group, they can be associated only with something that is equally common to all. Now the totemic emblem is the only thing satisfying this condition. By definition, it is common to all. During the ceremony, it is the centre of all regards. While generations change, it remains the same; it is the permanent element of the social life. So it is from it that those mysterious forces seem to emanate with which men feel that they are related, and thus they have been led to represent these forces under the form of the animate or inanimate being whose name the clan bears.

In fact, if left to themselves, individual consciousnesses are closed to each other; they can communicate only by means of signs which express their internal states. If the communication established between them is to become a real communion, that is to say, a fusion of all particular sentiments into one common sentiment, the signs expressing them must themselves be fused into one single and unique resultant. It is the appearance of this that informs individuals that they are in harmony and makes them conscious of their moral unity. It is by uttering the same cry, pronouncing the same word, or performing the same gesture in regard to some object that they become and feel themselves to be in unison. It is true that individual representations also cause reactions in the organism that are not without importance; however, they can be thought of apart from these physical reactions which accompany them or follow them, but which do not constitute them. But it is quite another matter with collective representations. They presuppose that minds act and react upon one another; they are the product of these actions and reactions which are themselves possible only through material intermediaries. These latter do not confine themselves to revealing the mental state with which they are associated; they aid in creating it. Individual minds cannot come in contact and communicate with each other except by coming out of themselves; but they cannot do this except by movements. So it is the homogeneity of these movements that gives the group consciousness of itself and consequently

makes it exist. When this homogeneity is once established and these movements have once taken a stereotyped form, they serve to symbolize the corresponding representations. But they symbolize them only because they have
aided in forming them.

Moreover, without symbols, social sentiments could have only a precarious
existence. Though very strong as long as men are together and influence each
other reciprocally, they exist only in the form of recollections after the assembly
has ended, and when left to themselves, these become feebler and feebler; for
since the group is now no longer present and active, individual temperaments
easily regain the upper hand. The violent passions which may have been released in the heart of a crowd fall away and are extinguished when this is
dissolved, and men ask themselves with astonishment how they could ever have
been so carried away from their normal character. But if the movements by
which these sentiments are expressed are connected with something that en-
dures, the sentiments themselves become more durable. These other things are
constantly bringing them to mind and arousing them; it is as though the cause
which excited them in the first place continued to act. Thus these systems of
emblems, which are necessary if society is to become conscious of itself, are no
less indispensable for assuring the continuation of this consciousness.

So we must refrain from regarding these symbols as simple artifices, as sorts
of labels attached to representations already made, in order to make them
more manageable: they are an integral part of them. Even the fact that collective sentiments are thus attached to things completely foreign to them is not
purely conventional: it illustrates under a conventional form a real characteristic of social facts, that is, their transcendence over individual minds. In fact, it
is known that social phenomena are born, not in individuals, but in the
group. Whatever part we may take in their origin, each of us receives them
from without. So when we represent them to ourselves as emanating from a
material object, we do not completely misunderstand their nature. Of course
they do not come from the specific thing to which we connect them, but
nevertheless, it is true that their origin is outside of us. If the moral force
sustaining the believer does not come from the idol he adores or the emblem
he venerates, still it is from outside of him, as he is well aware. The objectivity
of its symbol only translates its externalness.

Thus social life, in all its aspects and in every period of its history, is made
possible only by a vast symbolism. The material emblems and figurative representations with which we are more especially concerned in our present study,
are one form of this; but there are many others. Collective sentiments can just
as well become incarnate in persons or formulæ: some formulæ are flags,
while there are persons, either real or mythical, who are symbols.

The Circulation of Sentiments, Magic and Money
[1906–1934]

HENRI HUBERT AND MARCEL MAUSS

• In the Durkheimian tradition, society and its ritual density charge individuals with their emotional energies and ideas. But how does the individual fit into this? Henri Hubert and Marcel Mauss set out to show how the individual can act alone, independent of society or even against it. In tribal societies, the ritual presence of society is particularly strong; if individual forces can be found even there, their inner power should be revealed most sharply. Hubert and Mauss find the key to individualism in magic, a private appropriation of an emotional force that is, nevertheless, social in its origins. And by a strange dialectic, this appropriation is the beginning of an economy of individual exchanges. For it is magically charged objects (which is to say, those charged with social excitement and belief) that are the early form of money. Even today the money economy is ultimately a circulation of emotions of confidence, of payoffs expected from other people in the future. "J'attends," says Mauss. "I await, I expect: that is the definition itself of all actions of a collective nature." It is more fundamental than the expressions "constraint," "force," and "authority," which are its superficial forms.

There exists a considerable group of religious phenomena in which the double character of rites and beliefs—as both sacred and social—does not appear at first glance. This is magic. In order to generalize the results of our work on sacrifice [Hubert and Mauss, 1899] and also to verify them, we needed to assure ourselves that magic does not constitute an exception. Now magic presents us with an ensemble of rituals as efficacious as sacrifice. But they lack the formal adherence of society. They are practiced outside of society, and society keeps itself at a distance from them. Even more, sacrileges are impi-

From Henri Hubert and Marcel Mauss, "Introduction a l'analyse de quelques phénomènes religieux," *Revue de l'histoire des religions*, 58 (1906); Marcel Mauss, "Les Origins de la Notion de Monnaie," *Anthropologie* 25 (1914); Marcel Mauss, "Intervention a la suite d'une communication de Francois Simiand, 'La monnaie, realité sociale,' " *Annales Sociologiques* serie D, (1934). Translated by Randall Collins. I have omitted citations to Hubert and Mauss's anthropological sources and to most of their polemical opponents.

ous, or simply secular and technical, and lack at first glance the sacred character of the sacrifice. In magic there are also representations, from those of
gods and spirits to those of qualities and causes, that are invested with a
certitude equal to that of religious representations; there are myths whose
simple recitation acts like a charm [Hubert and Mauss, 1904] and notions like
those of nature, substance, force, *physis* and *dynamis*, whose merit was so
little contested that they were admitted by the sciences and technologies.
Nevertheless, neither these myths nor these abstract representations, whose
practical value is so high, are explicitly the object of the unanimous and
necessary accord of a society. And, finally, no more than the rites of magic do
these notions and myths seem to have for a principle the notion of the sacred.
Is the efficacy of magical practices then of the same genre as the efficacy of
technologies and the certitude of its notions and myths of the same kind as the
sciences?

At the time that we were posing ourselves these questions, the mental
operations from which magic derives were taken as given like natural sophisms
of the human spirit. Associations of ideas, analogical reasonings, false applica-
tions of the principle of causality: for Frazer and Jevons, these constituted the
entire mechanism. The English school of anthropologists arrived at results
completely opposed to those toward which we have been conducting our
investigations into religion. We were thus led to revise these works. Our
inquiry has established that all elements of magic—magicians, rituals, and
magical representations—are qualified by society to enter into magic.

The memoir that we are publishing on "The Origin of Magical powers in
Australian Societies" [Mauss, 1904] has furnished precisely the proof with
details concerning the consciousness [*conscience*] of the magician himself: the
magician is a functionary of society, often instituted by it, who never finds
within himself the source of his own power. We have been reproached for
having unduly extended what we have said about corporations of magicians.
But, in reality, individual magicians are connected by magical traditions and
form associations.

The magician does not invent rituals and representations each time. The
tradition that he observes is the guarantee of the efficacy of his gestures and
the authority of his ideas. Now who says tradition says society. In the second
place, if magic is not public like sacrifices, society is no less present. If the
magician retires and hides himself, it is from society; and if it drives him away,
it is because he is not a matter of indifference to it. Society is afraid of
magicians only because of the powers that it gives them, and they do not act
against society except as armed by it.

Finally, these powers and these qualities have all the same character and proceed from the same general idea. This notion we have given the name *mana*, borrowed from the Malayo-Polynesian tongues; this is how the general idea is designated in Melanesian magic, where Codrington revealed its existence. It is at one and the same time something of a power, of a cause, of a force, of a quality and a substance, even of a milieu. The word *mana* is simultaneously noun, adjective, and verb; and it designates attributes, actions, natures and things. It is applied to the rites, the actors, the materials, and the spirits of magic, as well as to those of religion.

It follows from this that magical rites and representations have the same social character as sacrifices, and they depend on a notion identical to, or analogous with, the notion of the sacred. Moreover, we began to demonstrate that there are some magical ceremonies in which are produced phenomena of collective psychology from which the notion of *mana* arises.

Because we did not dissimulate that we knew only a few authentic examples of this notion, Jevons has reproached us with founding all of magic on a principle whose explicit existence, in our opinion, is not absolutely universal. Our additional research permits us to affirm that this notion is very widespread.

The number of societies that do not notice this expressly has become more and more restricted.

In Africa, the Bantu, that is to say, the large and densest of the African families, possesses the all but identical notion of *nkissi* (or *moquissie*, as some of the old authors say). The Ehwé, who are a good part of the Negritos, have the notion of *dzo*. From this fact we conclude that in dealing with all of Africa it is necessary to replace the notion of fetish with that of *mana*. In America, we have already noted the Iroquois *orenda*, the Algonquin *manitou*, the Sioux *wakan*, the Pueblo *xube*, and the *naual* of central Mexico. It is necessary to join to this the *nauala* of the Kwakiutl. Our hypothesis, on the kinship that connects the notion of *brahman* in Vedic India with that of *mana*, was recently accepted by Strauss. As for the number of languages where the same notion is fragmented into several expressions, it is indefinite.

But we have another response to make to Jevons' criticism. It is not indispensible that a social phenomenon should achieve verbal expression for it to exist. What one language says in one word, other languages say in several. It is not even at all necessary that they express it: the notion of cause is not explicit in the transitive verb, but it is there nevertheless.

For the existence of a certain principle of mental operations to be sure, it is necessary and sufficient that these operations cannot be explained except by it. No one has taken it into his or her head to contest the universality of the notion of the sacred, yet it would be difficult to cite a word in Sanskrit or Greek that corresponds to the *sacer* of the Latins. One says: here, pure (*med-*

hya), sacrificial (*yajñiya*), divine (*devya*), terrible (*ghora*); there, *holy* (*ieros* or *agios*), venerable (*semnos*), just (*thesmos*), respectable (*aidesimos*). And, nevertheless, hadn't the Greeks and the Hindus a very just and strong consciousness of the sacred?

We have only published part of our work on magic; what mattered to us was to finish in order to get on with our research. It is enough for us to have shown that the phenomena of magic can be explained like those of religion. As we have not yet exposed the part of our theory that concerns the rapports between magic and religion, several misunderstandings have resulted.

We were the first to formulate, in this memoir, a distinction between positive and negative rites that we took from Durkheim. Two years after our publication, Frazer reached the same distinction from his side, but he considered all taboos as the negative rites that he calls sympathetic magic. We cannot accept the honor that Thomas and after him Marrett have made us of this generalization. We believe it erroneous. We have divided magic into positive and negative; the latter embraces taboos and, in particular, sympathetic taboos. But we have not said that all taboos were negative magic. We insisted without doubt on the interdictions of magic, because, by the very fact of prohibition, they carry, better than positive rules, the mark of social intervention. We did not deny at all that there might be religious taboos and that they were of another order.

Because we had not yet delimited the relations between magic and religion, we were drawn into another quarrel by Huvelin.

Huvelin [1907] attributes a magical origin to the bonds of primitive law; for him, magic has served powerfully in the constitution of what he calls the individual law (*droit*). What magic puts at the disposal of individuals are social and religious forces. He admits it. Nevertheless, he worries about a contradiction that he perceives in the terms that we use. How can magic, being social, that is to say, according to Huvelin, obligatory, be illicit? How, being religious and because it finds its place in the law—a phenomenon of public life—can it be antireligious at the same time? That is what he asks us to explain.

But a good part of the rituals and, above all, of the sanctions, which according to Huvelin come from magic, for us are bound up with religion. No more than the infernal gods are the imprecations and the *arai* by definition magical and outside of religion. Besides, in a good number of the cases cited, the magical sanction is only optimal. Religion, as well as magic, ties up with the bonds of individual law and with a formalism of the same nature.

The misunderstanding, in sum, comes uniquely from the abusive use of the word *magic* that Huvelin still makes. Between the facts of the system of magic and the facts of the system of religion, there is not the antinomy that he represents to himself and on the subject of which he takes us to task. There is, we have said, in all rites of magic as well as of religion a same mystical force that has been at other times falsely called magical. Huvelin has not repudiated this vice of nomenclature, and that is why he makes of magic the unique source of contracts.

It is not necessary to oppose magical phenomena to religious phenomena: in the latter, there are several systems, that of religion, that of magic, and still others; for example, divination and what is called folklore form systems of religious facts comparable to the foregoing ones. This classification corresponds better to the complexity of facts and to the variability of historical relations between magic and religion. But our definition of the system of magic remains the same, and we continue to consider as belonging to it only that which, putting aside folklore, *is not part of organized cults*. By virtue of this definition, for example, the *dharna*, the juridical suicide of which Huvelin speaks, has the effect of attaining the execution of a creditor; but this belongs to different law codes, the code of Manu [ancient India: Ed.] in particular; it does not appear in any magical manual, but depends on the funeral cult and has to do with religion and not with magic.

Finally, without being obligatory, the rites of magic are, nevertheless, social. Obligation, properly speaking, is for us not the distinctive character of social things, acts, and sentiments. For us, the illicit act of magic remains social, without there being any contradiction. The act is social because it takes its form from society, and it has no reason to exist [*raison d'être*] except by relation with it. Such is the case that Huvelin cites of the sacrificer who makes a sacrifice to kill an enemy. Moreover, magic is not necessarily illicit, and, in the law, in fact, it serves the public just as well as the individual right. Thus, in the Australian tribes, threats of spells are for the elders a means to make others respect their discipline. It is not without reason that Frazer relates the powers of magicians to the powers of the king.

Certainly Huvelin is right to show that magic has aided the formation of the techniques of law, as we have supposed it has done for other techniques [Hubert and Mauss, 1904]. We are in accord with him, when he alleges that, in the law, magic has facilitated individual action. Magic has in effect furnished the individual with means to make oneself valuable in one's own eyes and in the eyes of others, or else to evade the crowd, to escape from social pressure and routine. In the shelter of magic not only have juridical audacities been possible, but also experimental initiatives. The scientists [*savants*] are sons of the magicians.

We have frequently made allusions to the role that the individual plays in magic and to the place that it grants to him. These have been considered as prudent concessions, destined to compensate for the excessive rigor of a sociological theory that seems to deny in magic the autonomy of magicians. But there was neither concession nor contradiction. Our work had precisely as its object to determine the place of the individual in magic by relation to society.

We proposed to ourselves at the beginning of our studies, above all, to comprehend institutions, that is to say, some public rules of action and of thought. In the sacrifice, the public character of the institution, collective in action and representations, is quite clear. The magic whose acts are as little public as possible furnishes us with an occasion to push further our sociological analysis. It is important, above all, to know in what measure and how these facts were social. To put it another way: What is the attitude of the individual in social phenomena? What is the part of the society in the consciousness [*conscience*] of the individual? When individuals assemble, when they conform their gestures to a ritual, their ideas to a dogma; are they moved by purely individual motives or by motives of which the presence in their consciousness [*conscience*] is only explained by the presence of society? As society is composed of individuals organically assembled, we had to look for what they bring of themselves and what they receive from it and how they receive it. We believe we have isolated this process and shown how, in magic, the individual neither thinks nor acts except directed by tradition or pushed by a collective suggestion or certainly at least by a suggestion that he gives himself under the pressure of the collectivity.

Our theory being found thus verified, even for the difficult case of magic, where the acts of the individual are as laical and personal as possible, we are quite sure of our principles concerning sacrifice, prayer, and myth. One ought not then to oppose us to ourselves if, sometimes, we talk of renowned magicians who put practices in vogue or of strong religious personalities who found sects and religions. For it is always society that speaks by their mouth, and if they have some historical interest, it is because they act upon their societies.

THE ORIGINS OF THE NOTION OF MONEY

Money is not at all a material and physical fact, but essentially a social fact; its value is that of its power of purchase and the measure of confidence that one has in it. It is of the origin of a notion, an institution, a faith, that we are speaking.

It is not a question of showing an origin, that is to say, an absolute commencement, a birth so to speak out of nothing. Contrary to the general opinion, you will see that, in effect, it is not certain that there have been, among the societies that we know or that we can represent to ourselves by hypothesis, any that were completely unprovided with notions at least analogous to what we designate in practice today under the name of money. Hence we are not looking here for how humanity suddenly hit on the idea of money, to which it had previously been a stranger. We are looking for the most primitive, the most simple, to say it better, the most elementary form, under which one may fancy that the notion of money has presented itself in the lowest societies that we know.

I was working, about four years ago on the beautiful documents that the German missionaries to Togo have published on the Ehwé languages and nations of that region. I was not at all preoccupied at that moment with the question of the origins of money. On this subject I knew only the excellent little book of Schurtz, full of facts if not of ideas. And even if I have had to preoccupy myself with the definition of economic phenomena, I had never made these questions a particular object of my researches.

It was in reading these Ehwé documents, in handling the texts translated by Spieth and the dictionary of Westermann that several chance remarks furnished me with the hypothesis that I am going to present.

I was studying in particular the notion of *dzo*, equivalent to that of *mana*, which is that of magical power, substances, and actions among the Ehwé. And among the derivates of the radical *dzo*, I found in Westermann's dictionary, the word *dzonu* (*Zauberding*), magical thing. "All sorts of pearls or things in the form of a pearl, and so on." That is one of the names of the cowrie shells that are so much utilized in the magic and the religion of the Negro nations in general.

Around this fact, other facts crystallized very quickly and formed a sort of system. Here are some that came together as if by themselves.

The notion of *mana* in Melanesia is directly connected to the notion of money. At the Banks Isles and at Santa Cruz, one calls *rongo* (sacred red) the shell money that elsewhere carries the name of *diwarra*.

Another example of the notion of magical-religious power is the notion of *manitou* (more exactly *manido*) among the Algonquins. Now Father Thavenet says textually that the pearls of the traders were for the Algonquins the scales of a *manitou* fish.

Elsewhere the notion of money is allied to a more precise notion of the sacred. In New Guinea, as in the Bismark archipelago, money kept in the men's houses carries the title of *tambu*. On this point there is an old work of Schurtz.

Elsewhere it is more neatly connected with the notion of the talisman. That is the case in particular in the tribes of Northwest America, and especially among the Kwakiutl, where the name of *logwa* talisman, supernatural being and object, was the true name of the clans' paraphernalia, emblazoned blankets and coppers, a veritable money used in the course of the potlatches, a series of exchanges from clan to clan. Now the primitive sense of the word *logwa* is connected to a root *log*, which Boas translated as supernatural power.

In all these cases, the religious and magical character of money was strongly marked, and in a number of populations the notion of money was expressly attached through its name to that of magic power.

Since then we have followed our research, and we have hardly found any society, sufficiently close to its origins, where the cult and the magic of stones, of shells, and of precious metals did not give a true value to these objects. The religious uses of gold in antiquity, the lapidaries that made the tour of the civilizations of the ancient world, the name of the pearl in Arabic, *baraka* (benediction = good *mana*), all these facts crowd on us and are too well known for us to insist on them.

But let us descend lower in the scale of societies. For a long time we had been struck by the importance of crystals and, in particular, crystals of quartz in a very large number of societies either extremely primitive or highly civilized. We had already drawn attention to the facts that concern the acquisition of crystals by the Australian magicians [Mauss, 1904]. Since then we have found confirmation of our hypothesis, in a very bad book, in the account, very old to be sure, of an encounter between an old sorceress and a lieutenant of an English vessel. This gives the reason why the primitive imagination was so impressed by the fact that crystals decompose light: that this water passed through fire and become solid and cold is one of the first mysteries that humankind has recognized. We speak of it ourselves, in our century, like the old sorceress of Bas Murray.

But let us disregard this anecdote and this hypothesis. Isn't it striking that the myth of quartz, of the mountain of quartz as the source of talismans, is found in Northwest America almost in the equivalent terms that one finds in Australia?

Moreover, we have in Australia not only facts that are equivalent to those of an order that is purely magical and religious, but also to facts that are economic. Besides, the commerce in these stones of quartz and other talismans is as well attested as their value. Thus, among the Aruntas, Spencer and Gillen have established the use of the *lonka-lonka*, large shells procured from the Gulf of Carpentaria, and from which thunder is considered to have descended. The word *lonka-lonka* is, moreover, a word of the mixed native-European dialect and means "far, far."

An even more remarkable fact is that in these same tribes, it is not only these magical talismans that are objects of commerce, but even the sacred emblems of individuals, the *churinga*, are objects of exchange. We have the proof that it is necessary to see not only religious facts but also economic facts in the pilgrimages of which Spencer and Gillen have given us such lively descriptions, with their exchange and commerce of these totemic emblems; these visits involve numerous exchanges of gifts: food, enjoyment of women, and so on, or presents made for the occasion. But there is also another testimony than that of Spencer and Gillen, namely, that of Eylmann, who says expressly and without the shadow of a preconceived idea that the *churinga*, the sacred objects (which is the sense of the word), serve as a measure of value in these tribes. He tells an anecdote in which his guides, originating from very distant nations, told him spontaneously that this was "the money of the blacks."

That is perhaps the angle from which one can imagine the primitive forms of the notion of money. Money—whatever definition one adopts—is a value on display that is also a use value that is not fungible, that is permanent and transmissible, that is able to be the object of transactions and usages without deteriorating, but that can be the means to procure other values that are fungible, transitory, of consumption, and of gifts. Now the talisman and its possessor have, according to us, very early, without doubt since the most primitive societies, played this role of objects equally craved by all and of which the possession conferred on their holder a power that easily became a power of purchasing.

But, beyond this, isn't there something in this that derives from the nature of societies? Let us take an example. The word *mana* in the Malayo-Polynesian languages designates not only the power of magical substances and acts, but also the authority of humans. It designates just as well precious objects, the talismans of the tribe, which were the object of such exchanges, battles, and inheritances as are known. There is nothing irrational about this, if we know how to represent to ourselves the spirit in which these institutions have functioned. Isn't the purchasing power of money natural when it is attached to a talisman that can even constrain the subordinates of chiefs and the clients of magicians to make the presents that they demand? And, inversely, isn't it necessary, once the notion of riches intervened in however vague a form, that the riches of the chief and the magician reside, above all, in the emblems that incarnate their magic powers, in a word their authority, or that symbolize the force of the clan?

Schurtz very astutely remarks elsewhere, following Kubary, who has made observations in the Palaos Islands, that money was not primitively employed to acquire the means of consumption, but to acquire things of luxury and those of authority over people. The purchasing power of primitive money is, above all, according to us, the prestige that the talisman confers on whoever possesses it and that can be used to command others.

But isn't that a sentiment that is still very lively among ourselves? And the true faith that we nourish vis-à-vis gold and all the values that flow from its estimation, isn't this in large part the confidence that we have in its power? Doesn't the essence of faith in the value of gold reside in the belief that we can obtain, thanks to it, presents from our contemporaries—in goods or in services—that the state of the market permits us to exact?

This magical power of money, this prestige grows with the exchanges it undergoes. The famous "wampum" of the Iroquois circulated in the interior of the Five Nations and inside the phratries and among the clans. Now, the more it circulated, either because each collectivity added a new figure of pearls, or even without anyone augmenting the number of figures, the more price it acquired. This is the same fact that Malinowsky exposed apropos of the *kula* commerce in the Trobriand islands. These exotic moneys took on more value the more they circulated; in the same fashion that a family jewel augments its value with each generation, in the same fashion a large *écu* [an old French coin: Ed.]—as it is an *écu*, a veritable buckler in the form of an emblaisoned escutcheon—requires a large potlatch each time that it changes hands.

For after all, what we have arrived at is the importance of the notion of awaiting, of anticipation, which is precisely one of the forms of collective thought. Among ourselves, in society, we have to await each other for this or that result; that is the essential form of the community. Formerly we have been able to use the expressions constraint, force, authority, and they have their value; but this notion of collective awaiting is in my opinion one of the fundamental notions on which we ought to work. I know no other notion that generates the law and the economy: "I expect," "I await" [*J'attends*]: that is the definition itself of all actions of a collective nature. It is at the origin of theology: God will hear—I do not say will grant—my prayer.

The infractions of these collective expectations are measured for example by upsets in the economic realm, panics, social upheavals, and so forth.

Expectations, emotions, whims all quantify themselves. A panic on the Bourse [Paris stock exchange: Ed.] is quantified, the proof being the difference of prices. I would even add an example relating to the functioning of a tribe of the Belgian Congo in which by means of so many iron spearpoints, which represent so many heads of cattle, I can purchase a woman in order to have so many children. There the notion of quantification is this understanding that binds me to my mother-in-law by the most extraordinary proceedings—because, in effect, she is a horrible creditor. Expectations, even in that case, are quantified. The Bergsonian idea of the total difference between quantity and quality is not in Aristotle—Aristotle said that quality has degrees; consequently it is quantified; it is precisly this fundamental idea that we have.

What underlies the state of panic in which we live [France in the 1930s was in the midst of a governmental and economic crisis: Ed.] and which, perhaps due to an economic phenomenon or perhaps to something else—I don't know what—verges on abolishing expectations? It is measured by all sorts of things: by the fact that one doesn't travel; by the fact that one doesn't undertake enterprises, not even in works of sociology.

REFERENCES

Hubert, Henri, and Marcel Mauss. "Essai sur la nature et la fonction du sacrifice." *Année Sociologique*, 2 (1899), pp. 2–138.
———. 1904. "Esquisse d'une théorie génerale de la magie." *Année Sociologique* 7 (1904).
Huvelin, P. "Magie et droit individuel." *Année Sociologique* 10 (1907), pp. 1–47.
Mauss, Marcel. "L'origine des pouvoirs magiques dans les sociétés australiennes." Paris: Ecole Pratique des Hautes Études, 1904.

Kinship as Sexual Property Exchange [1949]

CLAUDE LÉVI-STRAUSS

• *The central argument of Claude Lévi-Strauss's great theory of kinship is diffusely spread through the 500 pages of* The Elementary Structures of Kinship (1949) *and is hard to follow or excerpt. The following analytical summary gives its main points, stressing especially its Maussian aspect and its points of linkage with the conflict tradition.*

The *Elementary Structures of Kinship* by no means gives an idealized picture of primitive social life. There are struggles for food, warfare and threats of violent death, quarrels, divorces, and all the other ills of human life in an imperfect world. Lévi-Strauss's view on this is as hard-nosed as the most cynical conflict theorist. The very basis of the kinship system is sexual domination. Males exert property rights over the bodies and labor of females, and exchange them with other males. Lévi-Strauss is thus the prime mover of a modern sociology of sexual stratification, as well as of alliance theory within modern treatments of kinship. To be sure, Lévi-Strauss states his position without regard for the variations in the degrees and kinds of sexual stratification across the whole range of history. But certainly his theory of alliances, augmented with a consideration of variations in other resources and motives for sexual domination, opens the way toward a more refined theory, which does not take male domination as a universal but as a condition that emerges under specific circumstances.

The purposes for which males dominate females in tribal societies are manifold. Aside from sexual gratification, there is also a struggle for food and livelihood itself; women as food providers are a major source of wealth. In the Australian desert, Lévi-Strauss remarks, the bachelor is a poor thing, a creature who barely eaks out his survival without a woman's help. The major value of women is that they determine alliances among groups. Alliances are necessary because of the constant danger of violence. Lévi-Strauss describes the way in which Australians encounter a stranger: They first ascertain his

From Randall Collins, *Sociology Since Midcentury* (New York: Academic Press, 1981), pp. 115–131. Reprinted with permission of Academic Press.

lineage and his marriage ties, because these divide friends from enemies. The man (the sexism is explicit here) without marriage ties is defenseless, thus marriages are the main means of military defense.

Lévi-Strauss continually emphasizes that exchange brings solidarity, and he distinguishes among various types of kinship exchange systems in terms of the amount of solidarity that they bring. But this is not a naïve pan-functionalist argument based on the society's demand for solidarity. Solidarity is important precisely because of the threat of conflict. It is the solidarity of various groups within the society, not of the total social order itself. It is the solidarity of warfare groups, as Lévi-Strauss explicitly remarks (1949/1969:149). Exchange is a crucial weapon of each group, and hence the object of its explicit strategizing.

Lévi-Strauss's most striking point, though, is that exchange both creates solidarity among groups and structures new conflicts among them. Exchange produces conflict itself, and not just in the obvious sense that the structure produced is a lineup of opposing alliances. Exchange also produces strains and potential conflicts within alliances. Gifts give grounds for grievances, if reciprocity is not properly lived up to. The strains in the marriage alliance system are still apparent even today, in our jokes about in-laws, and these were much more serious in societies in which the whole economic and political organization was based on such marriage connections. Many of the fights within tribal societies break out precisely over the way in which rights and gifts due from previous donations are not properly repaid (1949/1969:261). Part of this very instability is due to the fact that gifts are often used as a means of ending a conflict. A murder or an insult might be repaid by the gift of a woman, just as a truce in a feudal war could best be sealed by a diplomatic marriage (1949/1969:113). Marriage, then, is a way of containing quarrels, of keeping them from becoming more serious. This is one reason why tribal marriage ceremonies often involve competitive games or even mock fights (1949/1969:481). The ceremonial carrying-off of the bride is not a survivor of some bygone era of bride-capture, but an indicator of current realities. Lévi-Strauss quotes with approval the phrase "marriage is a socially regulated act of hostility [1949/1969:261]," and sums up his position with a telling remark: "Exchanges are peacefully resolved wars, and wars are the result of unsuccessful transactions [1949/1969:67]."

This interdependence of conflict and exchange is the structural key to historical change. As we shall see, from the existing structure of alliances, the lines of further conflicts and breakdowns of structure are predictable. History is a series of alliance structures, with their strains and conflictual transformations.

THE INCEST TABOO AS EXTERNALLY IMPOSED

The incest taboo itself, by implication, is explainable in these terms. All would agree that the incest taboo is crucial for establishing the larger, non-nuclear networks of society. But Lévi-Strauss's formulation about exchange does not leave us with the usual teleological functionalist explanation of the taboo in terms of its consequences. The logic of Lévi-Strauss's theme of the interdependence of exchange and conflict provides a sequential hypothesis for the creation of the incest taboo.

Men without daughters or sisters cannot get them within the nuclear group, and hence must go outside it to find women. Such situations must have happened often, due to sheer demographic accident. In the absence of exchange relations, raiding for women must have been a source of much warfare, even when there were no other natural scarcities due to an abundance of land. Although Lévi-Strauss does not mention it, the archaeological evidence certainly suggests that primitive humanoids killed one another quite frequently; many of the protohuman species were apparently made extinct in this way.

On the other hand, demographic change would have produced many groups with more than enough females for the men. Men in such groups would have found it advantageous to use this sexual surplus to gain alliances. Thus a gift-economy of women would have arisen. Perhaps the women were given in a purely defensive spirit: instead of being robbed and perhaps killed, better to give the plunder away. The more initiative in doing this, the more goodwill that could be created, and thus alliances would come into being. Eventually the families carrying out this strategy would become more powerful militarily than isolated nuclear families. The exogamous, alliance-making families would sooner or later drive the more traditional groups out of existence.

The incest taboo, then, is not a psychological phenomenon at all, nor is it merely a latently functional practice that first appeared by accident. The incest taboo is imposed from without: It reflects people's recognition that outsiders demand their women and will not allow them to be kept selfishly within the group. It is fear of other people that enforces the feeling that women must not become sexual property in their own families, and it is precisely conflict situations that enforce this feeling.

The theory has the merit of being testable. The larger the network of family-based alliances, the further the incest taboo—exogamy requirement extends among consanguineal relations. In a modern society with a bureaucratic state and impersonal economy, the family is no longer important for alliances; incest taboos shrink back to the minimum level of enforcement, which still requires women to be available in the general sexual marketplace. The mother–son taboo cannot be established in this way, of course, but it is easily explicable in terms of male domination: the father asserting exclusive sexual property rights over his wife against his most immediate male rival. The other incest taboos—on cousins, whole exogamous lineages and groups, and so forth—have narrowed their scope, and perhaps have also been less enforced even where they exist, as modern societies have moved further away from kinship-based economic and political organization. But the mother–son taboo survives, as the strongest and least violated prohibition, precisely because it is not based on exchange.

IDEAL STRATEGIES AND MATERIAL REALITIES

These conflicts are only the first step in human prehistory. They are followed by many more, whose contours are revealed by Lévi-Strauss. But already in the incest model, we can see a key dynamic of Lévi-Strauss's scheme. The demographic realities shift. Some of the proto-human nuclear families had no daughters, some had many. It is precisely this demographic variability that people must take into account in their social arrangements.

Lévi-Strauss has discussed this point intermittently, both in debates over his general method and throughout his writings on kinship and mythology. Lévi-Strauss has been accused of placing too much emphasis on the ideal side of kin structures. It is said that he has failed to attend to the distinction between preferential and prescriptive rules, and has ignored the empirical data of what marriages actually take place, since this data often show the rules being evaded in practice. These criticisms are misplaced.

1. Lévi-Strauss has directly replied that even if only a small percentage of marriages take place according to the kinship rules, this gives a certain tendency to the development of the social structure. Those families that do not or cannot obey the rules act essentially at random, and give rise to no sustained changes; it is those that do obey the rules that make social history (1949/1969:xxx-xxxv).

2. Furthermore, Lévi-Strauss argues that the natives themselves tend to see the rules in the same complex way that he does. Sometimes the rules are ideologies, upheld mainly as claims to prestige, not because they can always be carried out. He even remarks that the formal rules can be a kind of myth. Moreover, the natives can deliberately manipulate and change the rules. Australian tribal elders sit and discuss them at great length, devising possible changes to fit new problems. Lévi-Strauss sees such men as native intellectu-

als, producing deliberate strategies for coordinating pre-existing structures with new demographic problems and political aims (1949/1969:125). In his later reflections on his kinship theory (1962/1966:251), Lévi-Strauss remarks that he should have given even greater emphasis to this conscious creation of rules and myths.

Native intellectuals, in other words, knew what they were doing when they formulated the kinship rules. One can see this as they reformulate the rules to deal with current problems. One can thus infer that similar conscious decision-making went into formulating the earlier rules. We cannot necessarily recover the reasoning directly in the case of strategies that have been in effect for a long time. Kinship strategies are constantly in motion, contrary to the notion that tribal societies are structurally static. It is these new problems and strategies that occupy people's minds. Because of this, the older strategies that are not practically called into question are taken for granted. To focus on one thing necessarily defocuses everything else. Incest taboos would fall into that category, since they are still the fundamental basis of all other kinship alliances, but the reasoning behind them is no longer of interest. They have been thoroughly routinized for tens of thousands of generations.

3. Lévi-Strauss's accounts of the particular kinship patterns found at one point in time are frequently set in terms of their adaptations to changing demographic circumstances. From highly complicated structures, he reconstructs the sequence of changes that must have brought a particular pattern to its condition. The hypothesized causes are sometimes conflicts, sometimes demographic accidents. He mentions that some lineages die out, and that this must happen not infrequently; other groups grow large and split. Such changes have structural consequences to which the rest of the system must adjust. Even in his later work on the structure of myths, Lévi-Strauss applies the same analysis. A tribe might have had three clans, for example: bear—turtle—eagle (in this case reflecting a division among three elements: land—water—sky). If the bear clan dies out, the structural organization of the society can be re-established only by subdividing the larger of the remaining clans. The modern observer would thus find: yellow turtle—grey turtle—eagle (1962/1966:67). Lévi-Strauss comments: "Demographic evolution can shatter the structure but. . . . if the structural orientation survives the shock it has, after each upheaval, several means of reestablishing a system, which may not be identical with the earlier one but is at least formally of the same type [1962/1966:68]."

The basic process, then, is an interplay of raw demographic facts of nature with deliberate human attempts to strategically respond to them; it is this interplay that produces human history and culture. It is, in fact, by knowing this interplay that one can read the code of the myths. Lévi-Strauss remarks that it is precisely this emphasis upon material history that sets his position apart from that of Durkheim: "Although there is undoubtedly a dialectical relation between the social structure and systems of categories, the latter are not an effect or result of the former: each, at the cost of laborious mental adjustments, translates certain historical and local modalities of the relations between man and the world, which form their common substratum [1962/1966:214]."

Lévi-Strauss's full view, then, not only takes account of demographic accidents, but also builds this into the center of his model. We should add that such arguments refer not merely to demography in the narrow sense, but to the full range of conditions in which humanity interacts with the material environment, to "wars, epidemics, and famines [1962/1966:71]." Social structure is generally to be explained, as Lévi-Strauss remarks of a particular instance, "by the combined action of two forces, one of demographic origin which pushes it towards disorganization, and the other of speculative inspiration which pushes it towards a reorganization as closely as possible in line with the earlier state of affairs (1962/1966:71)." Lévi-Strauss is thus not merely paying lip-service to Marxism when he declares that the material infrastructure is basic grounds for all human action, while at the same time stating that his purpose is to contribute to the theory of superstructures. It is fully consistent with the thrust of this approach that we may broaden it further in this direction than Lévi-Strauss himself has done, to take account of variations in the abundance or scarcity of food and natural resources, and in the geographical dispersion or concentration of populations, and build an alliance theory of kinship upon a fuller treatment of these conditions.

Lévi-Strauss, then, is elaborating a Maussian theme. Women are currency in a gift exchange system which is really a system of communications. It is not, as mistakenly interpreted, a group mind talking to itself, even though Lévi-Strauss himself often gives grounds for this impression in his later works. The communications are among specific groups of allies. Mauss (1925/1962) showed that shells passing around a kula ring in symbolic ceremonies make possible mundane economic transactions within the structure of the ring; Lévi-Strauss shows that women passing around a kinship structure make possible political alliances. (One might add that this is an economic structure, too, since not only marriage payments, funeral contributions, and property inheritance pass through this network, but also many other and frequent deliveries of food and goods.) These exchanges are carried out under actual or potential threat of warfare, and its milder conflictual equivalent, the scramble for pres-

tige. Conflicts not only force exchanges, but exchanges also structure conflicts, as Mauss, too, was well aware. Exchanges can contain conflicts and
make them milder, but they also produce them in predictable ways.

From a mass of kinship data from many different societies, Lévi-Strauss has
tried to reconstruct the basic logic of such alliances and their transformations.
Although this project was left incomplete—and still remains so—it is a powerful and at least partially convincing effort. Let us look at its main outlines.

BASIC ELEMENTS: RESIDENCE AND LINEAGE

There are two basic elements of a kinship system. *Residence:* Where do the
husband, the wife, and their children live after their marriage? In the tribal
societies with which Lévi-Strauss was concerned, the main choices are patrilocal or matrilocal (with avunculocal—residence with the maternal
uncle—as a variant on the latter). *Lineage:* What group do the children
belong to? Again, for these tribes, the major choice is patrilineal or matrilineal. Bilineality is also a possibility, but an unimportant one in the
Lévi-Strauss model: not that it doesn't occur, but that nothing of structural
significance can come from it. We might note, in addition, that lineages
need not be narrow family chains in the modern sense, but can be organized
as entire clans or subclans, or subdivided into elaborate sectional systems, as
in many Australian societies.

These basic forms are by no means ideal constructs. Both are grossly behavioral and material; both in fact can be looked on as forms of property. This is
obvious in the case of lineage: In a matrilineal system, children inherit not
only their names but also their material goods from their mother's family,
while in a patrilineal system this property is inherited from the father's family.
But the children themselves are property as well: they are usable for exchange,
and hence for alliances, and matri–patrilineality tells us which family group
gets to use them as such.

Locality of residence is also a form of property: secondarily as property over
the children, but primarily as property over the wife. In a patrilocal system, the
woman goes to live with her husband and his kin. She is lost from her own
family and cut off from its support, and even her children are not her own. This
is an extreme form of male domination. In matrilocality (or its variant, avuncu-
locality), the woman stays with her own kinfolk, and the male is the one in the
midst of an alien group. Such practices take various forms: sometimes the males
only visit their wives for intercourse; sometimes they live there for a period but
later return home; sometimes the males actually move in, although this is rare

and confined to subservient relations, since it prevents a man from being with his own property in his sister's household. Although matrilocal groups are also dominated by men, the position of women within them is much stronger than in patrilocal ones. In terms of property relations, sexual property in the form of erotic access and labor service of married men from their wives is a good deal weaker in matrilocal than patrilocal arrangements.

In general, one might say that locality is sexual property as daily enacted; lineality is the long-term, macroaspect of sexual property.

On can infer from these circumstances something of the conditions under which these systems are likely to arise. Matrilocal residence is empirically rather rare. From a structural viewpoint, its rarity should not be surprising, since it is just barely one step away from an incest situation, in which no sexual trades and alliances are made at all. Matrilineality, too, is a good deal less common than patrilineality. (And in fact, both are less common statistically than bilineality.) These empirical distributions seem not to be widely known. The impression is often given in comparative surveys of social history that all societies of a primitive horticultural type are matrilineal. This is probably because, as Lévi-Strauss points out, matrilineal societies are more spectacular than patrilineal ones. They have been the subjects of some of the most famous anthropological studies, such as those of Malinowski. Why are they so dramatic? Not only because of the reversal of our familiar modern forms of kinship, but also because their atmosphere tends to be psychologically heavy, full of jealousies, divorces, conflicts, and their religious and symbolic expressions. In fact, matrilineal societies indicate a situation in which the women-giving groups do not give up very much: they strike a hard bargain in the marriage market. It is in effect a sellers' market.

If we ask, then, what causes these patterns, the answer is that matrilineal societies (and matrilocal ones as well, to the extent that we find them) are much more likely than patrilineal and patrilocal ones to exist in a situation of a high degree of warfare. More recent empirical comparisons confirm this judgment (Divale, 1975). An ecological factor also enters in: matrilineal societies are usually ones in which various exogenous groups live very close to each other, so that males are not greatly inconvenienced by their relative separation from their property. Patrilineality and patrilocality, however, fit well with situations where groups are geographically remote: the woman leaves her home once and for all, and there are few occasions for subsequent contact. Lévi-Strauss comments that these systems are best suited to creating long-distance alliances between culturally rather divergent groups (1949/1969:289).

Wars are probably both the cause and the effect of matrilineality, as the structure emerges from a situation of high distrust, and also tends to foster further quarrels. Variations in the scarcity of ecological conditions also enter into these determinations; more recent alliance theories have developed this point (e.g., Harris, 1979:81–84, 96–100).

HARMONIC AND DISHARMONIC SYSTEMS

The key structural difference, in Lévi-Strauss's scheme, is neither lineage nor residence *per se*, but their combination. Either patrilineal–patrilocal or matrilineal–matrilocal is called *harmonic*; matrilineal–patrilocal or patrilineal–matrilocal is called *disharmonic*. (In practice the second of each pair can be dropped as empirically rare or nonexistent.) In effect, this is the difference between a sexual property system dominated either by takers of wives (a buyer's market), or by the givers of wives (a seller's market). These two situations make possible quite different historical sequences.

THREE MARRIAGE STRATEGIES

Given these property situations, the native policymakers must decide on an optimum strategy for achieving family alliances. Strategies are put into practice by formulating marriage rules, be they preferential or prescribed, closely adhered to or widely violated, as discussed previously. There are three elementary sorts of marriage strategies. Most prominently, these involve cross-cousins: marriages that link a man either to his mother's or to his father's family.

Two of these strategies are asymmetrical:

• Man marries mother's brother's daughter (matrilateral cross-cousin marriage).
• Man marries father's sister's daughter (patrilateral cross-cousin marriage).

There is also a symmetrical form, in which either cross-cousin marriage is permitted. Such symmetrical systems can also work by equivalent rules, which do not specify the actual cross-cousin but someone from an equivalent place in the generational and lineage structure.

Even with the best intentions, of course, such marriages cannot always be made. There may not be any matrilateral cross-cousin in that particular generation, or there may be too many sons or daughters, or too few. All of these are historically specific contingencies through which these systems work themselves out. It is, in fact, these various contingencies, which are bound to come up over and over again across the generations, that prove the relative power of one or another type of marriage strategy.

The core of Lévi-Strauss's model is to work out the logical consequences of these different strategies.

SYMMETRICAL MARRIAGE AND RESTRICTED EXCHANGE

Symmetrical cross-cousin rules bring about a particular kind of social structure. If the rules are followed out consistently, they link the same two families together continuously, with a marriage in each direction, perhaps as often as several times in the same generation. The society is not linked together as a whole, but braided into independent and parallel strands: A⇆B C⇆D. The same result follows from other symmetrical rules that do not necessarily involve cross-cousins, such as those found in societies with dual organization, a division of the tribe into halves, quarters, eighths, and so on, with specific rules regarding preferred and prohibited marriages among members of these sections.

ASYMMETRICAL MARRIAGE AND GENERALIZED EXCHANGE

If marriage rules specify only one cross-cousin and prohibit the other, the system of exchange does not form braids but a long chain of families. The longest chain occurs if matrilateral cross-cousin marriage is consistently performed; A→B→C→D→. (Eventually the first in the chain also receives a wife by this system: →A.) This is the long cycle. It is simultaneously the most risky, in that there are many places in which the chain can be broken, either by conflict or by demographic accident. On the other hand, there is the most to gain; the widest network of alliances can be forged in this way. As we shall see, it is via this route that important historical changes occur. This form results in each lineage being linked to another, which always gives it wives but never takes any in return, and then of course to a second, to which it is wife-giver but not wife-taker. The structure is a system of permanent debts. It is out of this that the stratification of the system arises.

The other form of asymmetrical cross-cousin marriage, patrilateral, also creates chains. But in this case they are not very long ones. If followed out, each alternating generation receives a wife back for its previous gift to that particular family. The patrilateral strategy results in a discontinuous structure, with all accounts settled every second generation. Less is risked, but less is gained. It constitutes a short cycle.

WHY ONE ROUTE RATHER THAN ANOTHER?

The structural determinant of which way a system will go, Lévi-Strauss argues, is whether it is harmonic or disharmonic. *Disharmonic systems* (which are mostly of the matrilineal–patrilocal form) tend to follow the patrilateral cross-cousin strategy: they opt for a short cycle, and cut their risks. They are, of course, already in a high-conflict situation in their local relations, even within family groups themselves. This may seem sufficient reason for their unwillingness to invest in the long run. It is also possible to see a structural consequence of the patrilateral cross-cousin strategy in this situation: a man's grandchildren come back into his own descent group, and hence male line-ages can be covertly reestablished even though the official connection passes entirely through females (Harris, 1979:182). This amounts to a strategy for preserving some of the power of husbands over their own property, in a situation in which the wive's families otherwise tend to dominate. The strategy boils down to fighting for power within the family, and giving up on the possibility of long-term investments that would strengthen the position of the family as a whole.

Harmonic systems, on the other hand (mainly patrilineal–local), are much more likely to prefer the matrilateral cross-cousin strategy. For a patrilateral strategy here would not only create no more than a short cycle, but would also pass property to grandchildren back into the female's linage. The structural consequences of a patrilateral marriage strategy in a strongly male-dominated system would, paradoxically, undermine control by males (Harris, 1979:182). The matrilateral strategy, then, is much more widespread in these societies, and hence it is in these societies that long cycles of exchange are constituted. (Many patrilineal–patrilocal societies, however, especially in Africa, do not practice cross-cousin marriage at all, and hence fail to create these long alliance chains. Harmonic systems are a precondition, but not a sufficient determinant of this strategy.)

LONG-TERM CHANGES AND THE KINSHIP REVOLUTION

Which path a group starts down is fateful for the future of that society. Societies with symmetrical or short cycle exchanges produce restricted alliance patterns. A good deal of change can occur here, of course. But conflicts, demographic accidents, and environmental pressures, when they change such structures, nevertheless leave them within the orbit of restricted exchange. Particular family alliances come and go, and particular lineages or even ar-rangements of lineages appear and disappear. But the structural peculiarity of these forms is that changes are caught within the walls of a certain social type. Quarrels within a reciprocal exchange system, for example, frequently break out because of what their members think of as breaches of gift obligations. These can result in the groups breaking off contacts or going to war with each other. But the now-isolated groups can only go on to establish new alliances of the same sort with some other group (1949/1969:78–9). The very number of groups can change. Dual systems can become more complex, subdividing into further categories. Australian elders make quite elaborate policy decisions on such matters, creating new exchange rules and new subsections of their tribes to meet the political exigencies of the day. But the structures always change into another version of a restricted exchange system. Moieties may turn into eight-class systems, or sometimes eight-class systems devolve into four or two classes (1949/1969:152). Alliances are patched up, wars arranged, demographic accidents smoothed out. Much changes, but the scale of social organization—especially its form of stratification and its degree of political decentralization—stays the same.

A truly generalized exchange system, though, is unstable in a different way. Because of demographic accident, some groups will have more daughters than others, and they will be able to make more alliances. The returns on these investments take a longer time to materialize, but they are proportionately greater. A family embarked on a positive cycle as giver of wives puts increasing numbers of clients in its debt. In subsequent generations, it has more women coming in, which in turn allows it to get a demographic jump on its rivals in the next cycle. With excess claims on women, privileged families can become polygymous. Since women work, they are an increasing source of direct wealth, while the alliances that they bring make the family increasingly powerful militarily. On the other side, families that get behind in this cycle are likely to become steadily poorer, both demographically and economically. They have fewer women, and these become less desirable for other families as tokens of alliance. Marriages are made on increasingly unequal terms; poorer men marrying upper-lineage women become servitors of the powerful families, while upper-lineage men confine themselves to alliances with other powerful families. Social classes develop, and some groups may even become slaves.

As the system becomes stratified, its forms eventually break down. Exchanges are no longer substantially equal, and additional economic goods are added on as a kind of immediate recompense, through the institution of brideprice. This further exacerbates the stratifying tendencies of the system, because poorer families are less likely to be able to pay the brideprice, hence less likely to be able to produce more daughters. They fall increasingly further behind. Richer families, on the other hand, can afford to pay those prices, and hence increasingly monopolize the marriage (and the political alliance) market. The returns on this, in more daughters and more brideprices, make them richer still. Perhaps the brideprice was even deliberately instituted as a strategy by dominant families for this purpose, a kind of tax they were enforcing by their commanding position on the market.

Finally, both upper and lower classes are motivated to withdraw from the system. The lower-class families can no longer afford to make a marriage in the traditional way; they begin to withdraw among themselves and set up reciprocal exchanges with some other lineage. This at least gets wives for the men, but it seals the family's fate in the overall stratification picture. Upper-class families, on the other hand, are now embarked on an aristocratic scale of living, and on political alliances of major scope. Some are on their way to outright military and political rule. They begin to find their obligations to their lesser kin a drag on their own ambitions. They begin to make short-term alliances outside the kin network entirely, without using marriage politics. In this way, kings eventually arise. Through the feudal tendencies of an unstable system of generalized exchange, the state finally emerges.

THE STRUCTURALIST THEORY OF PREHISTORY

Lévi-Strauss thus allows us to infer the outlines of human history for the last half-million years or so, from the protohuman condition onwards through the emergence of stratified society and the state. The first major event was the development of a strategy of exogamous wife-giving, which enabled some nuclear groups to make alliances and to take an edge in the hostilities that pervaded this period. The incest taboo, as a strategy imposed by the threat of external raiding, eventually became the basis upon which more complex alliance strategies could emerge.

Subsequent history is full of a variety of kinship forms: bilateral and cognate lineages, the so-called "Crow-Omaha" types of purely negative kinship prohibitions, as well as the unilateral forms that Lévi-Strauss concentrated on. These pure unilateral forms may be statistically a minority, but if Lévi-Strauss is right, they are the ones that have an historical logic built into them. Bilateral marriage strategies, cognatic descent, and so forth all tend either to subdivide property, and hence dissipate it, or in effect to randomize and localize alliance patterns. The purer version of restricted exchange and short-cycle generalized exchange stand out with a greater structural elegance. Their histories are structurally more predictable, in that they fall within a given compass, although they are doomed to go around and around the same set of variations. Ironically, it is these pure forms that were especially locked into a kind of historyless eternity: if not strictly without histories, they made a major part of human prehistory into a sort of cyclical universe.

It is the pure form of patrilineal–patrilocal harmonic systems, then, that are the true makers of linear history. That is, they brought about the transformation of relatively egalitarian and small-scale groups into class-stratified societies and into incipient states. This emergence into modern-style history has an almost Marxian dialectic to it. This particular kind of kinship alliance system not only brought about a new society, but also broke down the very system on which it was formerly based. The long chains of matrilateral cross-cousin marriage were eventually repudiated both from below and above. The one structural path out of the cycles of purely kinship-based societies ended by overturning even the most dynamic type of kinship system itself. The first step was to institute a strategy that turned from a series of balanced exchanges to a set of imbalanced exchanges. The imbalanced system finally undermined kinship exchange itself. In its place emerged nonexchange domination: the state.

Is this the only way the state could, or did, come about? We are not sure. Certainly there are competing theories: conquest, hydraulic economies, incipient priesthoods, big-man redistribution systems. The evidence is not really in yet. The Lévi-Strauss theory has mainly been debated in terms of specialized anthropological interests in kinship, and the requisite cross-societal comparisons have not been produced. On the other hand, the rival theories have so far been formulated in general terms, and have not come to grips with the social realities of daily human interaction, and with human strategizing, the way Lévi-Strauss's model does. Surely conquest was often involved in the rise of the states that we know about. But how did the conquerors become organized into a sufficiently large and permanent group to rule, rather than to raid, and for that matter to win, rather than to chip away piecemeal? Again, how did a community become organized to be able to carry out irrigation projects? How could priesthoods break old bonds of religious allegiance and establish new ones? Where did the big man get the wealth to redistribute? Kinship politics was more than likely involved in all of these, and a full model would certainly have to be built up around a structural theory of alliances.

On the face of it, the Lévi-Strauss argument is supported by the existing distribution of kinship structures, which were founded around the world in historical times. Patrilineal–patrilocal systems are found across the major state-building areas of China, India, the Middle East, and Europe. (Exceptions within these areas may help prove the case: If these are the groups that failed to establish strong stratified structures, they would appear to have been held back by their kinship structure.) On the other side, the weakness of state formation in Africa, North America, and Australia fits the model in that these were the areas of bilateral marriage strategies or restricted or randomized exchange systems.

Certainly we know of societies within these large areas that do not follow the hypothesized kinship–state linkage. There were states in central and west Africa, or example, or the Mexican and Andean states, or the North American Indian confederations, that arose in response to European incursions. But a closer look at these may reveal kinship–alliance patterns that approximate those given in the structuralist model. This may be especially likely if we can break that model into a series of variations, predicting partial and weak stratifying tendencies as well as stronger ones. It is also possible, of course, that we will find evidence for other, nonkinship factors, which must be entered into a theory of the state. We may also have to make variant paths within a kinship–alliance theory that have not yet been envisioned: the patrilateral cross-cousin strategy within a harmonic system may not be the only one which has long-term structural consequences. In any case, this line of analysis can only bring an enrichment of our understanding.

A CONTEMPORARY PAYOFF

Finally, we might ask: Why should sociologists be interested in this? One answer is that sociology and anthropology are really the same discipline, and that all of human history and all types of human societies come into the purview of a science of society. Another answer is that the tide of structuralism now washing over American sociology from the other side of the Atlantic deserves a critical analysis aimed at finding its most valuable elements. But most essentially, I would suggest, there is a theoretical lesson in Lévi-Strauss's effort to explain the long-term patterns of change in "historyless" tribal societies.

Formalized kinship networks are no longer important in modern society, but alliances certainly are. Lévi-Strauss's structuralist version of exchange theory appears a much more promising route to understanding this phenomenon than the individual-level, utilitarian style of exchange theory we have seen so far of the type of Homans, Blau, et al. Neoclassical economics shares the same utilitarian assumptions, and ignores the structural–network side of theory, which is precisely the strength of the Durkheim–Mauss–Lévi-Strauss tradition. The merit of Lévi-Strauss's version is that it concentrates on the structures resulting from exchange, not just the form of bargaining at the individual level, and that it systematically accounts for the histories of various kinds of structures, instead of reducing everything structurally to one ideally open market.

The major elements in Lévi-Strauss, in fact, give us the range of types of economic systems. Restricted exchange is a barter system, in which little is risked, but little gained, while social structure remains fragmented and localized. The generalized exchange strategy works on extending credit, betting on getting it back manyfold in the long run. It is a direct parallel to Schumpeter's definition of capitalism: enterprise carried out with borrowed money. The particular formulations of Lévi-Strauss regarding kinship systems may not be precisely the analogies we need to solve problems in other sociological fields. But Lévi-Strauss's concepts, taken more abstractly, may provide just the right building blocks. We find then in his model, property in both a short-term enacted form and in the long-term form of an exchange strategy for reproducing it. We furthermore understand property as a variable institution, representing varying degrees of compromise among conflicting groups. There are strategies for property-enhancing alliances, which are consciously considered while they are on the forefront of pressing issues, but become taken-for-granted forms of prestige or taboo in their more deeply embedded forms. There are unintended consequences of various strategies as they are carried out over many trials: those that produce merely random shifts, those that lock the structure into endless permutations of a basic pattern, and those that give rise to revolutionary breaks.

These elements, taken more abstractly and reworked as needed, may be just what is wanted for a better theory of the alliances that make up modern politics and international relations, as well as interorganizational ties, business communities, friendship networks, and the intellectual world itself. A tremendous amount of the problems of modern sociology—community and national power structures, business elites, social movements, social mobility—hinge upon a successful theoretical conceptualization of the descriptive materials we have been amassing. Above all, we need to see in general terms the conditions under which these structures appear, give rise to new conflicts, and are transformed either in cyclical or revolutionary directions. Perhaps some Lévi-Strauss of the future will seize on this material and one day give us an elegant model beyond the narrow tribalisms of the ethnographers of modern society.

REFERENCES

Divale, William. 1975. "An explanation of matrilocal residence." In D. Raphael (ed.), *Being Female: Reproduction, Power, and Change*. The Hague: Mouton.
Harris, Marvin. 1979. *Cultural Materialism*. New York: Random House.

Lévi-Strauss, Claude. 1949/1969. *The Elementary Structures of Kinship*. Boston: Beacon Press.

Lévi-Strauss, Claude. 1962/1966. *The Savage Mind*. Chicago: University of Chicago Press.

Mauss, Marcel. 1925/1962. *The Gift*. New York: Norton.

The Nature of Deference and Demeanor [1956]

ERVING GOFFMAN

• *Erving Goffman is not usually thought of as a follower of the Durkheimian tradition. But the early works that made him famous are explicitly built on Durkheim's theory of rituals. Goffman shows that these crucial ceremonials still exist in the little microrituals of everyday life. Because our modern social structure has the crisscrossing complexity of social paths that promotes individualism, the "sacred object" that these rituals create and worship is, appropriately enough, the individual self. Goffman's deference and demeanor rituals also follow the pattern of Mauss's theory that social exchange proceeds from symbolic gifts: in this case, a kind of mutual obeisance among personal cults. Each individual, Goffman says, has become their own god, who nevertheless needs the worship of others to keep up their own reality.*

Under the influence of Durkheim and Radcliffe-Brown, some students of modern society have learned to look for the symbolic meaning of any given social practice and for the contribution of the practice to the integrity and solidarity of the group that employs it. However, in directing their attention away from the individual to the group, these students seem to have neglected a theme that is presented in Durkheim's chapter on the soul.[1] There he suggests that the individual's personality can be seen as one apportionment of the collective *mana*, and that (as he implies in later chapters), the rites performed to representations of the social collectivity will sometimes be performed to the individual himself.

In this paper I want to explore some of the senses in which the person in our urban secular world is allotted a kind of sacredness that is displayed and confirmed by symbolic acts. An attempt will be made to build a conceptual scaffold by stretching and twisting some common anthropological terms. This will be used to support two concepts which I think are central to this area: deference and demeanor. Through these reformulations I will try to

From Erving Goffman, "The Nature of Deference and Demeanor." Reproduced by permission of the American Anthropological Association from *American Anthropologist* 58 (3): 473–499, 1956.
[1] Emile Durkheim, *The Elementary Forms of the Religious Life*, tr. J. W. Swain (Free Press, Glencoe, Ill., 1954), pp. 240–72.

show that a version of Durkheim's social psychology can be effective in modern dress.

Data for the paper are drawn chiefly from a brief observational study of mental patients in a modern research hospital. I use these data on the assumption that a logical place to learn about personal properties is among persons who have been locked up for spectacularly failing to maintain them. Their infractions of propriety occur in the confines of a ward, but the rules broken are quite general ones, leading us outward from the ward to a general study of our Anglo-American society.

INTRODUCTION

A rule of conduct may be defined as a guide for action, recommended not because it is pleasant, cheap, or effective, but because it is suitable or just. Infractions characteristically lead to feelings of uneasiness and to negative social sanctions. Rules of conduct infuse all areas of activity and are upheld in the name and honor of almost everything. Always, however, a grouping of adherents will be involved—if not a corporate social life—providing through this a common sociological theme. Attachment to rules leads to a constancy and patterning of behavior; while this is not the only source of regularity in human affairs it is certainly an important one. Of course, approved guides to conduct tend to be covertly broken, side-stepped, or followed for unapproved reasons, but these alternatives merely add to the occasions in which rules constrain at least the surface of conduct.

Rules of conduct impinge upon the individual in two general ways: directly, as *obligations*, establishing how he is morally constrained to conduct himself; indirectly, as *expectations*, establishing how others are morally bound to act in regard to him. A nurse, for example, has an obligation to follow medical orders in regard to her patients; she has the expectation, on the other hand, that her patients will pliantly co-operate in allowing her to perform these actions upon them. This pliancy, in turn, can be seen as an obligation of the patients in regard to their nurse, and points up the interpersonal, actor-recipient character of many rules: what is one man's obligation will often be another's expectation.

Because obligations involve a constraint to act in a particular way, we sometimes picture them as burdensome or irksome things, to be fulfilled, if at all, by gritting one's teeth in conscious determination. In fact, most actions which are guided by rules of conduct are performed unthinkingly, the questioned actor saying he performs "for no reason" or because he "felt like doing so." Only when his routines are blocked may he discover that his neutral little actions have all along been consonant with the proprieties of his group and that his failure to perform them can become a matter of shame and humiliation. Similarly, he may so take for granted his expectations regarding others that only when things go unexpectedly wrong will he suddenly discover that he has grounds for indignation.

Once it is clear that a person may meet an obligation without feeling it, we can go on to see that an obligation which *is* felt as something that *ought* to be done may strike the obligated person either as a desired thing or as an onerous one, in short, as a pleasant or unpleasant duty. In fact, the same obligation may appear to be a desirable duty at one point and an undesirable one at another, as when a nurse, obliged to administer medication to patients, may be glad of this when attempting to establish social distance from attendants (who in some sense may be considered by nurses to be not "good enough" to engage in such activity), yet burdened by it on occasions when she finds that dosage must be determined on the basis of illegibly written medical orders. Similarly, an expectation may be perceived by the expectant person as a wanted or unwanted thing, as when one person feels he will deservedly be promoted and another feels he will deservedly be fired. In ordinary usage, a rule that strikes the actor or recipient as a personally desirable thing, apart from its propriety, is sometimes called a right or privilege, as it will be here, but these terms have additional implications, suggesting that special class of rules which an individual may invoke but is not required to do so. It should also be noted that an actor's pleasant obligation may constitute a recipient's pleasant expectation, as with the kiss a husband owes his wife when he returns from the office, but that, as the illustration suggests, all kinds of combinations are possible.

When an individual becomes involved in the maintenance of a rule, he tends also to become committed to a particular image of self. In the case of his obligations, he becomes to himself and others the sort of person who follows this particular rule, the sort of person who would naturally be expected to do so. In the case of his expectations, he becomes dependent upon the assumption that others will properly perform such of their obligations as affect him, for their treatment of him will express a conception of him. In establishing himself as the sort of person who treats others in a particular way and is treated by them in a particular way, he must make sure that it will be possible for him to act and be this kind of person. For example, with certain psychiatrists there seems to be a point where the obligation of giving psychotherapy to patients, *their* patients, is transformed into something they must do if they are to retain the image they have come to have of themselves. The effect of this transformation can be seen in the squirming some of them may do in the early phases of their careers when they may find themselves employed to do research, or administer a ward, or give therapy to those who would rather be left alone.

In general then, when a rule of conduct is broken we find that two individuals run the risk of becoming discredited: one with an obligation, who should have governed himself by the rule; the other with an expectation, who should have been treated in a particular way because of this governance. Both actor and recipient are threatened.

An act that is subject to a rule of conduct is, then, a communication, for it represents a way in which selves are confirmed—both the self for which the rule is an obligation and the self for which it is an expectation. An act that is subject to rules of conduct but does not conform to them is also a communication—often even more so—for infractions make news and often in such a way as to disconfirm the selves of the participants. Thus rules of conduct transform both action and inaction into expression, and whether the individual abides by the rules or breaks them, something significant is likely to be communicated. For example, in the wards under study, each research psychiatrist tended to expect his patients to come regularly for their therapeutic hours. When patients fulfilled this obligation, they showed that they appreciated their need for treatment and that their psychiatrist was the sort of person who could establish a "good relation" with patients. When a patient declined to attend his therapeutic hour, others on the ward tended to feel that he was "too sick" to know what was good for him, and that perhaps his psychiatrist was not the sort of person who was good at establishing relationships. Whether patients did or did not attend their hours, something of importance about them and their psychiatrist tended to be communicated to the staff and to other patients on the ward.

In considering the individual's participation in social action, we must understand that in a sense he does not participate as a total person but rather in terms of a special capacity or status; in short, in terms of a special self. For example, patients who happen to be female may be obliged to act shamelessly before doctors who happen to be male, since the medical relation, not the sexual one, is defined as officially relevant. In the research hospital studied, there were both patients and staff who were Negro, but this minority-group status was not one in which these individuals were officially (or even, in the main, unofficially) active. Of course, during face-to-face encounters individuals may participate officially in more than one capacity. Further, some unofficial weight is almost always given to capacities defined as officially irrelevant, and the reputation earned in one capacity will flow over and to a degree determine the reputation the individual earns in his other capacities. But these are questions for more refined analysis.

In dealing with rules of conduct it is convenient to distinguish two classes, symmetrical and asymmetrical. A symmetrical rule is one which leads an individual to have obligations or expectations regarding others that these others have in regard to him. For example, in the two hospital wards, as in most other places in our society, there was an understanding that each individual was not to steal from any other individual, regardless of their respective statuses, and that each individual could similarly expect not to be stolen from by anyone. What we call common courtesies and rules of public order tend to be symmetrical, as are such biblical admonitions as the rule about not coveting one's neighbor's wife. An asymmetrical rule is one that leads others to treat and be treated by an individual differently from the way he treats and is treated by them. For example, doctors give medical orders to nurses, but nurses do not give medical orders to doctors. Similarly, in some hospitals in America nurses stand up when a doctor enters the room, but doctors do not ordinarily stand up when a nurse enters the room.

Students of society have distinguished in several ways among types of rules, as for example, between formal and informal rules; for this paper, however, the important distinction is that between substance and ceremony.[2] A substantive rule is one which guides conduct in regard to matters felt to have significance in their own right, apart from what the infraction or maintenance of the rule expresses about the selves of the persons involved. Thus, when an individual refrains from stealing from others, he upholds a substantive rule which primarily serves to protect the property of these others and only incidentally functions to protect the image they have of themselves as persons with proprietary rights. The expressive implications of substantive rules are officially considered to be secondary; this appearance must be maintained, even though in some special situations everyone may sense that the participants were primarily concerned with expression.

A ceremonial rule is one which guides conduct in matters felt to have secondary or even no significance in their own right, having their primary importance—officially anyway—as a conventionalized means of communication by which the individual expresses his character or conveys his apprecia-

---

[2] I take this distinction from Durkheim (Emile Durkheim, "The Determination of Moral Facts," *Sociology and Philosophy*, tr. D. F. Pocock, Free Press, Glencoe, Ill., 1953, especially pp. 42–43); see also A. R. Radcliffe-Brown, "Taboo," *Structure and Function in Primitive Society* (Free Press, Glencoe, Ill., 1952, pp. 143–44), and Talcott Parsons, *The Structure of Social Action* (McGraw-Hill, New York, 1937, pp. 430–33); sometimes the dichotomy is phrased in terms of "intrinsic" or "instrumental" versus "expressive" or "ritual."

tion of the other participants in the situation.[3] This usage departs from the everyday one, where "ceremony" tends to imply a highly specified, extended sequence of symbolic action performed by august actors on solemn occasions when religious sentiments are likely to be invoked. In my attempt to stress what is common to such practices as tipping one's hat and coronations, I will perforce ignore the differences among them to an extent that many anthropologists might perhaps consider impracticable.

In all societies, rules of conduct tend to be organized into codes which guarantee that everyone acts appropriately and receives his due. In our society the code which governs substantive rules and substantive expressions comprises our law, morality, and ethics, while the code which governs ceremonial rules and ceremonial expressions is incorporated in what we call etiquette. All of our institutions have both kinds of codes, but in this paper attention will be restricted to the ceremonial one.

The acts or events, that is, the sign-vehicles or tokens which carry ceremonial messages, are remarkably various in character. They may be linguistic, as when an individual makes a statement of praise or depreciation regarding self or other, and does so in a particular language and intonation; gestural, as when the physical bearing of an individual conveys insolence or obsequiousness; spatial, as when an individual precedes another through the door, or sits on his right instead of his left; task-embedded, as when an individual accepts a task graciously and performs it in the presence of others with aplomb and dexterity; part of the communication structure, as when an individual speaks more frequently than the others, or receives more attentiveness than they do. The important point is that ceremonial activity, like substantive activity, is an

---

[3]While the substantive value of ceremonial acts is felt to be quite secondary it may yet be quite appreciable. Wedding gifts in American society provide an example. It is even possible to say in some cases that if a sentiment of a given kind is to be conveyed ceremonially it will be necessary to employ a sign-vehicle which has a given amount of substantive value. Thus in the American lower-middle class, it is understood that a small investment in an engagement ring, as such investments go, may mean that the man places a small value on his fiancee as these things go, even though no one may believe that women and rings are commensurate things. In those cases where it becomes too clear that the substantive value of a ceremonial act is the only concern of the participants, as when a girl or an official receives a substantial gift from someone not interested in proper relations, then the community may respond with a feeling that their symbol system has been abused.

An interesting limiting case of the ceremonial component of activity can be found in the phenomenon of "gallantry," as when a man calmly steps aside to let a strange lady precede him into a lifeboat, or when a swordsman, fighting a duel, courteously picks up his opponent's fallen weapon and proffers it to him. Here an act that is usually a ceremonial gesture of insignificant substantive value is performed under conditions where it is known to have unexpectedly great substantive value. Here, as it were, the forms of ceremony are maintained above and beyond the call of duty.

In general, then, we can say that all ceremonial gestures differ in the degree to which they have substantive value, and that this substantive value may be systematically used as part of the communication value of the act, but that still the ceremonial order is different from the substantive one and is so understood.

analytical element referring to a component or function of action, not to concrete empirical action itself. While some activity that has a ceremonial component does not seem to have an appreciable substantive one, we find that all activity that is primarily substantive in significance will nevertheless carry some ceremonial meaning, provided that its performance is perceived in some way by others. The manner in which the activity is performed, or the momentary interruptions that are allowed so as to exchange minor niceties, will infuse the instrumentally-oriented situation with ceremonial significance.

All of the tokens employed by a given social group for ceremonial purposes may be referred to as its ceremonial idiom. We usually distinguish societies according to the amount of ceremonial that is injected into a given period and kind of interaction, or according to the expansiveness of the forms and the minuteness of their specification; it might be better to distinguish societies according to whether required ceremony is performed as an unpleasant duty or, spontaneously, as an unfelt or pleasant one.

Ceremonial activity seems to contain certain basic components. As suggested, a main object of this paper will be to delineate two of these components, deference and demeanor, and to clarify the distinction between them.

DEFERENCE

By deference I shall refer to that component of activity which functions as a symbolic means by which appreciation is regularly conveyed to a recipient of this recipient, or of something of which this recipient is taken as a symbol, extension, or agent. These marks of devotion represent ways in which an actor celebrates and confirms his relation to a recipient. In some cases, both actor and recipient may not really be individuals at all, as when two ships greet each other with four short whistle blasts when passing. In some cases, the actor is an individual but the recipient is some object or idol, as when a sailor salutes the quarterdeck upon boarding ship, or when a Catholic genuflects to the altar. I shall only be concerned, however, with the kind of deference that occurs when both actor and recipient are individuals, whether or not they are acting on behalf of something other than themselves. Such ceremonial activity is perhaps seen most clearly in the little salutations, compliments, and apologies which punctuate social intercourse, and may be referred to as "status rituals" or "interpersonal rituals." I use the term "ritual" because this activity, however informal and secular, represents a way in which the individual must guard and design the symbolic implications of his acts while in the immediate presence of an object that has a special value for him.

There appear to be two main directions in which the study of deference rituals may go. One is to settle on a given ritual and attempt to discover factors common to all of the social situations in which it is performed, for it is through such an analysis that we can get at the "meaning" of the ritual. The other is to collect all of the rituals that are performed to a given recipient, from whomever the ritual comes. Each of these rituals can then be interpreted for the symbolically expressed meaning that is embodied in it. By piecing together these meanings we can arrive at the conception of the recipient that others are obliged to maintain of him to him.

The individual may desire, earn, and deserve deference, but by and large he is not allowed to give it to himself, being forced to seek it from others. In seeking it from others, he finds he has added reason for seeking them out, and in turn society is given added assurance that its members will enter into interaction and relationships with one another. If the individual could give himself the deference he desired there might be a tendency for society to disintegrate into islands inhabited by solitary cultish men, each in continuous worship at his own shrine.

The appreciation carried by an act of deference implies that the actor possesses a sentiment of regard for the recipient, often involving a general evaluation of the recipient. Regard is something the individual constantly has for others, and knows enough about to feign on occasion; yet in having regard for someone, the individual is unable to specify in detail what in fact he has in mind.

Those who render deference to an individual may feel, of course, that they are doing this merely because he is an instance of a category, or a representative of something, and that they are giving him his due not because of what they think of him "personally" but in spite of it. Some organizations, such as the military, explicitly stress this sort of rationale for according deference, leading to an impersonal bestowal of something that is specifically directed toward the person. By easily showing a regard that he does not have, the actor can feel that he is preserving a kind of inner autonomy, holding off the ceremonial order by the very act of upholding it. And of course in scrupulously observing the proper forms he may find that he is free to insinuate all kinds of disregard by carefully modifying intonation, pronunciation, pacing, and so forth.

In thinking about deference it is common to use as a model the rituals of obeisance, submission, and propitiation that someone under authority gives to someone in authority. Deference comes to be conceived as something a subordinate owes to his superordinate. This is an extremely limiting view of deference on two grounds. First, there are a great many forms of symmetrical deference which social equals owe to one another; in some societies, Tibetan for example, salutations between high-placed equals can become prolonged displays of ritual conduct, exceeding in duration and expansiveness the kind of obeisance a subject may owe his ruler in less ritualized societies. Similarly, there are deference obligations that superordinates owe their subordinates; high priests all over the world seem obliged to respond to offerings with some equivalent of "Bless you, my son." Secondly, the regard in which the actor holds the recipient need not be one of respectful awe; there are other kinds of regard that are regularly expressed through interpersonal rituals also, such as trust, as when an individual welcomes sudden strangers into his house, or capacity-esteem, as when the individual defers to another's technical advice. A sentiment of regard that plays an important role in deference is that of affection and belongingness. We see this in the extreme in the obligation of a newly married man in our society to treat his bride with affectional deference whenever it is possible to twist ordinary behavior into a display of this kind. We find it more commonly, for example, as a component in many farewells where, as in our middle-class society, the actor will be obliged to infuse his voice with sadness and regret, paying deference in this way to the recipient's status as someone whom others can hold dearly. In "progressive" psychiatric establishments, a deferential show of acceptance, affection, and concern may form a constant and significant aspect of the stance taken by staff members when contacting patients. On Ward B, in fact, the two youngest patients seemed to have become so experienced in receiving such offerings, and so doubtful of them, that they would sometimes reply in a mocking way, apparently in an effort to re-establish the interaction on what seemed to these patients to be a more sincere level.

It appears that deference behavior on the whole tends to be honorific and politely toned, conveying appreciation of the recipient that is in many ways more complimentary to the recipient than the actor's true sentiments might warrant. The actor typically gives the recipient the benefit of the doubt, and may even conceal low regard by extra punctiliousness. Thus acts of deference often attest to ideal guide lines to which the actual activity between actor and recipient can now and then be referred. As a last resort, the recipient has a right to make a direct appeal to these honorific definitions of the situation, to press his theoretic claims, but should he be rash enough to do so, it is likely that his relationship to the actor will be modified thereafter. People sense that the recipient ought not to take the actor literally or force his hand, and ought to rest content with the show of appreciation as opposed to a more substantive expression of it. Hence one finds that many automatic acts of deference contain a vestigial meaning, having to do with activity in which no one is any longer engaged and implying an appreciation long since not expected—and yet we know these antique tributes cannot be neglected with impunity.

In addition to a sentiment of regard, acts of deference typically contain a kind of promise, expressing in truncated form the actor's avowal and pledge to treat the recipient in a particular way in the on-coming activity. The pledge affirms that the expectations and obligations of the recipient, both substantive and ceremonial, will be allowed and supported by the actor. Actors thus promise to maintain the conception of self that the recipient has built up from the rules he is involved in. (Perhaps the prototype here is the public act of allegiance by which a subject officially acknowledges his subservience in certain matters to his lord.) Deferential pledges are frequently conveyed through spoken terms of address involving status-identifiers, as when a nurse responds to a rebuke in the operating room with the phrase, "yes, Doctor," signifying by term of address and tone of voice that the criticism has been understood and that, however unpalatable, it has not caused her to rebel. When a putative recipient fails to receive anticipated acts of deference, or when an actor makes clear that he is giving homage with bad grace, the recipient may feel that the state of affairs which he has been taking for granted has become unstable, and that an insubordinate effort may be made by the actor to reallocate tasks, relations, and power. To elicit an established act of deference, even if the actor must first be reminded of his obligations and warned about the consequence of discourtesy, is evidence that if rebellion comes it will come slyly; to be pointedly refused an expected act of deference is often a way of being told that open insurrection has begun.

I have mentioned four very common forms of presentational deference; salutations, invitations, compliments, and minor services. Through all of these the recipient is told that he is not an island unto himself and that others are, or seek to be, involved with him and with his personal private concerns. Taken together, these rituals provide a continuous symbolic tracing of the extent to which the recipient's ego has not been bounded and barricaded in regard to others.

Two main types of deference have been illustrated: presentational rituals through which the actor concretely depicts his appreciation of the recipient; and avoidance rituals, taking the form of proscriptions, interdictions, and taboos, which imply acts the actor must refrain from doing lest he violate the right of the recipient to keep him at a distance. We are familiar with this distinction from Durkheim's classification of ritual into positive and negative rites.[4]

In suggesting that there are things that must be said and done to a recipient, and things that must not be said and done, it should be plain that there is an inherent opposition and conflict between these two forms of deference. To ask

[4]Durkheim, *The Elementary Forms*, p. 299.

[handwritten top margin: Deference = appreciation through avoidance rituals + presentational rituals]

[handwritten: Offer someone a chair or drink]

after an individual's health, his family's well-being, or the state of his affairs, is
to present him with a sign of sympathetic concern; but in a certain way to make *[handwritten right margin: How you do it is demeanor]*
this presentation is to invade the individual's personal reserve, as will be made
clear if an actor of wrong status asks him these questions, or if a recent event has
made such a question painful to answer. As Durkheim suggested, "The human
personality is a sacred thing; one dare not violate it nor infringe its bounds,
while at the same time the greatest good is in communion with others."[5]

[handwritten: Ceremonial behavior conveyed through deportment, dress, bearing = desirable + undesirable qualities]

DEMEANOR =
It was suggested that the ceremonial component of concrete behavior has at
least two basic elements, deference and demeanor. Deference, defined as the
appreciation an individual shows of another to that other, whether through
avoidance rituals or presentational rituals, has been discussed and demeanor
may now be considered.

By demeanor I shall refer to that element of the individual's ceremonial
behavior typically conveyed through deportment, dress, and bearing, which
serves to express to those in his immediate presence that he is a person of
certain desirable or undesirable qualities. In our society, the "well" or "properly" demeaned individual displays such attributes as: discretion and sincerity;
modesty in claims regarding self; sportsmanship; command of speech and
physical movements; self-control over his emotions, his appetites, and his
desires; poise under pressure; and so forth.

When we attempt to analyze the qualities conveyed through demeanor,
certain themes become apparent. The well-demeaned individual possesses the
attributes popularly associated with "character training" or "socialization,"
these being implanted when a neophyte of any kind is housebroken. Rightly or
wrongly, others tend to use such qualities diagnostically, as evidence of what
the actor is generally like at other times and as a performer of other activities.
In addition, the properly demeaned individual is someone who has closed off
many avenues of perception and penetration that others might take to him,
and is therefore unlikely to be contaminated by them. Most importantly,
perhaps, good demeanor is what is required of an actor if he is to be transformed into someone who can be relied upon to maintain himself as an
interactant, poised for communication, and to act so that others do not en-
danger themselves by presenting themselves as interactants to him.

It should be noted once again that demeanor involves attributes derived
from interpretations others make of the way in which the individual handles

[5]Emile Durkheim, "The Determination of Moral Facts," p. 37.

himself during social intercourse. The individual cannot establish these attributes for his own by verbally avowing that he possesses them, though sometimes he may rashly try to do this. (He can, however, contrive to conduct himself in such a way that others, through their interpretation of his conduct, will impute the kinds of attributes to him he would like others to see in him.) In general, then, through demeanor the individual creates an image of himself, but properly speaking this is not an image that is meant for his own eyes. Of course this should not prevent us from seeing that the individual who acts with good demeanor may do so because he places an appreciable value upon himself, and that he who fails to demean himself properly may be accused of having "no self-respect" or of holding himself too cheaply in his own eyes.

As in the case of deference, an object in the study of demeanor is to collect all the ceremonially relevant acts that a particular individual performs in the presence of each of the several persons with whom he comes in contact, to interpret these acts for the demeanor that is symbolically expressed through them, and then to piece these meanings together into an image of the individual, an image of him in others' eyes.

Rules of demeanor, like rules of deference, can be symmetrical or asymmetrical. Between social equals, symmetrical rules of demeanor seem often to be prescribed. Between unequals many variations can be found. For example, at staff meetings on the psychiatric units of the hospital, medical doctors had the privilege of swearing, changing the topic of conversation, and sitting in undignified positions; attendants, on the other hand, had the right to attend staff meetings and to ask questions during them (in line with the milieu-therapy orientation of these research units) but were implicitly expected to conduct themselves with greater circumspection than was required of doctors. (This was pointed out by a perceptive occupational therapist who claimed she was always reminded that a mild young female psychiatrist was really an M.D. by the fact that this psychiatrist exercised these prerogatives of informal demeanor.) The extreme here perhaps is the master-servant relation as seen in cases where valets and maids are required to perform in a dignified manner services of an undignified kind. Similarly, doctors had the right to saunter into the nurses' station, lounge on the station's dispensing counter, and engage in joking with the nurses; other ranks participated in this informal interaction with doctors, but only after doctors had initiated it.

DEFERENCE AND DEMEANOR

Deference and demeanor are analytical terms; empirically there is much overlapping of the activities to which they refer. An act through which the individual gives or withholds deference to others typically provides means by which he expresses the fact that he is a well or badly demeaned individual. Some aspects of this overlapping may be cited. First, in performing a given act of presentational deference, as in offering a guest a chair, the actor finds himself doing something that can be done with smoothness and aplomb, expressing self-control and poise, or with clumsiness and uncertainty, expressing an irresolute character. This is, as it were, an incidental and adventitious connection between deference and demeanor. It may be illustrated from recent material on doctor-patient relationships, where it is suggested that one complaint a doctor may have against some of his patients is that they do not bathe before coming for an examination; while bathing is a way of paying deference to the doctor it is at the same time a way for the patient to present himself as a clean, well demeaned person. A further illustration is found in acts such as loud talking, shouting, or singing, for these acts encroach upon the right of others to be let alone, while at the same time they illustrate a badly demeaned lack of control over one's feelings.

The same connection between deference and demeanor has had a bearing on the ceremonial difficulties associated with intergroup interaction: the gestures of deference expected by members of one society have sometimes been incompatible with the standards of demeanor maintained by members of another. For example, during the nineteenth century, diplomatic relations between Britain and China were embarrassed by the fact that the *Kot'ow* demanded of visiting ambassadors by the Chinese Emperor was felt by some British ambassadors to be incompatible with their self-respect.

A second connection between deference and demeanor turns upon the fact that a willingness to give others their deferential due is one of the qualities which the individual owes it to others to express through his conduct, just as a willingness to conduct oneself with good demeanor is in general a way of showing deference to those present.

In spite of these connections between deference and demeanor, the analytical relation between them is one of "complementarity," not identity. The image the individual owes to others to maintain of himself is not the same type of image these others are obliged to maintain of him. Deference images tend to point to the wider society outside the interaction, to the place the individual has achieved in the hierarchy of this society. Demeanor images tend to point to qualities which any social position gives its incumbents a chance to display during interaction, for these qualities pertain more to the way in which the individual handles his position than to the rank and place of that position relative to those possessed by others.

Further, the image of himself the individual owes it to others to maintain through his conduct is a kind of justification and compensation for the image of him that others are obliged to express through their deference to him. Each of the two images in fact may act as a guarantee and check upon the other. In an interchange that can be found in many cultures, the individual defers to guests to show how welcome they are and how highly he regards them; they in turn decline the offering at least once, showing through their demeanor that they are not presumptuous, immodest, or over-eager to receive favor. Similarly, a man starts to rise for a lady, showing respect for her sex; she interrupts and halts his gesture, showing she is not greedy of her rights in this capacity but is ready to define the situation as one between equals. In general, then, by treating others deferentially one gives them an opportunity to handle the indulgence with good demeanor. Through this differentiation in symbolizing function the world tends to be bathed in better images than anyone deserves, for it is practical to signify great appreciation of others by offering them deferential indulgences, knowing that some of these indulgences will be declined as an expression of good demeanor.

There are still other complementary relations between deference and demeanor. If an individual feels he ought to show proper demeanor in order to warrant deferential treatment, then he must be in a position to do so. He must, for example, be able to conceal from others aspects of himself which would make him unworthy in their eyes, and to conceal himself from them when he is in an indignified state, whether of dress, mind, posture, or action. The avoidance rituals which others perform in regard to him give him room to maneuver, enabling him to present only a self that is worthy of deference; at the same time, this avoidance makes it easier for them to assure themselves that the deference they have to show him is warranted.

To show the difference between deference and demeanor, I have pointed out the complementary relation between them, but even this kind of relatedness can be overstressed. The failure of an individual to show proper deference to others does not necessarily free them from the obligation to act with good demeanor in his presence, however disgruntled they may be at having to do this. Similarly, the failure of an individual to conduct himself with proper demeanor does not always relieve those in his presence from treating him with proper deference. It is by separating deference and demeanor that we can appreciate many things about ceremonial life, such as that a group may be noted for excellence in one of these areas while having a bad reputation in the other. Hence we can find a place for arguments such as De Quincey's, that an Englishman shows great self-respect but little respect for others while a Frenchman shows great respect for others but little respect for himself.

We are to see, then, that there are many occasions when it would be improper for an individual to convey about himself what others are ready to convey about him to him, since each of these two images is a warrant and justification for the other, and not a mirror image of it. The Meadian notion that the individual takes toward himself the attitude others take to him seems very much an oversimplification. Rather the individual must rely on others to complete the picture of him of which he himself is allowed to paint only certain parts. Each individual is responsible for the demeanor image of himself and the deference image of others, so that for a complete man to be expressed, individuals must hold hands in a chain of ceremony, each giving deferentially with proper demeanor to the one on the right what will be received deferentially from the one on the left. While it may be true that the individual has a unique self all his own, evidence of this possession is thoroughly a product of joint ceremonial labor, the part expressed through the individual's demeanor being no more significant than the part conveyed by others through their deferential behavior toward him.

CONCLUSIONS

The rules of conduct which bind the actor and the recipient together are the bindings of society. But many of the acts which are guided by these rules occur infrequently or take a long time for their consummation. Opportunities to affirm the moral order and the society could therefore be rare. It is here that ceremonial rules play their social function, for many of the acts which are guided by these rules last but a brief moment, involve no substantive outlay, and can be performed in every social interaction. Whatever the activity and however profanely instrumental, it can afford many opportunities for minor ceremonies as long as other persons are present. Through these observances, guided by ceremonial obligations and expectations, a constant flow of indulgences is spread through society, with others who are present constantly reminding the individual that he must keep himself together as a well demeaned person and affirm the sacred quality of these others. The gestures which we sometimes call empty are perhaps in fact the fullest things of all.

It is therefore important to see that the self is in part a ceremonial thing, a sacred object which must be treated with proper ritual care and in turn must be presented in a proper light to others. As a means through which this self is established, the individual acts with proper demeanor while in contact with others and is treated by others with deference. It is just as important to see that if the individual is to play this kind of sacred game, then the field must be suited to it. The environment must ensure that the individual will not pay too high a price for acting with good demeanor and that deference will be accorded him. Deference and demeanor practices must be institutionalized so that the individual will be able to project a viable, sacred self and stay in the game on a proper ritual basis.

An environment, then, in terms of the ceremonial component of activity, is a place where it is easy or difficult to play the ritual game of having a self. Where ceremonial practices are thoroughly institutionalized, as they were on Ward A, it would appear easy to be a person. Where these practices are not established, as to a degree they were not in Ward B, it would appear difficult to be a person. Why one ward comes to be a place in which it is easy to have a self and another ward comes to be a place where this is difficult depends in part on the type of patient that is recruited and the type of regime the staff attempts to maintain.

One of the bases upon which mental hospitals throughout the world segregate their patients is degree of easily apparent "mental illness." By and large this means that patients are graded according to the degree to which they violate ceremonial rules of social intercourse. There are very good practical reasons for sorting patients into different wards in this way, and in fact that institution is backward where no one bothers to do so. This grading very often means, however, that individuals who are desperately uncivil in some areas of behavior are placed in the intimate company of those who are desperately uncivil in others. Thus, individuals who are the least ready to project a sustainable self are lodged in a milieu where it is practically impossible to do so.

It is in this context that we can reconsider some interesting aspects of the effect of coercion and constraint upon the individual. If an individual is to act with proper demeanor and show proper deference, then it will be necessary for him to have areas of self-determination. He must have an expendable supply of the small indulgences which his society employs in its idiom of regard—such as cigarettes to give, chairs to proffer, food to provide, and so forth. He must have freedom of bodily movement so that it will be possible for him to assume a stance that conveys appropriate respect for others and appropriate demeanor on his own part; a patient strapped to a bed may find it impractical not to befoul himself, let alone to stand in the presence of a lady. He must have a supply of appropriate clean clothing if he is to make the sort of appearance that is expected of a well demeaned person. To look seemly may require a tie, a belt, shoe laces, a mirror, and razor blades—all of which the authorities may deem unwise to give him. He must have access to the eating utensils which his society defines as appropriate ones for use, and may find that meat cannot be circumspectly eaten with a cardboard spoon. And finally, without too much cost to himself he must be able to decline certain kinds of work, now sometimes classified as "industrial therapy," which his social group considers *infra dignitatem*.

When the individual is subject to extreme constraint he is automatically forced from the circle of the proper. The sign vehicles or physical tokens through which the customary ceremonies are performed are unavailable to him. Others may show ceremonial regard for him, but it becomes impossible for him to reciprocate the show or to act in such a way as to make himself worthy of receiving it. The only ceremonial statements that are possible for him are improper ones.

The history of the care of mental cases is the history of constricting devices: constraining gloves, camisoles, floor and seat chains, handcuffs, "biter's mask," wet-packs, supervised toileting, hosing down, institutional clothing, forkless and knifeless eating, and so forth. The use of these devices provides significant data on the ways in which the ceremonial grounds of selfhood can be taken away. By implication we can obtain information from this history about the conditions that must be satisfied if individuals are to have selves. Unfortunately, today there are still mental institutions where the past of other hospitals can be empirically studied now. Students of interpersonal ceremony should seek these institutions out almost as urgently as students of kinship have sought out disappearing cultures.

Throughout this paper I have assumed we can learn about ceremony by studying a contemporary secular situation—that of the individual who has declined to employ the ceremonial idiom of his group in an acceptable manner and has been hospitalized. In a crosscultural view it is convenient to see this as a product of our complex division of labor which brings patients together instead of leaving each in his local circle. Further, this division of labor also brings together those who have the task of caring for these patients.

We are thus led to the special dilemma of the hospital worker: as a member of the wider society he ought to take action against mental patients, who have transgressed the rules of ceremonial order; but his occupational role obliges him to care for and protect these very people. When "milieu therapy" is stressed, these obligations further require him to convey warmth in response to hostility; relatedness in response to alienation.

We have seen that hospital workers must witness improper conduct without applying usual negative sanctions, and yet that they must exercise disrespectful coercion over their patients. A third peculiarity is that staff members may be obliged to render to patients services such as changing socks, tying shoelaces or trimming fingernails, which outside the hospital generally convey elaborate deference. In the hospital setting, such acts are likely to convey something inappropriate since the attendant at the same time exerts certain kinds of power and moral superiority over his charges. A final peculiarity in the ceremonial life of mental hospitals is that individuals collapse as units of minimal ceremonial substance and others learn that what had been taken for granted as ultimate entities are really held together by rules that can be broken with some kind of impunity. Such understanding, like one gained at war or at a kinsman's funeral, is not much talked about but it tends, perhaps, to draw staff and patients together into an unwilling group sharing undesired knowledge.

In summary, then, modern society brings transgressors of the ceremonial order to a single place, along with some ordinary members of society who make their living there. These dwell in a place of unholy acts and unholy understandings, yet some of them retain allegiance to the ceremonial order outside the hospital setting. Somehow ceremonial people must work out mechanisms and techniques for living without certain kinds of ceremony.

In this paper I have suggested that Durkheimian notions about primitive religion can be translated into concepts of deference and demeanor, and that these concepts help us to grasp some aspects of urban secular living. The implication is that in one sense this secular world is not so irreligious as we might think. Many gods have been done away with, but the individual himself stubbornly remains as a deity of considerable importance. He walks with some dignity and is the recipient of many little offerings. He is jealous of the worship due him, yet, approached in the right spirit, he is ready to forgive those who may have offended him. Because of their status relative to his, some persons will find him contaminating while others will find they contaminate him, in either case finding that they must treat him with ritual care. Perhaps the individual is so viable a god because he can actually understand the ceremonial significance of the way he is treated, and quite on his own can respond dramatically to what is proffered him. In contacts between such deities there is no need for middlemen; each of these gods is able to serve as his own priest.

Social Control in Science [1965]

WARREN O. HAGSTROM

• *Warren O. Hagstrom's* The Scientific Community *(1965) was one of the first works to state a systematic sociological theory of science, and it helped to set off the modern wave of research in the sociology of science. The basic theory, presented here, attempts to show that science is held together by the same mechanism of symbolic gift-exchanges that Marcel Mauss had analyzed as at the foundation of primitive economies. Science is not a collection of self-motivated individuals making discoveries, but a tightly regulated system such as is found wherever "sacred" rather than secular values are at stake.*

A common view of the organization of science, held implicitly or explicitly by most scientists, is that the individual characteristics [of being "self-starting" and "self-controlling"] are sufficient to account for conformity to scientific values and norms. It is often asserted that the scientist does what he wishes to do, attempts to solve problems that are intrinsically interesting and important, and is guided by aesthetic considerations. His social relations with others either interfere with this or are happy, but secondary consequences of it.

This highly individualistic view is incomplete. It leads to no propositions about the actual scientific community as we know it, except perhaps that the socialization of recruits plays an unusually important part in the community's activities, and the importance of socialization is also consistent with other theoretical approaches. Some facts, which will be presented more fully in succeeding chapters, are inconsistent with the view of the scientist assumed by an individualistic theory. For instance, scientists seek to publish their accomplishments and are greatly disturbed if proper recognition for them is not forthcoming. Moreover, scientists who experience prolonged isolation from their colleagues cease being productive. A more obvious objection to this individualistic approach is that scientists seldom consciously set to work on problems that they know others have solved. If scientists received their major

From Warren O. Hagstrom, *The Scientific Community* (New York: Basic Books, 1965), pp. 11–22, 52. Reprinted by permission of the author.

gratifications from problem-solving alone, the mere fact that others have solved the problem should not deter them from solving it themselves. (Although mountaineers receive egoistic gratifications from being the first to climb a peak, they receive similar gratifications from climbing peaks already climbed: it demonstrates their abilities. Similarly, the egoistic scientist can demonstrate his abilities by solving previously solved problems, yet he seldom chooses to do so, since he also desires social recognition for his discoveries.)

Not only is the extremely individualistic view directly controverted by obvious facts about the scientific community, but there is every theoretical reason to expect this to be so. First, the autonomy of the scientific community cannot be taken for granted; it must be maintained by internal social controls, among other things. Without them, scientists would tend to respond more readily to the goals and standards of nonscientists. Second, communities of autonomous specialists tend to be rigid; they incorporate new goals and standards only with difficulty, for the socialization that produces commitment to norms and values at the highest levels also produces commitment to more specific norms. The scientific training that produces committed scientists also tends to commit them to techniques and particular theories. Since change is intrinsic in any community incorporating scientific values, if science is to thrive, scientists must respond to discoveries by continually changing their goals, techniques, and theories. Third, commitments to norms tend to erode in the absence of reinforcement. Many of the procedures known collectively as the "scientific method" are important only because they make possible communication among scientists. In the absence of sanctions, deviance from such norms would be common.

We may conclude that the socialization of scientists must be supplemented by a dynamic system of social control, if the values and effectiveness of science are to be maintained. Negative arguments are unsatisfying; the best reason for studying social control in science is that it leads one to discover the characteristic tensions within the scientific community, and this endeavor makes meaningful many varieties of scientific behavior that are otherwise unseen or dismissed as idiosyncratic and the consequence of aberrant personalities.

THE SOCIAL RECOGNITION OF DISCOVERY

Manuscripts submitted to scientific periodicals are often called "contributions," and they are, in fact, gifts. Authors do not usually receive royalties or other payments, and their institutions may even be required to aid in the financial support of the periodical. On the other hand, manuscripts for which the scientific authors do receive financial payments, such as textbooks and popularizations, are, if not despised, certainly held in much lower esteem than articles containing original research results.

Gift-giving by scientists is thus similar to one of the most common modes of allocating resources to science, for this often takes the form of gifts from wealthy individuals or organizations. This has been true from the time of Cosimo de Medici to today, the time of the Rockefeller and Ford foundations. The gift status of moneys spent by industrial firms and governments on research is ambiguous; usually money seems to be spent with specific goals in mind, but the vast sums spent on space programs, particle accelerators, radiotelescopes, and so forth often seem like a potlatch by the community of nations. Neil Smelser has suggested that the gift mode of exchange is typical not only of science but of all institutions concerned with the maintenance and transmission of common values, such as the family, religion, and communities.[1]

In general, the acceptance of a gift by an individual or a community implies a recognition of the status of the donor and the existence of certain kinds of reciprocal rights.[2] These reciprocal rights may be to a return gift of the same kind and value, as in many primitive economic systems, or to certain appropriate sentiments of gratitude and deference. In science, the acceptance by scientific journals of contributed manuscripts establishes the donor's status as a scientist—indeed, status as a scientist can be achieved *only* by such gift-giving—and it assures him of prestige within the scientific community. The remainder of this chapter concerns the nature and forms of this allocation of prestige.

The organization of science consists of an exchange of social recognition for information. But, as in all gift-giving, the expectation of return gifts (of recognition) cannot be publicly acknowledged as the motive for making the gift. A gift is supposed to be given, not in the expectation of a return, but as an expression of the sentiment of the donor toward the recipient. Thus, in the kula expeditions of the Melanesians:

> The ceremony of transfer is done with solemnity. The object given is disdained or suspect; it is not accepted until it is thrown on the ground. The donor affects an exaggerated modesty. Solemnly bearing his gift, accompanied by the blowing of a conch-shell, he apologizes for bringing only his leavings and throws the objects at his partner's feet. . . .

[1]Neil J. Smelser, "A Comparative View of Exchange Systems," *Economic Development and Cultural Change*, 7 (1959), 173–182.
[2]Cf. Alvin W. Gouldner, "The Norm of Reciprocity," *American Sociological Review*, 25 (1960), 161–178; and Marcel Mauss, *The Gift: Forms and Functions of Exchange in Primitive Societies* (Glencoe, Ill.: Free Press, 1954), pp. 40 f., 73, *et passim*.

Pains are taken to show one's freedom and autonomy as well as one's magnanimity, yet all the time one is actuated by the mechanisms of obligation which are resident in the gifts themselves.[3]

Gift-giving is capable of cynical manipulation; if this is publicly expressed, however, the exchange of gifts ceases, perhaps to be succeeded by contractual exchange. Consequently, scientists usually deny that they are strongly motivated by a desire for recognition, or that this desire influences their research decisions.

Nevertheless, the public disavowal of the expectation of recognition in return for scientific contributions should no more be taken to mean that the expectation is absent than the magnanimous front of the kula trader can be taken to mean that he does not expect a return gift. In both instances, this is made clearest when the expected response is not forthcoming. In primitive societies, failure to present return gifts often means warfare.[4] In science, the failure to recognize discovery may give rise, if not to warfare, at least to strong antagonisms and, at times, to intense controversy. A historical summary and analysis of priority controversies has been given by Robert K. Merton,[5] who pointed out that the failure to recognize previous work threatens the system of incentives in science. The pattern is not infrequent today. Of my seventy-nine informants, at least nine admitted to having been involved in questions of disputed priority either as the culprit or the victim.

The desire to obtain social recognition induces the scientist to conform to scientific norms by contributing his discoveries to the larger community. Thomas Sprat, writing near the dawn of modern science, perceived the importance of this: "If neither *Chance*, nor *Friendship*, nor *Treachery* of Servants, have brought such Things out; yet we see *Ostentation* alone to be every day powerful enough to do it. This Desire of Glory, and to be counted Authors, prevails on all. . . ."[6]

Not only does the desire for recognition induce the scientist to communicate his results; it also influences his selection of problems and methods. He will tend to select problems the solution of which will result in greater recognition, and he will tend to select methods that will make his work acceptable to his colleagues.

[3]Mauss, *op. cit.*, p. 21, reporting the work of Malinowski.
[4]Mauss, *op. cit.*, p. 3 *et passim.*
[5]Merton, "Priorities in Scientific Discovery," *American Sociological Review*, 22 (1957), 635–659.
[6]Sprat, *The History of the Royal Society of London* (London, 1673), pp. 74 f. See also Karl Mannheim on the importance of the desire for recognition in science and other cultural pursuits: *Essays on the Sociology of Knowledge* (London: Routledge and Kegan Paul, 1952), ch. VI, especially pp. 239, 242–243, 272.

Another type of sanction is not primarily important in science, although it is often alleged to be. This consists of extrinsic rewards, primarily position and money. It is alleged that scientists publish, select problems, and select methods in order to maximize these rewards. University policies that base advancement and salary on quantity of publication sometimes seem to imply that this is true, that scientists' research contributions are not freely given gifts at all but are, instead, services in return for salary. While it is important for extrinsic rewards to be more or less consistent with recognition, the ideal seems to be that they should follow recognition, and this seems to be the general practice. In any case, an explanation of scientific behavior in terms of extrinsic rewards is weakened by the fact that many scientists in elite positions, whose extrinsic rewards will be unaffected by their behavior, continue to be highly productive and to conform to scientific goals and norms. Furthermore, scientists usually feel that it is degrading and improper to submit manuscripts for publication primarily to gain position without really caring if the work is read by others.

But why should gift-giving be important in science when it is essentially obsolete as a form of exchange in most other areas of modern life, especially the most distinctly "civilized" areas? Gift-giving, because it tends to create particularistic obligations, usually reduces the rationality of economic action. Rationality is maximized when "costs" of alternative courses of action can be assessed, and such costs are usually established in free-market exchanges or in the plans of central directing agencies. When participants are paid a money wage or salary for their efforts, and when this effectively controls their behavior, the system is more flexible than when controls derive from traditional or gift obligations. Why, then, does this frequently inefficient and irrational form of control persist in science? To be sure, it also tends to persist in other professions. Professionals are expected to be motivated by a desire to serve others. For example, physicians do receive a fee for service, yet they are expected to have a "sliding scale" and serve the indigent at reduced fees or for no fees at all. The larger community recognizes two types of public dependence on professions: professional services are regarded as essential, concerned with values that should be realized regardless of a client's ability to pay; and nonprofessionals are unable to evaluate professional services, which makes them vulnerable to exploitation by unqualified persons. The rationale for the norm of service is usually the former type of dependence. In science, for example, the fact that a community has no one willing and able to pay for an important item of useless knowledge is not supposed to interfere with its ability to acquire the knowledge. But the idea of the gift and the norm of service is also related to the dependence of the public that follows from its inability to evaluate services.

The rationality of professional services is not the same as the rationality of the market. In contractual exchanges, when services are rewarded on a direct financial or barter basis, the client abdicates, to a considerable degree, his *moral control* over the producer. In return, the client is freed from personal ties with the producer, and he is able to choose rationally between alternative sources of supply. In the professions, and especially in science, the abdication of moral control would disrupt the system. The producer of professional services must be strongly committed to higher values. He must be responsible for his products, and it is fitting that he not be alienated from them. The scientist, for example, must be concerned with maintaining and correcting existing theories in his field, and his work should be oriented to this end. The exchange of gifts for recognition tends to maintain such orientations. On the one hand, the recipient of the gifts finds it difficult to refuse them (they are "free"), and, on the other, the donor is held responsible for adhering to central norms and values. The maxim, *caveat emptor*, is inapplicable.[7] Furthermore, the donor is not alienated from his gift, but retains a lasting interest in it. It is, in a sense, his property.[8] One indication of this is the frequent practice of eponymy, the affixing of the name of the scientist to all or part of what he has found.[9]

Emphasis on gifts and services occurs frequently in social life, and we can get at the root of this generality by focusing on certain paradoxical elements implicit in the argument presented thus far. It has been argued that scientists are oriented to receiving recognition from colleagues and that this orientation influences their research decisions. Yet evidence that scientists themselves deny this has also been presented. There is a normative component to this denial, one that appears more clearly in analyzing scientific fashions. It is felt that, if a scientist's decisions are influenced by the probability of being recognized, he will tend to deviate from certain central scientific norms—he will fail to be original and critical. Thus, while it is true that scientists are motivated by a desire to obtain social recognition, and while it is true that only work on certain types of problems and with certain techniques will receive

[7]This does not mean that scientists are not supposed to be skeptical; that they should be skeptical about their own work as well as that of their colleagues is one of the more important institutionalized norms of science. Cf. Robert K. Merton, *Social Theory and Social Structure* (Glencoe, Ill.: Free Press, 1949), pp. 315 f. It does mean that unlike the consumer in the free market, the "consumer" of scientific products can hold the producer morally responsible for "defective products."

[8]Cf. Merton, "Priorities in Scientific Discovery," *op. cit.*, pp. 640 f., and *Social Theory and Social Structure*, *op. cit.*, pp. 312 f. Mauss pointed out that members of some "archaic societies" felt gifts somehow remained part of the donor and that this belief was reinforced by further existential beliefs, e.g., the gift itself possessed the power to harm the recipient if it was not reciprocated. Mauss, *op. cit.*, pp. 41 ff. *et passim*.

[9]Cf. Merton, "Priorities in Scientific Discovery," *op. cit.*, pp. 642–644.

recognition at any particular time, it is also true that, if a scientist were to admit being influenced in his choices of problems and techniques by the probability of being recognized, he would be considered deviant. That is, if scientists conform to norms about problems and techniques as a result of this specific form of social control, they are thereby deviants.

This apparent paradox, that people deviate in the very act of conforming, is common whenever people are expected to be strongly committed to values. In general, *whenever strong commitments to values are expected, the rational calculation of punishments and rewards is regarded as an improper basis for making decisions.* Citizens who refrain from treason merely because it is against the law are, by that fact, of questionable loyalty; parents who refrain from incest merely because of fear of community reaction are, by that fact, unfit for parenthood; and scientists who select problems merely because they feel that in dealing with them they will receive greater recognition from colleagues are, by that fact, not "good" scientists. In all such cases the sanctions are of no obvious value: they evidently do not work for the deviants, and none of those who conform admit to being influenced by them. But this does not mean that the sanctions are of no importance; it does mean that more than overt conformity to norms is demanded, that inner conformity is regarded as equally, or more, important.

Thus, the gift exchange (or the norm of service), as opposed to barter or contractual exchange, is particularly well suited to social systems in which great reliance is placed on the ability of well-socialized persons to operate independently of formal controls. The prolonged and intensive socialization scientists experience is reinforced and complemented by their practice of the exchange of information for recognition. The socialization experience produces scientists who are strongly committed to the values of science and who need the esteem and approval of their peers. The reward of recognition for information reinforces this commitment but also makes it flexible. Recognition is given for kinds of contributions the scientific community finds valuable, and different kinds of contributions will be found valuable at different times.

The scientist's denial of recognition as an important incentive has other consequences related to those already mentioned. When peers exchange gifts, the denial of the expectation of reciprocity in kind implies an expectation of gratitude, a highly diffuse response.[10] It will be shown that this kind of gift

[10]As Georg Simmel says, gratitude "establishes the bond of interaction, of the reciprocity of service and return service, even where they are not guaranteed by external coercion." *The Sociology of Georg Simmel*, Kurt Wolff, ed. and trans. (Glencoe, Ill.: Free Press, 1950), p. 387. He goes on to note that persons make great efforts to avoid receiving gifts in order not to make such commitments to others. Something like this may occur in science.

exchange occurs among scientists, although the more important form of scientific contribution is directed to the larger scientific community.[11] In this case the denial of the pursuit of recognition serves to emphasize the universality of scientific standards: it is not a particular group of colleagues at a particular time that should be addressed, but all possible colleagues at all possible periods. These sentiments were expressed with his typical fervor by Johannes Kepler:

> I have robbed the golden vessels of the Egyptians to make out of them a tabernacle for my God, far from the frontiers of Egypt. If you forgive me, I shall rejoice. If you are angry, I shall bear it. Behold, I have cast the dice, and I am writing a book either for my contemporaries, or for posterity. It is all the same to me. It may wait a hundred years for a reader, since God has also waited six thousand years for a witness.[12]

While this orientation is consistent with the scientist's need for autonomy—being dependent on the favors of particular others is terrifying—it also contains a strong element of the tragic. Scientists learn to *expect* injustice, the inequitable allocation of rewards. Occasionally one of them makes this explicit. Max Weber addressed students on "Science as a Vocation" in the following way:

> I know of hardly any career on earth where chance plays such a role. . . . If the young scholar asks for my advice with regard to habilitation, the responsibility of encouraging him can hardly be borne . . . one must ask every . . . man: Do you in all conscience believe that you can stand seeing mediocrity after mediocrity, year after year, climb beyond you, without becoming embittered and without coming to grief? Naturally, one always receives the answer: "Of course, I live only for my calling." Yet, I have found that only a few men could endure this situation without coming to grief.[13]

More common than such an explicit statement is the myth of the hero who is recognized only after his death. This myth is important in science, as in art, because it strengthens universal standards against tendencies to become depen-

---

[11]In other words, the scientific contribution is closely approximated by the sacrificial model of the gift. Cf. Emile Durkheim, *The Elementary Forms of Religious Life*, J. W. Swain, trans. (London: George Allen and Unwin, 1915), pp. 342 f.: "The sacrifice is partially a communion; but it is also, and no less essentially, a gift and an act of renouncement."

[12]Quoted in Arthur Koestler, *The Sleepwalkers* (London: Hutchinson, 1959), pp. 393 f.

[13]Hans H. Gerth and C. Wright Mills, trans. and eds. *From Max Weber: Essays in Sociology* (New York: Oxford University Press, 1946), pp. 132, 134. Weber was partly concerned with the particular aspects of science in German universities, but the entire essay shows that he was also concerned with the more universal aspects of science as a profession.

dent on particular communities. Thus, mathematics has such heroes as Galois, who wrote the major part of his great mathematical opus the night before he was killed in a duel at the age of twenty-one; Abel, who died of tuberculosis as his greatness was coming to be recognized; and Cantor, who died mad, believing his ideas were spurned by others.[14] The stories of Copernicus, receiving his revolutionary book the day he died, and Mendel, rediscovered years after his death, are well known in the larger society, where they perhaps serve a function similar to that performed in science, albeit more general.

SUMMARY

The thesis presented here is that social control in science is exercised in an exchange system, a system wherein gifts of information are exchanged for recognition from scientific colleagues. Because scientists desire recognition, they conform to the goals and norms of the scientific community. Such control reinforces and complements the socialization process in science. It is partly dependent on the socialization of persons to become sensitive to the responses of their colleagues. By rewarding conformity, this exchange system reinforces commitment to the higher goals and norms of the scientific community, and it induces flexibility with regard to specific goals and norms. The very denial by scientists of the importance of recognition as an incentive can be seen to involve commitments to higher norms, including an orientation to a scientific community extending beyond any particular collection of contemporaries.

[14]Cf. Eric T. Bell, *Men of Mathematics* (New York: Simon and Schuster, 1937), for these and others.

Symbolic Violence and Cultural Capital [1972]

PIERRE BOURDIEU

• *With Pierre Bourdieu, the French Durkeimian tradition arrives at last at an explicit connection with the conflict tradition of Marx and Weber. For Bourdieu, the issue is how culture acts as a stratifying device. A good deal of his research has dealt with the stratifying effects of education, as well as of elite and mass culture, in modern France. In these selections, he uses his anthropological field research among the Kabyle tribe of the Algerian mountains to demonstrate that symbolic and ritual practices have the same kind of economic logic as the competitiveness of modern capitalism. Culture circulates as "cultural capital" or "symbolic capital"; the main difference between tribal societies and modern societies is that in the latter much of the culture takes a written form and is produced by specialized culture-producing institutions, especially the school system. The reproduction of this culture from generation to generation and its periodic conversion into hard economic assets and thence back into cultural capital constitute the reproduction of the class system. Culture thus can be characterized as "symbolic violence," "the gentle, invisible form of violence that is never recognized as such," because it insidiously creates and recreates relationships of domination and subordination. Among the Kabyle tribespeople, these cultural exchanges take the form of gifts and countergifts of the sort described by Mauss, as well as the sexual property exchanges in marriages that make up a Lévi-Straussian alliance system. There is also the vendetta, a symbolic gift-exchange of "throats lent" to be cut and "throats returned" in countermurders, all of which Bourdieu sees as taking place on a second level, reflecting the "symbolic violence" that creates the stratification of honor.*

[A] *restricted definition of economic interest* . . . in its explicit form, is the historical product of capitalism: the constitution of relatively autonomous

From Pierre Bourdieu, *Outline of a Theory of Practice*, translated by Richard Nice (New York: Cambridge University Press, 1977), pp. 177–192, 195–97. Reprinted by permission of Cambridge University Press.

areas of practice is accompanied by a process through which symbolic interests (often described as "spiritual" or "cultural") come to be set up in opposition to strictly economic interests as defined in the field of economic transactions by the fundamental tautology "business is business"; strictly "cultural" or "aesthetic" interest, disinterested interest, is the paradoxical product of the ideological labour in which writers and artists, those most directly interested, have played an important part and in the course of which symbolic interests become autonomous by being opposed to material interests, that is, by being symbolically nullified as interests. Economism knows no other interest than that which capitalism has produced, through a sort of concrete application of abstraction, by establishing a universe of relations between man and man based, as Marx says, on "callous cash payment." Thus it can find no place in its analyses, still less in its calculations, for the strictly symbolic interest which is occasionally recognized (when too obviously entering into conflict with "interest" in the narrow sense, as in certain forms of nationalism or regionalism) only to be reduced to the irrationality of feeling or passion. In fact, in a universe characterized by the more or less perfect interconvertibility of economic capital (in the narrow sense) and symbolic capital, the *economic calculation* directing the agents' strategies takes indissociably into account profits and losses which the narrow definition of economy unconsciously rejects as *unthinkable* and *unnameable*, that is, as economically irrational. In short, contrary to naively idyllic representations of "pre-capitalist" societies (or of the "cultural" sphere of capitalist societies), practice never ceases to conform to economic calculation even when it gives every appearance of disinterestedness by departing from the logic of interested calculation (in the narrow sense) and playing for stakes that are non-material and not easily quantified.

Thus the theory of strictly economic practice is simply a particular case of a general theory of the economics of practice. The only way to escape from the ethnocentric naiveties of economism, without falling into populist exaltation of the generous naivety of earlier forms of society, is to carry out in full what economism does only partially, and to extend economic calculation to *all* the goods, material and symbolic, without distinction, that present themselves as *rare* and worthy of being sought after in a particular social formation—which may be "fair words" or smiles, handshakes or shrugs, compliments or attention, challenges or insults, honour or honours, powers or pleasures, gossip or scientific information, distinction or distinctions, etc. Economic calculation has hitherto managed to appropriate the territory objectively surrendered to the remorseless logic of what Marx calls "naked self-interest" only by setting aside a "sacred" island miraculously spared by the "icy water of egoistical calculation" and left as a sanctuary for the priceless or worthless things it cannot assess. But an accountancy of symbolic exchanges would itself lead to a distorted representation of the archaic economy if it were forgotten that, as the product of a principle of differentiation alien to the universe to which it is applied—the distinction between economic and symbolic capital—the only way in which such accountancy can apprehend the undifferentiatedness of economic and symbolic capital is in the form of their perfect interconvertibility. If the constitution of art *qua* art, accompanying the development of a relatively autonomous artistic field, leads one to conceive of certain primitive or popular practices as aesthetic, one inevitably falls into the ethnocentric errors unavoidable when one forgets that those practices cannot be conceived as such from within; similarly, any partial or total objectification of the ancient economy that does not include a theory of the *theorization effect* and of the social conditions of objective apprehension, together with a theory of that economy's relation to its objective reality (a relation of misrecognition), succumbs to the subtlest and most irreproachable form of ethnocentrism.

In its full definition, the patrimony of a family or lineage includes not only their land and instruments of production but also their kin and their clientele, the network of alliances, or, more broadly, of relationships, to be kept up and regularly maintained, representing a heritage of commitments and debts of honour, a capital of rights and duties built up in the course of successive generations and providing an additional source of strength which can be called upon when extra-ordinary situations break in upon the daily routine. For all its power to regulate the routine of the ordinary course of events through ritual stereotyping, and to overcome crises by producing them symbolically or ritualizing them as soon as they appear, the archaic economy is nonetheless familiar with the opposition between ordinary and extraordinary occasions, between the regular needs which the household can satisfy and the exceptional needs for material and symbolic goods and services (in unusual circumstances of economic crisis, political conflict, or simply urgent farm work) requiring the unpaid assistance of a more extended group. If this is so, it is because, contrary to what Max Weber suggests when he draws a crude contrast between the traditionalist type and the charismatic type, the ancient economy has its discontinuities, not only in the political sphere, with conflicts which may start with a chance incident and escalate into tribal war through the interplay of the "leagues," but also in the economic sphere, with the opposition between the *labour period*, which in traditional cereal cultivation is particularly short, and the *production period*—an opposition giving rise to one of the basic contradictions of that social formation and also, in consequence, to the strategies designed to overcome it. The strategy of accumulating a capital of honour and prestige, which produces the clients as much as they produce it, provides the optimal solution to the problem the group would face if it had to *maintain continuously* (throughout the production period as well) the whole (human and animal) workforce it needs during the labour period: it allows the great families to make use of the maximum workforce during the labour period, and to reproduce consumption to a minimum during the unavoidably long production period. Both human and animal consumption are cut, the former by the reduction of the group to the minimal unit, the family; and the latter through hire contracts, such as the *charka* of an ox, by which the owner lends his animal in exchange for nothing more than compensation in cash or in kind for "depreciation of the capital." These services, provided at precise moments and limited of periods of intense activity, such as harvest time, are repaid either in the form of labour, at other times of the year, or with other services such as protection, the loan of animals, and so on.

Thus we see that symbolic capital, which in the form of the prestige and renown attached to a family and a name is readily convertible back into economic capital, is perhaps *the most valuable form of accumulation* in a society in which the severity of the climate (the major work—ploughing and harvesting—having to be done in a very short space of time) and the limited technical resources (harvesting is done with the sickle) demand collective labour. Should one see in it a disguised form of purchase of labour power, or a covert exaction of corvées? By all means, as long as the analysis holds together what holds together in practice, the *double reality* of intrinsically *equivocal, ambiguous* conduct. This is the pitfall awaiting all those whom a naively dualistic representation of the relationship between practice and ideology, between the "native" economy and the "native" representation of that economy, leads into self-mystifying demystifications: the complete reality of this appropriation of services lies in the fact that it *can only* take place in the disguise of the voluntary assistance which is also a corvée and is thus a voluntary corvée and forced assistance, and that, to use a geometrical metaphor, it implies a double half-rotation returning to the starting-point, that is, a conversion of material capital into symbolic capital itself reconvertible into material capital.

The acquisition of a clientele, even an inherited one, implies considerable *labour* devoted to making and maintaining relations, and also substantial material and symbolic *investments*, in the form of political aid against attack, theft, offence, and insult, or economic aid, which can be very costly, especially in times of scarcity. As well as material wealth, *time* must be invested, for the value of symbolic labour cannot be defined without reference to the time devoted to it, *giving* or *squandering time* being one of the most precious of gifts. It is clear that in such conditions symbolic capital can only be accumulated at the expense of the accumulation of economic capital. Combining with the objective obstacles stemming from the inefficiency of the means of production, the action of the social mechanisms inclining agents to repress or disguise economic interest and tending to make the accumulation of symbolic capital the only recognized, legitimate form of accumulation, was sufficient to restrain and even prohibit the accumulation of material capital; and it was no doubt rare for the assembly to have to step in and order someone "not to get any richer." It is a fact that collective pressure—with which the wealthy members of the group have to reckon, because they draw from it not only their authority but also, at times, political power, the strength of which ultimately reflects their capacity to mobilize the group for or against individuals or groups—requires the rich not only to pay the largest share of the cost of ceremonial exchanges but also to make the biggest contributions to the maintenance of the poor, the lodging of strangers, and the organization of festivals. Above all, wealth implies duties. "The generous man", it is said, "is the friend of God." Belief in immanent justice, which inspires a number of practices (such as collective oath-swearing), no doubt helps to make of generosity a sacrifice designed to win in return the blessing of prosperity: "Eat, you who are used to feeding others"; "Lord, give unto me that I may give." But the two forms of capital are so inextricably linked that the mere exhibition of the material and symbolic strength represented by prestigious affines is likely to be in itself a source of material profit in a good-faith economy in which good repute is the best, if not the only, economic guarantee: it is easy to see why the great families never miss a chance (and this is one reason for their predilection for distant marriages and vast processions) to organize exhibitions of symbolic capital (in which conspicuous consumption is only the most visible aspect), with processions of relatives and friends to solemnize the pilgrim's departure or return; the bride's escort, assessed in terms of the number of "rifles" and the intensity of the salutes fired in the couple's honour; prestigious gifts, including sheep, given on the occasion of the marriage; witnesses and guarantors who can be mobilized at any time and place, to attest the good faith of a market transaction or to strengthen the position of the lineage in matrimonial negotiation and to solemnize the contract. Once one realizes that symbolic capital is always *credit*, in the widest sense of the word, that is, a sort of advance which the group alone can grant those who give it the best material and symbolic *guarantees*, it can be seen that the exhibition of symbolic capital (which is always very expensive in economic terms) is one of the mechanisms which (no doubt universally) make capital go to capital.

It is thus by drawing up a *comprehensive balance-sheet* of symbolic profits, without forgetting the undifferentiatedness of the symbolic and material aspects of the patrimony, that it becomes possible to grasp the economic rationality of conduct which economism dismisses as absurd: the decision to buy a second pair of oxen after the harvest, on the grounds that they are needed for treading out the grain—which is a way of making it known the crop has been plentiful—only to have to sell them again for lack of fodder, before the autumn ploughing, when they would be technically necessary, seems economically aberrant only if one forgets all the material and symbolic profit accruing from this (albeit fictitious) addition to the family's symbolic capital in the late-summer period in which marriages are negotiated. The perfect rationality of this strategy of bluff lies in the fact that marriage is the occasion for an (in the widest sense) economic circulation which cannot be seen purely in terms of material goods; the profit a group can expect to draw from the transaction rises with its material and especially its symbolic patrimony, in other words, its standing in the eyes of other groups. This standing, which depends on the capacity of the group's point of honour to guarantee the invulnerability of its honour, and constitutes an undivided whole indissolubly uniting the quantity and quality of its goods and the quantity and quality of the men capable of turning them to good account, is what enables the group, mainly through marriage, to acquire powerful affines (i.e., wealth in the form of "rifles," measured not only by the number of men but also by their quality, that is, their point of honour), and defines the group's capacity to preserve its land and honour, and in particular the honour of its women (i.e., the capital of material and symbolic strength which can actually be mobilized for market transactions, contests of honour, or work on the land). Thus the interest at stake in the conduct of honour is one for which economism has no name, and which has to be called symbolic, although it is such as to inspire actions which are very directly material; just as there are professions, like law and medicine, in which those who practise them must be "above suspicion," so a family has a vital interest in keeping its capital of honour, i.e. its capital of honourability, safe from suspicion. And the hypersensitivity to the slightest slur or innuendo, and the multiplicity of strategies designed to belie or avert them, can be explained by the fact that symbolic capital is less easily measured and counted than land or livestock and that the group, ultimately the only source of credit for it, will readily withdraw that credit and direct its suspicions at the strongest members, as if in matters of honour, as in land, one man's greater wealth made the others that much poorer.

Thus, the homologies established between the circulation of land sold and bought, the circulation of "throats" "lent" and "returned" (murder and vengeance), and the circulation of women given and received, that is, between the different forms of capital and the corresponding modes of circulation, oblige us to abandon the dichotomy of the economic and the non-economic which stands in the way of seeing the science of economic practices as a particular case of a *general science of the economy of practices*, capable of treating all practices, including those purporting to be disinterested or gratu-itous, and hence non-economic, as economic practices directed towards the maximizing of material or symbolic profit. The capital accumulated by groups, the energy of social dynamics—in this case their capital of physical strength (related to their mobilizing capacity, and hence to the number of men and their readiness to fight), their economic capital (land and livestock) and their symbolic capital, always additionally associated with possession of the other kinds of capital, but susceptible of increase or decrease depending on how they are used—can exist in *different forms* which, although subject to strict laws of equivalence and hence mutually convertible, produce specific effects. Symbolic capital, a transformed and thereby *disguised* form of physical "economic" capital, produces its proper effect inasmuch, and only inasmuch, as it conceals the fact that it originates in "material" forms of capital which are also, in the last analysis, the source of its effects.

MODES OF DOMINATION

In societies which have no "self-regulating market" (in Karl Polyani's sense), no educational system, no juridical apparatus, and no State, relations of domination can be set up and maintained only at the cost of strategies which must be endlessly renewed, because the conditions required for a *mediated, lasting appropriation* of other agents' labour, services, or homage have not been brought together. By contrast, domination no longer needs to be exerted in a direct, personal way when it is entailed in possession of the means (economic or cultural capital) of appropriating the mechanisms of the field of production and the field of cultural production, which tend to assure their own reproduction by their very functioning, independently of any deliberate intervention by the agents. So, it is in the degree of objectification of the accumulated social capital that one finds the basis of all the pertinent differ-ences between the modes of domination: that is, very schematically, between, on the one hand, social universes in which relations of domination are made, unmade, and remade in and by the interactions between persons, and on the other hand, social formations in which, mediated by objective, institutional-ized mechanisms, such as those producing and guaranteeing the distribution of "titles" (titles of nobility, deeds of possession, academic degrees, etc.), relations of domination have the opacity and permanence of things and escape the grasp of individual consciousness and power. Objectification guarantees the permanence and cumulativity of material and symbolic acquisitions which can then subsist without the agents having to recreate them continuously and in their entirety by deliberate action; but, because the profits of these institutions are the object of differential appropriation, objectification also and inseparably ensures the reproduction of the structure of the distribution of the capital which, in its various forms, is the precondition for such appropriation, and in so doing, reproduces the structure of the relations of domination and dependence.

Paradoxically, it is precisely because there exist relatively autonomous fields, functioning in accordance with rigorous mechanisms capable of imposing their necessity on the agents, that those who are in a position to command these mechanisms and to appropriate the material and/or symbolic profits accruing from their functioning are able to *dispense with* strategies aimed *expressly* (which does not mean manifestly) and directly (i.e. without being mediated by the mechanisms) at the domination of individuals, a domination which in this case is the condition of the appropriation of the material and symbolic profits of their labour. The saving is a real one, because strategies designed to establish or maintain lasting relations of dependence are generally very expensive in terms of material goods (as in the potlatch or in charitable acts), services, or simply *time*; which is why, by a paradox constitutive of this mode of domination, the means eat up the end, and the actions necessary to ensure the continuation of power themselves help to weaken it.

Economic power lies not in wealth but in the relationship between wealth and a field of economic relations, the constitution of which is inseparable from the development of a *body of specialized agents*, with specific interests; it is in this relationship that wealth is constituted, in the form of capital, that is, as the instrument for appropriating the institutional equipment and the mechanisms indispensable to the functioning of the field, and thereby also appropriating the profits from it. Thus Moses Finley convincingly shows that the ancient economy lacked not resources but the means "to overcome the limits of individual resources." "There were no proper credit instruments—no negotiable paper, no book clearance, no credit payments. . . . There was money-lending in plenty but it was concentrated on small usurious loans to peasants or consumers, and in large borrowings to enable men to meet the political or other conventional expenditures of the upper classes. . . . Similarly in the field of business organization: there were no long-term partnerships or corporations, no brokers or agents, no guilds—again with the occasional and unimportant exception. In short, both the organizational and the operational devices were lacking for the mobilization of private capital resources." This analysis is even more relevant to ancient Kabylia, which lacked even the most elementary instruments of an economic institution. Land was in fact more or less totally excluded from circulation (though, occasionally serving as security, it was liable to pass from one group to another). Village and tribal markets remained isolated and there was no way in which they could be linked up in a single mechanism. The opposition made by traditional morality between the "sacrilegious cunning" customary in market transactions and the good faith appropriate to exchanges among kinsmen and friends—which was marked by the spatial distinction between the place of residence, the village, and the place of transactions, the market—must not be allowed to mask the opposition between the small local market, still "embedded in social relationships," as Polyani puts it, and the market when it has become the "dominant transactional mode."

Just as economic wealth cannot function as capital until it is linked to an economic apparatus, so cultural competence in its various forms cannot be constituted as cultural capital until it is inserted into the objective relations between the system of economic production and the system producing the producers (which is itself constituted by the relation between the school system and the family). When a society lacks both the literacy which would enable it to preserve and accumulate in objectified form the cultural resources it has inherited from the past, and also the educational system which would give its agents the aptitudes and dispositions required for the symbolic reappropriation of those resources, it can only preserve them *in their incorporated state.* Consequently, to ensure the perpetuation of cultural resources which would otherwise disappear along with the agents who bear them, it has to resort to systematic inculcation, a process which, as is shown by the case of the bards, may last as long as the period during which the resources are actually used. The transformations made possible by an instrument of cultural communication such as writing have been abundantly described: by detaching cultural resources from persons, literacy enables a society to move beyond immediate human limits—in particular those of individual memory—and frees it from the constraints implied by mnemonic devices such as poetry, the preservation technique par excellence in non-literate societies; it enables a society to accumulate culture hitherto preserved in embodied form, and correlatively enables particular groups to practise *primitive accumulation of cultural capital,* the partial or total monopolizing of the society's symbolic resources in religion, philosophy, art, and science, by monopolizing the instruments for appropriation of those resources (writing, reading, and other decoding techniques) henceforward preserved not in memories but in texts.

But the objectification effects of literacy are nothing in comparison with those produced by the educational system. Without entering into detailed analysis, it must suffice to point out that academic qualifications are to cultural capital what money is to economic capital. By giving the same value to all holders of the same certificate, so that any one of them can take the place of any other, the educational system minimizes the obstacles to the free circulation of cultural capital which result from its being incorporated in individual persons (without, however, sacrificing the advantages of the charismatic ideology of the irreplaceable individual); it makes it possible to relate all qualification-holders (and also, negatively, all unqualified individuals) to a single standard, thereby setting up a *single market* for all cultural capacities and guaranteeing the convertibility of cultural capital into money, at a determinate cost in labour and time. Academic qualifications, like money, have a conventional, fixed value which, being guaranteed by law, is freed from local limitations (in contrast to scholastically uncertified cultural capital) and temporal fluctuations: the cultural capital which they in a sense guarantee once and for all does not constantly need to be proved. The objectification accomplished by academic degrees and diplomas and, in a more general way, by all forms of credentials, is inseparable from the objectification which the law guarantees by defining *permanent positions* which are distinct from the biological individuals holding them, and may be occupied by agents who are biologically different but interchangeable in terms of the qualifications required. Once this state of affairs is established, relations of power and domination no longer exist directly between individuals; they are set up in pure objectivity between institutions, that is, between socially guaranteed qualifications and socially defined positions, and through them, between the social mechanisms which produce and guarantee both the social value of the qualifications and the positions and also the distribution of these social attributes, among biological individuals.

Law does no more than symbolically consecrate—by *recording* it in a form which renders it both eternal and universal—the structure of the power relation between groups and classes which is produced and guaranteed practically by the functioning of these mechanisms. For example, it records and legitimates the distinction between the position and the person, the power and its holder, together with the relationship obtaining at a particular moment between qualifications and jobs (reflecting the relative bargaining power of the buyers and sellers of qualified, i.e., scholastically guaranteed, labour power) which appears concretely in a particular distribution of the material and symbolic profits assigned to the holders (or non-holders) of qualifications. The law thus contributes its own (specifically symbolic) force to the action of the various mechanisms which render it superfluous constantly to reassert power relations by overtly resorting to force.

Thus the task of legitimating the established order does not fall exclusively to the mechanisms traditionally regarded as belonging to the order of ideology, such as law. The system of symbolic goods production and the system producing the producers fulfil in addition, that is, by the very logic of their normal functioning, ideological functions, by virtue of the fact that the mechanisms through which they contribute to the reproduction of the established order and to the perpetuation of domination remain hidden. The educational system helps to provide the dominant class with what Max Weber terms "a theodicy of its own privilege," not so much through the ideologies it produces or inculcates (as those who speak of "ideological apparatuses" would have it); but rather through the practical justification of the established order which it achieves by using the overt connection between qualifications and jobs as a smokescreen for the connection—which it *records surreptitiously*, under cover of formal equality—between the qualifications people obtain and the cultural capital they have inherited—in other words, through the legitimacy it confers on the transmission of this form of heritage. The most successful ideological effects are those which have no need of words, and ask no more than complicitous silence. It follows, incidentally that any analysis of ideologies, in the narrow sense of "legitimating discourses," which fails to include an analysis of the corresponding institutional mechanisms is liable to be no more than a contribution to the efficacy of those ideologies: this is true of all internal (semiological) analyses of political, educational, religious, or aesthetic ideologies which forget that the political function of these ideologies may in some cases be reduced to the effect of displacement and diversion, camouflage and legitimation, which they produce by reproducing—through their oversights and omissions, and in their deliberately or involuntarily complicitous silences—the effects of the objective mechanisms.

It has been necessary at least to sketch an analysis of the objective mechanisms which play a part both in setting up and in concealing lasting relations of domination, in order to understand fully the radical difference between the different modes of domination and the different political strategies for conservation characteristic of social formations whose accumulated social energy is unequally objectified in mechanisms. On the one side there are social relations which, not containing within themselves the principle of their own reproduction, must be kept up through nothing less than a process of continuous creation; on the other side, a social world which, containing within itself the principle of its own continuation, frees agents from the endless work of creating or restoring social relations. This opposition finds expression in the history or prehistory of sociological thought. In order to "ground social being in nature," as Durkheim puts it, it has been necessary to break with the propensity to see it as founded on the arbitrariness of individual wills, or, with Hobbes, on the arbitrariness of a sovereign will: "For Hobbes," writes Durkheim, "it is an act of will which gives birth to the social order and it is a perpetually renewed act of will which upholds it." And there is every reason to believe that the break with this artificialist vision, which is the precondition for scientific apprehension, could not be made before the constitution, in reality, of objective mechanisms like the self-regulating market, which, as Polyani points out, was intrinsically conducive to belief in determinism. But social reality had another trap in store for science: the existence of mechanisms capable of reproducing the political order, independently of any deliberate intervention, makes it possible to recognize as political, amongst the different types of conduct directed towards gaining or keeping power, only such practices as tacitly exclude control over the reproduction mechanisms from the area of legitimate competition. In this way, social science, taking for its object the sphere of legitimate politics (as so-called "political science" does nowadays) adopted the preconstructed object which reality foisted upon it.

The greater the extent to which the task of reproducing the relations of domination is taken over by objective mechanisms, which serve the interests of the dominant group without any conscious effort on the latter's part, the more indirect and, in a sense, impersonal, become the strategies objectively oriented towards reproduction: it is not by lavishing generosity, kindness, or politeness on his charwoman (or on any other "socially inferior" agent), but by choosing the best investment for his money, or the best school for his son, that the possessor of economic or cultural capital perpetuates the relationship of domination which objectively links him with his charwoman and even her descendants. Once a system of mechanisms has been constituted capable of objectively ensuring the reproduction of the established order by its own motion, the dominant class have only to *let the system they dominate take its own course* in order to exercise their domination; but until such a system exists, they have to work directly, daily, personally, to produce and reproduce conditions of domination which are even then never entirely trustworthy. Because they cannot be satisfied with appropriating the profits of a social machine which has not yet developed the power of self-perpetuation, they are obliged to resort to *the elementary forms of domination*, in other words, the direct domination of one person by another, the limiting case of which is appropriation of persons, that is, slavery. They cannot appropriate the labour, services, goods, homage, and respect of others without "winning" them personally, "tying" them—in short, creating a bond between persons.

Thus this system contains only two ways (and they prove in the end to be just one way) of getting and keeping a lasting hold over someone: gifts or debts, the overtly economic obligations of debt, or the "moral," "affective" obligations created and maintained by exchange, in short, [overt (physical or economic) violence,] or symbolic violence—*censored, euphemized*, that is, unrecognizable, socially recognized violence. There is an intelligible relation—not a contradiction—between these two forms of violence, which coexist in the same social formation and sometimes in the same relationship: when domination can only be exercised in its *elementary form*, that is, directly, between one person and another, it cannot take place overtly and must be disguised under the veil of enchanted relationships, the official model of which is presented by relations between kinsmen; in order to be socially recognized it must get itself misrecognized. The reason for the pre-capitalist economy's great need for symbolic violence is that the only way in which relations of domination can be set up, maintained, or restored, is through strategies which, being expressly oriented towards the establishment of relations of personal dependence, must be disguised and transfigured lest they destroy themselves by revealing their true nature; in a word, they must be *euphemized*. Hence the *censorship* to which the overt manifestation of violence, especially in its naked economic form, is subjected by the logic characteristic of an economy in which interests can only be satisfied on condition that they be disguised in and by the strategies aiming to satisfy them. It would be a mistake to see a contradiction in the fact that violence is here both more present and more hidden. Because the pre-capitalist economy cannot count on the implacable, hidden violence of objective mechanisms, it resorts *simultaneously* to forms of domination which may strike the modern observer as more brutal, more primitive, more barbarous, or at the same time, as gentler, more humane, more respectful of persons. This coexistence of overt physical and economic violence and of the most refined symbolic violence is found in all the institutions characteristic of this economy, and at the heart of every social relationship: it is present both in the debt and in the gift, which, in spite of their apparent opposition, have in common the power of founding either dependence (and even slavery) or solidarity, depending on the strategies within which they are deployed. The fundamental ambiguity of all the institutions which modern taxonomies tend to present as economic is evidence that contrary strategies, which, as we have also seen in the case of the master—*khammes* [sharecropper] relationship, may coexist under the same name, are interchangeable ways of performing the same function, with the "choice" between overt violence and gentle, hidden violence depending on the relative strengths of the two parties at a particular time, and on the degree of integration and ethical integrity of the arbitrating group. In a society in which overt violence, the violence of the usurer or the merciless master, meets with collective reprobation and is liable either to provoke a violent riposte from the victim or to force him to flee (that is to say, in either case, in *the absence of any other recourse*, to provoke the annihilation of the very relationship which was intended to be exploited), symbolic violence, the gentle, invisible form of violence, which is never recognized as such, and is not so much undergone as chosen, the violence of credit, confidence, obligation, personal loyalty, hospitality, gifts, gratitude, piety—in short, all the virtues honoured by the code of honour—cannot fail to be seen as the most economical mode of domination, that is, the mode which best corresponds to the economy of the system.

Gentle, hidden exploitation is the form taken by man's exploitation of man whenever overt, brutal exploitation is impossible. It is as false to identify this essentially *dual* economy with its official reality (generosity, mutual aid, etc.), that is, the form which exploitation has to adopt in order to take place, as it is to reduce it to its objective reality, seeing mutual aid as a corvée, the *khammes* as a sort of slave, and so on. The gift, generosity, conspicuous distribution— the extreme case of which is the potlatch—are operations of social alchemy which may be observed whenever the direct application of overt physical or economic violence is negatively sanctioned, and which tend to bring about the transmutation of economic capital into symbolic capital. Wastage of money, energy, time, and ingenuity is the very essence of the social alchemy through which an interested relationship is transmuted into a disinterested, gratuitous relationship, overt domination into misrecognized, "socially recognized" domination, in other words, *legitimate authority*.

Goods are for giving. The rich man is "rich so as to be able to give to the poor," say the Kabyles. This is an exemplary disclaimer: because giving is also a way of possessing (a gift which is not matched by a counter-gift creates a lasting bond, restricting the debtor's freedom and forcing him to adopt a peaceful, co-operative, prudent attitude); because in the absence of any juridical guarantee, or any coercive force, one of the few ways of "holding" someone is to *keep up* a lasting asymmetrical relationship such as indebtedness; and because the only recognized, legitimate form of possession is that achieved by dispossessing oneself—that is, obligation, gratitude, prestige, or personal loyalty. Wealth, the ultimate basis of power, can exert power and exert it durably, only in the form of symbolic capital; in other words, economic capital can be accumulated only in the form of symbolic capital, the unrecognizable, and hence socially recognizable, form of the other kinds of capital. The chief is indeed, in Malinowski's phrase, a "tribal banker," amassing food only to lavish it on others, in order to build up a capital of obligations and debts which will be repaid in the form of homage, respect, loyalty, and, when the opportunity arises, work and services, which may be the bases of a new accumulation of material goods. Processes of circular circulation, such as the levying of a tribute followed by hierarchical redistribution, would appear absurd but for the effect they have of transmuting the nature of the social relation between the agents or groups involved. Wherever they are observed, these *consecration cycles* perform the fundamental operation of social alchemy, the transformation of arbitrary relations into legitimate relations, *de facto* differences into officially recognized distinctions. Distinctions and lasting associations are founded in the circular circulation from which the legitimation of power arises as a symbolic surplus value. If, like Lévi-Strauss, one considers only the *particular case* of exchanges of material and/or symbolic goods intended to legitimate relations of reciprocity, one is in danger of forgetting that all structures of inseparably material and symbolic exchange (i.e., involving both circulation and communication) function as ideological machines whenever the *de facto* state of affairs which they tend to legitimate by transforming a contingent social relationship into a recognized relationship is an unequal balance of power.

The endless reconversion of economic capital into symbolic capital, at the cost of a wastage of social energy which is the condition for the permanence of domination, cannot succeed without the complicity of the whole group: the work of denial which is the source of social alchemy is, like magic, a collective undertaking. As Mauss puts it, the whole society pays itself in the false coin of its dream. The collective misrecognition which is the basis of the ethic of honour, a collective denial of the economic reality of exchange, is only possible because, when the group lies to itself in this way, there is neither deceiver nor deceived: the peasant who treats his *khammes* as an associate, because that is the custom and because honour requires him to do so, deceives himself as much as he deceives his *khammes*, since the *only* form in which he can serve his interest is the euphemistic form presented by the ethic of honour; and nothing suits the *khammes* better than to play his part in an interested fiction which offers him an honourable representation of his condition. Thus the mechanisms responsible for reproducing the appropriate habitus are here an integral part of an apparatus of production which could not function without them. Agents lastingly "bind" each other, not only as parents and children, but also as creditor and debtor, master and *khammes*, only through the dispositions which the group inculcates in them and continuously reinforces, and which render *unthinkable* practices which would appear as legitimate and even be taken for granted in the disenchanted economy of "naked self-interest."

The official truth produced by the collective work of euphemization, an elementary form of the labour of objectification which eventually leads to the juridical definition of acceptable behaviour, is not simply the group's means of saving its "spiritualistic point of honour"; it also has a practical efficacy, for, even if it were contradicted by everyone's behaviour, like a rule to which every case proved an exception, it would still remain a true description of such behaviour as is intended to be acceptable. The code of honour weighs on each agent with the weight of all the other agents, and the disenchantment which leads to the progressive unveiling of repressed meanings and functions can only result from a collapse of the social conditions of the *cross-censorship* to which each agent submits with impatience but which he imposes on all the others.

If it be true that symbolic violence is the gentle, hidden form which violence takes when overt violence is impossible, it is understandable why symbolic forms of domination should have progressively withered away as objective mechanisms came to be constituted which, in rendering superfluous the work of euphemization, tended to produce the "disenchanted" dispositions their development demanded. It is equally clear why the progressive uncovering and neutralization of the ideological and practical effects of the mechanisms assuring the reproduction of the relations of domination should determine a return to forms of symbolic violence again based on dissimulation of the mechanisms of reproduction through the conversion of economic into symbolic capital: it is through legitimacy-giving redistribution, public ("social" policies) and private (financing of "disinterested" foundations, grants to hospitals and to academic and cultural institutions), which they make possible, that the efficacy of the mechanisms of reproduction is exerted.

To these forms of legitimate accumulation, through which the dominant groups or classes secure a capital of "credit" which seems to owe nothing to the logic of exploitation, must be added another form of accumulation of symbolic capital, the collection of luxury goods attesting the taste and distinction of their owner. The denial of economy and of economic interest, which in pre-capitalist societies at first took place on a ground from which it had to be expelled in order for economy to be constituted as such, thus finds its favourite refuge in the domain of art and culture, the site of pure consumption—of money, of course, but also of time convertible into money. The world of art, a sacred island systematically and ostentatiously opposed to the profane, everyday world of production, a sanctuary for gratuitous, disinterested activity in a universe given over to money and self-interest, offers, like theology in a past epoch, an imaginary anthropology obtained by denial of all the negations really brought about by the economy.

III THE MICROINTERACTIONIST TRADITION

Some Main Points of the Microinteractionist Tradition

1870–1900	American pragmatists: Peirce, James	German objectivists: Brentano, Meinong
1900–1930	Dewey Cooley Thomas Mead	Husserl
1930–1960	Symbolic Interactionism: Blumer Theories of deviance, occupations, and professions: Everett Hughes	Schutz existentialism: Heidegger Sartre
1960–	Role theory	Ethnomethodology: Garfinkel Conversational analysis Cognitive sociology
	Goffman's frame analysis	

Society Is in the Mind [1902]

CHARLES HORTON COOLEY

• *Charles Horton Cooley is the earliest professional sociologist in
the distinctively American tradition of social psychology. In this
excerpt from 1902, he attempts to show that social interaction
takes place only within each individual's mind, as he or she
imagines other people's attitudes and possible responses. "All real
persons are imaginery" in a certain sense, according to Cooley;
and in a famous conclusion, he asserts: "The imaginations which
people have of one another are the solid facts of society, and . . .
to observe and interpret these must be a chief aim of sociology."*

When left to themselves children continue the joys of sociability by means of
an imaginary playmate. Although all must have noticed this who have observed children at all, only close and constant observation will enable one to
realize the extent to which it is carried on. It is not an occasional practice,
but, rather, a necessary form of thought, flowing from a life in which personal
communication is the chief interest and social feeling the stream in which,
like boats on a river, most other feelings float. Some children appear to live in
personal imaginations almost from the first month; others occupy their minds
in early infancy mostly with solitary experiments upon blocks, cards, and other
impersonal objects, and their thoughts are doubtless filled with the images of
these. But, in either case, after a child learns to talk and the social world in all
its wonder and provocation opens on his mind, it floods his imagination so
that all his thoughts are conversations. He is never alone. Sometimes the
inaudible interlocutor is recognizable as the image of a tangible playmate,
sometimes he appears to be purely imaginary. Of course each child has his
own peculiarities.

The main point to note here is that these conversations are not occasional and
temporary effusions of the imagination, but are the naïve expression of a
socialization of the mind that is to be permanent and to underlie all later
thinking. The imaginary dialogue passes beyond the thinking aloud of little

From Charles Horton Cooley, *Human Nature and the Social Order* (New York: Scribners', 1902),
pp. 88–92, 95–97, 118–28, 143.

children into something more elaborate, reticent, and sophisticated; but it never ceases. Grown people, like children, are usually unconscious of these dialogues; as we get older we cease, for the most part, to carry them on out loud, and some of us practise a good deal of apparently solitary meditation and experiment. But, speaking broadly, it is true of adults as of children, that the mind lives in perpetual conversation. It is one of those things that we seldom notice just because they are so familiar and involuntary; but we can perceive it if we try to. If one suddenly stops and takes note of his thoughts at some time when his mind has been running free, as when he is busy with some simple mechanical work, he will be likely to find them taking the form of vague conversations. This is particularly true when one is somewhat excited with reference to a social situation. If he feels under accusation or suspicion in any way he will probably find himself making a defense, or perhaps a confession, to an imaginary hearer. A guilty man confesses "to get the load off his mind"; that is to say, the excitement of his thought cannot stop there but extends to the connected impulses of expression and creates an intense need to tell somebody. Impulsive people often talk out loud when excited, either "to themselves," as we say when we can see no one else present, or to any one whom they can get to listen. Dreams also consist very largely of imaginary conversations; and, with some people at least, the mind runs in dialogue during the half-waking state before going to sleep. There are many other familiar facts that bear the same interpretation—such, for instance, as that it is much easier for most people to compose in the form of letters or dialogue than in any other; so that literature of this kind has been common in all ages. . . . The fact is that language, developed by the race through personal intercourse and imparted to the individual in the same way, can never be dissociated from personal intercourse in the mind; and since higher thought involves language, it is always a kind of imaginary conversation. The word and the interlocutor are correlative ideas.

It is worth noting here that there is no separation between real and imaginary persons; indeed, to be imagined is to become real, in a social sense, as I shall presently point out. An invisible person may easily be more real to an imaginative mind than a visible one; sensible presence is not necessarily a matter of the first importance. A person can be real to us only in the degree in which we imagine an inner life which exists in us, for the time being, and which we refer to him. The sensible presence is important chiefly in stimulating us to do this. All real persons are imaginary in this sense. If, however, we use imaginary in the sense of illusory, an imagination not corresponding to fact, it is easy to see that visible presence is no bar to illusion. Thus I meet a stranger on the steamboat who corners me and tells me his private history. I care nothing for it, and he half knows that I do not; he uses me only as a lay figure to sustain the agreeable illusion of sympathy, and is talking to an imaginary companion quite as he might if I were elsewhere. So likewise good manners are largely a tribute to imaginary companionship, a make-believe of sympathy which it is agreeable to accept as real, though we may know, when we think, that it is not. To conceive a kindly and approving companion is something that one involuntarily tries to do, in accordance with that instinctive hedonizing inseparable from all wholesome mental processes, and to assist in this by at least a seeming of friendly appreciation is properly regarded as a part of good breeding. To be always sincere would be brutally to destroy this pleasant and mostly harmless figment of the imagination.

Thus the imaginary companionship which a child of three or four years so naïvely creates and expresses is something elementary and almost omnipresent in the thought of a normal person. In fact, thought and personal intercourse may be regarded as merely aspects of the same thing: we call it personal intercourse when the suggestions that keep it going are received through faces or other symbols present to the senses; reflection when the personal suggestions come through memory and are more elaborately worked over in thought. But both are mental, both are personal. Personal images, as they are connected with nearly all our higher thought in its inception, remain inseparable from it in memory. The mind is not a hermit's cell, but a place of hospitality and intercourse. We have no higher life that is really apart from other people. It is by imagining them that our personality is built up; to be without the power of imagining them is to be a low-grade idiot; and in the measure that a mind is lacking in this power it is degenerate. Apart from this mental society there is no wisdom, no power, justice, or right, no higher existence at all. The life of the mind is essentially a life of intercourse.

So far as the study of immediate social relations is concerned the personal idea is the real person. That is to say, it is in this alone that one man exists for another, and acts directly upon his mind. My association with you evidently consists in the relation between my idea of you and the rest of my mind. If there is something in you that is wholly beyond this and makes no impression upon me it has no social reality in this relation. *The immediate social reality is the personal idea*; nothing, it would seem, could be much more obvious than this.

Society, then, in its immediate aspect, *is a relation among personal ideas*. In order to have society it is evidently necessary that persons should get together somewhere; and they get together only as personal ideas in the mind. Where else? What other possible *locus* can be assigned for the real contact of persons, or in what other form can they come in contact except as impressions or ideas formed in this common *locus*? Society exists in my mind as the contact and reciprocal influence of certain ideas named "I," Thomas, Henry, Susan, Bridget, and so on. It exists in your mind as a similar group, and so in every mind. Each person is immediately aware of a particular aspect of society: and so far as he is aware of great social wholes, like a nation or an epoch, it is by embracing in this particular aspect ideas or sentiments which he attributes to his countrymen or contemporaries in their collective aspect. In order to see this it seems to me only necessary to discard vague modes of speech which have no conceptions back of them that will bear scrutiny, and look at the facts as we know them in experience.

Yet most of us, perhaps, will find it hard to assent to the view that the social person is a group of sentiments attached to some symbol or other characteristic element, which keeps them together and from which the whole idea is named. The reason for this reluctance I take to be that we are accustomed to talk and think, so far as we do think in this connection, as if a person were a material rather than a psychical fact. Instead of basing our sociology and ethics upon what a man really is as part of our mental and moral life, he is vaguely and yet grossly regarded as a shadowy material body, a lump of flesh, and not as an ideal thing at all. But surely it is only common sense to hold that the social and moral reality is that which lives in our imaginations and affects our motives. As regards the physical it is only the finer, more plastic and mentally significant aspects of it that imagination is concerned with, and with them chiefly as a nucleus or centre of crystallization for sentiment. Instead of perceiving this we commonly make the physical the dominant factor, and think of the mental and moral only by a vague analogy to it.

Persons and society must, then, be studied primarily in the imagination. It is surely true, *prima facie*, that the best way of observing things is that which is most direct; and I do not see how any one can hold that we know persons directly except as imaginative ideas in the mind. These are perhaps the most vivid things in our experience, and as observable as anything else, though it is a kind of observation in which accuracy has not been systematically cultivated. The observation of the physical aspects, however important, is for social purposes quite subsidiary: there is no way of weighing or measuring men which throws more than a very dim side-light on their personality. The physical factors most significant are those elusive traits of expression already discussed, and in the observation and interpretation of these physical science is only indirectly helpful. What, for instance, could the most elaborate knowledge of his weights and measures, including the anatomy of his brain, tell us of the character of Napoleon? Not enough, I take it, to distinguish him with certainty from an imbecile. Our real knowledge of him is derived from reports of his conversation and manner, from his legislation and military dispositions, from the impression made upon those about him and by them communicated to us, from his portraits and the like; all serving as aids to the imagination in forming a system that we call by his name.

I conclude, therefore, that the imaginations which people have of one another are the *solid facts* of society, and that to observe and interpret these must be a chief aim of sociology. I do not mean merely that society must be studied *by* the imagination—that is true of all investigations in their higher reaches—but that the *object* of study is primarily an imaginative idea or group of ideas in the mind, that we have to imagine imaginations. The intimate grasp of any social fact will be found to require that we divine what men think of one another. Charity, for instance, is not understood without imagining what ideas the giver and recipient have of each other; to grasp homicide we must, for one thing, conceive how the offender thinks of his victim and of the administrators of the law; the relation between the employing and hand-laboring classes is first of all a matter of personal attitude which we must apprehend by sympathy with both, and so on. In other words, we want to get at motives, and motives spring from personal ideas. There is nothing particularly novel in this view; historians, for instance, have always assumed that to understand and interpret personal relations was their main business; but apparently the time is coming when this will have to be done in a more systematic and penetrating manner than in the past. Whatever may justly be urged against the introduction of frivolous and disconnected "personalities" into history, the understanding of persons is the aim of this and all other branches of social study.

It is important to face the question of persons who have no corporeal reality, as for instance the dead, characters of fiction or the drama, ideas of the gods and the like. Are these real people, members of society? I should say that in so far as we imagine them they are. Would it not be absurd to deny social reality to Robert Louis Stevenson, who is so much alive in many minds and so potently affects important phases of thought and conduct? He is certainly more real in this practical sense than most of us who have not yet lost our corporeity, more alive, perhaps, than he was before he lost his own, because of his wider influence. And so Colonel Newcome, or Romola, or Hamlet is real to the imaginative reader with the realest kind of reality, the kind that works directly upon his personal character. And the like is true of the conceptions of supernatural beings handed down by the aid of tradition among all peoples. What, indeed, would society be, or what would any one of us be, if we associated only with corporeal persons and insisted that no one should enter our company who could not show his power to tip the scales and cast a shadow?

On the other hand, a corporeally existent person is not socially real unless he is imagined. If the nobleman thinks of the serf as a mere animal and does not attribute to him a human way of thinking and feeling, the latter is not real to him in the sense of acting personally upon his mind and conscience. And if a man should go into a strange country and hide himself so completely that no one knew he was there, he would evidently have no social existence for the inhabitants.

In saying this I hope I do not seem to question the independent reality of persons or to confuse it with personal ideas. The man is one thing and the various ideas entertained about him are another; but the latter, the personal idea, is the immediate social reality, the thing in which men exist for one another, and work directly upon one another's lives. Thus any study of society that is not supported by a firm grasp of personal ideas is empty and dead— mere doctrine and not knowledge at all.

I believe that the vaguely material notion of personality, which does not confront the social fact at all but assumes it to be the analogue of the physical fact, is a main source of fallacious thinking about ethics, politics, and indeed every aspect of social and personal life. It seems to underlie all four of the ways of conceiving society and the individual alleged in the first chapter to be false. If the person is thought of primarily as a separate material form, inhabited by thoughts and feelings conceived by analogy to be equally separate, then the only way of getting a society is by adding on a new principle of socialism, social faculty, altruism, or the like. But if you start with the idea that the social person is primarily a fact in the mind, and observe him there, you find at once that he has no existence apart from a mental whole of which all personal ideas are members, and which is a particular aspect of society. Every one of these ideas, as we have seen, is the outcome of our experience of all the persons we have known, and is only a special aspect of our general idea of mankind.

To many people it would seem mystical to say that persons, as we know them, are not separable and mutually exclusive, like physical bodies, so that what is part of one cannot be part of another, but that they interpenetrate one another, the same element pertaining to different persons at different times, or even at the same time: yet this is a verifiable and not very abstruse fact. The sentiments which make up the largest and most vivid part of our idea of any person are not, as a rule, peculiarly and exclusively his, but each one may be entertained in conjunction with other persons also. It is, so to speak, at the point of intersection of many personal ideas, and may be reached through any one of them.

As regards one's self in relation to other people, I shall have more to say in a later chapter; but I may say here that there is no view of the self, that will bear examination, which makes it altogether distinct, in our minds, from other persons. If it includes the whole mind, then, of course, it includes all the persons we think of, all the society which lives in our thoughts. If we confine ' to a certain part of our thought with which we connect a distinctive emotion c sentiment called self-feeling, as I prefer to do, it still includes the persons wit whom we feel most identified. *Self and other do not exist as mutually exclusiv social facts*, and phraseology which implies that they do, like the antithesis egoism *versus* altruism, is open to the objection of vagueness, if not of falsity. It seems to me that the classification of impulses as altruistic and egoistic, with or without a third class called, perhaps, ego-altruistic, is empty; and I do not see how any other conclusion can result from a concrete study of the matter. There is no class of altruistic impulses specifically different from other impulses: all our higher, socially developed sentiments are indeterminately personal, and may be associated with self-feeling, or with whatever personal symbol may happen to arouse them. Those feelings which are merely sensual and have not been refined into sentiments by communication and imagination are not so much egoistic as merely animal: they do not pertain to social persons, either first or second, but belong in a lower stratum of thought. Sensuality is not to be confused with the social self. As I shall try to show later we do not think "I" except with reference to a complementary thought of other persons; it is an idea developed by association and communication.

The egoism-altruism way of speaking falsifies the facts at the most vital point possible by assuming that our impulses relating to persons are separable into two classes, the I impulses and the You impulses, in much the same way that physical persons are separable; whereas a primary fact throughout the range of sentiment is a fusion of persons, so that the impulse belongs not to one or the other, but precisely to the common ground that both occupy, to their inter-course or mingling. Thus the sentiment of gratitude does not pertain to me as against you, nor to you as against me, but springs right from our union, and so with all personal sentiment.

According to this view of the matter society is simply the collective aspect of personal thought. Each man's imagination, regarded as a mass of personal impressions worked up into a living, growing whole, is a special phase of society; and Mind or Imagination as a whole, that is human thought con-sidered in the largest way as having a growth and organization extending throughout the ages, is the *locus* of society in the widest possible sense.

Thought as Internalized Conversation [1934]

GEORGE HERBERT MEAD

> • *George Herbert Mead was for many years a professor of philosophy at the University of Chicago. His greatest influence was not on philosophy but on the sociologists who came to hear his lectures, among them Herbert Blumer, who developed the ideas of Mead and others into the sociological theory of symbolic interactionism. In this excerpt from Mead's posthumously published lectures, Mead argues that the self is not one's physical body, but, in fact, a complicated set of attitudes that one derives from outside and that can be turned in various directions, both inward and outward. We are multiple selves as we have multiple social relationships, and on these we build yet another degree of multiplicity through reflexive relationships among our own selves. For Mead, the thinking mind is itself social, an internalized conversation among the different parts of the self, the "I," "me," and "generalized other." Symbolism would not be possible without the generalization of perspectives that comes from taking the role of another. "A person who is saying something is saying to himself what he says to others," Mead proposes; "otherwise he does not know what he is talking about."*

We can distinguish very definitely between the self and the body. The body can be there and can operate in a very intelligent fashion without there being a self involved in the experience. The self has the characteristic that it is an object to itself, and that characteristic distinguishes it from other objects and from the body. It is perfectly true that the eye can see the foot, but it does not see the body as a whole. We cannot see our backs; we can feel certain portions of them, if we are agile, but we cannot get an experience of our whole body. There are, of course, experiences which are somewhat vague and difficult of location, but the bodily experiences are for us organized about a self. The foot and hand belong to the self. We can see our feet, especially if we look at them from the wrong end of an opera glass, as strange things which we have

From George Herbert Mead, *Mind, Self, and Society*, edited by Charles W. Morris (University of Chicago Press, 1934), pp. 136–42, 145–62, 175–78. Copyright 1934 by the University of Chicago. Copyright 1962 by Charles W. Morris. Reprinted with permission of University of Chicago Press.

difficulty in recognizing as our own. The parts of the body are quite distinguishable from the self. We can lose parts of the body without any serious invasion of the self. The mere ability to experience different parts of the body is not different from the experience of a table. The table presents a different feel from what the hand does when one hand feels another, but it is an experience of something with which we come definitely into contact. The body does not experience itself as a whole, in the sense in which the self in some way enters into the experience of the self.

It is the characteristic of the self as an object to itself that I want to bring out. This characteristic is represented in the word "self," which is a reflexive, and indicates that which can be both subject and object. This type of object is essentially different from other objects, and in the past it has been distinguished as conscious, a term which indicates an experience with, an experience of, one's self. It was assumed that consciousness in some way carried this capacity of being an object to itself. In giving a behavioristic statement of consciousness we have to look for some sort of experience in which the physical organism can become an object to itself.[1]

When one is running to get away from someone who is chasing him, he is entirely occupied in this action, and his experience may be swallowed up in the objects about him, so that he has, at the time being, no consciousness of self at all. We must be, of course, very completely occupied to have that take place, but we can, I think, recognize that sort of a possible experience in which the self does not enter. . . . In such instances there is a contrast between an experience that is absolutely wound up in outside activity in which the self as an object does not enter, and an activity of memory and imagination in which the self is the principal object. The self is then entirely distinguishable from an organism that is surrounded by things and acts with reference to things, including parts of its own body. These latter may be objects like other objects, but they are just objects out there in the field, and they do not involve a self that is an object to the organism. This is, I think, frequently overlooked. It is that fact which makes our anthropomorphic reconstructions of animal life so fallacious. How can an individual get outside himself (experientially) in such a way as to become an object to himself? This is the essential psychological problem of selfhood or of self-consciousness; and its solution is to be found by referring to the process of social conduct or activity in which

[1] Man's behavior is such in his social group that he is able to become an object to himself, a fact which constitutes him a more advanced product of evolutionary development than are the lower animals. Fundamentally it is this social fact—and not his alleged possession of a soul or mind with which he, as an individual, has been mysteriously and supernaturally endowed, and with which the lower animals have not been endowed—that differentiates him from them.

the given person or individual is implicated. The apparatus of reason would not be complete unless it swept itself into its own analysis of the field of experience; or unless the individual brought himself into the same experiential field as that of the other individual selves in relation to whom he acts in any given social situation. Reason cannot become impersonal unless it takes an objective, non-affective attitude toward itself; otherwise we have just consciousness, not *self*-consciousness. And it is necessary to rational conduct that the individual should thus take an objective, impersonal attitude toward himself, that he should become an object to himself. For the individual organism is obviously an essential and important fact or constituent element of the empirical situation in which it acts; and without taking objective account of itself as such, it cannot act intelligently, or rationally.

The individual experiences himself as such, not directly, but only indirectly, from the particular standpoints of other individual members of the same social group, or from the generalized standpoint of the social group as a whole to which he belongs. For he enters his own experience as a self or individual, not directly or immediately, not by becoming a subject to himself, but only in so far as he first becomes an object to himself just as other individuals are objects to him or in his experience; and he becomes an object to himself only by taking the attitudes of other individuals toward himself within a social environment or context of experience and behavior in which both he and they are involved.

The importance of what we term "communication" lies in the fact that it provides a form of behavior in which the organism or the individual may become an object to himself. It is that sort of communication which we have been discussing—not communication in the sense of the cluck of the hen to the chickens, or the bark of a wolf to the pack, or the lowing of a cow, but communication in the sense of significant symbols, communication which is directed not only to others but also to the individual himself. So far as that type of communication is a part of behavior it at least introduces a self. Of course, one may hear without listening; one may see things that he does not realize; do things that he is not really aware of. But it is where one does respond to that which he addresses to another and where that response of his own becomes a part of his conduct, where he not only hears himself but responds to himself, talks and replies to himself as truly as the other person replies to him, that we have behavior in which the individuals become objects to themselves.

The self, as that which can be an object to itself, is essentially a social structure, and it arises in social experience. After a self has arisen, it in a certain sense provides for itself its social experiences, and so we can conceive of an absolutely solitary self. But it is impossible to conceive of a self arising outside of social experience. When it has arisen we can think of a person in solitary confinement for the rest of his life, but who still has himself as a companion, and is able to think and to converse with himself as he had communicated with others. That process to which I have just referred, of responding to one's self as another responds to it, taking part in one's own conversation with others, being aware of what one is saying and using that awareness of what one is saying to determine what one is going to say there-after—that is a process with which we are all familiar. We are continually following up our own address to other persons by an understanding of what we are saying, and using that understanding in the direction of our continued speech. We are finding out what we are going to say, what we are going to do, by saying and doing, and in the process we are continually controlling the process itself. In the conversation of gestures what we say calls out a certain response in another and that in turn changes our own action, so that we shift from what we started to do because of the reply the other makes. The conversation of gestures is the beginning of communication. The individual comes to carry on a conversation of gestures with himself. He says something, and that calls out a certain reply in himself which makes him change what he was going to say. One starts to say something, we will presume an unpleasant something, but when he starts to say it he realizes it is cruel. The effect on himself of what he is saying checks him; there is here a conversation of gestures between the individual and himself. We mean by significant speech that the action is one that affects the individual himself, and that the effect upon the individual himself is part of the intelligent carrying-out of the conversation with others. Now we, so to speak, amputate that social phase and dispense with it for the time being, so that one is talking to one's self as one would talk to another person.[2]

This process of abstraction cannot be carried on indefinitely. One inevitably

---

[2]It is generally recognized that the specifically social expressions of intelligence, or the exercise of what is often called "social intelligence," depend upon the given individual's ability to take the rôles of, or "put himself in the place of," the other individuals implicated with him in given social situations; and upon his consequent sensitivity to their attitudes toward himself and toward one another. These specifically social expressions of intelligence, of course, acquire unique significance in terms of our view that the whole nature of intelligence is social to the very core—that this putting of one's self in the places of others, this taking by one's self of their rôles or attitudes, is not merely one of the various aspects or expressions of intelligence or of intelligent behavior, but is the very essence of its character. Spearman's "X factor" in intelligence—the unknown factor which, according to him, intelligence contains—is simply (if our social theory of intelligence is correct) this ability of the intelligent individual to take the attitude of the other, or the attitudes of others, thus realizing the significations or grasping the meanings of the symbols or gestures in terms of which thinking proceeds; and thus being able to carry on with himself the internal conversation with these symbols or gestures which thinking involves.

seeks an audience, has to pour himself out to somebody. In reflective intelligence one thinks to act, and to act solely so that this action remains a part of a social process. Thinking becomes preparatory to social action. The very process of thinking is, of course, simply an inner conversation that goes on, but it is a conversation of gestures which in its completion implies the expression of that which one thinks to an audience. One separates the significance of what he is saying to others from the actual speech and gets it ready before saying it. He thinks it out, and perhaps writes it in the form of a book; but it is still a part of social intercourse in which one is addressing other persons and at the same time addressing one's self, and in which one controls the address to other persons by the response made to one's own gesture. That the person should be responding to himself is necessary to the self, and it is this sort of social conduct which provides behavior within which that self appears. I know of no other form of behavior than the linguistic in which the individual is an object to himself, and, so far as I can see, the individual is not a self in the reflexive sense unless he is an object to himself. It is this fact that gives a critical importance to communication, since this is a type of behavior in which the individual does so respond to himself.

We realize in everyday conduct and experience that an individual does not mean a great deal of what he is doing and saying. We frequently say that such an individual is not himself. We come away from an interview with a realization that we have left out important things, that there are parts of the self that did not get into what was said. What determines the amount of the self that gets into communication is the social experience itself. Of course, a good deal of the self does not need to get expression. We carry on a whole series of different relationships to different people. We are one thing to one man and another thing to another. There are parts of the self which exist only for the self in relationship to itself. We divide ourselves up in all sorts of different selves with reference to our acquaintances. We discuss politics with one and religion with another. There are all sorts of different selves answering to all sorts of different social reactions. It is the social process itself that is responsible for the appearance of the self; it is not there as a self apart from this type of experience.

The peculiar character possessed by our human social environment belongs to it by virtue of the peculiar character of human social activity; and that character, as we have seen, is to be found in the process of communication, and more particularly in the triadic relation on which the existence of meaning is based: the relation of the gesture of one organism to the adjustive response made to it by another organism, in its indicative capacity as pointing to the completion or resultant of the act it initiates (the meaning of the gesture being thus the response of the second organism to it as such, or as a gesture). What, as it were, takes the gesture out of the social act and isolates it as such—what makes it something more than just an early phase of an individual act—is the response of another organism, or of other organisms, to it. Such a response is its meaning, or gives it its meaning. The social situation and process of behavior are here presupposed by the acts of the individual organisms implicated therein. The gesture arises as a separable element in the social act, by virtue of the fact that it is selected out by the sensitivities of other organisms to it; it does not exist as a gesture merely in the experience of the single individual. The meaning of a gesture by one organism, to repeat, is found in the response of another organism to what would be the completion of the act of the first organism which that gesture initiates and indicates.

We sometimes speak as if a person could build up an entire argument in his mind, and then put it into words to convey it to someone else. Actually, our thinking always takes place by means of some sort of symbols. It is possible that one could have the meaning of "chair" in his experience without there being a symbol, but we would not be thinking about it in that case. We may sit down in a chair without thinking about what we are doing, that is, the approach to the chair is presumably already aroused in our experience, so that the meaning is there. But if one is thinking about the chair he must have some sort of a symbol for it. It may be the form of the chair, it may be the attitude that somebody else takes in sitting down, but it is more apt to be some language symbol that arouses this response. In a thought process there has to be some sort of a symbol that can refer to this meaning, that is, tend to call out this response, and also serve this purpose for other persons as well. It would not be a thought process if that were not the case.

Our symbols are all universal. You cannot say anything that is absolutely particular; anything you say that has any meaning at all is universal. You are saying something that calls out a specific response in anybody else provided that the symbol exists for him in his experience as it does for you. There is the language of speech and the language of hands, and there may be the language of the expression of the countenance. One can register grief or joy and call out certain responses. There are primitive people who can carry on elaborate conversations just by expressions of the countenance. Even in these cases the person who communicates is affected by that expression just as he expects somebody else to be affected. Thinking always implies a symbol which will call out the same response in another that it calls out in the thinker. Such a symbol is a universal of discourse; it is universal in its character. We always assume that the symbol we use is one which will call out in the other person the same response, provided it is a part of his mechanism of conduct. A person who is saying something is saying to himself what he says to others; otherwise he does not know what he is talking about.

Among primitive people, as I have said, the necessity of distinguishing the self and the organism was recognized in what we term the "double": the individual has a thing-like self that is affected by the individual as it affects other people and which is distinguished from the immediate organism in that it can leave the body and come back to it. This is the basis for the concept of the soul as a separate entity.

We find in children something that answers to this double, namely, the invisible, imaginary companions which a good many children produce in their own experience. They organize in this way the responses which they call out in other persons and call out also in themselves. Of course, this playing with an imaginary companion is only a peculiarly interesting phase of ordinary play. Play in this sense, especially the stage which precedes the organized games, is a play at something. A child plays at being a mother, at being a teacher, at being a policeman; that is, it is taking different rôles, as we say. We have something that suggests this in what we call the play of animals: a cat will play with her kittens, and dogs play with each other. Two dogs playing with each other will attack and defend, in a process which if carried through would amount to an actual fight. There is a combination of responses which checks the depth of the bite. But we do not have in such a situation the dogs taking a definite rôle in the sense that a child deliberately takes the rôle of another. This tendency on the part of the children is what we are working with in the kindergarten where the rôles which the children assume are made the basis for training. When a child does assume a rôle he has in himself the stimuli which call out that particular response or group of responses. He may, of course, run away when he is chased, as the dog does, or he may turn around and strike back just as the dog does in his play. But that is not the same as playing at something. Children get together to "play Indian." This means that the child has a certain set of stimuli which call out in itself the responses that they would call out in others, and which answer to an Indian. In the play period the child utilizes his own responses to these stimuli which he makes use of in building a self. The response which he has a tendency to make to these stimuli organizes them. He plays that he is, for instance, offering himself something, and he buys it; he gives a letter to himself and takes it away; he addresses himself as a parent, as a teacher; he arrests himself as a policeman. He has a set of stimuli which call out in himself the sort of responses they call out in others. He takes this group of responses and organizes them into a certain whole. Such is the simplest form of being another to one's self. It involves a temporal situation. The child says something in one character and responds in another character, and then his responding in another character is a stimulus to himself in the first character, and so the conversation goes on. A certain organized structure arises in him and in his other which replies to it, and these carry on the conversation of gestures between themselves.

If we contrast play with the situation in an organized game, we note the essential difference that the child who plays in a game must be ready to take the attitude of everyone else involved in that game, and that these different rôles must have a definite relationship to each other. Taking a very simple game such as hide-and-seek, everyone with the exception of the one who is hiding is a person who is hunting. A child does not require more than the person who is hunted and the one who is hunting. If a child is playing in the first sense he just goes on playing, but there is no basic organization gained. In that early stage he passes from one rôle to another just as a whim takes him. But in a game where a number of individuals are involved, then the child taking one rôle must be ready to take the rôle of everyone else. If he gets in a ball nine he must have the responses of each position involved in his own position. He must know what everyone else is going to do in order to carry out his own play. He has to take all of these roles. They do not all have to be present in consciousness at the same time, but at some moments he has to have three or four individuals present in his own attitude, such as the one who is going to throw the ball, the one who is going to catch it, and so on. These responses must be, in some degree, present in his own make-up. In the game, then, there is a set of responses of such others so organized that the attitude of one calls out the appropriate attitudes of the other.

This organization is put in the form of the rules of the game. Children take a great interest in rules. They make rules on the spot in order to help themselves out of difficulties. Part of the enjoyment of the game is to get these rules. Now, the rules are the set of responses which a particular attitude calls out. You can demand a certain response in others if you take a certain attitude. These responses are all in yourself as well. There you get an organized set of such responses as that to which I have referred, which is something more elaborate than the rôles found in play. Here there is just a set of responses that follow on each other indefinitely. At such a stage we speak of a child as not yet having a fully developed self. The child responds in a fairly intelligent fashion to the immediate stimuli that come to him, but they are not organized. He does not organize his life as we would like to have him do, namely, as a whole. There is just a set of responses of the type of play. The child reacts to a certain stimulus, and the reaction is in himself that is called out in others, but he is not a whole self. In his game he has to have an organization of these rôles; otherwise he cannot play the game. The game represents the passage in the life of the child from taking the rôle of others in play to the organized part that is essential to self-consciousness in the full sense of the term.

PLAY, THE GAME, AND THE GENERALIZED OTHER

The fundamental difference between the game and play is that in the latter the child must have the attitude of all the others involved in that game. The attitudes of the other players which the participant assumes organize into a sort of unit, and it is that organization which controls the response of the individual. The illustration used was of a person playing baseball. Each one of his own acts is determined by his assumption of the action of the others who are playing the game. What he does is controlled by his being everyone else on that team, at least in so far as those attitudes affect his own particular response. We get then an "other" which is an organization of the attitudes of those involved in the same process.

The organized community or social group which gives to the individual his unity of self may be called "the generalized other." The attitude of the generalized other is the attitude of the whole community. Thus, for example, in the case of such a social group as a ball team, the team is the generalized other in so far as it enters—as an organized process or social activity—into the experience of any one of the individual members of it.

If the given human individual is to develop a self in the fullest sense, it is not sufficient for him merely to take the attitudes of other human individuals toward himself and toward one another within the human social process, and to bring that social process as a whole into his individual experience merely in these terms: he must also, in the same way that he takes the attitudes of other individuals toward himself and toward one another, take their attitudes toward the various phases or aspects of the common social activity or set of social undertakings in which, as members of an organized society or social group, they are all engaged; and he must then, by generalizing these individual attitudes of that organized society or social group itself, as a whole, act toward different social projects which at any given time it is carrying out, or toward the various larger phases of the general social process which constitutes its life and of which these projects are specific manifestations. This getting of the broad activities of any given social whole or organized society as such within the experiential field of any one of the individuals involved or included in that whole is, in other words, the essential basis and prerequisite of the fullest development of that individual's self: only in so far as he takes the attitudes of the organized social group to which he belongs toward the organized, co-operative social activity or set of such activities in which that group as such is engaged, does he develop a complete self or possess the sort of complete self he has developed. And on the other hand, the complex co-operative processes and activities and institutional functionings of organized human society are also possible only in so far as every individual involved in them or belonging to that society can take the general attitudes of all other such individuals with reference to these processes and activities and institutional functionings, and to the organized social whole of experiential relations and interactions thereby constituted—and can direct his own behavior accordingly.

It is in the form of the generalized other that the social process influences the behavior of the individuals involved in it and carrying it on, that is, that the community exercises control over the conduct of its individual members; for it is in this form that the social process or community enters as a determining factor into the individual's thinking. In abstract thought the individual takes the attitude of the generalized other toward himself, without reference to its expression in any particular other individuals; and in concrete thought he takes that attitude in so far as it is expressed in the attitudes toward his behavior of those other individuals with whom he is involved in the given social situation or act. But only by taking the attitude of the generalized other toward himself, in one or another of these ways, can he think at all; for only thus can thinking—or the internalized conversation of gestures which constitutes thinking—occur. And only through the taking by individuals of the attitude or attitudes of the generalized other toward themselves is the existence of a universe of discourse, as that system of common or social meanings which thinking presupposes at its context, rendered possible.

I have pointed out, then, that there are two general stages in the full development of the self. At the first of these stages, the individual's self is constituted simply by an organization of the particular attitudes of other individuals toward himself and toward one another in the specific social acts in which he participates with them. But at the second stage in the full development of the individual's self that self is constituted not only by an organization of these particular individual attitudes, but also by an organization of the social attitudes of the generalized other or the social group as a whole to which he belongs. These social or group attitudes are brought within the individual's field of direct experience, and are included as elements in the structure or constitution of his self, in the same way that the attitudes of particular other individuals are; and the individual arrives at them, or succeeds in taking them, by means of further organizing, and then generalizing, the attitudes of particular other individuals in terms of their organized social bearings and implications. So the self reaches its full development by organizing these individual attitudes of others into the organized social or group attitudes, and by thus becoming an individual reflection of the general systematic pattern of social or group behavior in which it and the others are all involved—a pattern which enters as a whole into the individual's experience in terms of these organized group attitudes which, through the mechanism of his central nervous system, he takes toward himself, just as he takes the individual attitudes of others.

The game has a logic, so that such an organization of the self is rendered possible: there is a definite end to be obtained; the actions of the different individuals are all related to each other with reference to that end so that they do not conflict; one is not in conflict with himself in the attitude of another man on the team. If one has the attitude of the person throwing the ball he can also have the response of catching the ball. The two are related so that they further the purpose of the game itself. They are interrelated in a unitary, organic fashion. There is a definite unity, then, which is introduced into the organization of other selves when we reach such a stage as that of the game, as over against the situation of play where there is a simple succession of one rôle after another, a situation which is, of course, characteristic of the child's own personality. The child is one thing at one time and another at another, and what he is at one moment does not determine what he is at another. That is both the charm of childhood as well as its inadequacy. You cannot count on the child; you cannot assume that all the things he does are going to determine what he will do at any moment. He is not organized into a whole. The child has no definite character, no definite personality.

The game is then an illustration of the situation out of which an organized personality arises. In so far as the child does take the attitude of the other and allows that attitude of the other to determine the thing he is going to do with reference to a common end, he is becoming an organic member of society. He is taking over the morale of that society and is becoming an essential member of it. He belongs to it in so far as he does allow the attitude of the other that he takes to control his own immediate expression. What is involved here is some sort of an organized process. That which is expressed in terms of the game is, of course, being continually expressed in the social life of the child, but this wider process goes beyond the immediate experience of the child himself. The importance of the game is that it lies entirely inside of the child's own experience, and the importance of our modern type of education is that it is brought as far as possible within this realm. The different attitudes that a child assumes are so organized that they exercise a definite control over his response, as the attitudes in a game control his own immediate response. In the game we get an organized other, a generalized other, which is found in the nature of the child itself, and finds its expression in the immediate experience of the child. And it is that organized activity in the child's own nature controlling the particular response which gives unity, and which builds up his own self.

Such is the process by which a personality arises. I have spoken of this as a process in which a child takes the rôle of the other, and said that it takes place essentially through the use of language. Language is predominantly based on the vocal gesture by means of which co-operative activities in a community are carried out. Language in its significant sense is that vocal gesture which tends to arouse in the individual the attitude which it arouses in others, and it is this perfecting of the self by the gesture which mediates the social activities that gives rise to the process of taking the rôle of the other. The latter phrase is a little unfortunate because it suggests an actor's attitude which is actually more sophisticated than that which is involved in our own experience. To this degree it does not correctly describe that which I have in mind. We see the process most definitely in a primitive form in those situations where the child's play takes different rôles. Here the very fact that he is ready to pay out money, for instance, arouses the attitude of the person who receives money; the very process is calling out in him the corresponding activities of the other person involved. The individual stimulates himself to the response which he is calling out in the other person, and then acts in some degree in response to that situation. In play the child does definitely act out the rôle which he himself has aroused in himself. It is that which gives, as I have said, a definite content in the individual which answers to the stimulus that affects him as it affects somebody else. The content of the other that enters into one personality is the response in the individual which his gesture calls out in the other.

We may illustrate our basic concept by a reference to the notion of property. If we say, "This is my property, I shall control it," that affirmation calls out a certain set of responses which must be the same in any community in which property exists. It involves an organized attitude with reference to property which is common to all the members of the community. One must have a definite attitude of control of his own property and respect for the property of others. Those attitudes (as organized sets of responses) must be there on the part of all, so that when one says such a thing he calls out in himself the response of the others. He is calling out the response of what I have called a generalized other. That which makes society possible is such common responses, such organized attitudes, with reference to what we term property, the cults of religion, the process of education, and the relations of the family. Of course, the wider the society the more definitely universal these objects must be. In any case there must be a definite set of responses, which we may speak of as abstract, and which can belong to a very large group. Property is in itself a very abstract concept. It is that which the individual himself can control and nobody else can control. The attitude is different from that of a dog toward a bone. A dog will fight any other dog trying to take the bone. The dog is not taking the attitude of the other dog. A man who says, "This is my property," is taking an attitude of the other person. The man is appealing to his rights because he is able to take the attitude which everybody else in the group has with reference to property, thus arousing in himself the attitude of others.

The "I" is the response of the organism to the attitudes of the others; the "me" is the organized set of attitudes of others which one himself assumes. The attitudes of the others constitute the organized "me," and then one reacts toward that as an "I." I now wish to examine these concepts in greater detail.

There is neither "I" nor "me" in the conversation of gestures; the whole act is not yet carried out, but the preparation takes place in this field of gesture. Now, in so far as the individual arouses in himself the attitudes of the others, there arises an organized group of responses. And it is due to the individual's ability to take the attitudes of these others in so far as they can be organized that he gets self-consciousness. The taking of all of those organized sets of attitudes gives him his "me"; that is the self he is aware of. He can throw the ball to some other member because of the demand made upon him from other members of the team. That is the self that immediately exists for him in his consciousness. He has their attitudes, knows what they want and what the consequence of any act of his will be, and he has assumed responsibility for the situation. Now, it is the presence of those organized sets of attitudes that constitutes that "me" to which he as an "I" is responding. But what that response will be he does not know and nobody else knows. Perhaps he will make a brilliant play or an error. The response to that situation as it appears in his immediate experience is uncertain, and it is that which constitutes the "I."

The "I" is his action over against that social situation within his own conduct, and it gets into his experience only after he has carried out the act. Then he is aware of it. He had to do such a thing and he did it. He fulfils his duty and he may look with pride at the throw which he made. The "me" arises to do that duty—that is the way in which it arises in his experience. He had in him all the attitudes of others, calling for a certain response; that was the "me" of that situation, and his response is the "I."

The "I," then, in this relation of the "I" and the "me," is something that is, so to speak, responding to a social situation which is within the experience of the individual. It is the answer which the individual makes to the attitude which others take toward him when he assumes an attitude toward them. Now, the attitudes he is taking toward them are present in his own experience, but his response to them will contain a novel element. The "I" gives the sense of freedom, of initiative. The situation is there for us to act in a self-conscious fashion. We are aware of ourselves, and of what the situation is, but exactly how we will act never gets into experience until after the action takes place.

Such is the basis for the fact that the "I" does not appear in the same sense in experience as does the "me." The "me" represents a definite organization of the community there in our own attitudes, and calling for a response, but the response that takes place is something that just happens. There is no certainty in regard to it. There is a moral necessity but no mechanical necessity for the act. When it does take place then we find what has been done. The above account gives us, I think, the relative position of the "I" and "me" in the situation, and the grounds for the separation of the two in behavior. The two are separated in the process but they belong together in the sense of being parts of a whole. They are separated and yet they belong together. The separation of the "I" and the "me" is not fictitious. They are not identical, for, as I have said, the "I" is something that is never entirely calculable. The "me" does call for a certain sort of an "I" in so far as we meet the obligations that are given in conduct itself, but the "I" is always something different from what the situation itself calls for. So there is always that distinction, if you like, between the "I" and the "me." The "I" both calls out the "me" and responds to it. Taken together they constitute a personality as it appears in social experience. The self is essentially a social process going on with these two distinguishable phases. If it did not have these two phases there could not be conscious responsibility, and there would be nothing novel in experience.

Symbolic Interactionism [1969]

HERBERT BLUMER

• *Herbert Blumer coined the term* symbolic interactionism *"in an offhand way in an article written in 1937." He calls it "a somewhat barbaric neologism," but "the term somehow caught on and is now in general use." Blumer's symbolic interactionism is built on Mead and Cooley, as well as on W. I. Thomas, John Dewey, and others. In Blumer's hands, it turned into a full-fledged dynamic sociology, as well as a militant intellectual movement critical of opposing approaches. In one of his later statements, Blumer sums up its principles.*

Symbolic interactionism rests in the last analysis on three simple premises. The first premise is that human beings act toward things on the basis of the meanings that the things have for them. Such things include everything that the human being may note in his world—physical objects, such as trees or chairs; other human beings, such as a mother or a store clerk; categories of human beings, such as friends or enemies; institutions, as a school or a government; guiding ideals, such as individual independence or honesty; activities of others, such as their commands or requests; and such situations as an individual encounters in his daily life. The second premise is that the meaning of such things is derived from, or arises out of, the social interaction that one has with one's fellows. The third premise is that these meanings are handled in, and modified through, an interpretative process used by the person in dealing with the things he encounters. I wish to discuss briefly each of these three fundamental premises.

It would seem that few scholars would see anything wrong with the first premise—that human beings act toward things on the basis of the meanings which these things have for them. Yet, oddly enough, this simple view is ignored or played down in practically all of the thought and work in contemporary social science and psychological science. Meaning is either taken for granted and thus pushed aside as unimportant or it is regarded as a mere neutral link between the factors responsible for human behavior and this

From Herbert Blumer, *Symbolic Interactionism: Perspective and Method*, copyright 1969, pp. 2–21, 60. Reprinted by permission of Prentice-Hall, Inc., Englewood Cliffs, N.J.

behavior as the product of such factors. We can see this clearly in the predominant posture of psychological and social science today. Common to both
of these fields is the tendency to treat human behavior as the product of
various factors that play upon human beings; concern is with the behavior and
with the factors regarded as producing them. Thus, psychologists turn to such
factors as stimuli, attitudes, conscious or unconscious motives, various kinds
of psychological inputs, perception and cognition, and various features of
personal organization to account for given forms or instances of human conduct. In a similar fashion sociologists rely on such factors as social position,
status demands, social roles, cultural prescriptions, norms and values, social
pressures, and group affiliation to provide such explanations. In both such
typical psychological and sociological explanations the meanings of things for
the human beings who are acting are either bypassed or swallowed up in the
factors used to account for their behavior. If one declares that the given kinds
of behavior are the result of the particular factors regarded as producing them,
there is no need to concern oneself with the meaning of the things toward
which human beings act; one merely identifies the initiating factors and the
resulting behavior. Or one may, if pressed, seek to accommodate the element
of meaning by lodging it in the initiating factors or by regarding it as a neutral
link intervening between the initiating factors and the behavior they are alleged to produce. In the first of these latter cases the meaning disappears by
being merged into the initiating or causative factors; in the second case meaning becomes a mere transmission link that can be ignored in favor of the
initiating factors.

The position of symbolic interactionism, in contrast, is that the meanings
that things have for human beings are central in their own right. To ignore
the meaning of the things toward which people act is seen as falsifying the
behavior under study. To bypass the meaning in favor of factors alleged to
produce the behavior is seen as a grievous neglect of the role of meaning in
the formation of behavior.

The simple premise that human beings act toward things on the basis of the
meaning of such things is much too simple in itself to differentiate symbolic
interactionism—there are several other approaches that share this premise. A
major line of difference between them and symbolic interactionism is set by
the second premise, which refers to the source of meaning. There are two
well-known traditional ways of accounting for the origin of meaning. One of
them is to regard meaning as being intrinsic to the thing that has it, as being a
natural part of the objective makeup of the thing. Thus, a chair is clearly a
chair in itself, a cow a cow, a cloud a cloud, a rebellion a rebellion, and so
forth. Being inherent in the thing that has it, meaning needs merely to be

disengaged by observing the objective thing that has the meaning. The meaning emanates, so to speak, from the thing and as such there is no process involved in its formation; all that is necessary is to recognize the meaning that is there in the thing. It should be immediately apparent that this view reflects the traditional position of "realism" in philosophy—a position that is widely held and deeply entrenched in the social and psychological sciences. The other major traditional view regards "meaning" as a psychical accretion brought to the thing by the person for whom the thing has meaning. This psychical accretion is treated as being an expression of constituent elements of the person's psyche, mind, or psychological organization. The constituent elements are such things as sensations, feelings, ideas, memories, motives, and attitudes. The meaning of a thing is but the expression of the given psychological elements that are brought into play in connection with the perception of the thing; thus one seeks to explain the meaning of a thing by isolating the particular psychological elements that produce the meaning. One sees this in the somewhat ancient and classical psychological practice of analyzing the meaning of an object by identifying the sensations that enter into perception of that object; or in the contemporary practice of tracing the meaning of a thing, such as let us say prostitution, to the attitude of the person who views it. This lodging of the meaning of things in psychological elements limits the processes of the formation of meaning to whatever processes are involved in arousing and bringing together the given psychological elements that produce the meaning. Such processes are psychological in nature, and include perception, cognition, repression, transfer of feelings, and association of ideas.

Symbolic interactionism views meaning as having a different source than those held by the two dominant views just considered. It does not regard meaning as emanating from the intrinsic makeup of the thing that has meaning, nor does it see meaning as arising through a coalescence of psychological elements in the person. Instead, it sees meaning as arising in the process of interaction between people. The meaning of a thing for a person grows out of the ways in which other persons act toward the person with regard to the thing. Their actions operate to define the thing for the person. Thus, symbolic interactionism sees meanings as social products, as creations that are formed in and through the defining activities of people as they interact. This point of view gives symbolic interactionism a very distinctive position, with profound implications that will be discussed later.

The third premise mentioned above further differentiates symbolic interactionism. While the meaning of things is formed in the context of social interaction and is derived by the person from that interaction, it is a mistake to think that the use of meaning by a person is but an application of the meaning so derived. This mistake seriously mars the work of many scholars who otherwise follow the symbolic interactionist approach. They fail to see that the use of meanings by a person in his action involves an interpretative process. In this respect they are similar to the adherents of the two dominant views spoken of above—to those who lodge meaning in the objective makeup of the thing that has it and those who regard it as an expression of psychological elements. All three are alike in viewing the use of meaning by the human being in his action as being no more than an arousing and application of already established meanings. As such, all three fail to see that the use of meanings by the actor occurs through *a process of interpretation*. This process has two distinct steps. First, the actor indicates to himself the things toward which he is acting; he has to point out to himself the things that have meaning. The making of such indications is an internalized social process in that the actor is interacting with himself. This interaction with himself is something other than an interplay of psychological elements; it is an instance of the person engaging in a process of communication with himself. Second, by virtue of this process of communicating with himself, interpretation becomes a matter of handling meanings. The actor selects, checks, suspends, regroups, and transforms the meanings in the light of the situation in which he is placed and the direction of his action. Accordingly, interpretation should not be regarded as a mere automatic application of established meanings but as a formative process in which meanings are used and revised as instruments for the guidance and formation of action. It is necessary to see that meanings play their part in action through a process of self-interaction.

It is not my purpose to discuss at this point the merits of the three views that lodge meaning respectively in the thing, in the psyche, and in social action, nor to elaborate on the contention that meanings are handled flexibly by the actor in the course of forming his action. Instead, I wish merely to note that by being based on these three premises, symbolic interaction is necessarily led to develop an analytical scheme of human society and human conduct that is quite distinctive. It is this scheme that I now propose to outline.

Symbolic interactionism is grounded on a number of basic ideas, or "root images," as I prefer to call them. These root images refer to and depict the nature of the following matters: human groups or societies, social interaction, objects, the human being as an actor, human action, and the interconnection of the lines of action. Taken together, these root images represent the way in which symbolic interactionism views human society and conduct. They constitute the framework of study and analysis. Let me describe briefly each of these root images.

NATURE OF HUMAN SOCIETY OR HUMAN GROUP LIFE

Human groups are seen as consisting of human beings who are engaging in action. The action consists of the multitudinous activities that the individuals perform in their life as they encounter one another and as they deal with the succession of situations confronting them. The individuals may act singly, they may act collectively, and they may act on behalf of, or as representatives of, some organization or group of others. The activities belong to the acting individuals and are carried on by them always with regard to the situations in which they have to act. The import of this simple and essentially redundant characterization is that fundamentally human groups or society *exists in action* and must be seen in terms of action. This picture of human society as action must be the starting point (and the point of return) for any scheme that purports to treat and analyze human society empirically. Conceptual schemes that depict society in some other fashion can only be derivations from the complex of ongoing activity that constitutes group life. This is true of the two dominant conceptions of society in contemporary sociology—that of culture and that of social structure. Culture as a conception, whether defined as custom, tradition, norm, value, rules, or such like, is clearly derived from what people do. Similarly, social structure in any of its aspects, as represented by such terms as social position, status, role, authority, and prestige, refers to relationships derived from how people act toward each other. The life of any human society consists necessarily of an ongoing process of fitting together the activities of its members. It is this complex of ongoing activity that establishes and portrays structure or organization. A cardinal principle of symbolic interactionism is that any empirically oriented scheme of human society, however derived, must respect the fact that in the first and last instances human society consists of people engaging in action. To be empirically valid the scheme must be consistent with the nature of the social action of human beings.

NATURE OF SOCIAL INTERACTION

Group life necessarily presupposes interaction between the group members; or, put otherwise, a society consists of individuals interacting with one another. The activities of the members occur predominantly in response to one another or in relation to one another. Even though this is recognized almost universally in definitions of human society, social interaction is usually taken for granted and treated as having little, if any, significance in its own right. This is evident in typical sociological and psychological schemes—they treat social interaction as merely a medium through which the determinants of behavior pass to produce the behavior. Thus, the typical sociological scheme ascribes behavior to such factors as status position, cultural prescriptions, norms, values, sanctions, role demands, and social system requirements; explanation in terms of such factors suffices without paying attention to the social interaction that their play necessarily presupposes. Similarly, in the typical psychological scheme such factors as motives, attitudes, hidden complexes, elements of psychological organization, and psychological processes are used to account for behavior without any need of considering social interaction. One jumps from such causative factors to the behavior they are supposed to produce. Social interaction becomes a mere forum through which sociological or psychological determinants move to bring about given forms of human behavior. I may add that this ignoring of social interaction is not corrected by speaking of an interaction of societal elements (as when a sociologist speaks of an interaction of social roles or an interaction between the components of a social system) or an interaction of psychological elements (as when a psychologist speaks of an interaction between the attitudes held by different people). Social interaction is an interaction between actors and not between factors imputed to them.

Symbolic interactionism does not merely give a ceremonious nod to social interaction. It recognizes social interaction to be of vital importance in its own right. This importance lies in the fact that social interaction is a process that *forms* human conduct instead of being merely a means or a setting for the expression or release of human conduct. Put simply, human beings in interacting with one another have to take account of what each other is doing or is about to do; they are forced to direct their own conduct or handle their situations in terms of what they take into account. Thus, the activities of others enter as positive factors in the formation of their own conduct; in the face of the actions of others one may abandon an intention or purpose, revise it, check or suspend it, intensify it, or replace it. The actions of others enter to set what one plans to do, may oppose or prevent such plans, may require a revision of such plans, and may demand a very different set of such plans. One has to *fit* one's own line of activity in some manner to the actions of others. The actions of others have to be taken into account and cannot be regarded as merely an arena for the expression of what one is disposed to do or sets out to do.

We are indebted to George Herbert Mead for the most penetrating analysis of social interaction—an analysis that squares with the realistic account just given. Mead identifies two forms or levels of social interaction in human society. He refers to them respectively as "the conversation of gestures" and "the use of significant symbols"; I shall term them respectively "non-symbolic interaction" and "symbolic interaction." Non-symbolic interaction takes place when one responds directly to the action of another without interpreting that action; symbolic interaction involves interpretation of the action. Non-symbolic interaction is most readily apparent in reflex responses, as in the case of a boxer who automatically raises his arms to parry a blow. However, if the boxer were reflectively to identify the forthcoming blow from his opponent as a feint designed to trap him, he would be engaging in symbolic interaction. In this case, he would endeavor to ascertain the meaning of the blow—that is, what the blow signifies as to his opponent's plan. In their association human beings engage plentifully in non-symbolic interaction as they respond immediately and unreflectively to each other's bodily movements, expressions, and tones of voice, but their characteristic mode of interaction is on the symbolic level, as they seek to understand the meaning of each other's action.

Mead's analysis of symbolic interaction is highly important. He sees it as a presentation of gestures and a response to the meaning of those gestures. A gesture is any part or aspect of an ongoing action that signifies the larger act of which it is a part—for example, the shaking of a fist as an indication of a possible attack, or the declaration of war by a nation as an indication of a posture and line of action of that nation. Such things as requests, orders, commands, cues, and declarations are gestures that convey to the person who recognizes them an idea of the intention and plan of forthcoming action of the individual who presents them. The person who responds organizes his response on the basis of what the gestures mean to him; the person who presents the gestures advances them as indications or signs of what he is planning to do as well as of what he wants the respondent to do or understand. Thus, the gesture has meaning for both the person who makes it and for the person to whom it is directed. When the gesture has the same meaning for both, the two parties understand each other. From this brief account it can be seen that the meaning of the gesture flows out along three lines (Mead's triadic nature of meaning): It signifies what the person to whom it is directed is to do; it signifies what the person who is making the gesture plans to do; and it signifies the joint action that is to arise by the articulation of the acts of both. Thus, for illustration, a robber's command to his victim to put up his hands is (a) an indication of what the victim is to do; (b) an indication of what the robber plans to do, that is, relieve the victim of his money; and (c) an indication of the joint act being formed, in this case a holdup. If there is confusion or misunderstanding along any one of these three lines of meaning, communication is ineffective, interaction is impeded, and the formation of joint action is blocked.

One additional feature should be added to round out Mead's analysis of symbolic interaction, namely, that the parties to such interaction must necessarily take each other's roles. To indicate to another what he is to do, one has to make the indication from the standpoint of that other; to order the victim to put up his hands the robber has to see this response in terms of the victim making it. Correspondingly, the victim has to see the command from the standpoint of the robber who gives the command; he has to grasp the intention and forthcoming action of the robber. Such mutual role-taking is the *sine qua non* of communication and effective symbolic interaction.

The central place and importance of symbolic interaction in human group life and conduct should be apparent. A human society or group consists of people in association. Such association exists necessarily in the form of people acting toward one another and thus engaging in social interaction. Such interaction in human society is characteristically and predominantly on the symbolic level; as individuals acting individually, collectively, or as agents of some organization encounter one another they are necessarily required to take account of the actions of one another as they form their own action. They do this by a dual process of indicating to others how to act and of interpreting the indications made by others. Human group life is a vast process of such defining to others what to do and of interpreting their definitions; through this process people come to fit their activities to one another and to form their own individual conduct. Both such joint activity and individual conduct are formed *in* and *through* this ongoing process; they are not mere expressions or products of what people bring to their interaction or of conditions that are antecedent to their interaction. The failure to accommodate to this vital point constitutes the fundamental deficiency of schemes that seek to account for human society in terms of social organization or psychological factors, or of any combination of the two. By virtue of symbolic interaction, human group life is necessarily a formative process and not a mere arena for the expression of pre-existing factors.

NATURE OF OBJECTS

The position of symbolic interactionism is that the "worlds" that exist for human beings and for their groups are composed of "objects" and that these objects are the product of symbolic interaction. An object is anything that can be indicated, anything that is pointed to or referred to—a cloud, a book, a legislature, a banker, a religious doctrine, a ghost, and so forth. For purposes of convenience one can classify objects in three categories: (a) physical objects, such as chairs, trees, or bicycles; (b) social objects, such as students, priests, a president, a mother, or a friend; and (c) abstract objects, such as moral principles, philosophical doctrines, or ideas such as justice, exploitation, or compassion. I repeat that an object is anything that can be indicated or referred to. The nature of an object—of any and every object—consists of the meaning that it has for the person for whom it is an object. This meaning sets the way in which he sees the object, the way in which he is prepared to act toward it, and the way in which he is ready to talk about it. An object may have a different meaning for different individuals: a tree will be a different object to a botanist, a lumberman, a poet, and a home gardener; the President of the United States can be a very different object to a devoted member of his political party than to a member of the opposition; the members of an ethnic group may be seen as a different kind of object by members of other groups. The meaning of objects for a person arises fundamentally out of the way they are defined to him by others with whom he interacts. Thus, we come to learn through the indications of others that a chair is a chair, that doctors are a certain kind of professional, that the United States Constitution is a given kind of legal document, and so forth. Out of a process of mutual indications common objects emerge—objects that have the same meaning for a given set of people and are seen in the same manner by them.

Several noteworthy consequences follow from the foregoing discussion of objects. First, it gives us a different picture of the environment or milieu of human beings. From their standpoint the environment consists *only* of the objects that the given human beings recognize and know. The nature of this environment is set by the meaning that the objects composing it have for those human beings. Individuals, also groups, occupying or living in the same spatial location may have, accordingly, very different environments; as we say, people may be living side by side yet be living in different worlds. Indeed, the term "world" is more suitable than the word "environment" to designate the setting, the surroundings, and the texture of things that confront them. It is the world of their objects with which people have to deal and toward which they develop their actions. It follows that in order to understand the action of people it is necessary to identify their world of objects—an important point that will be elaborated later.

Second, objects (in the sense of their meaning) must be seen as social creations—as being formed in and arising out of the process of definition and interpretation as this process takes place in the interaction of people. The meaning of anything and everything has to be formed, learned, and transmitted through a process of indication—a process that is necessarily a social process. Human group life on the level of symbolic interaction is a vast process in which people are forming, sustaining, and transforming the objects of their world as they come to give meaning to objects. Objects have no fixed status except as their meaning is sustained through indications and definitions that people make of the objects. Nothing is more apparent than that objects in all categories can undergo change in their meaning. A star in the sky is a very different object to a modern astrophysicist than it was to a sheepherder of biblical times; marriage was a different object to later Romans than to earlier Romans; the president of a nation who fails to act successfully through critical times may become a very different object to the citizens of his land. In short, from the standpoint of symbolic interactionism human group life is a process in which objects are being created, affirmed, transformed, and cast aside. The life and action of people necessarily change in line with the changes taking place in their world of objects.

THE HUMAN BEING AS AN ACTING ORGANISM

Symbolic interactionism recognizes that human beings must have a makeup that fits the nature of social interaction. The human being is seen as an organism that not only responds to others on the non-symbolic but as one that makes indications to others and interprets their indications. He can do this, as Mead has shown so emphatically, only by virtue of possessing a "self." Nothing esoteric is meant by this expression. It means merely that a human being can be an object of his own action. Thus, he can recognize himself, for instance, as being a man, young in age, a student, in debt, trying to become a doctor, coming from an undistinguished family and so forth. In all such instances he is an object to himself; and he acts toward himself and guides himself in his actions toward others on the basis of the kind of object he is to himself. This notion of oneself as an object fits into the earlier discussion of objects. Like other objects, the self-object emerges from the process of social interaction in which other people are defining a person to himself. Mead has traced the way in which this occurs in his discussion of role-taking. He points out that in order to become an object to himself a person has to see himself from the outside. One can do this only by placing himself in the position of others and viewing himself or acting toward himself from that position. The roles the person takes range from that of discrete individuals (the "play stage"), through that of discrete organized groups (the "game stage") to that of the abstract community (the "generalized other"). In taking such roles the person is in a position to address or approach himself—as in the case of a young girl who in "playing mother" talks to herself as her mother would do, or in the case of a young priest who sees himself through the eyes of the priesthood. We form our objects of ourselves through such a process of role-taking. It follows that we see ourselves through the way in which others see or define us—or, more precisely, we see ourselves by taking one of the three types of roles of others that have been mentioned. That one forms an object of himself through the ways in which others define one to himself is recognized fairly well in the literature today, so despite its great significance I shall not comment on it further.

There is an even more important matter that stems from the fact that the human being has a self, namely that this enables him to interact with himself. This interaction is not in the form of interaction between two or more parts of a psychological system, as between needs, or between emotions, or between ideas, or between the id and the ego in the Freudian scheme. Instead, the interaction is social—a form of communication, with the person addressing himself as a person and responding thereto. We can clearly recognize such interaction in ourselves as each of us notes that he is angry with himself, or that he has to spur himself on in his tasks, or that he reminds himself to do this or that, or that he is talking to himself in working out some plan of action. As such instances suggest, self-interaction exists fundamentally as a process of making indications to oneself. This process is in play continuously during one's waking life, as one notes and considers one or another matter, or observes this or that happening. Indeed, for the human being to be conscious or aware of anything is equivalent to his indicating the thing to himself—he is identifying it as a given kind of object and considering its relevance or importance to his line of action. One's waking life consists of a series of such indications that the person is making to himself, indications that he uses to direct his action.

We have, then, a picture of the human being as an organism that interacts with itself through a social process of making indications to itself. This is a radically different view of the human being from that which dominates contemporary social and psychological science. The dominant prevailing view sees the human being as a complex organism whose behavior is a response to factors playing on the organization of the organism. Schools of thought in the social and psychological sciences differ enormously in which of such factors they regard as significant, as is shown in such a diverse array as stimuli, organic drives, need-dispositions, conscious motives, unconscious motives, emotions, attitudes, ideas, cultural prescriptions, norms, values, status demands, social roles, reference group affiliations, and institutional pressures. Schools of thought differ also in how they view the organization of the human being, whether as a kind of biological organization, a kind of psychological organization, or a kind of imported societal organization incorporated from the social structure of one's group. Nevertheless, these schools of thought are alike in seeing the human being as a responding organism, with its behavior being a product of the factors playing on its organization or an expression of the interplay of parts of its organization. Under this widely shared view the human being is "social" only in the sense of either being a member of social species, or of responding to others (social stimuli), or of having incorporated within it the organization of his group.

The view of the human being held in symbolic interactionism is fundamentally different. The human being is seen as "social" in a much more profound sense—in the sense of an organism that engages in social interaction with itself by making indications to itself and responding to such indications. By virtue of engaging in self-interaction the human being stands in a markedly different relation to his environment than is presupposed by the widespread conventional view described above. Instead of being merely an organism that responds to the play of factors on or through it, the human being is seen as an organism that has to deal with what it notes. It meets what it so notes by engaging in a process of self-indication in which it makes an object of what it notes, gives it a meaning, and uses the meaning as the basis for directing its action. Its behavior with regard to what it notes is not a response called forth by the presentation of what it notes but instead is an action that arises out of the interpretation made through the process of self-indication. In this sense, the human being who is engaging in self-interaction is not a mere responding organism but an acting organism—an organism that has to mold a line of action on the basis of what it takes into account instead of merely releasing a response to the play of some factor on its organization.

NATURE OF HUMAN ACTION

The capacity of the human being to make indications to himself gives a distinctive character to human action. It means that the human individual confronts a world that he must interpret in order to act instead of an environment to which he responds because of his organization. He has to cope with the situations in which he is called on to act, ascertaining the meaning of the actions of others and mapping out his own line of action in the light of such interpretation. He has to construct and guide his action instead of merely releasing it in response to factors playing on him or operating through him. He may do a miserable job in constructing his action, but he has to construct it.

This view of the human being directing his action by making indications to himself stands sharply in contrast to the view of human action that dominates current psychological and social science. This dominant view, as already implied, ascribes human action to an initiating factor or a combination of such factors. Action is traced back to such matters as motives, attitudes, need-dispositions, unconscious complexes, stimuli configurations, status demands, role requirements, and situational demands. To link the action to one or more of such initiating agents is regarded as fulfilling the scientific task. Yet, such an approach ignores and makes no place for the process of self-interaction through which the individual handles his world and constructs his action. The door is closed to the vital process of interpretation in which the individual notes and assesses what is presented to him and through which he maps out lines of overt behavior prior to their execution.

Fundamentally, action on the part of a human being consists of taking account of various things that he notes and forging a line of conduct on the basis of how he interprets them. The things taken into account cover such matters as his wishes and wants, his objectives, the available means for their achievement, the actions and anticipated actions of others, his image of himself, and the likely result of a given line of action. His conduct is formed and guided through such a process of indication and interpretation. In this process, given lines of action may be started or stopped, they may be abandoned or postponed, they may be confined to mere planning or to an inner life of reverie, or if initiated, they may be transformed. My purpose is not to analyze this process but to call attention to its presence and operation in the formation of human action. We must recognize that the activity of human beings consists of meeting a flow of situations in which they have to act and that their action is built on the basis of what they note, how they assess and interpret what they note, and what kind of projected lines of action they map out. This process is not caught by ascribing action to some kind of factor (for example, motives, need-dispositions, role requirements, social expectations, or social rules) that is thought to initiate the action and propel it to its conclusion; such a factor, or some expression of it, is a matter the human actor takes into account in mapping his line of action. The initiating factor does not embrace or explain how it and other matters are taken into account in the situation that calls for action. One has to get inside of the defining process of the actor in order to understand his action.

This view of human action applies equally well to joint or collective action in which numbers of individuals are implicated. Joint or collective action constitutes the domain of sociological concern, as exemplified in the behavior of groups, institutions, organizations, and social classes. Such instances of societal behavior, whatever they may be, consist of individuals fitting their lines of action to one another. It is both proper and possible to view and study such behavior in its joint or collective character instead of in its individual components. Such joint behavior does not lose its character of being constructed through an interpretative process in meeting the situations in which the collectivity is called on to act. Whether the collectivity be an army engaged in a campaign, a corporation seeking to expand its operations, or a nation trying to correct an unfavorable balance of trade, it needs to construct its action through an interpretation of what is happening in its area of operation. The interpretative process takes place by participants making indications to one another, not merely each to himself. Joint or collective action is an outcome of such a process of interpretative interaction.

INTERLINKAGE OF ACTION

As stated earlier, human group life consists of, and exists in, the fitting of lines of action to each other by the members of the group. Such articulation of lines of action gives rise to and constitutes "joint action"—a societal organization of conduct of different acts of diverse participants. A joint action, while made up of diverse component acts that enter into its formation, is different from any one of them and from their mere aggregation. The joint action has a distinctive character in its own right, a character that lies in the articulation or linkage as apart from what may be articulated or linked. Thus, the joint action may be identified as such and may be spoken of and handled without having to break it down into the separate acts that comprise it. This is what we do when we speak of such things as marriage, a trading transaction, war, a parliamentary discussion, or a church service. Similarly, we can speak of the collectivity that engages in joint action without having to identify the individual members of that collectivity, as we do in speaking of a family, a business corporation, a church, a university, or a nation. It is evident that the domain of the social scientist is constituted precisely by the study of joint action and of the collectivities that engage in joint action.

In dealing with collectivities and with joint action one can easily be trapped in an erroneous position by failing to recognize that the joint action of the collectivity is an interlinkage of the separate acts of the participants. This failure leads one to overlook the fact that a joint action always has to undergo a process of formation; even though it may be a well-established and repetitive form of social action, each instance of it has to be formed anew. Further, this career of formation through which it comes into being necessarily takes place through the dual process of designation and interpretation that was discussed above. The participants still have to guide their respective acts by forming and using meanings.

With these remarks as a background I wish to make three observations on the implications of the interlinkage that constitutes joint action. I wish to consider first those instances of joint action that are repetitive and stable. The preponderant portion of social action in a human society, particularly in a settled society, exists in the form of recurrent patterns of joint action. In most situations in which people act toward one another they have in advance a firm understanding of how to act and of how other people will act. They share common and pre-established meanings of what is expected in the action of the participants, and accordingly each participant is able to guide his own behavior by such meanings. Instances of repetitive and pre-established forms of joint action are so frequent and common that it is easy to understand why scholars have viewed them as the essence or natural form of human group life. Such a view is especially apparent in the concepts of "culture" and "social order" that are so dominant in social science literature. Most sociological schemes rest on the belief that a human society exists in the form of an established order of living, with that order resolvable into adherence to sets of rules, norms, values, and sanctions that specify to people how they are to act in their different situations.

Several comments are in order with regard to this neat scheme. First, it is just not true that the full expanse of life in a human society, in any human society, is but an expression of pre-established forms of joint action. New situations are constantly arising within the scope of group life that are problematic and for which existing rules are inadequate. I have never heard of any society that was free of problems nor any society in which members did not have to engage in discussion to work out ways of action. Such areas of unprescribed conduct are just as natural, indigenous, and recurrent in human group life as are those areas covered by pre-established and faithfully followed prescriptions of joint action. Second, we have to recognize that even in the case of pre-established and repetitive joint action each instance of such joint action has to be formed anew. The participants still have to build up their lines of action and fit them to one another through the dual process of designation and interpretation. They do this in the case of repetitive joint action, of course, by using the same recurrent and constant meanings. If we recognize this, we are forced to realize that the play and fate of meanings are what is important, not the joint action in its established form. Repetitive and stable joint action is just as much a result of an interpretative process as is a new form of joint action that is being developed for the first time. This is not an idle or pedantic point; the meanings that underlie established and recurrent joint action are themselves subject to pressure as well as to reinforcement, to incipient dissatisfaction as well as to indifference; they may be challenged as well as affirmed, allowed to slip along without concern as well as subjected to infusions of new vigor. Behind the facade of the objectively perceived joint action the set of meanings that sustains that joint action has a life that the social scientists can ill afford to ignore. A gratuitous acceptance of the concepts of norms, values, social rules, and the like should not blind the social scientist to the fact that any one of them is subtended by a process of social interaction—a process that is necessary not only for their change but equally well for their retention in a fixed form. It is the social process in group life that creates and upholds the rules, not the rules that create and uphold group life.

The second observation on the interlinkage that constitutes joint action refers to the extended connection of actions that make up so much of human group life. We are familiar with these large complex networks of action involving an interlinkage and interdependency of diverse actions of diverse people—as in the division of labor extending from the growing of grain by the farmer to an eventual sale of bread in a store, or in the elaborate chain extending from the arrest of a suspect to his eventual release from a penitentiary. These networks with their regularized participation of diverse people by diverse action at diverse points yields a picture of institutions that have been appropriately a major concern of sociologists. They also give substance to the idea that human group life has the character of a system. In seeing such a large complex of diversified activities, all hanging together in a regularized operation, and in seeing the complementary organization of participants in well-knit interdependent relationships, it is easy to understand why so many scholars view such networks or institutions as self-operating entities, following their own dynamics and not requiring that attention be given to the participants within the network. Most of the sociological analyses of institutions and social organization adhere to this view. Such adherence, in my judgment, is a serious mistake. One should recognize what is true, namely, that the diverse array of participants occupying different points in the network engage in their actions at those points on the basis of using given sets of meanings. A network or an institution does not function automatically because of some inner dynamics or system requirements; it functions because people at different points do something, and what they do is a result of how they define the situation in which they are called on to act. A limited appreciation of this point is reflected today in some of the work on decision-making, but on the whole the point is grossly ignored. It is necessary to recognize that the sets of meanings that lead participants to act as they do at their stationed points in the network have their own setting in a localized process of social interaction—and that these meanings are formed, sustained, weakened, strengthened, or transformed, as the case may be, through a socially defining process. Both the functioning and the fate of institutions are set by this process of interpretation as it takes place among the diverse sets of participants.

A third important observation needs to be made, namely, that any instance of joint action, whether newly formed or long established, has necessarily arisen out of a background of previous actions of the participants. A new kind of joint action never comes into existence apart from such a background. The participants involved in the formation of the new joint action always bring to that formation the world of objects, the sets of meanings, and the schemes of interpretation that they already possess. Thus, the new form of joint action always emerges out of and is connected with a context of previous joint action. It cannot be understood apart from that context; one has to bring into one's consideration this linkage with preceding forms of joint action. One is on treacherous and empirically invalid grounds if he thinks that any given form of joint action can be sliced off from its historical linkage, as if its makeup and character arose out of the air through spontaneous generation instead of growing out of what went before. In the face of radically different and stressful situations people may be led to develop new forms of joint action that are markedly different from those in which they have previously engaged, yet even in such cases there is always some connection and continuity with what went on before. One cannot understand the new form without incorporating knowledge of this continuity into one's analysis of the new form. Joint action not only represents a horizontal linkage, so to speak, of the activities of the participants, but also a vertical linkage with previous joint action.

SUMMARY REMARKS

The general perspective of symbolic interactionism should be clear from our brief sketch of its root images. This approach sees a human society as people engaged in living. Such living is a process of ongoing activity in which participants are developing lines of action in the multitudinous situations they encounter. They are caught up in a vast process of interaction in which they have to fit their developing actions to one another. This process of interaction consists in making indications to others of what to do and in interpreting the indications as made by others. They live in worlds of objects and are guided in their orientation and action by the meaning of these objects. Their objects, including objects of themselves, are formed, sustained, weakened, and transformed in their interaction with one another. This general process should be seen, of course, in the differentiated character which it necessarily has by virtue of the fact that people cluster in different groups, belong to different associations, and occupy different positions. They accordingly approach each other differently, live in different worlds, and guide themselves by different sets of meanings. Nevertheless, whether one is dealing with a family, a boy's gang, an industrial corporation, or a political party, one must see the activities of the collectivity as being formed through a process of designation and interpretation.

CONCLUSION

My conclusion . . . is indeed brief. It can be expressed as a simple injunction: Respect the nature of the empirical world and organize a methodological stance to reflect that respect. This is what I think symbolic interactionism strives to do.

The Ethnomethodology of the Human Reality Constructor [1975]

HUGH MEHAN AND HOUSTON WOOD

• *Ethnomethodology is notoriously difficult material for outsiders to get a feeling for, and that is especially true of the writings of its inspirational center, Harold Garfinkel. Ethnomethodology is in many ways more of an oral, face-to-face, intellectual analysis than it is a written discipline; given the nature of its insights into the social process of reality-constructing, perhaps that is not surprising. "Signed objects" (objects that have been turned into social symbols and signs, like language) have always irretrievably lost something of the qualities of "lebenswelt objects" of ordinary, unreflective experience. Ethnomethodology investigates the laws of that transformation. The word itself alludes to its mission: "ethno"—the ethnographic description of—"methodology," the folk-methods people use in their everyday, practical reasoning, conversation, and work. The following selection, by Hugh Mehan and Houston Wood, is an unusually lucid résumé of ethnomethodology's central discoveries and of the famous "breaching experiments" Garfinkel used to point up some of them.*

Much ethnomethodological theorizing has explored the work entailed in achieving the object constancy belief and other fundamental propositions of daily life. The ethnomethodologist finds that persons are constructing social structures without being aware of this work. This reality work is explicated by the construction of a "model of the actor."

In the normative model, rules, actors, and situations are assumed to be independent entities. In the ethnomethodological model, persons are treated as reality constructors. Rules are dependent upon the ceaseless, ongoing activities of persons within social situations. The ethnomethodological model is a characteristization of the way persons *create* situations and rules, and so at once create themselves and their social realities.[1]

From Hugh Mehan and Houston Wood, *The Reality of Ethnomethodology*, pp. 98–114. Copyright 1975, John Wiley and Sons. Reprinted by permission of John Wiley and Sons, Inc.

[1] Ethnomethodologists adopted this research program from Schutz (1962, 1964), who spoke of the construction of "homunculi" and "puppets" as the theorists' solution of theoretical problems. Trading off a more recent metaphor, Crowle (1971) has suggested that the model is analogous to an android, that is, an automated simulated human (cf. Sacks, 1963).

A CONSTRUCTION OF A REALITY CONSTRUCTOR

I will now attribute some minimal requisites for social interaction to a model of the actor. The attributions are *constitutive*. They both create interaction and the possibility of interaction. These features have been culled from the writings of Schutz (1962, 1964, 1966, 1967, 1970a), from Garfinkel's (1963, 1967a) distillation of these writings, and from Cicourel's (1973a) further elaboration of this work.[2] My purpose is not to provide an accurate historical sequence in the development of the model. It is rather to provide a single, unified formulation so that the use of this device can be better understood.

This model of the reality constructor is composed of (1) social knowledge and (2) interpretive procedures that operate on that social knowledge.

Social Knowledge

The properties of social knowledge can be summarized as follows:

1. Social knowledge provides *a practical interest* in the world. Garfinkel describes this feature as follows:

> Events, their relationships, their causal texture are not for [the person] matters of theoretic interest. He does not sanction the notion that in dealing with them it is correct to address them with the interpretive rule that he knows nothing, or that he can assume that he knows nothing "just to see where it leads." In everyday situations what he knows is an integral feature of his social competence (1967a:273).

That is, as people conduct the affairs of their daily life, they are *not* constrained by the canons of the "scientific rationalities" (Garfinkel, 1967a:262–283). They are *not* concerned with semantic or conceptual clarity for its own sake, or insuring that their actions conform to the demands of formal logic.

---

[2]Garfinkel has on numerous occasions attempted to codify and systematize Schutz's various discussions of the attitude of everyday life. His first attempt at this synthesis appears in his dissertation (Garfinkel, 1952). In his "Documentary Method" paper (Garfinkel, 1967a:89–94), he speaks in terms of the "findings" of an experiment reported there. In his 1960 paper on the "Rationalities" (1967a:272–279), he offers another summary of the "presuppositions of everyday life." A far more complex listing appears in his "Trust" paper (1963), where 8 presuppositions are listed and described. This list is repeated again as 11 presuppositions in the 1964 "Routine Grounds" paper (1967a:55–56).

Cicourel's treatment of the "interpretive procedures" has a similar history. His first writing (1968, in 1973a:42–73) made a strong analogy to linguistics; six interpretive procedures were "deep" rules to normative "surface rules." A discussion of "role theory" (1970, in 1973a:11–41) distributes the interpretive procedures into three "basic rules." Still another formulation (1969, in 1973a:74–98) produces four interpretive procedures.

2. Social knowledge is *socially distributed*. Garfinkel describes this feature as follows:

> There corresponds, thereby, to the common intersubjective world of communication, unpublicized knowledge which in the eyes of the actor is distributed among persons as grounds of their actions, that is, of their motives or, in the radical sense of the term, their "interests," as constituent features of the social relationships of interaction. He assumes that there are matters that one person knows that he assumes others do not know. The ignorance of one party consists in what another knows that is motivationally relevant to the first. Thereby matters that are known in common are informed in their sense by the personal reservations, the matters that are selectively withheld. Thus the events of everyday situations are informed by this integral background of "meanings held in reserve," of matters known about self and others that are none of somebody else's business; in a word, the private life (Ibid.:276).

This feature of social knowledge provides that some people know some things, but not everybody knows all things. Interactants recognize this. Nonetheless, biographically specific meanings are treated as irrelevant for the purposes of communicating the here-and-now event to others.

3. Social knowledge is *tacit*. Garfinkel points out that any "event means for both the witness and the other more than the witness can say" (Ibid.:56). This feature of social knowledge provides that what both persons know in common cannot be said in so many words. This common, tacit knowing is used by people to build interaction.

4. Social knowledge *takes the world for granted*. Garfinkel writes:

> a relationship of undoubted correspondence is the sanctioned relationship between the-presented-appearance-of-the-object and the-intended-object-that-presents-itself-in-the-perspective-of-the-particular-appearance (Ibid.:55).

And he writes elsewhere:

> Schutz finds that in everyday situations the "practical theorist" achieves an ordering of events while seeking to retain and sanction the presupposition that the objects of the world are as they appear. The person coping with everyday affairs seeks an interpretation of these affairs while holding a line of "official neutrality" towards the interpretive rule that one may doubt the objects of the world as they appear. The actor's assumption consists in the expectation that a relationship of

undoubted correspondence exists between the particular appearances of an object and the intended-object-that-appears-in-this-particular-fashion (Ibid.:272).

That is, people expect the world beyond to be accurately pictured by their way of looking at it. This feature of social knowledge makes it possible for objects to be accepted for what they appear to be on the surface.

This discussion establishes that the reality constructor has social knowledge, but this conception is static. People do not use all their knowledge in every situation. They do not apply all that they (tacitly) know at once. Therefore, our model must have a mechanism that activates the situationally relevant aspects of this constantly changing stock of knowledge.

Borrowing from Schutz, this feature has been talked about in various ways: as "constitutive rules" (Garfinkel, 1963), as "interpretive rules" (Garfinkel, 1967a), as "interpretive procedures" or "basic rules" (Cicourel, 1973a).[3] I will use the term "procedure," because it best conveys the sense that these are descriptions of interactional activities that are *done* by people in interaction.

Interpretive Procedures

Three interpretive procedures have been described by the ethnomethodologist:

1. *Searching for a normal form.* Cicourel (1973a:86) describes this interpretive procedure as follows:

> when discrepancies or ambiguities appear, speakers will attempt to normalize the presumed discrepancies . . . this commonsense principle provides each member with instructions for unwittingly (and sometimes deliberately) evaluating and striving for a reciprocally assumed normal form judgment of his utterances and perceptions.

2. *Doing a reciprocity of perspectives.* Cicourel (Ibid.:85–86) describes the reciprocity of perspectives as doing the work of sustaining the assumption that:

> (i) each would have the same experiences if they were to change places, and (ii) that until further notice they can disregard any differences that might arise from their respective personal ways of assigning meaning to objects and events.

[3] In this talk, these theorists continually refer to the assumptions that the actor makes in interaction. They do *not* mean that the actor is consciously making choices prior to doing things. Postulating "assumptions" is one way the ethnomethodologist has for talking about the necessary aspects of interaction. There is no necessary commitment to a cognitive formulation.

3. *Employing the et cetera principle.* Cicourel (Ibid.:87) describes this interpretive procedure as follows:

> The participants to a conversation must "fill in" meanings throughout the exchange and after the exchange when attempting to recall or reconstruct what happened because of the inadequacies of oral and non-oral communication, and the routine practice of leaving many intentions unstated (Garfinkel, 1964). Vague or ambiguous or truncated expressions are located by members, given meaning contextually and across contexts, by their retrospective-prospective sense of occurrence. Present utterances or descriptive accounts that contain ambiguous or promissory overtones can be examined prospectively by the speaker-hearer for their possible meaning in some future sense under the assumption of filling in meanings now and imagining the kinds of intentions that can be expected later. Or, past remarks can now be seen as clarifying present utterances.

Hence, the et cetera principle has three interrelated parts. In some versions of the model, these features are treated as separate entities.

a. Unclear information is allowed to pass while clarifying information is sought.

ŀ Contextual information is sought over time to fill in the ambiguity of ind xical expressions.

. The filling in is accomplished by retrospective-prospective means. When va ue, ambiguous, or unclear utterances occur, the vagueness is not immediat ly challenged or questioned. The hearer allows the unclear utterance to pass. He assumes that subsequent events will clarify the present ambiguity. If and when subsequent information becomes available, that present information is used to clarify the previously unclear events.

DISPLAYING THE REALITY CONSTRUCTOR

The model of the reality constructor can be used as an analytic tool. I will illustrate this by providing a hypothetical account of an everyday event. A man driving to work sees a fuzzy object. After several minutes during which the object's appearance baffles him, he determines that it is a freeway sign. To account for this occurrence, I will attribute to the model of a freeway driver some of the elements necessary for driving the freeway in an acceptable manner.

Before this man can begin driving his car, in fact, even before he can leave his bed in the morning, put on his clothes, or drink his coffee, he must assume that objects are what they appear to be on the surface. If the motorist had scientifically rational doubts about the nature of objects appearing before him, he would not be able to act at all. If the motorist doubts that the floor under his bed is a floor, he will be unable to stand on that floor. If our motorist does not see the long ribbon of black ooze as a "freeway," the brightly colored mass hurtling toward him as a "car" with a competent driver who will drive past, not at him, he may be unable to negotiate the roadway.[4] These suggest the taken-for-granted features of social knowledge I summarized above.

As the motorist drives the freeway, he is confronted by swirls of colors and sounds. Our motorist must transform these stimuli into meaningful wholes. This is the interpretive procedure "searching for a normal form." As an individual goes through a social situation (as the motorist drives his car), the individual searches for and selects features of the world which can be placed in a familiar schemata. Casting for coherent forms is an interpretive procedure performed on all knowledge systems.

When first confronted by swirling colors, the motorist sensed the presence of a "something," but its specific form, content, and dimensions were unknown. The assumed presence of *"some* object there" enabled the motorist to continue to look for features that would help him identify "the something" as a *specific* thing. In the language of the interpretive procedures discussed above, the motorist allowed unclear events to pass while seeking clarification. He waited to see what the object would mean then.

Although an object may not have a *specific* meaning at the time that it is initially apprehended, it has some meaning. For example, it is "an unclear object." Its specific meaning may become clear with subsequent events. After these events occur, the motorist is able to see in retrospect what the object was "all along." This retrospective filling in is an aspect of the interpretive procedure: employing the et cetera principle.

Of course, this now specific, clear meaning is also subject to subsequent reinterpretation. The object may not be a freeway sign, but a scaffold, or a truck; any subsequent determination will modify previous ones. "What it is now" will be "what it was all along."

The meaning of an object, event, or utterance is also "prospective." When a person does not immediately know the normal form meaning of an object,

---

[4]I cannot help but reflect on how difficult it is to talk about "meaninglessness." The very words we use to talk about "meaninglessness" are themselves meaningful. The expression "black ooze" does not refer to a meaningless object. Although the expression does not carry a noun as specific as "asphalt," "black ooze" nevertheless is meaningful.

It may in fact be impossible to suspend or "get behind" the meanings provided to us by language and culture to "pure sensation." Layers of meaning may be stripped off (so that "freeway sign" becomes "bright shiny object," then "green flashes"), but each successive account requires a tie to a meaningful category to be processed. As Merleau-Ponty said: "We are condemned to meaning."

he assumes that its meaning will become clear later. The practice of "waiting until later to see what was intended now" is the "prospective" interpretive procedure.

The motorist knows this swirling object was a sign all along. He also knows that this object will be the same object the next time he confronts it. It will be the same object on all subsequent occasions. It will be the same object to any and all others who look at it. He maintains this knowledge by employing the "reciprocity of perspectives" interpretive procedure.

Now suppose our motorist needs to go from one part of the city to another. He might ask a gas station attendant for directions:

How do I get to Jack-in-the-Box from here?

The gas station attendant might give the following directions: "See this street here? That takes you to the freeway. Stay on the freeway until you see the sign for Mazeville Road. Get off there. Jack-in-the-Box will be on your right, a few blocks down."

In order for the gas station attendant to tell our motorist this, the attendant must treat the freeway sign as a constant object. That is, the gas station attendant must also employ the reciprocity of perspectives interpretive procedure, which provides that the meaning of the objects, utterances, or events that he has encountered are the same that others have encountered. And, in order for the motorist to follow those directions, he must treat the signs, streets, and buildings he encounters and calls by certain names, as the same objects the gas station attendant or anybody else names in the same way.

Now, the motorist who follows these instructions may have had peculiar experiences with that particular street exit. For example, he may once have had a flat tire or an accident there. The gas station attendant may be having "a bad day," or he may have just won money at the racetrack. But the motorist is not interested in these biographical features. He is interested in getting to Jack-in-the-Box. If the gas station attendant were to begin to provide the motorist with the details about his declining business, the rising prices of his products, or what he will do with his winnings, the motorist would see that as strange. Likewise, the gas station attendant is not interested in *why* the motorist wants to go to Jack-in-the-Box. It is irrelevant for his purpose of giving instructions whether the motorist is going to Jack-in-the-Box to make a purchase, to meet someone, or to rob it. Both the motorist and the gas station attendant must treat any such biographically specific meanings as irrelevant for the purposes at hand. They must employ the socially distributed aspect of social knowledge.

The motorist who asks the gas station attendant for directions has a "practical interest in the world" (see the first property of social knowledge, above). He wants to go from one place to another. That practical problem occupies his time. He is not interested in theoretical matters about the journey, the freeway, or the sign, such as the laws of physics that explain how the sign is able to stand in high winds, or the principle that explains how the asphalt is able to support the weight of cars on it, or the kinetic theory that explains why the sign "lights up" when headlights shine on the sign at night. Theoretical reflection and practical problem-solving are separate activities. It is difficult to engage in both simultaneously. On another occasion, at another time, say, when the motorist and a friend are sipping coffee after dinner, they might engage in a discussion of the physical principles of light reflection. But at the moment when the motorist is trying to navigate unfamiliar streets and heavy traffic, he is hardly interested in such theoretical matters.

The motorist is able to concentrate on his practical concerns of finding streets and signs and does not need to worry about asphalt strength and principles of light reflection because he "knows" that other people have these theoretical matters as *their* practical concerns. This is another facet of the social distribution of social knowledge. No member of society need know all society's knowledge in order to interact. But in order to function in everyday life, each must rely on the fact that some people have some knowledge of the world, and that others have other knowledge.

Likewise, no person need have a *formal* acquaintance with any of that knowledge. Just as a speaker of a language need not know the rules of grammar to speak that language (Chomsky, 1965), a person need not be able to list the rules of society to act in it. This illumines the meaning of the "tacit" feature of social knowledge.

Now let us examine the conversation between the motorist and the gas station attendant, especially the instruction the gas station attendant gave to the motorist so that he could go from one part of town to another.

Motorist:	How do I get to Jack-in-the-Box from here?
Gas station attendant:	See this street here? That takes you to the freeway. Stay on the freeway until you see the sign for Mazeville Road. Get off there. Jack-in-the-Box will be on your right, a few blocks down.

To ask the gas station attendant for directions, the motorist would need to know at least the following about socially distributed social knowledge: that there are people who can legitimately be asked for directions; that there are places where directions can be legitimately asked; and that there are times when such questions can legitimately be asked. If a priest hearing confession were asked for directions to Jack-in-the-Box, the person asking the question might be considered bizarre, a stranger, or incompetent. Knowing that there are people who can and cannot be asked for instructions, and knowing that there are those who *can* legitimately be asked for directions, and knowing that such a person has certain obligations to respond is presumably knowledge that "everyone (who is a competent member of society) knows."

The ethnomethodologist is not interested in compiling a list of the "background" knowledge required for successful interaction. The list I have begun above for the motorist merely scratches the surface of what he would have to know to ask that question. As I explain in a later section of this chapter, it seems unlikely that a complete list could ever be constructed.

To ask for directions, the motorist must consult his normal forms, which guide his selection of a person who would be likely to help him. The initial selection is prospective, for the person selected for instructions may be a stranger, a pathological liar, or a robber. Subsequent events will retrospectively inform the motorist if his initial prospective selection was accurate.

What does the gas station attendant's instruction tell the motorist? It seems to tell him everything that he needs to know. It tells him to turn at a certain street of a certain freeway. But notice that far more is implied by the utterance than is stated in words. The utterance assumes that the hearer can supply contextual information (see interpretive procedure 3b)—for example, that he knows the meaning of "freeway" and can recognize one when he sees one, and that he knows what a car is and can use one. It assumes that the person knows about making turns, and can make one, et cetera.

The instruction refers to a few landmarks, a freeway, and a particular sign. It does not provide a detailed map on which every building and street is identified with its dimensions, age, and number of dollars spent in its conruction. The hearer must go beyond the information given in the instruction self and fill in with particulars from his own past experience, and with ormal forms that he gains along the way. Thus, the instructions . . . are incomplete. The operation of interpretive procedures on social knowledge show how such symbolic forms are managed by the actor.

EXPLORING THE MODEL THROUGH ETHNOGRAPHIES

No studies describing the use of social knowledge and interpretive procedures in actual settings have been conducted. However, the model of the reality constructor need not be restricted to free inventions. It is a schemata that enables actual social scenes to be examined at a greater depth than is usual in sociological field studies. It suggests a way of investigating particular scenes in order to *see general* features. Sociology presently searches particular scenes for *particular* features.

Consider, for example, the works of Becker, Whyte, and Goffman, acknowledged masters of the field study technique. Becker's (1953) analysis of marijuana users is typical. He describes how jazz musicians use "the smoke" to get "high" and improve their performance. Becker's (1968) later analysis of LSD use also describes how particular activities get done. He is not interested in using those particular activities as a vehicle for exploring the general features of all activities. Whyte (1955) provides descriptions of how gang members behave on street corners. Goffman's (1959, 1961, 1969) work reaches toward a deeper level, but it does not to seek features that appear in all situations.[5]

The model of the reality constructor, like Goffman's model, is "only" a schemata. However, it differs from Goffman, Becker and Whyte in directing the researcher's attention to transsituational features of particular situations. It provides a method for attempting ethnographies of the general problem of social order.

The choice between these alternative approaches must be made on extratheoretical grounds. The model of the reality constructor is *not* a higher ontological truth. (I return to this ontological issue at the end of this chapter.) For those interested in the particular features of particular scenes, traditional field work schemata are efficacious. For those interested in the general problem of social order, a model like the reality constructor is indicated.

EXPLORING THE MODEL THROUGH BREACHING

Field work studies are only one method of refining the reality constructor model. A second method is the use of "incongruity" or "breaching" procedures . . . The logic of the procedures derives from the claim that social structures are created by social structuring activities, work that is not apparent under normal circumstances. A corollary of this suggests that suppressing any of the models' features should "produce anomic effects and increase disorga-

---

[5]Garfinkel (1967a:116–185) . . . explored some differences between situated "passing" practices and Goffman's "management" practices in his "Agnes" study (see especially Garfinkel, 1967a: 164–185). Garfinkel argues that Goffman's dramaturgical model presupposes a world of constant objects. Goffman does not describe how such objects are ceaselessly created. Garfinkel shows that no amount of "staging" or strategic planning before social scenes was sufficient to account for Agnes's creation of her female sexuality.

nization" (Garfinkel, 1963:215). I will adapt Garfinkel's breaching procedures to illustrate the necessity of the features of social knowledge, and interpretive procedures.

Breaching Social Knowledge

One of the features of everyday knowledge is that it provides a practical interest in the world . . . Garfinkel (1964, in 1967a:41–44) instructed a number of persons to converse while repressing this feature. He told them to adopt a *theoretic* interest in the conversation. This entailed seeking meanings "for their own sake," "just to see where it might lead." They were to show no regard for the practical circumstances surrounding the conversation.

The people who followed this procedure typically found that social order halted. This is the report of one person (*E*) who attempted to suppress the practical interest feature of social knowledge:

> *E:* My friend and I were talking about a man whose overbearing attitude annoyed us. My friend expressed his feeling:
> *S:* I'm sick of him.
> *E:* Would you explain what is wrong with you that you are sick?
> *S:* Are you kidding me? You know what I mean.
> *E:* Please explain your ailment.
> *S:* (He listened to me with a puzzled look.) What came over you? We never talk this way, do we? (Ibid.:44).

The experimenter is not allowing what he knows to be "an integral feature" (Ibid.:273) of the scene. As a result, the ongoing interaction is swiftly disrupted. The subject demands to know "what came over" the experimenter, and points out that "We never talk this way." The repression of this feature of social knowledge breaches the subject's sense of normality, indicating that this feature is vital for the construction of everyday scenes.

A second feature of social knowledge is that it is socially distributed . . . Persons recognize that some persons know some things that others do not. These *personal* disparities in knowledge are supposed to be irrelevant in everyday interaction. Where they are not, it is assumed that the party with relevant personal knowledge will inform the other.

Garfinkel (Ibid.:75) demonstrated the importance of this feature by using the following procedure:

> the experimenter engaged others in conversation while he had a wire recorder hidden under his coat. In the course of the conversation the

experimenter opened his jacket to reveal the recorder saying, "See what I have?" An initial pause was almost invariably followed by the question, "What are you doing with it?" . . . The fact that the conversation was revealed to have been recorded motivated new possibilities which the parties then sought to bring under the jurisdiction of an agreement that they had never specifically mentioned and that indeed did not previously exist.

The subjects knew that the experimenter knew things they did not, just as they knew they had knowledge the experimenter did not. But the subjects assumed as well that these disparities in knowledge were irrelevant to the interaction at hand. The appearance of the tape recorder made this taken-for-granted feature visible. By breaching it, Garfinkel demonstrated its importance to everyday interactions where it exists but is unnoticed. (For allied procedures breaching this feature, see Garfinkel, 1963:201–206; 1967a:71–73.)

The third feature of social knowledge I described above (p. 100) is its tacitness. Social knowledge is assumed to be shared by parties to an interaction. Though this shared knowledge is never exhaustively articulated, persons assume that they know a single world in common.

Garfinkel (1967a:51) designed a procedure to reveal the importance of this feature of social knowledge:

> Students were instructed to engage someone in conversation and to imagine and act on the assumption that what the other person was saying was directed by hidden motives which were his real ones.

In other words, students were asked to suspend the assumption that a body of knowledge was being tacitly held in common. The other person was seen as having a hidden body of knowledge ("motives") which were coloring all that person was doing.

Reviewing 35 instances of the implementation of this breaching procedure, Garfinkel concludes:

> The attitude was difficult to sustain and carry through. Students reported acute awareness of being "in an artificial game," of being unable to "live the part," and of frequently being "at a loss as to what to do next." . . . One student spoke for several when she said she was unable to get any results because so much of her effort was directed to maintaining an attitude of distrust that she was unable to follow the conversation. She said she was unable to imagine how her fellow conversationalist might be deceiving her because they were talking about such inconsequential matters (Ibid.).

In sum, students found that they could not suppress the belief that they held a corpus of knowledge in common with the other. Even attempting to breach this feature disrupted the interaction. Common tacit knowledge is thus indicated to be essential to social scenes.

A fourth and final feature of social knowledge is that it takes the world for granted . . . A real world exists independent of the knowledge of the world. This world is in direct correspondence with the knowledge. Knowledge and world picture each other (cf. Wittgenstein, 1921).

Garfinkel (Ibid.:46) breached this feature by asking subjects to enter their homes with the attitude of a boarder. The home was a familiar world. The attitude of a boarder required the use of unfamiliar knowledge. The procedure was designed to explore the clash of foreign knowledge and a familiar world.

Some of the students were instructed only to observe their homes as a boarder. They were not to act on this attitude:

> Many reported that the attitude was difficult to sustain because with it quarreling, bickering, and hostile motivations became discomfitingly visible. Frequently an account that recited newly visible troubles was accompanied by the student's assertion that his account of family problems was not a "true" picture; the family was *really* a very happy one. Students were convinced that the view from the boarder's attitude was not their real home environment (Ibid.).

The fourth feature of knowledge maintains that there is an undoubted correspondence between knowledge and world. Thus, students found that if they adopted a boarder's knowledge, they experienced a boarder's world. They were anxious to assure themselves that the world that appeared under the aegis of the different knowledge was not the "real" world. That new world offered troubles that were not visible through a family member's knowledge.

Garfinkel's procedure does not suggest that one or the other of these experiences of the home is true. It suggests instead that any knowledge will produce the experience of a world that corresponds with that knowledge. An omnipresent feature of all social knowledge is that it matches a real and external reality.

Breaching Interpretive Procedures

The first of three interpretive procedures I described was "searching for a normal form" . . . This refers to the work people do to transform discrepan-

cies and ambiguities into similar patterns. I have adapted another of Garfinkel's (1963:229–235; 1967a:59–67) procedures to illustrate the results of frus-
trating normal forming.

Garfinkel's subjects were 28 premedical students. They were separately introduced to a purported expert on medical school admissions, who said he was
interested in decreasing student anxiety over medical school admissions interviews. He solicited the student's opinion on how this might be done.

After a casual hour's discussion, the interviewer asked the students if they
would like to hear a recording of an actual admissions interview. All of the
students had such interviews in their future and leaped at the opportunity as a
possible means of increasing their chances of admission.

The applicant the students heard was excessively boorish. He used poor
grammar and was stupid. He was pushy and abrasive, contradicting the interviewer when not being evasive. He degraded other schools and professions.
On top of it all, he demanded to be told at the end of the interview how he
had done. At this point the recording ended.

The students were asked to write a detailed assessment of this tape-recorded
applicant's performance. They described him much as I did above. This was,
then, a first and initially successful attempt at normal forming. The inter-
viewer-experimenter then breached this procedure. He presented the subject
with the fake applicant's "official records," which showed superior grades and
recommendations. Before the subjects could begin to attempt to normalize
this information, they were inundated with more. They were handed the fake
interviewer's assessment, which showed that the interviewer had rated the
applicant highly. Subjects were given the opinions of a "panel of psychiatrists," who, along with other premedical students, were alleged to have also
listened to the recording. These materials, which were individually arranged,
contradicted almost adjective by adjective the assessment the subjects had
originally offered.

The procedures of normal forming were thus rendered inoperative. Three
of the 28 subjects resolved the situation by deciding it was all "a joke" or
"merely an experiment." But for the majority who were unable to normalize
in these ways, the world became "specifically senseless" (Garfinkel, 1963:189).
They were bewildered. They exhibited great anxiety and discomfort. Some
wondered if they had "gone crazy." It was as if once the normal forming
procedures were rendered unsuccessful, they found themselves with "an am-
nesia for social structure" (Ibid.).

Garfinkel (Ibid.:223–226) designed another procedure that illustrates the
importance of the interpretive procedure that I have labeled "doing a reciproc-

ity of perspectives" . . . This procedure indicates that persons normally act to
maintain that they share the same worlds and knowledge. To make this procedure fail:

> students were asked to enter a store, to select a customer, and to treat
> the customer as a clerk while giving no recognition that the subject was
> any other person than the experimenter took him to be and without
> giving any indication that the experimenter's treatment was anything
> other than perfectly reasonable and legitimate (Ibid.:223).

. . . The other results offered by Garfinkel display the anomia exhibited [in
another experiment]. A physics professor, it will be remembered, becomes the
unsuspecting subject of an experimenter, who "mistakes" him for a mâitre d'
and persists in her error despite his attempts to create a reciprocity of perspectives. He tells her afterward "I haven't been so shaken since———denounced
my theory of———in 19—" (Ibid.: 226). These studies indicate that if the
reciprocity of perspectives is not accepted by other interactants, social scenes
are severely disrupted.

I labeled the third interpretive procedure "employing the et cetera principle" (see p. 304 above). Although this procedure has three subfeatures, the
breaching experiment I use as an example seems to explore the importance of
only one of them. This feature suggests that normal interactants must permit
unclear information to pass while waiting for later clarifying information.
Garfinkel (Ibid.:221–223) instructed students to converse without letting any
statements pass that they did not immediately feel they understood. Here is
one of the cases that resulted from this procedure:

> *Case 4.* During a conversation (with the E's fiancée) the E ques-
> tioned the meaning of various words used by the subject. For the first
> minute and a half the subject responded to the questions as if they
> were legitimate inquiries. Then she responded with "Why are you
> asking me these questions?" . . . She became nervous and jittery, her
> face and hand movements . . . uncontrolled. She appeared bewildered
> and complained that I was making her nervous and demanded that I
> "Stop it!"

The fiancée at last covered her face with a magazine and refused to talk. Their
orderly relations had been temporarily anomicized by the experimenter's refusal to employ one of the et cetera procedures. His refusal forced the other
interactant into simulating schizophrenia.

The Empirical Status of the Breaching Studies

Breaching procedures such as these are not experiments. Instead, Garfinkel (1967a:65) has suggested that they be called *demonstrations*, to emphasize their "results do no more than illustrate what I am talking about" (italics omitted). The linkage between any specific incongruity demonstration and a feature of social knowledge or interpretive procedure is obscure. The logic of the demonstrations does not follow from the theory in any determinate way. One must not look to these breaching studies as a way of building a theory of the reality constructor that will be comparable to the theories of the truly experimental sciences.

The value of such demonstrations is great nonetheless. Deep disruptions of the social order are possible at any moment, in any scene. These demonstrations strongly suggest that ceaseless reality work is necessary for social order to persist.

A serious problem with the breaching procedures is that they became too potent . . . Refinements on several of the techniques I mentioned led to anomia that threatened to linger for days. *Interested persons are strongly advised not to undertake any new breaching studies.* It is immoral to inflict them on others. However, there are ways that one can breach one's own sense of social order. This is not immoral, though it may be foolish. . . .

THE REALITY CONSTRUCTOR

Objective and constraining social structures are constructed by social structuring activities. To determine the nature of this reality work, the ethnomethodologist constructs a "model of the actor." The procedures he attributes to the model are descriptions of activities that display the objective and constraining social structures.

Thus the ethnomethodological theory of the reality constructor is about the *procedures* that accomplish reality. It is not about any specific reality. Social scientists often adopt a privileged position about their pursuits. They claim that their findings are about the reality they study. Making connections between social class and occupation, for example, social scientists propose that social class is actually the reason a person has a certain job.

My ethnomethodology makes no such claim. I do not assume a correspondence between my theory and particular realities. The reality constructor is not a picture of actual persons. Jennings (personal communication) once proposed that the ultimate model of the reality constructor would be a machine that could engage in interaction with humans without detection. If the technological problems of such an operation could be overcome, and the ethnomethodologist was actually able to "plug in" the social knowledge and interpretive procedures sufficient for the machine to "pass," there would be no claim that the way the machine engages in interaction is the way a person engages in interaction.

Ethnomethodology is not a method of pursuing the truth about the world. Rather, it examines the many versions, including its own, of the way the world is assembled. Ethnomethodology is not concerned with the truth value of statements about the world except as phenomena. It tries to determine the practices that make any statement true.

To this point we have discussed two kinds of "rules": normative rules (including legal, linguistic, and social science rules . . .), and interpretive rules or procedures. Interpretive rules can be used as a theoretical device for understanding normative rule use. Interpretive procedures "fill in" the essential incompleteness of normative rules. Though interpretive procedures can be used in this way, it would be inconsistent to conclude that they are immune from the feature of incompleteness found in normative rules. In fact, each interpretive procedure exhibits the same feature of incompleteness.

The specter of incompleteness neither jeopardizes the enterprise nor spells its end. It is a source of mystery and wonder.

Looked at this way, constructing a list of interpretive procedures, or constructing any finite model is like fashioning a ladder, a tool to carry us upward. At some point, the ladder can be tossed away, as we will no longer depend on it for our climb (Wittgenstein, 1921).

REFERENCES

Becker, Howard
    1953   Outsiders—Studies in the Sociology of Deviance. New York: The Free Press.
    1968   History, Culture and Subjective Experience: An Exploration of the Social Bases of Drug-Induced Experiences. Journal of Health and Human Behavior 8:961–968.
Chomsky, Noam
    1965   Aspects of the Theory of Syntax. Cambridge: The M.I.T. Press.
Cicourel, Aaron V.
    1964   Method and Measurement in Sociology. New York: The Free Press.
    1968   The Social Organization of Juvenile Justice. New York: John Wiley & Sons.
    1970   Language as a Variable in Social Research. Sociological Focus 3:2.

1972   Cross Modal Communication. Paper presented at the 23rd Annual Soci-
        olinguistics Roundtable: Language and Linguistics, Georgetown Univer-
        sity, March 16–18, 1972. In Roger Shuy (ed.), *Monograph 25, Linguis-
        tics and Language Science*. Washington, D.C.: Georgetown University
        Press, 1973.

1973a   *Cognitive Sociology*. London: Macmillan & Co.

Crowle, Anthony

1971   Post Experimental Interviews: An Experiment and a Sociolinguistic
        Analysis. Unpublished Ph.D. dissertation. University of California, Santa
        Barbara.

Goffman, Erving

1959   *The Presentation of Self in Everyday Life*. Garden City; N.Y.: Doubleday
        & Company; Anchor Books.

1961   *Encounters*. Indianapolis: The Bobbs-Merrill Co.

1969   *Strategic Interaction*. Philadelphia: University of Pennsylvania Press.

Garfinkel, Harold

1952   Perception of the Other. Unpublished Ph.D. dissertation. Harvard Uni-
        versity.

1956a   Conditions of Successful Degradation Ceremonies. *American Journal of
        Sociology* 61:420–424.

1956b   Some Sociological Concepts of Methods for Psychiatrists. *Psychiatric Re-
        search Reports* 6:181–195.

1959   Aspects of the Problem of Common Sense Knowledge of Social Struc-
        tures. *Transactions of the Fourth World Congress of Sociology*, 4:51–65.
        Milan: Stressa.

1960   The Rational Properties of Scientific and Common Sense Activities. *Be-
        havioral Science* 5:72–83. (Chapter 8 in Garfinkel, 1967a.)

1962   Common Sense Knowledge of Social Structures: The Documentary
        Method of Interpretation. In Jordan M. Scher (ed.), *Theories of the Mind*.
        New York: The Free Press.

1963   A Conception of and Experiments with "Trust" as a Condition of Con-
        certed Stable Actions. In O.J. Harvey (ed.), *Motivation and Social Inter-
        action*. New York: The Ronald Press Company.

1964   Studies of the Routine Grounds of Everyday Activities. *Social Problems*
        11:225–250 (Chapter 2 in Garfinkel, 1967a.)

1967a   *Studies in Ethnomethodology*. New York: Prentice-Hall.

Sacks, Harvey

1963   Sociological Description. *Berkeley Journal of Sociology* 8:1–17.

1965–
1968   Unpublished lectures at University of California, Los Angeles and Irvine.

1966   The Search for Help: No One to Turn to. Unpublished Ph.D. disserta-
        tion. University of California, Berkeley.

Schutz, Alfred

1962   *Collected Papers I: The Problem of Social Reality*. The Hague: Martinus
        Nijhoff.

1964   *Collected Papers II: Studies in Social Theory*. The Hague: Martinus
        Nijhoff.

1966   *Collected Papers III: Studies in Phenomenological Philosophy*. The Hague: Martinus Nijhoff.

1967   *The Phenomenology of the Social World*. Evanston, Ill.: Northwestern University Press.

1970a   *On Phenomenology and Social Relations*. Chicago: University of Chicago Press.

Whyte, W. H.

1955   *Street Corner Society*. Chicago: University of Chicago Press.

Wittgenstein, Ludwig

[1921]

1961   *Tractatus Logico-Philosphicus*. London: Basil Blackwell, & Mott.

Frame Analysis [1974]

ERVING GOFFMAN

• *Goffman, as we have seen (pp. 215–232 above), began as a Durkheimian anthropologist, donning his pith helmet to investigate the rituals of modern everyday life. Never very friendly to situationalism and mental constructionism of the symbolic interactionists (who lack the emphasis of the ritualists on the emotional and moral aspect of society), Goffman reacted more sharply when the ethnomethodologists arose in the 1960s and invaded his turf with a more extreme Husserlian phenomenology. Frame Analysis is Goffman's counterattack. Intellectually strong, it also shows Goffman's command of writing style, a theatrical performance by the master of sociological staging at the height of his powers.*

There is a venerable tradition in philosophy that argues that what the reader assumes to be real is but a shadow, and that by attending to what the writer says about perception, thought, the brain, language, culture, a new methodology, or novel social forces, the veil can be lifted. That sort of line, of course, gives as much a role to the writer and his writings as is possible to imagine and for that reason is pathetic. (What can better push a book than the claim that it will change what the reader thinks is going on?) A current example of this tradition can be found in some of the doctrines of social psychology and the W. I. Thomas dictum: "If men define situations as real, they are real in their consequences." This statement is true as it reads but false as it is taken. Defining situations as real certainly has consequences, but these may contribute very marginally to the events in progress: in some cases only a slight embarrassment flits across the scene in mild concern for those who tried to define the situation wrongly. All the world is not a stage—certainly the theater isn't entirely. (Whether you organize a theater or an aircraft factory, you need to find places for cars to park and coats to be checked, and these had better be real places, which, incidentally, had better carry real insurance against theft.) Presumably, a "definition of the situation" is almost always to be found, but

Erving Goffman, *Frame Analysis* (New York: Harper & Row, 1974), pp. 1–20. Reprinted by permission of the executrix of Erving Goffman's estate.

those who are in the situation ordinarily do not *create* this definition, even though their society often can be said to do so; ordinarily, all they do is to assess correctly what the situation ought to be for them and then act accordingly. True, we personally negotiate aspects of all the arrangements under which we live, but often once these are negotiated, we continue on mechanically as though the matter had always been settled. So, too, there are occasions when we must wait until things are almost over before discovering what has been occurring and occasions of our own activity when we can considerably put off deciding what to claim we have been doing. But surely these are not the only principles of organization. Social life is dubious enough and ludicrous enough without having to wish it further into unreality.

Within the terms, then, of the bad name that the analysis of social reality has, this book presents another analysis of social reality. I try to follow a tradition established by William James in his famous chapter "The Perception of Reality,"[1] first published as an article in *Mind* in 1869. Instead of asking what reality is, he gave matters a subversive phenomenological twist, italicizing the following question: *Under what circumstances do we think things are real?* The important thing about reality, he implied, is our sense of its realness in contrast to our feeling that some things lack this quality. One can then ask under what conditions such a feeling is generated, and this question speaks to a small, manageable problem having to do with the camera and not what it is the camera takes pictures of.

In his answer, James stressed the factors of selective attention, intimate involvement and noncontradiction by what is otherwise known. More important, he made a stab at differentiating the several different "worlds" that our attention and interest can make real for us, the possible subuniverses, the "orders of existence" (to use Aron Gurwitsch's phrase), in each of which an object of a given kind can have its proper being: the world of the senses, the world of scientific objects, the world of abstract philosophical truths, the worlds of myth and supernatural beliefs, the madman's world, etc. Each of these subworlds, according to James, has "its own special and separate style of existence,"[2] and "each world, *whilst it is attended to*, is real after its own fashion; only the reality lapses with the attention."[3] Then, after taking this radical stand, James copped out; he allowed that the world of the senses has a special status, being the one we judge to be the realest reality, the one that retains our liveliest belief, the one before which the other worlds must give

---

[1]William James, *Principles of Psychology*, vol. 2 (New York: Dover Publications, 1950), chap. 21, pp. 283–324. Here, as throughout, italics in quoted materials are as in the original.
[2]*Ibid.*, p. 291.
[3]*Ibid.*, p. 293.

way.[4] James in all this agreed with Husserl's teacher, Brentano, and implied, as phenomenology came to do, the need to distinguish between the content of a current perception and the reality status we give to what is thus enclosed or bracketed within perception.[5]

James' crucial device, of course, was a rather scandalous play on the word "world" (or "reality"). What he meant was not *the* world but a particular person's current world—and, in fact, as will be argued, not even that. There was no good reason to use such billowy words. James opened a door; it let in wind as well as light.

In 1945 Alfred Schutz took up James' theme again in a paper called "On Multiple Realities."[6] His argument followed James' surprisingly closely, but more attention was given to the possibility of uncovering the conditions that must be fulfilled if we are to generate one realm of "reality," one "finite province of meaning," as opposed to another. Schutz added the notion, interesting but not entirely convincing, that we experience a special kind of "shock" when suddenly thrust from one "world," say, that of dreams, to another, such as that of the theater:

> There are as many innumerable kinds of different shock experiences as there are different finite provinces of meaning upon which I may bestow the accent of reality. Some instances are: the shock of falling asleep as the leap into the world of dreams; the inner transformation we endure if the curtain in the theater rises as the transition into the world of the stageplay; the radical change in our attitude if, before a painting, we permit our visual field to be limited by what is within the frame as the passage into the pictorial world; our quandary, relaxing into laughter, if, in listening to a joke, we are for a short time ready to

[4]James' interest in the varieties-of-worlds problem was not fleeting. In his *Varieties of Religious Experience* (New York: Longmans, Green & Co., 1902) he approached the same question but through a different route.

[5]"But who does not see that in a disbelieved or doubted or interrogative or conditional proposition, the ideas are combined in the same identical way in which they are in a proposition which is solidly believed" (James, *Principles of Psychology*, 2:286). Aron Gurwitsch in his *The Field of Consciousness* (Pittsburgh: Duquesne University Press, 1964) makes a similar comment in a discussion of Husserl:

> Among such characters we mentioned those concerning modes of presentation, as when a thing is one time perceived, another time remembered or merely imagined, or when a certain state of affairs (the identical matter of a proposition) is asserted or denied, doubted, questioned, or deemed probable. [p. 327]

[6]First appearing in *Philosophy and Phenomenological Research*, V (1945): 533–576; reprinted in his *Collected Papers*, 3 vols. (The Hague: Martinus Nijhoff, 1962), 1:207–259.) A later version is "The Stratification of the Life-World," in Alfred Schutz and Thomas Luckmann, *The Structures of the Life-World*, trans. Richard M. Zaner and H. Tristram Engelhardt, Jr. (Evanston, Ill.: Northwestern University Press, 1973), pp. 21–98. An influential treatment of Schutz's ideas is Peter L. Berger and Thomas Luckmann, *The Social Construction of Reality* (Garden City, N.Y.: Doubleday & Company, Anchor Books, 1966).

accept the fictitious world of the jest as a reality in relation to which the world of our daily life takes on the character of foolishness; the child's turning toward his toy as the transition into the play-world; and so on. But also the religious experiences in all their varieties—for instance, Kierkegaard's experience of the "instant" as the leap into the religious sphere—are examples of such a shock, as well as the decision of the scientist to replace all passionate participation in the affairs of "this world" by a disinterested contemplative attitude.[7]

And although, like James, he assumed that one realm—the "working world"—had a preferential status, he was apparently more reserved than James about its objective character:

We speak of provinces of *meaning* and not of subuniverses because it is the meaning of our experience and not the ontological structure of the objects which constitute reality,[8]

attributing its priority to ourselves, not the world:

For we will find that the world of everyday life, the common-sense world, has a paramount position among the various provinces of reality, since only within it does communication with our fellow-men become possible. But the common-sense world is from the outset a sociocultural world, and the many questions connected with the intersubjectivity of the symbolic relations originate within it, are determined by it, and find their solution within it.[9]

and to the fact that our bodies always participate in the everyday world whatever our interest at the time, this participation implying a capacity to affect and be affected by the everyday world.[10] So instead of saying of a subuniverse that it is generated in accordance with certain structural principles, one says it has a certain "cognitive style."

Schutz's paper (and Schutz in general) was brought to the attention of ethnographic sociologists by Harold Garfinkel, who further extended the argument about multiple realities by going on (at least in his early comments) to look for rules which, when followed, allow us to generate a "world" of a given kind. Presumably a machine designed according to the proper specifications

[7]Schutz, *Collected Papers*, 1:231.

[8]*Ibid.*, p. 230. See also Alfred Schutz, *Reflections on the Problem of Relevance*, ed. Richard M. Zaner (New Haven, Conn.: Yale University Press, 1970), p. 125. On matters Schutzian I am indebted to Richard Grathoff.

[9]From "Symbol, Reality, and Society," Schutz, *Collected Papers*, 1:294.

[10]*Ibid.*, p. 342.

could grind out the reality of our choice. The conceptual attraction here is obvious. A game such as chess generates a habitable universe for those who can follow it, a plane of being, a cast of characters with a seemingly unlimited number of different situations and acts through which to realize their natures and destinies. Yet much of this is reducible to a small set of interdependent rules and practices. If the meaningfulness of everyday activity is similarly dependent on a closed, finite set of rules, then explication of them would give one a powerful means of analyzing social life. For example, one could then see (following Garfinkel) that the significance of certain deviant acts is that they undermine the intelligibility of everything else we had thought was going on around us, including all next acts, thus generating diffuse disorder. To uncover the informing, constitutive rules of everyday behavior would be to perform the sociologist's alchemy—the transmutation of any patch of ordinary social activity into an illuminating publication. It might be added that although James and Schutz are convincing in arguing that something like the "world" of dreams is differently organized from the world of everyday experience, they are quite unconvincing in providing any kind of account as to how many different "worlds" there are and whether everyday, wide-awake life can actually be seen as but one rule-produced plane of being, if so seen at all. Nor has there been much success in describing constitutive rules of everyday activity.[11] One is faced with the embarrassing methodological fact that the announcement of constitutive rules seems an open-ended game that any number can play forever. Players usually come up with five or ten rules (as I will), but there are no grounds for thinking that a thousand additional assumptions might not be listed by others. Moreover, these students neglect to make clear that what they are often concerned with is not an individual's sense of what is

---

[11]Schutz's various pronouncements seem to have hypnotized some students into treating them as definitive rather than suggestive. His version of the "cognitive style" of everyday life he states as follows:

1. a specific tension of consciousness, namely, wide-awakeness, originating in full attention to life;
2. a specific *epoché*, namely suspension of doubt;
3. a prevalent form of spontaneity, namely working (a meaningful spontaneity based upon a project and characterized by the intention of bringing about the projected state of affairs by bodily movements gearing into the outer world);
4. a specific form of experiencing one's self (the working self as the total self);
5. a specific form of sociality (the common intersubjective world of communication and social action);
6. a specific time-perspective (the standard time originating in an interaction between *durée* and cosmic time as the universal temporal structure of the intersubjective world).

These are at least some of the features of the cognitive style belonging to this particular province of meaning. As long as our experiences of this world—the valid as well as the invalidated ones—partake of this style we may consider this province of meaning as real, we may bestow upon it the accent of reality. [*Ibid.*, pp. 230–231.]

real, but rather what it is he can get caught up in, engrossed in, carried away by; and this can be something he can claim is really going on and yet claim is not real. One is left, then, with the structural similarity between everyday life—neglecting for a moment the possibility that no satisfactory catalog might be possible of what to include therein—and the various "worlds" of make-believe but no way of knowing how this relationship should modify our view of everyday life.

Interest in the James-Schutz line of thought has become active recently among persons whose initial stimulus came from sources not much connected historically with the phenomenological tradition: The work of those who created what has come to be called "the theater of the absurd," most fully exhibited in the analytical dramas of Luigi Pirandello. The very useful paper by Gregory Bateson, "A Theory of Play and Phantasy,"[12] in which he directly raised the question of unseriousness and seriousness, allowing us to see what a startling thing experience is, such that a bit of serious activity can be used as a model for putting together unserious versions of the same activity, and that, on occasion, we may not know whether it is play or the real thing that is occurring. (Bateson introduced his own version of the notion of "bracketing," a usable one, and also the argument that individuals can intentionally produce framing confusion in those with whom they are dealing; it is in Bateson's paper that the term "frame" was proposed in roughly the sense in which I want to employ it.)[13] The work of John Austin, who, following Wittgenstein,[14] suggested again that what we mean by "really happening" is complicated, and that although an individual may dream unrealities, it is still proper to say of him on that occasion that he is really dreaming.[15] (I have also drawn on the work of a student of Austin, D. S. Schwayder, and his fine book, *The Stratification of Behavior*.)[16] The efforts of those who study (or at least publish on) fraud, deceit, misidentification, and other "optical" effects, and the work of those who study "strategic interaction," including the way in which concealing and revealing bear upon definitions of the situation. The useful paper by Barney Glaser and Anselm Strauss, "Awareness Contexts and Social Inter-

[12]*Psychiatric Research Reports* 2, American Psychiatric Association (December 1955), pp. 39–51. Now reprinted in his *Steps to an Ecology of Mind* (New York: Ballantine Books, 1972), pp. 177–193. A useful exegesis is William F. Fry, Jr., *Sweet Madness: A Study of Humor* (Palo Alto, Calif.: Pacific Books, 1968).

[13]Edward T. Cone, in the first chapter of his *Musical Form and Musical Performance* (New York: W. W. Norton & Company, 1968), quite explicitly uses the term "frame" in much the same way that Bateson does and suggests some of the same lines of inquiry, but I think quite independently.

[14]See, for example, Ludwig Wittgenstein, *Philosophical Investigations*, trans. G. E. M. Anscombe (Oxford: Basil Blackwell, 1958), pt. 2, sec. 7.

[15]See, for example, chap. 7 in his *Sense and Sensibilia* (Oxford: Oxford University Press, 1962).

[16]London: Routledge & Kegan Paul, 1965.

action."[17] Finally, the modern effort in linguistically oriented disciplines to employ the notion of a "code" as a device which informs and patterns all events that fall within the boundaries of its application.

I have borrowed extensively from all these sources, claiming really only the bringing of them together. My perspective is situational, meaning here a concern for what one individual can be alive to at a particular moment, this often involving a few other particular individuals and not necessarily restricted to the mutually monitored arena of a face-to-face gathering. I assume that when individuals attend to any current situation, they face the question: "What is it that's going on here?" Whether asked explicitly, as in times of confusion and doubt, or tacitly, during occasions of usual certitude, the question is put and the answer to it is presumed by the way the individuals then proceed to get on with the affairs at hand. Starting, then, with that question, this volume attempts to limn out a framework that could be appealed to for the answer.

Let me say at once that the question "What is it that's going on here?" is considerably suspect. Any event can be described in terms of a focus that includes a wide swath or a narrow one and—as a related but not identical matter—in terms of a focus that is close-up or distant. And no one has a theory as to what particular span and level will come to be the ones employed. To begin with, I must be allowed to proceed by picking my span and level arbitrarily, without special justification.[18]

A similar issue is found in connection with perspective. When participant roles in an activity are differentiated—a common circumstance—the view that one person has of what is going on is likely to be quite different from that of another. There is a sense in which what is play for the golfer is work for the caddy. Different interests will—in Schutz's phrasing—generate different motivational relevances. (Moreover, variability is complicated here by the fact that those who bring different perspectives to the "same" events are likely to employ different spans and levels of focus.) Of course, in many cases some of those who are committed to differing points of view and focus may still be willing to acknowledge that theirs is not the official or "real" one. Caddies work at golf, as do instructors, but both appreciate that their job is special, since it has to do with servicing persons engaged in play. In any case, again I will initially assume the right to pick my point of view, my motivational relevancies, only limiting this choice of perspective to one that participants would easily recognize to be valid.

[17]*American Sociological Review*, XXIX (1964): 669–679.

[18]See the discussion by Emanuel A. Schegloff, "Notes on a Conversational Practice: Formulating Place," in David Sudnow, ed., *Studies in Social Interaction* (New York: The Free Press, 1972), pp. 75–119. There is a standard criticism of "role" as a concept which presents the same argument.

Further, it is obvious that in most "situations" many different things are happening simultaneously—things that are likely to have begun at different moments and may terminate dissynchronously.[19] To ask the question "What is *it* that's going on here?" biases matters in the direction of unitary exposition and simplicity. This bias, too, I must be temporarily allowed.

So, too, to speak of the "current" situation (just as to speak of something going on "here") is to allow reader and writer to continue along easily in their impression that they clearly know and agree on what they are thinking about. The amount of time covered by "current" (just as the amount of space covered by "here") obviously can vary greatly from one occasion to the next and from one participant to another; and the fact that participants seem to have no trouble in quickly coming to the same apparent understanding in this matter does not deny the intellectual importance of our trying to find out what this apparent consensus consists of and how it is established. To speak of something happening before the eyes of observers is to be on firmer ground than usual in the social sciences; but the ground is still shaky, and the crucial question of how a seeming agreement was reached concerning the identity of the "something" and the inclusiveness of "before the eyes" still remains.

Finally, it is plain that retrospective characterization of the "same" event or social occasion may differ very widely, that an individual's role in an undertaking can provide him with a distinctive evaluative assessment of what sort of an instance of the type the particular undertaking was. In that sense it has been argued, for example, that opposing rooters at a football game do not experience the "same" game,[20] and that what makes a party a good one for a participant who is made much of is just what makes it a bad one for a participant who thereby is made little of.

All of which suggests that one should even be uneasy about the easy way in which it is assumed that participants in an activity can be terminologically identified and referred to without issue. For surely, a "couple" kissing can also be a "man" greeting his "wife" or "John" being careful with "Mary's" makeup.

I only want to claim that although these questions are very important, they are not the only ones, and that their treatment is not necessarily required before one can proceed. So here, too, I will let sleeping sentences lie.

My aim is to try to isolate some of the basic frameworks of understanding available in our society for making sense out of events and to analyze the

[19]Nicely described by Roger G. Barker and Herbert F. Wright, *Midwest and Its Children* (Evanston, Ill.: Row, Peterson & Company, 1964), chap. 7, "Dividing the Behavior Stream," pp. 225–273.

[20]Presented perhaps overstrongly in a well-known early paper by Albert H. Hastorf and Hadley Cantril, "They Saw a Game: A Case Study," *Journal of Abnormal and Social Psychology*, XLIX (1954): 129–234.

special vulnerabilities to which these frames of reference are subject. I start with the fact that from an individual's particular point of view, while one thing may momentarily appear to be what is really going on, in fact what is actually happening is plainly a joke, or a dream, or an accident, or a mistake, or a misunderstanding, or a deception, or a theatrical performance, and so forth. And attention will be directed to what it is about our sense of what is going on that makes it so vulnerable to the need for these various rereadings.

Elementary terms required by the subject matter to be dealt with are provided first. My treatment of these initial terms is abstract, and I am afraid the formulations provided are crude indeed by the standards of modern philosophy. The reader must initially bestow the benefit of mere doubt in order for us both to get to matters that (I feel) are less dubious.

The term "strip" will be used to refer to any arbitrary slice or cut from the stream of ongoing activity, including here sequences of happenings, real or fictive, as seen from the perspective of those subjectively involved in sustaining an interest in them. A strip is not meant to reflect a natural division made by the subjects of inquiry or an analytical division made by students who inquire; it will be used only to refer to any raw batch of occurrences (of whatever status in reality) that one wants to draw attention to as a starting point for analysis.

And of course much use will be made of Bateson's use of the term "frame." I assume that definitions of a situation are built up in accordance with principles of organization which govern events—at least social ones—and our subjective involvement in them; frame is the word I use to refer to such of these basic elements as I am able to identify. That is my definition of frame. My phrase "frame analysis" is a slogan to refer to the examination in these terms of the organization of experience.

In dealing with conventional topics, it is usually practical to develop concepts and themes in some sort of logical sequence: nothing coming earlier depends on something coming later, and, hopefully, terms developed at any one point are actually used in what comes thereafter. Often the complaint of the writer is that linear presentation constrains what is actually a circular affair, ideally requiring simultaneous introduction of terms, and the complaint of the reader is that concepts elaborately defined are not much used beyond the point at which the fuss is made about their meaning. In the analysis of frames, linear presentation is no great embarrassment. Nor is the defining of terms not used thereafter. The problem, in fact, is that once a term is introduced (this occurring at the point at which it is first needed), it begins to have too much bearing, not merely applying to what comes later, but reapplying in each chapter to what it has already applied to. Thus each succeeding section of the study becomes more entangled, until a step can hardly be made because of what must be carried along with it. The process closely follows the horrors of repetition songs, as if—in the case of frame analysis—what Old MacDonald had on his farm were partridge and juniper trees.

Discussions about frame inevitably lead to questions concerning the status of the discussion itself, because here terms applying to what is analyzed ought to apply to the analysis also. I proceed on the commonsense assumption that ordinary language and ordinary writing practices are sufficiently flexible to allow anything that one wants to express to get expressed.[21] Here I follow Carnap's position:

> The sentences, definitions, and rules of the syntax of a language are concerned with the forms of that language. But, now, how are these sentences, definitions, and rules themselves to be correctly expressed? Is a kind of super-language necessary for the purpose? And, again, a third language to explain the syntax of this superlanguage, and so on to infinity? Or is it possible to formulate the syntax of a language within that language itself? The obvious fear will arise that in the latter case, owing to certain reflexive definitions, contradictions of a nature seemingly similar to those which are familiar both in Cantor's theory of transfinite aggregates and in the pre-Russellian logic might make their appearance. But we shall see later that without any danger of contradictions or antinomies emerging it is possible to express the syntax of a language in that language itself, to an extent which is conditioned by the wealth of means of expression of the language in question.[22]

Thus, even if one took as one's task the examination of the use made in the humanities and the less robust sciences of "examples," "illustrations," and "cases in point," the object being to uncover the folk theories of evidence which underlie resort to these devices, it would still be the case that examples and illustrations would probably have to be used, and they probably could be without entirely vitiating the analysis.

In turning to the issue of reflexivity and in arguing that ordinary language is an adequate resource for discussing it, I do not mean that these particular linguistic matters should block all other concerns. Methodological self-consciousness that is full, immediate, and persistent sets aside all study and analysis except that of the reflexive problem itself, thereby displacing fields of inquiry instead of contributing to them. Thus, I will throughout use quota-

[21]*Wovan man nicht sprechen kann, ist nicht der satz,* "*Wovan man nicht sprechen kann, darüber muss man schweigen.*" [Of that which one cannot speak, it is *not* the case: "of that which one cannot speak, one must keep silent."—Ed.]
[22]Rudolf Carnap, *The Logical Syntax of Language*, trans. Amethe Smeaton (London: Kegan Paul, Trench, Trubner & Co., 1937), p. 3.

tion marks to suggest a special sense of the word so marked and not concern myself systematically with the fact that this device is routinely used in a variety of quite different ways,[23] that these seem to bear closely on the question of frame, and that I must assume that the context of use will automatically lead my readers and me to have the same understanding, although neither I nor they might be able to explicate the matter further. So, too, with the warning and the lead that ordinary language philosophers have given us. I know that the crucial term "real" may have been permanently Wittgensteined into a blur of slightly different uses, but proceed on the assumption that carefulness can gradually bring us to an understanding of basic themes informing diversity, a diversity which carefulness itself initially establishes, and that what is taken for granted concerning the meaning of this word can safely so be done until it is convenient to attend to what one has been doing.

A further caveat. There are lots of good grounds for doubting the kind of analysis about to be presented. I would do so myself if it weren't my own. It is too bookish, too general, too removed from fieldwork to have a good chance of being anything more than another mentalistic adumbration. And, as will be noted throughout, there are certainly things that cannot be nicely dealt with in the arguments that follow. (I coin a series of terms—some "basic"; but writers have been doing that to not much avail for years.) Nonetheless, some of the things in this world seem to urge the analysis I am here attempting, and the compulsion is strong to try to outline the framework that will perform this job, even if this means some other tasks get handled badly.

Another disclaimer. This book is about the organization of experience—something that an individual actor can take into his mind—and not the organization of society. I make no claim whatsoever to be talking about the core matters of sociology—social organization and social structure. Those matters have been and can continue to be quite nicely studied without refer-

---

[23]I. A. Richards, for example, has a version in his *How to Read a Page* (New York: W.W. Norton & Company, 1942):

> We all recognize—more or less unsystematically—that quotation marks serve varied purposes:
> 1. Sometimes they show merely that we are quoting and where our quotation begins and ends.
> 2. Sometimes they imply that the word or words within them are in some way open to question and are only to be taken in some special sense with reference to some special definition.
> 3. Sometimes they suggest further that what is quoted is nonsense or that there is really no such thing as the thing they profess to name.
> 4. Sometimes they suggest that the words are improperly used. The quotation marks are equivalent to *the so-called*.
> 5. Sometimes they only indicate that we are talking of the words as distinguished from their meanings. "Is" and "at" are shorter than "above." "Chien" means what "dog" means, and so forth.
>
> There are many other uses.. . . . [p. 66]

ence to frame at all. I am not addressing the structure of social life but the structure of experience individuals have at any moment of their social lives. I personally hold society to be first in every way and any individual's current involvements to be second; this report deals only with matters that are second. This book will have weaknesses enough in the areas it claims to deal with; there is no need to find limitations in regard to what it does not set about to cover. Of course, it can be argued that to focus on the nature of personal experiencing—with the implication this can have for giving equally serious consideration to all matters that might momentarily concern the individual—is itself a standpoint with marked political implications, and that these are conservative ones. The analysis developed does not catch at the differences between the advantaged and disadvantaged classes and can be said to direct attention away from such matters. I think that is true. I can only suggest that he who would combat false consciousness and awaken people to their true interests has much to do, because the sleep is very deep. And I do not intend here to provide a lullaby but merely to sneak in and watch the way the people snore.

Finally, a note about the materials used. First, there is the fact that I deal again in this book with what I have dealt with in others—another go at analyzing fraud, deceit, con games, shows of various kinds, and the like. There are many footnotes to and much repetition of other things I've written.[24] I am trying to order my thoughts on these topics, trying to construct a general statement. That is the excuse.

Second, throughout the book very considerable use is made of anecdotes cited from the press and from popular books in the biographical genre.[25] There could hardly be data with less face value. Obviously, passing events that are typical or representative don't make news just for that reason; only extraordinary ones do, and even these are subject to the editorial violence routinely employed by gentle writers. Our understanding of the world precedes these stories, determining which ones reporters will select and how the ones that are selected will be told. Human interest stories are a caricature of evidence in the very degree of their interest, providing a unity, coherence, pointedness, self-completeness, and drama only crudely sustained, if at all, by everyday living. Each is a cross between an *experimentum crucim* and a sideshow. That is their point. The design of these reported events is fully responsive to our demands—which are not for facts but for typifications. Their telling demon-

[24]So much so that I use source abbreviations, a list of which can be found on p. xi.

[25]An analysis of incidentally published stories—"fillers"—is provided by Roland Barthes along with an exhibition of literary license in "Structure of *Fait-Divers*," in his *Critical Essays*, trans. Richard Howard (Evanston, Ill.: Northwestern University Press, 1972), pp. 185–195.

strates the power of our conventional understandings to cope with the bizarre potentials of social life, the furthest reaches of experience. What appears, then, to be a threat to our way of making sense of the world turns out to be an ingeniously selected defense of it. We press these stories to the wind; they keep the world from unsettling us. By and large, I do not present these anecdotes, therefore, as evidence or proof, but as clarifying depictions, as frame fantasies which manage, through the hundred liberties taken by their tellers, to celebrate our beliefs about the workings of the world. What was put into these tales is thus what I would like to get out of them.

These data have another weakness. I have culled them over the years on a hit-or-miss basis using principles of selection mysterious to me which, furthermore, changed from year to year and which I could not recover if I wanted to. Here, too, a caricature of systematic sampling is involved.

In addition to clippings as a source of materials, I draw on another, one as questionable as the first. Since this study attempts to deal with the organization of experience as such, whether "actual" or of the other kinds, I will have recourse to the following: cartoons, comics, novels, the cinema, and especially, it turns out, the legitimate stage. I am here involved in no horrors of bias different from the ones already exhibited in the selection of bits of human interest news. But I am led to draw on materials that writers in other traditions use, whether in literary and dramatic criticism of current "high" culture or in the sort of sociological journalism which attempts to read from surface changes in commercially available vicarious experience to the nature of our society at large. In consequence, many of the things I have to say about these materials will have already been said many times and better by fashionable writers. My excuse for brazenly dipping into this preempted domain is that I have a special interest, one that does not recognize a difference in value between a good novel and a bad one, a contemporary play or an ancient one, a comic strip or an opera. All are equally useful in explicating the character of strips of experienced activity. I end up quoting from well-known works recognized as setting standards, and from minor works current at the time of writing, but not because I think these examples of their genre have special cultural worth and warrant endorsement. Critics and reviewers cite the classics of a genre in dealing with current works in order to explicate what if anything is significant and artful in them. I draw clumsily on the same materials—as well as critiques of them—simply because that is what is easy to hand. Indeed, these materials are easy to everyone's hand, providing something of a common fund of familiar experience, something that writers can assume readers know about.

* * * * * *

That is the introduction. Writing one allows a writer to try to set the terms of what he will write about. Accounts, excuses, apologies designed to reframe what follows after them, designed to draw a line between deficiencies in what the author writes and deficiencies in himself, leaving him, he hopes, a little better defended than he might otherwise be.[26] This sort of ritual work can certainly disconnect a hurried pedestrian from a minor inconvenience he might cause a passing stranger. Just as certainly, such efforts are optimistic when their purpose is to recast the way in which a long book is to be taken. (And more optimistic still in the case of a second edition's preface to an already prefaced edition, this being an attempt to recast a recasting.)

* * * * * *

But what about comments on prefaces? Where does such a topic taken up at such a point leave the writer and the reader (or a speaker and an audience)? Does that sort of talk strike at the inclination of the reader to discount or

---

[26]There is a useful article by Jacob Brackman called "The Put-On" (*The New Yorker*, June 24, 1967, pp. 34–73). In his twelve-page introduction to the paperback edition he writes:

> Updating. If "updating" this essay were to mean exchanging more current jokes and performers for ones since disappeared, and appending how there came to be "put-on" head boutiques, and TV game shows, and a Sears Put-On clothing shop, and publishers crowing "This is the novel that makes you ask: *Is the author putting me on?*", and thousands of winkful commercials that seemed to say, "I know that you know that I'm trying to sell you. Let's you and me both goof on the product together."—if I were to "update" along these lines, and if I were to add little exegeses of Tiny Tim's wedding, Paul Morrissey's movies, Paul McCartney's death, then the piece would begin to stink of inauthenticity.
>
> I think you must let a piece like this stand—not in its syntax, necessarily, but within the limits of its original awareness—as a fragment of cultural history. It may have been valid to the precise present for a matter of months, or days; who will quibble now that time is so short? Once the vision's devoured, mulched and incorporated, unless it has been frozen somewhere, its moment—when only so much had happened, when only so much had been revealed—is lost forever. All we have left are "updated" reports, grotesquely stretched, debased and freshened up, as what played itself out between haircuts is made to seem the rage of a decade. If I were to do this piece today (which would itself be impossible) hardly anything in it would stay the same. Of things in the real world about which one can try to write, sensibility may be the slipperiest. If I won't write the new piece now, how can I go back and meddle with the old one? [*The Put-On* (New York: Bantam Books, 1972), pp. 10–11.]

Brackman also argues that current items of cultural interest date very rapidly and fully, and, by implication, that writings concerned with these items will date quickly, too. He also suggests that the point of such writings is to bring the not quite consciously appreciated to awareness, and to do this first, and that once again a restatement or republication will sound stale. All of this I think has some truth and correctly describes the contingencies of that kind of subject matter, there being inevitably an unstated element of the reader's interest that derives from the current interest of the item. This element will decline rather quickly, leaving the writer having written something that can no longer be read with interest. In fact, every analyst of jokes has faced this problem, since the current version of a basic joke which he writes about today will sound very dated tomorrow. But given what Brackman is stuck with reprinting, his introduction does the framing work that introductions can do to segregate the producer from his product, in this case arguing that the piece was an expression of his sensibility *then*, not now.

criticize prefacing as an activity? And if it turns out that the preface was written in bad faith, tailored from the beginning to exemplify this use that will have come to be made of it? Will the preface then be retrospectively reframed by the reader into something that really isn't a preface at all but an inappropriately inserted illustration of one? Or if an admission of bad faith is made unconvincingly, leaving open the possibility that the disclosure was an afterthought? What then?

* * * * * *

And does the last comment excuse me in any degree from having been puerile and obvious in commenting on prefaces, as when, in a book analyzing jokes, the writer is excused the badness of the cited jokes but not the badness of the analysis of them? (A novelist who nowadays injects direct address in the body of his work—"Dear Reader, if you've gone this far, you'll know I hate that character . . ."—easily fails to change the footing we allow him; but what if he writes that he would like to succeed in such a device but knows we will not let him?)

* * * * * *

And what about discussions about being puerile and obvious? A word incorrectly spelled can, I think, be successfully used by the misspeller as an illustration of incorrect spelling and analyzed as such. But can a writer posture in his writing and then effectively claim that all along he was only providing an illustration of bad taste and lack of sophistication? Would it be necessary for him to show, and if so, how would he, that his claims were not merely a device hit upon after the fact to make the best out of what he was not able to prevent from being a bad thing?

* * * * * *

And if in the first pages after acknowledging colleagues who had helped, I had said: "Richard C. Jeffrey, on the other hand, did not help." And if I had gone on here (in these later pages) to suggest that the aim had been to make a little joke and incidentally bring awareness to a tacit constraint on acknowledgment writing? Then the explication of this aim could be seen as bad faith—either a post-hoc effort to hedge on having tried to be witty or an admission of having entrapped the reader into accepting a plant, that is, a statement whose reason for inclusion would later be shown to have not been apparent. But if, as is in fact the case, the whole matter is enclosed as a question within a section of the introduction dealing with a consideration of introductions and is therefore not to be seen as having an initial character as a simple, straightforward introduction, what then?

And after all of this, can I get the point across that Richard C. Jeffrey in fact didn't help? Does this last sentence do it? And if so, had a conditional been used, as in: "And after all of this, could I get the point across . . . etc." What then? And would this last comment transform an assertion into an illustration and so once again cast the matter of Richard C. Jeffrey in doubt?

*   *   *   *   *   *

And if the preface and the comments on the preface and the comments on the comments on the preface are put in question, what about the asterisks which divide up and divide off the various sections in which this is managed? And if the orthography had still been intact, would this last question itself have undermined these framing devices, including the ones which bracket this sentence with the prior one?

*   *   *   *   *   *

And if above I had said: "What about the * * * * * *which divide up and divide off . . ."; would this be a proper use of print, and can an easy rule be formulated? Given the motivational relevancies of orthographers, a book on orthography can properly use a batch of print to illustrate print, to the neglect of saying something with its meaning. Similarly, a geography book can properly switch from words to maps. But when a mystery writer has his hero find a coded message on a torn bit of paper and then shows the clue to the reader by insetting it in the center of the page as though it were a map in a geography book, so that the reader sees the tear as well as the message, what sort of shift to a nonfictional frame has the writer asked the reader to make, and was he quite within his rights to ask it? Is it overly cute for an anthropologist reporting on the role of metaphor (with special reference to animal sources) to write, "One always feels a bit sheepish, of course, about bringing the metaphor concept into the social sciences and perhaps that is because one always feels there is something soft and wooly about it"?[27] Similarly, if I try to get dodgy with prefaces, is this not different from writing about tricks done with prefaces (which characteristically need not be undertaken at the beginning of a study)? Is this not the difference between doing and writing about the doing? And in considering all of these matters, can I properly draw on my own text ("And if above I had said: 'What about the * * * * * * that divide up and divide off . . .'; would this be . . .") as an illustration? And in this last sentence has not all need to be hesitant about the right to use actual asterisks disappeared, for after all, a doubtful usage cited as an example of doubtful usage ceases to be something that is doubtful to print?

[27]James W. Fernandez, "Persuasions and Performances: Of the Beast in Every Body . . . And the Metaphors of Everyman," *Daedalus*, Winter 1972, p. 41.

*　*　*　*　*　*

And if I wanted to comment on the next to last sentence, the one containing a parenthesized quoted sentence and questionably real asterisks, could I quote *that* sentence effectively, that is, employ the apparently required punctuation marks and yet allow the reader an easy comprehension of what was being said about what? Would the limits of doing things in print have been reached?

*　*　*　*　*　*

That is what frame analysis is about.